Encounter with the Middle East

Winston Burdett

ENCOUNTER WITH THE MIDDLE EAST

An Intimate Report on What Lies Behind

The Arab-Israeli Conflict

NEW YORK   Atheneum   1969

FOR

Cristina

AND

Ricky

Foreword

IT MAY SOMETIMES befall a correspondent in the course of his work to cover an event or a segment of contemporary history that remains for him a signal and moving personal experience. Many others are more qualified than I by knowledge and training to trace the events of the tragic and unfinished encounter which this book attempts to describe. But after the Arab-Israeli war in June, 1967, having represented CBS News through the years as a roving correspondent on both sides of the lines in the Middle East, I found myself impelled to write it by the force of the attachment I had felt, for so long, to the theme of the Israelis and their destiny and of the Arabs and theirs. No one, I think, can be close to that encounter, in a role large or small, without feeling in some sense a participant. No one can stand aside as an indifferent witness.

This is a personal book both in its impulse and in its delineation of events. It does not pretend to assess events with dispassionate detachment. It seeks to tell a faithful story, but it reflects a single reporter's experiences and observations, his fallible judgments and his unconcealed sympathies. It is a reporter's book and not a historian's. It lays no claim to finality or scholarship. A scholar's sources of information are the accumulated records left by governments and by the actors and witnesses of history. A reporter's sources are living men who do not know what is going to happen next but who do know much more about a particular subject than he does. He assembles and sifts their testimony and their judgments and makes what he can of them. The historian may sometimes rashly aspire to write a definitive work; the reporter's labors must always be provisional and tentative. I have drawn unashamedly on the works of wise and scholarly men who have written about the history of the Arabs and the Jews; and for the body of the narrative I have turned to those who were more knowledgeable than I, since they were either close observers of the events or active participants in them: in short, a reporter's sources. This book is based largely on my conversations with them, though I should not forget, either, my countless long, inquiring and rewarding talks with fellow correspondents.

The historian and the reporter have this in common, that they are prompted by curiosity to discover what really happened and to understand, through the reconstruction of history, its inward meaning. The third Arab-Israeli war, unwanted by those who did the most to bring it about and unanticipated until it was too late, was the violent issue of a succession of events that offered such a challenge to curiosity. After the war I returned to the Middle East and then went on to Washington and New York to make the inquiry that is the substance of this book. The events of the recent past are fluid and, as it were, still in movement; and those that I relate are still surrounded by a wide, uncertain area that only deduction and surmise can enter. Not all the facts, by any means, are in; and from the same strands of fact different observers may weave different patterns of perception. Evidently, my sources for this story did not all agree on what had really happened. Even those who saw events from the same national position offered varying approaches and varying interpretations. From the views and experiences of others I have sought to make a consistent summing-up which in the end is my own view and own interpretation, though I could never have reached it without the help of those who gave me so much of their time and thought, of old friends and new, and of generous colleagues.

Rome
January 14, 1969

Contents

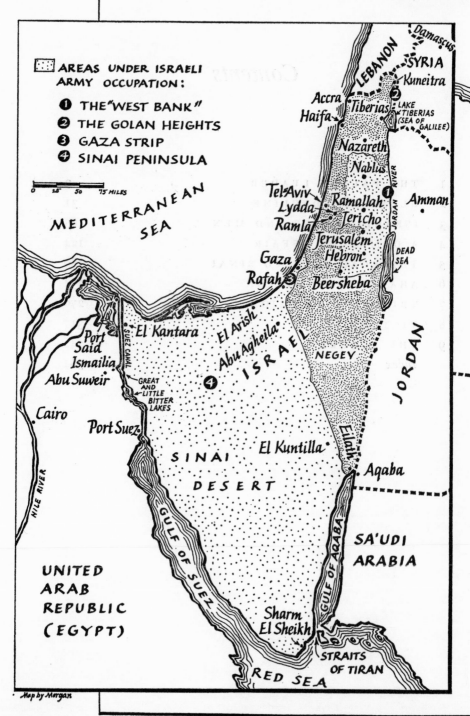

AREAS UNDER ISRAELI
ARMY OCCUPATION:

1 THE "WEST BANK"
2 THE GOLAN HEIGHTS
3 GAZA STRIP
4 SINAI PENINSULA

0   25   50   75 MILES

MEDITERRANEAN SEA

CRETE

Damascus

LEBANON

SYRIA

Kuneitra

Accra

Haifa

Tiberias

LAKE TIBERIAS
(SEA OF GALILEE)

Nazareth

Nablus

Tel-Aviv

Ramallah

Amman

Lydda

Jericho

Ramla

JORDAN RIVER

Jerusalem

Hebron

DEAD SEA

Gaza

Rafah **3**

Beersheba

JORDAN

El Kantara

El Arish

Abu Agheila

ISRAEL

NEGEV

Port Said

SUEZ CANAL

Ismailia

Abu Suweir

GREAT AND LITTLE BITTER LAKES

4

Cairo

Port Suez

El Kuntilla

Eilath

Aqaba

SINAI DESERT

NILE RIVER

GULF OF SUEZ

GULF OF AQABA

SA'UDI ARABIA

UNITED ARAB REPUBLIC (EGYPT)

Sharm El Sheikh

STRAITS OF TIRAN

RED SEA

Map by Morgan

0   50   100   200   300   400 MILES

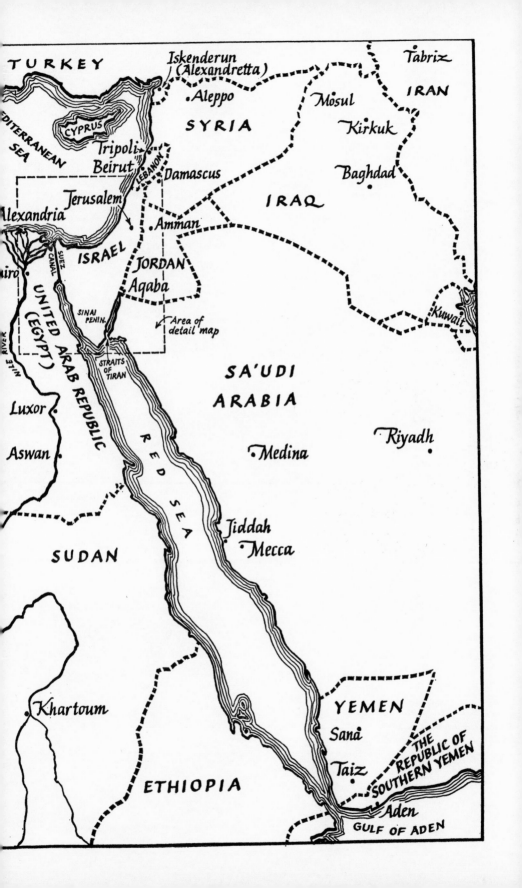

Encounter with the Middle East

1

The Fallen Leader

THE CITY THAT HAD BEEN the stage of so many vivid and exhilarating spectacles and so many boisterous triumphs a few days before sank back into silence and, in the warm air and fading light of a June evening, under the blow of the catastrophe, withdrew into itself and waited. No voices rose from the streets below us, no distant hum from the boulevards, not even the nearby sound of early evening traffic that normally sped headlong and without interruption along the broad corniche that frames the river. The bridges across the Nile were bare. Eastward from our balcony the city presented its broken skyline of electric billboards, minarets and rooftops, a tattered tableau with the dusky grandeur of Mohammed Ali's mosque and the brown ramparts of Saladdin's citadel in the background, wavering in the haze of unsettled dust but still distinct against the lighter desert brown of the Moquattam Hills. The wide stage of the vivacious city was empty. The imposing panorama lay still. Yet even so, with no sound of footsteps from the streets, no sight of passers-by and no hint of movement in the houses and gardens we looked down on, the scene we beheld was alive with expectancy. There were listeners behind the walls; and in the silence of streets, buildings, windows, there was boding and repression. The holiday was over and the spectacles were ended. The banners so profusely and so hopefully strung from lamppost to lamppost on the downtown avenues, celebrating in the gay and cursive letters of the Arabic script a victory that never came, had vanished at a nod from authority. Everybody had returned indoors, with feelings one could only guess at after so great a débâcle: bafflement, anger, disbelief and, possibly, a touch of awe.

It was a measureless defeat. The masterly planning of the Israeli General Staff and the courage of a new generation of young Israelis had demonstrated to the world that, ten years after their last encounter on the same ground in the Sinai Desert, the gap in fighting capacity between the opposing armies was greater than ever. The entire Sinai Peninsula, the meeting place of Africa and Asia, was in the hands of the victorious citizens' army, which now stood eighty miles away on the eastern bank of the Suez Canal, with no military power to halt or to challenge it should its commanders choose to cross the Canal and pursue their advance through the Nile Delta to the capital. With the irremediable collapse of Egyptian arms, the road was open.

We were gathered that evening on a bedroom balcony of the hotel where we had been interned, the five of us sharing one transistor radio and waiting for the music of Cairo Radio to stop and the voice of Gamal Abdel Nasser to begin. Throughout the city, in homes and offices, at ministries and army camps, in the back rooms of neighborhood shops and at the headquarters of the Supreme Command, people were listening to that music and waiting for that voice. He was the caved-in hero, but his voice was still the only one that counted, the only one that commanded belief; and the fact that it had kept silent throughout the four days of the war in Sinai was, for Egyptians, a more ominous and oppressive sign than all the others: more telling than the sudden disappearance of the victory streamers, or the hedging sentences of the army communiqués, or the choked voices of the news announcers. Few Egyptians realized the magnitude of the defeat, but sooner or later, in weeks or months, the truth would come creeping back; the soldiers home from the rout, the hospitals filled with the wounded, and those who would never come back to town or village; the word spreading, the rumors surging through the bazaars; and sooner or later, sometime, somehow, we thought, there would have to be a reckoning.

We had been locked into our hotel three days earlier, twenty-one American correspondents and cameramen formally expelled from the country by the government. But Egypt had no physical means to expel us, since the airports had been closed by the onslaught of the Israeli Air Force and the movement of trains through the Delta halted by order of the Egyptian Command. They interned us in the hotel, instead, and put a policeman at the door. We were cut off, except for our transistors.

The announced hour of seven-thirty had already passed and the music played on. Nasser was late. We wondered what he would find to say. He would have to say something to head off the course of the disaster. Would he acknowledge its extent? Whom would he blame? He would have to offer an outlet for the emotions of a frustrated people. Now that everything was over, would he persist in his charge that war planes of the United States and Britain had intervened on behalf of Israel, with the irresistible inference that the Arabs had been robbed? "He can't possibly survive a collapse like this," somebody said; and we reminded him that once before Nasser had pulled political victory out of military defeat, with a degree of astuteness, self-control and sustained agility that had made it seem like a conjurer's trick. "He will step down, announce his retirement," someone exclaimed, in a tone that was more one of challenge than conviction. "Yield power? Never. He can't," was the answer. "It's against his nature." And that was the judgment of the rest of us.

The dusk thickened over the city. This would be our last night in Cairo. The Embassy had laid on a special train for the following day and chartered a ship from Alexandria to evacuate the last of the Americans. We were more than five hundred, about a third of us confined in this hotel: educators, oil engineers, the representatives of charity foundations, clergymen who had known Egypt for years and loved it well; and various birds of passage about whom one was not sure—travelers caught in the tumble of events, teen-age girls seeing the world. I had to admit that this time, like them, I would be glad to go, even though I had always been glad to come, and on my visits through the years had always returned to Cairo with the sense of adventure and challenge that one feels when approaching a great city. I had always looked forward to it. There was the prospect of pleasant evenings at friends' homes in houseboats along the tree-lined quay of Gezira Island; the early morning walks to the center of town, the radiating avenues with their teahouses and carpet shops, their overloaded trams and scurrying traffic; the variety of the morning crowd, the immaculate white shirts of office workers and the tired galabias of

waiters and hawkers; the shouting and populous life of the boulevards; the chaotic indolence of the back streets. There was the familiar look of dingy stairways as one made the rounds of newspaper and
government offices, avoiding if one could the unreliable elevators and
wondering whether the editor or official one wanted to see would
really be there at the appointed hour and thinking of the cups of Turkish coffee one would drink if he were. There were those visits to the
old Arab city behind the Opera House, the roofed alleys of the Muski
and the sharp eyes of the shopkeepers waiting for custom; the dilapi-
dated taxis, Detroit or Stuttgart castoffs that hurtled along like cap-
sules out of orbit on the way back to the hotel; and the longer visits to
what was still the one absolute, undebunkable thing, the row of pyra-
mids at Giza. There was the poetry of river and desert. There were the
people of Cairo, easygoing, excitable, impudent and waggish. There
was the gradual lifting of the heat after four o'clock in the afternoon,
layer after layer rising in slow but perceptible degrees, like blankets
successively removed; and then the cool night and the black band of
the Nile catching the lights. There was the flavor of intrigue.

My American and European friends who lived there said that I
romanticized Cairo and, of course, they were right. It is a city hard on
the nerves of the Westerner who has to make his life there, businessman or diplomat or journalist who on some level or other must cope
with the Egyptian bureaucracy and find his way through that vast
nightmare of obstruction and indifference. The winds of propaganda
blow day in and day out and after a time they are deafening. The ma-
nipulations of mass feeling, the shrill discourses of Cairo Radio and
the lectures of the controlled press are wearing on the spirit of those
who have to take them for long. The world seen at a cockeyed angle
through the narrow lens of the political propagandist is a depressing
and claustrophobic place. The stimulations of Cairo begin to lose
their edge, and isolation sets in. Even the visitor is soon made aware
of the all-watching, soft-treading presence of the police—the locked
briefcase that has been forcibly opened, the papers that have disappeared from the drawer; aware that the security police, in one or another of their several embodiments, pervade Egyptian society and are
probably the single brilliantly efficient set of professional people in the
country. Or is it simply that so many Egyptians, whatever their jobs in
hotel or restaurant or ministry, are also policemen? The secret police
set a permanent barrier to any more cordial relations you might hope

to have with the Egyptians you have met. The well-placed government official you have known for years, who once spent twenty-eight months in jail because, it was said, he was so well liked by so many Americans, will greet you with pleasure when you visit him at his office and will enjoy the reunion over coffee; but he will not join you for dinner. The great political difference between a ritual coffee at his desk and a relaxed dinner in a public restaurant is known both to him and you, and the knowledge sets a check on your conversation with him. You would like to remind him of the kindness and quick thinking he once showed in helping you out of a tight corner in the old days before he went to jail, but delicacy discourages the impulse. After the opening exchanges, the conversation falters and soon reaches the line beyond which it cannot pass. It is the blight of the police state.

Yet, for diplomats and correspondents and all those whose trade is politics, Cairo keeps its fascination. So much history has brushed its walls and traveled down its streets; for so long and from so many directions, it has been under the bombardment of events; and still, today, it seems destined to be the scene of a larger action. Even under an authoritarian regime, it keeps its personality, capricious, jaded, unpredictable, toward which one feels in continual reaction, good or bad —one cannot be indifferent to it. Cairo is the stage and thoroughfare of the Arab Middle East. Of all the cities of that region, so arbitrarily and so oddly divided against itself by frontiers drawn half a century ago to suit the policy needs and whims of European powers, this is the only one that holds its ground as the capital of a recognizable nation with an identifiable national history. Compared to it, Beirut is a nightclub, Damascus a capital in search of a nation, Riyadh a desert upstart, Amman an unhappy hybrid and Baghdad a resonant name for a place that has lost nearly all echoes of its past.

It was a quarter to eight. We were tuned in to the English-language station. The shadows were closing over the city when the music stopped and a woman announcer introduced the President. We leaned forward over the transistor.

The voice was measured, earnest and low. After the first few words, the woman translated.

Brothers. We have been accustomed in time of victory and in time of ordeal, in happy hours and in bitter hours, to sit together and to talk with open hearts. We have been accustomed to tell each other everything. . . .

The cadence was elegiac. Even an untrained ear could catch the rhythm of the sentences, the refrains and repetitions of Arabic speech.

We cannot hide from ourselves the fact that we have met with a grave setback in the past few days. But I am confident that we can all overcome our difficult situation in a short time, though we will need much patience, wisdom, moral courage and concerted action.

A grave setback . . . The words were too well chosen and too precisely nuanced to have sprung from a simultaneous translation. The announcer was reading from an English text.

A careful estimate of enemy power indicated that our armed forces, with the standard they had attained in equipment and in training, were capable of repulsing the enemy. We were well aware of the possibility of armed conflict and we accepted the risk.

He appeared to dwell ruefully on one point: both the President of the United States and the Soviet Ambassador in Cairo had requested Egypt not to be the first to open fire.

On the morning of last Monday, June the fifth, came the enemy blow. If we may now say that it was more powerful than we expected, we may also affirm that it came with more power than the enemy possesses.

Ten and a half years earlier, after the Sinai campaign, he had told his people that Egypt had been defeated by France and Britain and not at all by Israel. The Israelis had merely conquered empty desert as the Egyptian Army withdrew from Sinai to face the imminent French and British invasion at Port Said. This version of events had stood the test of time in Arab minds.

The enemy we expected to come from the east and the north came from the west. This proved without any doubt that facilities had been granted to him beyond his ability and far in excess of the calculated extent of his forces. . . . It is now certain that American and British aircraft carriers were close to the enemy coasts, strengthening his military effort. . . . It may be said without either exaggeration or emotion that the enemy was operating with an air force three times its normal strength.

The new myth of Western intervention would be more difficult to maintain than the old myth of 1956. The old myth was a deception that damaged no one. The new myth was a calumny.

Our ground troops which were fighting ferocious battles with great courage found themselves in the most difficult situation. The nature of the desert did not permit a full defense, particularly in the face of a hostile superiority in the air. . . .

The enemy concentrated mainly on the Egyptian Front.

The story unfolded. Defeat, yes. But we all fought like lions, against insurmountable odds. And it was not just Israel who defeated us.

As we listened, we had a presentiment of something more. We could feel his innate political skill at work in some unexpected way to turn the disaster to account.

The earnest voice continued at the same even pace, with the woman translating:

I will tell you frankly . . . I am ready to bear the entire responsibility. I have taken a decision and I wish you to help me with it. I have decided to give up completely and finally every official post and every political role, and to return to the ranks of the masses to do my duty with them like every other citizen.

Even now, after the enormous reverse, he kept his touch. There was wizardry in the way he drew his listeners into his circle. Suddenly he widened the scope of the drama to embrace them all in the magic of a name:

The powers of imperialism imagine that Gamal Abdel Nasser is their enemy. I wish it to be clear to them that it is the whole Arab nation and not just Gamal Abdel Nasser. The powers opposing Arab nationalism always regard it as Abdel Nasser's empire. This is not true. The aspirations for Arab unity began before Gamal Abdel Nasser and will remain after Gamal Abdel Nasser.

Now that he had renounced power and become a simple citizen, he could proudly invoke the hero's name and meditate on his role. He was the servant of the Arab nation and the expression of its will. He was the instrument of his people and he belonged to them.

In accordance with Article 110 of the provisional Constitution issued in March, 1964, I have entrusted my colleague, my friend and my brother, Zakaria Mohieddin, to take over the post of President of the Republic. . . .

The city was murky in the early evening blackout. The sirens had sounded at some earlier moment during the speech—unaccountably, since there was no air raid and evidently no Israeli planes were on their way across the Delta. The war was over, but this was to be another night of blackout. With the wail of the alert, there had been movement below our balcony as a troop of Egyptian policemen, white-uniformed, slipped quietly into the street to take up positions around the unlit hotel that was now the internment camp and the waiting room for so many Americans. A second troop of policemen, more numerous, appeared and passed on, the white figures fading out in the direction of the American Embassy. We listened in darkness to the concluding words.

The members of our armed forces gave an honorable example to the Arabs for all time and all places. . . . The glorious feats that our officers and soldiers have written in blood will ever remain an inextinguishable torch in our history and a guide to the future. The people were faithful as always, genuine and faithful as always. . . .

My heart is with you and I want all your hearts to be with me. May God be with us and guide us.

A few moments passed. A volley of shooting lights burst into the night sky. After the alert, an antiaircraft barrage? Or a gala fireworks, a celebration? At first we could not tell. The fire was too widely dispersed at too many random angles of elevation to be a barrage; and coming all at once from so many places in the city, and directed at so many scattered points in the sky, it had no discoverable target. The blaze of red and yellow shells was directed at the night at large. It was a blaze of tracers, as we soon realized; a make-believe response to a make-believe raid; an army demonstration produced by army camps about town. The tracers crisscrossed overhead; some leaped straight upward; others arched so low over the rooftops that the profiles of buildings flashed in the gloom. A measure of discipline to keep people off the streets? A demonstration to discourage demonstrations? The lights soared and tossed and sparkled, and from the balcony we watched until the last of them shot up over the darkened city, flickered and went out.

There was silence and then a sharp knock at the door. We hesitated before unlocking. The bedroom was pitch-dark; they had cut off the hotel electricity to keep us from violating the blackout. We had no desire to be routed from the privacy of that room, but the knocking was insistent and we realized from its authoritative and angry note that the hotel employee on the other side of the door was there on the instructions of the police, and had come to herd us downstairs to the basement, where, in due course, we and the others would be served supper in the delivery and storage rooms of the garage that had been

cleared for the purpose. It was a security measure. We unlocked the
door and followed our guide, other inmates joining us on the way in
the darkness of the stair well. Our mess hall was at the end of a narrow service corridor behind the cashier's counter. We would certainly
be no safer there, crowded into a small space, elbow to elbow at five
long wooden tables, than in the quiet of our separate rooms, but this
was the rule of the blackout; the rigidities of the police mind required
that we all be marched to a single place and assembled under the eyes
of the hotel staff. It would be a long wait for supper, as cooks and
waiters, like room boys and reception clerks, had been listening to
Nasser. We could see it in their faces. Sharing as they did the emotions of that night, sensing the force of the reaction that was bound to
come, and feeling a troubled sense of responsibility for us, they knew
that any American flag, any American residence, any American at all
would be a target; and they were concerned both for us and for themselves. They were tense but not unfriendly, and they knew their helplessness. The taciturn Sudanese waiters, tall, heavy and graceful in
their galabias, were having the same thoughts and listening for the
same thing as the rest of us, aware of the vulnerability of this hotel,
with the thin line of policemen who presumably were still standing
just outside the bolted garage door as our protection, in case of need,
against the mob. We waited while the cooks worked. Perhaps ten,
perhaps fifteen minutes had gone by since the end of the speech when,
sitting by candlelight at the five tables, we heard the sound.

It was not a mechanical sound, the crack of shots; nor a human
sound, the cry of voices; but more a sound of nature, like a wind or a
swell of tide or a flood heard from far off, large and enveloping but
muffled; a broad impersonal rumor in the air that the ear could not
break down or analyze. Even as it came closer, it kept its impersonal
quality; and even as it grew louder, it seemed to come out of wide
space, from no identifiable direction. We began to think closely of the
layout of the city around the hotel, the only building on its small, egg-
shaped block. The front of the hotel was on a side street that curved
back at a sharp angle from the Nile corniche, a few steps away; then
there was the other bending street at the rear of the hotel, where our
garage was; and we thought of the turn this street made as it went on
and passed the somewhat unkempt grounds of glum but stately man-
sions and, a little farther down, reached an intersection and the thick
blue-white walls that announced the British Embassy, splendidly

withdrawn in its handsome compound. Kitty-corner at the next crossing was the smaller, more intimate compound of the Embassy of the
United States. It was four or five minutes away at an easy walk. We
had this picture of the neighborhood firmly in our minds as we tried to
measure the distance and plot the direction of the sound. Its pitch rose
and grew more urgent, but we could still not be certain it was coming
our way. Then suddenly, in its passage, it acquired a shape. It was the
noise of a multiple rush, and somewhere inside it there were sounds of
another kind, harsh ejaculations, repeated shouts that seemed to give
it a rhythm. It acquired a source; we could place it in our mental picture; it was coming from the direction of the American Embassy. We
strained our ears and we thought, though we could not be sure, that
we heard cries of "Nasser! Nasser!" For a few minutes the sound
maintained its volume and its pitch, and then subsided. The beat
went out of it, the shouts were reabsorbed and the pitch fell. It was
again the toneless and impersonal sound of a far-off tide. It traveled
on in the night, diminishing, leaving the Embassy and us behind it,
apparently seeking a new object.

Others, in other parts of the city not far from us, heard the same
noise and felt it coming. From the glass-enclosed outside stairway of
the Hilton Hotel, where the second large group of Americans was
quartered, they looked down into the blacked-out expanse of Liberation Square and heard the flood under them: the sound that was both
a hum and a roar, the note of urgency and movement, and the other
odd, reiterated sounds that broke across it. The square was not entirely black. Sectors and patches of it glimmered in a pale-blue light—
the gleam of headlights, crudely and hastily painted over with daubs
of blue for the war emergency. By that illumination and at that closer
range, the people on the stairway were able to take in all that was
happening. The sound of rush, unanalyzable and unsubdividable,
toneless and liquid, was the sound of thousands of running feet, now
dimly caught in the headlights; and the harsh reiteration was the chant
of the running men.

"Abdel Nasser el Khebir . . . Abdel Nasser el Khebir . . ."—
Abdel Nasser the Great. Ceaselessly repeated.

Fifteen years earlier on a January day the people of Cairo, enraged
by a series of injuries and humiliations that had ended with the
slaughter of seventy Egyptian policemen by British troops then stationed in the Canal Zone, had flowed in riot through the streets of the

capital, invaded the vast salons and rambling hallways of Shepheard's Hotel, a landmark that in popular symbolism stood for the arrogance of British wealth and power, and, with torches and gasoline, burned it to the ground. Those on the Hilton stairway who knew their Egyptian history were the most afraid. The decision they had to make was whether to go upstairs or down, whether to seek shelter in private rooms on the upper stories or descend to the lobby and take their chances on making a getaway in the event of fire. The decision was made for them by the hotel management, again in compliance with the orders of the police. They were rounded up from the stairway landings and escorted to the lobby and thence to the underground garage, where they remained under guard.

In all parts of Cairo, in the squares and boulevards of the modern city, in the labyrinth of the old Arab quarter, on the island of Gezira, in Dokki on the other side of the river, and on the Nile bridges, the tide rose. Men and boys issued from the night and roamed, shouting, through the streets. The currents of running feet converged. For a time they became a torrent in Liberation Square behind the Hilton, where ten streets meet; but not for long. Even the torrent receded. The moment of danger passed. The demonstrators moved on, toward another object.

For the roaming had a destination and a will. The noise came, swelled and passed on. Every section of Cairo, it appeared, sent its tributary to the stream that rolled on in the night and did not stop until it reached a point three miles from the center of the city. It was the seat of the Government of the United Arab Republic, the office of the Presidency, Kubbeh Palace. On the grounds of that large and ornate structure, in a mighty demonstration, they chanted their plea: "No leader but Abdel Nasser! . . . Abdel Naser, come back! . . ."

Some went on from there, another mile along the suburban avenues of Abbassieh to the home of the President. Again they cried, "Abdel Nasser, come back!" and then, in chorus: "Our hearts are with you!"

Supper was over at last in our garage mess hall. Conversation had picked up during the meal, after the sound had gone, but had lapsed again during the long waits between courses; and it was time to leave that airless room. We walked back, groping, through the service corridor and out into the candlelit lobby that had been our living room for the past three days and our major source of second- and third-hand news, conveyed by the hotel clerks or brought in from the outside by visiting friends—British and Italian colleagues who were permitted in, even though we were not permitted out. It was a forlorn lobby in the best of times, and now it reeked of living and the litter of tin ashtrays. There was an assortment of cheap wooden tables and an acute short-age of chairs; and on the wall between two windows, a faded color photograph of a much younger Nasser, the same that was tacked to the walls of thousands of shops and offices the length and breadth of Egypt, in three-quarter profile, his quiet gaze fixed on the distance and his jaw out.

A man from the Embassy came to see how we were and to alert us to the new order of battle. The Egyptian Foreign Ministry had abruptly changed its mind, informing the Embassy that it must collect its entire staff and prepare to leave at once, in the dead of night, tak-ing the American colony with it. There had been a small concession in the end: five lower-echelon men at the Embassy would be allowed to remain as a skeleton caretaking staff; everyone else, from the Ambas-sador and the political officers down, would have to go. A possible interpretation of the order was that the government was beginning to fear it could not answer for our safety much longer. The train that would take us to Alexandria was already at the station. A convoy of Egyptian police trucks would come to the hotel and start picking us up at the door at two A.M. I went up to my room to pack.

It was an unusually thick and sultry night, but I had to observe the blackout. I closed the wooden shutters of my window, drew the blind and, turning, bent over the bed and felt under the mattress. On our first day the hotel staff had carefully stolen all our candles, informing us later, when we protested, that they were strictly forbidden because we might use them to signal to enemy aircraft. An Italian friend had smuggled in a fresh supply that was clandestinely distributed among us. I found the candle and lit it, settled it on an ashtray, piled my clothes and papers on the bed and considered the problem. The Egyp-tian customs at Alexandria were not likely to be kind to us the next morning. What would they make of all these books and documents, the copies of speeches and the handwritten notes, the guilty-looking scripts of news broadcasts with hasty last-minute corrections made in longhand and entire paragraphs neatly lined out by the censor? If I hid them away under the shirts and suits and the customs man found them, he would righteously confiscate the lot. If I put them in full view on top, I would have the jump and be able to argue it out. I decided to put them on top.

The telephone rang. It was a colleague, calling from the lobby.

"Nasser's back," he said. "We just heard. That is, he's reconsidering. He'll go before the National Assembly tomorrow and announce his decision." Nasser, my friend said, had issued the announcement himself, calling on the people to "wait until the morning"—that is, to go home—"for the sake of the nation and for my sake."

It was past one o'clock and I went back to my packing. So we would miss the scenes at the National Assembly in the morning. And the scenes of acclamation in the streets. The return of the leader. Triumphant reinstatement. Servant of his people.

An hour later in the lobby, among the heaps of luggage, we waited our turn to go out the door for our last trip through Cairo. One truck left with a load of tired passengers; another replaced it at the door; the baggage in the interval disappeared in a third. It was astonishing how many of us were able to climb into and disappear in the medium-sized vehicle they had for us, a closed police truck with collapsed wooden benches along either side—the kind of truck, I imagined, that they used for rounding up undesired demonstrators; uncomfortable, but to the purpose. Standing and sitting, we must have been more than forty persons. A police officer climbed in beside the driver, the back doors were slammed to and we pulled away from the curb. The city turned and twisted past us, sped along easily for a few moments (it must have been the corniche) and then, losing speed, seemed to go around and around us in wide circles. I lost my bearings. It was three o'clock, and the city outside our cabin was still. I reflected that this exodus of several hundred persons in the middle of the night, ordered on such short notice and carried out with such dispatch, showed remarkable organization on the part of somebody. They were in a hurry to get us out.

The truck stopped and we climbed out of it. We were at one side of the station, close to our platform. From somewhere behind us, perhaps a block away, came the cries of a crowd. The last of the demonstrators going home. We could not see them and they did not see us as we walked in to the train.

It was a long train of exceptional luxury, clean and fresh, composed entirely of air-conditioned parlor cars. There were swivel armchairs, cloth-upholstered, with deep-cushioned seats into which you could sensibly sink; there was room for everyone's legs; there was no fuss or worry over baggage, since it had all been taken to the baggage car and we would not see it again until we reached the docks at Alexandria.

We sighed with pleasure and regained our spirits, and I wondered who
it was at the Embassy who had produced this train out of the wilderness of that night. Muscles relaxed and conversation quickened under
the effect of the air conditioning. Everyone had a story to tell or an
incident to recall or a shadowy piece of inside information to confide,
unconfirmed and unconfirmable. The talk passed from chair to chair
and soon was general up and down the aisle. We began to savor the
luxury of physical and mental relief, the contentment of those who
have shared in the experience of a dramatic event and now, with the
strain past but nerves still alive to its excitements, with the vexations
over but memories and impressions still whirling in the mind, are
eager to share it again, in comfort and secure from harassment.
Everyone aboard the train had had his share. The Ambassador who
had come so recently to Cairo on his first diplomatic assignment, arriving less than three weeks earlier in the middle of the prewar crisis;
the political officers, old hands in Egypt; the military attachés, who
had given the Israelis ten days (at the outside) to sweep all before
them and reach the Canal in the event of war; the Marine Guards; the
Embassy women, whom the Guards, a few hours earlier that night,
had corralled into a seventh-story apartment, barricading the stairway
with furniture and arming themselves with tear-gas bombs against the
crowd as it passed that way; the wives and the children; the tourists
who had somehow managed to find their way back from Luxor to the
capital; the technicians, the newsmen—each of us had been caught up
in the event, seen his or her part of it and lived it, more or less intensely.

We still felt the stimulation and the daze. But now, in the cool of
the train, as we waited to leave, there was time to sit back and reconsider. The train apparently was in no hurry to go. One piece of information we had picked up was that Ali Sabry, Nasser's lieutenant and,
at the time, secretary-general of the country's only political party, the
Arab Socialist Union, was apparently connected with the demonstrations that had taken place that night. There had been a certain amount
of forethought and planning. The A.S.U. had lent a hand and given a
push. Some demonstrators, it was said, had stepped forth into the
night with posters ready in their hands. Others had been provided with
transport. A truckload of them had been seen coming across one of
the Nile bridges from Gezira. All this was probably true, and yet I
wondered whether it was relevant. We also knew, from friends who

had been there, that in the crowded pressroom of the U.A.R. Radio and Television Building, men went to the walls when the speech was over, cradled their heads in their arms and wept. If the party apparatus had prepared the ground and given the signal, the entire city had responded; and it was the response of a population that felt totally bereft. Nasser was the last prize of his people, the only one they had left after the immense débâcle; and the genius of his speech lay in his ability to make them feel their loneliness without him. He offered a mighty release for emotion—a release not of anger but of grief.

Grief and loneliness were stronger than anger during those first hours, and that, I supposed, was why the police had had such a relatively easy time protecting the obvious American targets in the city. The great disappointment after the great expectations was a bewildering blow; the presumed Anglo-American intervention an outrage; the loss of Sinai an insult; the loss of the Egyptian Air Force and the destruction of the army a humiliation, as well as a scandal which even the most ignorant must have sensed; but the loss of Nasser was a loss of identity.

Thus, in that frustrated world of dreams and images in which so many Arabs seem to live, the emotional image was again predominant, and again determined the course of events. There was, I thought, a kind of sense and inevitability in Nasser's return to power, if one could accept the terms of the Arab character and look at events for a moment through the same emotional prism. Nasser was the author of the disaster; he had failed, even on a surge of Arab support; he had conned and cozened his people; he had led them straight into the abyss of a vast defeat; and even his comeback was fraudulent, for he had used a trick and a calumny. He was the impotent hero. But he was Gamal Abdel Nasser still, as he had cannily reminded everyone, and his people wanted him back because it was he, after all, who in the course of the years had given them their most intense experience of confidence, identity and triumph.

Of all the people on the train, I thought, those who had been closest to the center of events and had felt the strain most deeply were the diplomats. The political officers at the Embassy, the four or five men at the top, had had to deal with the events directly. They had had the day-by-day knowledge of what was happening—the messages received and delivered, the replies that came and that failed to come, the interventions, the attempts to gain time, the dilatory devices pro-

posed by Washington—and because of this knowledge, they had been
subject, in a more intimate way than any of the rest of us, to the
stress of crisis. It showed in their faces. They were thoughtful and preoccupied, and under the worry there was a weary expression of puz-
zlement. They, too, were puzzled. As much as we. Why and how had
it happened? A month earlier, on May 9, no one had seen a war on
the horizon and no one had been thinking of it. There had been alarms
and accusations of a kind that was standard in this part of the world,
border raids followed by threats of reprisals, and expressions of "concern" in various quarters. The Arab-Israeli conflict was a permanent
threat to the peace and someday it might lead to another war, but no
one in Washington or Moscow, New York or Tel-Aviv had foreseen
this war, this year, in the spring of 1967. Now, as we talked it over,
we realized that the particular conditions for this particular war had
existed all along, though we had not seen them at the time; that they
had matured, probably, over a rather long period, and in the end had
started to converge, drawn together by some chain of circumstance,
and then, unexpectedly and very rapidly, had produced the war. But
what were the precise conditions? What were the links in the chain?
How far afield would one have to go in order to retrace the blurred
line of cause and effect?

The train slid into motion and, slowly gaining speed, pulled out of
the station without a jolt. It was half past four. We were to arrive at
the port in Alexandria at nine and then, after who knew how many
hours clearing our mountains of baggage through customs, the Greek
ship and the passage to Piraeus . . .

Some of us went on with our talk. There were so many unanswered
questions. Why had Nasser gone overboard? Why had he challenged
Israel to war? What had made him think he was ready? Of course, in
his speech, he said he had known what he was doing; the re-equipped
and re-established Egyptian armed forces would be able to repulse the
enemy. But how could he possibly have believed it? "He broke out of
pattern," one of the diplomats said. "He felt hemmed in and he went
for broke." But if there were any questions that puzzled the men from
the Embassy, they were these.

After all, Nasser was their job. They had been concentrating on
him, with all their wits and discernment, for many years. They had
thought about him intently every time they sat down to draft a policy
recommendation for Washington. Indeed, for fifteen years, through all

the violent ups and downs of our relations with Egypt and all the oscillations of our Egyptian policy, experienced men had been coming out to Cairo to figure out Nasser. It seemed they had never quite caught up with him, he was always out ahead; and their view of him was always ambivalent. Running after him was a trying job, but one that had its compensations and keen professional interest. It had the human interest of a character study, with an especially provocative character as its subject, and the speculative interest of a political study that consisted in watching a gifted man in the exercise of power.

He was a political animal first and foremost, combining in an extraordinary way the instincts and habits of the conspirator, the skills of the statesman and the psychic gifts of the mass leader. The conspirator in him was restless and watchful, prompt in decision and ruthless in action, always quick to exploit the occasion, full of ruse and resilience. Caught in a corner, he was certain to gamble. He was a master of improvisation, animated by a will to strike, redress, overturn, dominate. He had only one method of dealing with his enemies, and that was to eliminate them. He was probably no more ruthless than many another political or military leader in a region where conspiracy was endemic. But his reflexes were faster, his resources greater and his ambitions more far-reaching. The figure of the conspirator was written large in his public life, and not only in the tireless subversion he practiced throughout the Arab world and beyond. His great public triumphs, the stepping stones in his ascent to glory that gave to the Arabs the momentary illusion of strength and unity, were nearly always astonishing deeds that bore the conspirator's mark of swiftness and surprise.

The statesman added a set of talents of a more sophisticated kind. There were the suppleness of the brilliant tactician and the boldness of the imaginative strategist in the manipulation of power. The fact that these were natural talents was demonstrated by the rapidity with which he developed and displayed them. He showed his insight into the workings of power as soon as he acquired it, dispersing and disarming the opposition and establishing his personal ascendancy on the Egyptian scene. He took his measure of the competing powers in the world around him and moved on to the wider arena of the Cold War. His success in balancing the world's two greatest powers against each other and, at times, in extracting the maximum profit from each required more than virtuosity. It was, above all, to the liveliness and power of his political imagination that he owed his emergence as a world figure. From then on, when he spoke, the capitals of the world listened. He won the title of statesman, the only real statesman in the Arab world: a title freely accorded by friends and foes in East and West, and by none more freely than the Israelis, who recognized in him their only credible enemy.

He was an engaging man to meet. He was equally endowed with natural charm and natural cunning, and he used his charm advantageously. His visitors were immediately at their ease. He was the incorruptible puritan revolutionary who never lost the simplicity of his tastes or the naturalness of his manners; the autocrat who disliked elaborate formalities and used the relaxed approach of democracy. He spurned the insignia of rank and power, the usual marks of the military regime, the uniformed retinues, the ostentatious bodyguards. Unlike Habib Bourghiba, an Arab leader much closer to the West by intellectual formation and experience, he never built himself a marble presidential palace of polychrome mosaic. His holiday palace was a family-size, mouse-gray stucco villa by the sea at Alexandria. He lived with a republican sobriety that was remarkable in the Orient, where display and opulence are the normal companions of authority. The only touch of grandeur one could sense was in his republican title. Most of the old friends and fellow conspirators of the band of "free officers" who had sent King Farouk into exile and proclaimed the revolution had themselves been banished to political oblivion, withdrawn, set aside, shunted to insignificant and toothless posts. Only four remained at this time, and one of them, Field Marshal Abdel Hakim Amer, was about to go. Ten years had passed since any of the four had addressed Nasser as Gamal. He was Mr. President. There was no second-in-command.

He was always ready to talk at length, and informatively, of the condition of his people—of the poverty, ignorance and physical debility of the fellahin, of the degradation of those who had to live on wheat, kerosene and tea. His feelings as an Egyptian patriot and his ambitions as a pan-Arab nationalist were of a very different order. He was attached to his own people. He appeared to have, at best, an invincible mistrust and, at worst, an exasperated contempt for all other Arabs. He was welcomed like a god in Damascus in 1958, at the celebrations marking the foundation of the United Arab Republic, the merger of Egypt and Syria; but when he returned to Cairo, he told the

American Ambassador, "I feel better here by the Nile." The name of the United Arab Republic was retained in Cairo, in defiance of reality, even after the Republic collapsed. It expressed both a political nostalgia and an imperious political ambition; in any case, a formal commitment. But he loved the name and land of Egypt.

He had taken great pains, through the years, to improve his English, and, for his purposes, he had conquered it. He spoke it with pleasure and handled it ably, always making his thought clear, often with grace and irony and never tricked by the foreign syntax or vocabulary into saying something he did not intend to say. At times, when the conversation touched some old wound or grievance (chiefly, the stubborn indifference of "the West" to the rights and justice of the Arab cause), his sentences would meander without apparent beginning or end, moving back and forth over the same ground with obsessive repetitions. He read the Western, and particularly the British, press with a diligence that must to some degree have been compulsive. He always had to know what the old British enemy was saying about him, still the archenemy in his imagination although Britain had folded most of her Middle Eastern tents and history had reassigned her role to the United States. But what was true of the great majority of educated Egyptians, for whom English was the second language, was true also of him: his interests and the direction of his thoughts, as well as his grievances, lay westward. This was evident in small things as well as large. When the time came for his eldest daughter to begin her higher education, he sent her to the American University in Cairo. When she became engaged to a young army officer and he had to make plans for their honeymoon, he did not think of the Crimea or even Beirut. A secretary summoned the political officer of the American Embassy (at a time when relations with the United States were beginning to seethe with mistrust and rancor) and requested that the daughter and son-in-law of the President be enabled to go to Disneyland and Las Vegas, incognito. It was so arranged and so done.

The qualities of mind and feeling that in time were to find expression in the acclaimed mass leader were stirring in him long before he conceived his ambition to bring the Arab Middle East under the hegemony of Egypt. Already as a young man, he dreamed grandly. He felt the call of large horizons and of the beckoning "vital spheres" in which, he said, his country lived. Fate had willed that Egypt should be at the crossroads of the world. He pondered on his country's role

when he was a company staff officer, sitting by himself in the trenches
and dugouts of the 1948 Palestine War, and, as he later recalled, "I
traveled far in my imagination." After the Palestine battles he came
home with the "whole region in my mind one complete whole." They
were vague thoughts, dreamily ambitious thoughts with no political
conclusion; but they were signposts on the road his imagination was
traveling, and after the Revolution he gave them a more formal definition. History had destined Egypt to assume the responsibilities of her
role, for she lived in three circles of which she formed part: the Arab
circle, the circle of Africa and the circle of Islam. And then, in the
reminiscences of his *Philosophy of the Revolution,* he wrote his celebrated line: "I always imagine that in this region in which we live
there is a role wandering aimlessly about, seeking an actor to play
it."

Aimlessly. The word expressed the impatience of a man who by
now had demonstrated his capacity for action. His republican Revolution, with its promise of a new era for a new generation, had awakened hope and enthusiasm in Arab countries far beyond the borders
of Egypt. He heard the call of pan-Arab nationalism, which had origi-
nated not in Egypt but in the lands of Arab Asia on the other side of
Israel. But what was this pan-Arab nationalist movement with its impassioned cry of unity—supposedly the strongest political force in the
region, stronger than kings or politicians or governments—but in fact
only a baseless dream and an aimless fiction, with no actor to play it?
On the stage of politics, as events unfolded, it was a movement that
found its most vivid expression in the ecstatic response which the
Arab world accorded to the triumphs of Nasser in his battles with the
West. This response opened new paths to his imagination. Intuitively,
he perceived that Arab nationalism expressed, above all, a craving for
self-respect and a claim to recognition, and he responded to that need
with all his leader's sense of psychology and occasion. What in others
was a craving and a dream was in him a demand. The struggle against
Western imperialism became a pan-Arab drama, and he the protagonist. The Arabs applauded and were grateful. Instead of frustrations,
he gave them victories; instead of self-abasement, self-esteem; and
instead of an embittered sense of inferiority, his own promptness to
react, his boldness in riposte, his spirit of defiance and his ferocity
of pride.

So the hero was born, and as his role grew, so did his appetite. One consequence of the new role was that he had to assume a militant and uncompromising stand against Israel; as he realized somewhat belatedly, he could not aspire to primacy in the Arab world without being in the forefront of that battle. His major imperative was to establish the unity of the Arab Middle East under the leadership of Egypt; and so began that fateful series of foreign adventures, of plot, counterplot, insurrection and war that in the course of a decade wasted the resources of Egypt and at one time or another distracted the energies of every other country in the region. He proclaimed the Arab Revolution and made Cairo its headquarters; the city became the base for a flock of terrorist undergrounds and shadowy liberation movements that were often in fierce competition with each other. The leaders of these movements—sometimes public men, sometimes anonymous and faceless figures—went to Cairo for arms, money and asylum; and if, as happened on several occasions, they were not the leaders Nasser wanted at the time, they were removed from circulation, placed under house arrest and kept there, for weeks or months, at his pleasure. He was the father of the Revolution and they were its children. He was a tyrannical father.

The military agent and organizer of the Revolution, the supplier of finance and arms, was the Egyptian Army Intelligence. The pulpit of the Revolution was Cairo Radio. "The Voice of the Arabs," amplified by the acquisition of four 150,000-watt transmitters from Czechoslovakia, was the principal instrument of mass agitation; it was under the control and direction of the President's office and received instructions in political action propaganda from a five-man board headed by Ali Sabry during the period when he was Minister of State for Presidential Affairs. The "Voice" mobilized the power of the streets, raising the mob in the city or inciting the Arab Palestinian refugees in their camps. But historically it served the larger purpose of effecting an unprecedented revolution in the Arab lands. It created a public opinion where none had existed a few years before, among the illiterate and semiliterate masses of the Arab world from its northern reaches in the Fertile Crescent of Syria and Iraq to the bazaars of Aden and the desolate sands of the Pirates' coast. Neither illiteracy nor distance was a barrier to the spoken word.

Nasser equipped himself with an ideology, but his interest was never intellectual. Ideology gave scope, drama and the breadth of historic purpose to his action; his battle with the dynasts of Arabia became part of the unfolding global struggle with Western imperialism. His talent lay in sensing the usefulness of ideological tags in the game of power; positive neutralism, anti-imperialism, socialism, decolonialization and the rest were weapons in the contest for mastery of the Middle East. He used them tactically and often changed them as the pressures of the time suggested, depending on his estimate of who happened to be his most dangerous enemy at the moment. "Anti-imperialism" remained the permanent cry and expressed a permanent conviction; but as frustrations mounted, "imperialism" degenerated into a propaganda bogey, the mystic word that was used to explain everything and excuse everything, designating the wickedness of anyone who dared to oppose him. Yet it was not entirely propaganda; the bogey was often believed in. The British bogey continued as a force to reckon with long after the British had retired from the scene; it was somehow impossible to believe they had really gone and would not find a way to come back. Later the American bogey, popularly identified as the C.I.A., was believed guilty of the most monstrous plots. Imperialism was the hidden enemy constantly at work to thwart the dream of Arab unity.

Neither the statesman nor the conspirator was able to consummate that dream. The adventures of the hero accomplished nothing. The record of his extraordinary career in international subversion that made every Arab country's business his business and sent his arms and his agents everywhere, a quest for supremacy that was forever foiled and forever renewed with insufficient means, is without a parallel in our times. It is a record of misbegotten enterprises, botched exploits and chimerical designs. The passionate personalism of inter-Arab politics made it a fertile and tempting field for the conspirator. He was forever lured on. He had his general political purposes and the rudiments of an ideology, but he worked opportunistically from plot to plot, with no prepared strategy and no progressive plan of action. He recognized this trait in himself (though there is no evidence he saw it as a failing) and often said, reflecting on his behavior, "I do not act. I react." So he had reacted when he had scored his major triumphs on the international scene; but his comment served equally as the epitaph for his ambitious failures in the Arab world. By the end of the decade he had become one of the most frustrated as well as one of the most brilliant politicians of the age.

All his major enemies were still at their posts and ranged against him. Between him and the sources of Arab wealth in the East stood the elderly, implacable figure of King Feisal, the guardian of the Holy Places of Islam and of the oil of the Persian Gulf. Feisal was, in addition, the custodian of a religious code so fiercely puritanical that it forbade the showing of movies or of any other image of man, graven or printed, and banned from the realm of Saudi Arabia the phonograph records and alcoholic refreshments of the Western world. In each of these protecting roles he looked with steadfast and high-minded hostility on the republican upstart in Cairo who threatened his overlordship of the Arabian Peninsula by making war in Yemen and arming terrorism in the sheikhdoms and sultanates of the Aden Protectorate. Feisal was an austere and heavy-lidded man; his face was a patrician landscape, the eyes slow and melancholy, the beard fastidiously sharp and the prominent nose expressing a magisterial disdain. His austerity was softened by the graciousness of his gestures and the occasional gleam of humor in his eye. But, above all, he was a remote lord of the desert, where men do not contend with time and where silence in company creates no embarrassment. So Feisal, when a question was put to him, could be silent for so long that one wondered whether he had heard it. The answer, when it came, was solemn and circuitous. Even amid the imported European comforts of his royal palace in Riyadh, where he presided with aloof and desiccated dignity on a Louis Seize chair in an air-conditioned room, the impression of the tribal patriarch was so strong that the visitor saw him, rather, sitting in the heat of a desert tent, motionless and possibly silent for minutes at a time. He ruled over an immense kingdom that had no rivers or forests and was bounded by the desert and the sea; a country of sand waste and frowning mountains, hard desert and scattered oases, with few communications, seldom visited by the monsoons. It had seemed for a time, under the loose and prodigal rule of his elder brother, King Saud, that this archaic dominion might crumble in financial disorder, as its wealth was being dissipated by the Cadillac set of royal princes, the legion of his progeny, made innumerable by the practice of polygamy. But Feisal had come to the rescue (in what was decorously called a "transfer of power"), taking tightly in hand the finances of the royal family and impressing his people with building projects. After further upheavals in the royal house, he had finally deposed his profligate brother. There was no doubt that, with him, there was a firm wrist of control in Riyadh. He, too, could send arms to his side in the Yemen war. He, too, could deal in conspiracy and subversion. His country and his monarchy lived on, sustained by their share of the revenues from the fabulous gift of oil with which geology had blessed the Persian Gulf region, and protected, no doubt, against domestic surprise or sudden uprising by the vast isolation of the Arabian desert. In vain Nasser pounded at the doors of the House of Saud.

Barring his way to the Arab heartland of the Fertile Crescent, a young king sat on the Hashimite throne of the impoverished state of Jordan. The assaults on his rule were so numerous and unrelenting and came from so many directions, and the danger of an assault on his life was so real, that a less spirited man would have shunned these hazards and gone to live peacefully with his wife and children in Switzerland. But King Hussein represented a royal house far more illustrious than that of King Feisal. He was the direct descendant of Mohammed in the male line from the Prophet's daughter, Fatima; and the Hashimite family, the noblest of Arabia, had for centuries carried the title of Grand Sherif of Mecca and ruled over the Hejaz, the birthplace of Islam. With such blood in his veins and with the sense of mission that the memory of such forebears instilled in so brave and romantic a man, Hussein took his Arab honor seriously and yearned for acceptance as a genuine leader of Arab nationalism, whatever Nasser might say of him. His kingdom was an anomaly created by the British to provide a throne for his dispossessed grandfather, who had been chased from the Hejaz by King Ibn Saud, the warlike father of Feisal. It was a portion of the desert shaped like a primitive arrowhead, later made more anomalous still by the acquisition of a region west of the Jordan River including the Old City of Jerusalem, that part of historic Palestine which we know as the West Bank. The Hashemite Kingdom thus came to straddle the great cultural divide represented by the narrow stream of the Jordan, with a population of loyal Bedouin tribesmen on the desert side and, to the west, the Arab Palestinians, who looked down on the uncultured Bedouins and felt no allegiance whatever to Hussein. Cooped up with their hopes and fears in the towns and refugee camps of the West Bank, the Palestinians lived in limbo, in a truncated part of what had once been their homeland. The rest of that homeland now belonged to the Israelis.

By this time, in the early fifties, history had given an unexpected turn to the destinies of Jordan. The curious state with no claim to

nationhood, created by the British for reasons of dynastic convenience, had attained an importance its creators had never foreseen. Its
existence became a necessity. Peace in the Middle East depended on
the preservation of a weak Arab state as a buffer between Israel
and the rest of the Arab world. Jordan's strategic virtue in the precarious balance of war and peace was her military weakness, while her
general feebleness as a state attracted the solicitous economic help of
Western powers who were anxious to maintain the balance.

Hussein faced the risks of both foreign conspiracy and internal betrayal. Among his enemies he counted the Syrians, the Egyptians, the
Communists, the Palestinians and Arab nationalist zealots of every
variety. But among his friends he could count the Bedouin tribes, who
sent their sons to his army, and the United States, of whom Jordan
became the permanent pensioner. Hussein himself was the Supreme
Commander of the Jordan Legion, in fact as well as in name, handling
arms negotiations with the United States, taking the initiative in the
formation of new brigades and dealing with problems of organization
and training. For Nasser, it was bad enough that the soldiers of the
Legion were considered, man for man, the finest in the Arab Middle
East; worse, that the loyalty of these desert tribesmen held the country together and maintained Hussein on his throne; most galling of all,
that Jordan's existence was tacitly underwritten by the armed forces
of Israel. The soldiers of the Legion were Jordan's national police;
their main function was to guard its internal security. But the army of
the Israelis, who would never permit a foreign intrusion that might
change the status quo on their longest and most vulnerable border,
was in fact the military force that guaranteed the integrity of Jordan.
In vain Cairo Radio inveighed against the "thrones of treason" in
Amman and Riyadh; in vain Nasser wove his schemes to unseat or
ensnare the last of the Hashimites. Buoyant and shrewd, Hussein
seemed possessed of a miraculous charm that gave him a thousand
lives.

It was not only the kings of Arabia who resisted the leader of the
Arab Revolution. The Arab states of the "revolutionary" camp were
equally loath to submerge their sovereign interests or yield up their
identities for his sake. Syria, for a time, was the one remarkable exception. Nasser's agents in the Arab world; his various political mis-
sionaries; his Army Intelligence, with its far-ranging dissemination of
arms and disbursement of moneys; his military attachés, plotting sub-

version or insurrection with their clandestine contacts in the countries
to which they were assigned; his loyal friends and supporters, the
bands and cliques of Nasserist "free officers" who, if they were not
shot down, went to jail or into exile for him; the newspaper editors
who accepted his bribery; the blasts of his propaganda, the winds of
Cairo Radio—all of these were not enough to upset or blow down the
House of the Middle East. The moral of the story was manifest: his
ends were beyond his means. He had all the weapons with which to
achieve or impose Arab unity except the obvious indispensable one of
military force. When Syria seceded from the United Arab Republic,
he lacked even the force to bring her back.

In the name of unity, he brought division; and in the name of revolution, a barren tumult. During the decade or more of his adventures,
Arab politics would have been volatile and discordant enough even
had another man been President of Egypt. The coup d'état in which
another Feisal, Hussein's cousin, the King of Iraq, lost his life in
1958, and General Abdel Karim Kassem came to power, and the
countercoup of 1963 in which Kassem in turn was slain, would probably have happened even had there been no Nasser. Of the long succession of coups that made Damascus the most feverish of Arab capitals, Nasser was responsible for none, except in the sense that his
despotic rule of the United Arab Republic provoked the Syrians to
bring that experiment to a sudden end. Even without Nasser there
would have been pan-Arab liberation movements, terrorist undergrounds, republican uprisings; and he was never alone in conspiracy.
The only Arab country that did not plot against her neighbors, by
encouraging and promoting armed subversion, was Lebanon. She was
in no position to do so. The make-up of her population, so evenly
balanced between Christian and Moslem, dictated a policy of treading
softly and being all things to all men, in order to preserve that domestic peace and large measure of prosperity that had made Beirut the
commercial hub of the Arab East and a bankers' paradise. All the
others plotted: Syria against Lebanon and Jordan, Jordan and Saudi
Arabia against Syria, Iraq against Syria and Syria against Iraq, Saudi
Arabia against Egypt. Nasser's distinction was that he plotted against
them all, as well as against several others. During those years, from
1955 to 1966, Egyptian military attachés were expelled from Morocco, Tunisia, Libya, the Sudan (in this case, together with the Egyptian Ambassador and the rest of the Embassy staff), Jordan, Syria

(before the union with Egypt), Iraq, Saudi Arabia and, since the Arab world was not enough, from Ethiopia. Nasser was unable to fly arms to the Congo, to help the breakaway pro-Russian government of Antoine Gizenga, only because the government of the Sudan denied him the overflight rights.

In the end, the only powerful weapon that remained to him was peculiarly his own. It was his capacity to mobilize emotion. Collective emotion alone remained. Arab politics became more than ever a dreamlike fiction, with the frustrated actor now searching for a role to play. In the minds of Arab revolutionaries, even of those who resisted him and wanted to get along without him, he was still the spiritual head of the Arab nationalist movement. He was the lawgiver, high judge and chief executive of the Revolution. Even the radical young men of Damascus, who claimed to be more nationalist, more pan-Arab and more socialist than anyone else, and who feared his domination, felt the need to draw closer to him (though not too close) to enhance their credit and win the seal of nationalist legitimacy that only he could give. He was the protector, the providential man, the commanding symbol. It was a dreamlike position if only because his prestige so far outran his power. More than any other politician of his prominence, he lived by prestige; and, it seemed, by prestige alone. He could not allow it to decline; he could not tolerate the fading of the image. He was the hero who always had to prove himself. Every challenge required a response; every stroke a counterstroke; every affront a reprisal. The initiative must be his; he could not be crowded or boxed in. It was in his nature to strike out, and he seemed most certain to strike when he was backed into a corner, most audacious when he was put on the spot and most unpredictable when he was threatened.

And yet, as the diplomats had been able to observe, he had many high qualities of statesmanship. He often impressed them with his statesman's sense of reality and his head-on approach to problems, intuitive and practical, working from the facts up and accepting the restraints that they imposed. As for the prospect of war with Israel, he seemed to recognize and to appreciate thoroughly all the important military facts. His pan-Arab role had formally committed him to an eventual "war of liberation" of Palestine. His realism expressed itself in his determination never to go to war until he was militarily ready. The impatience of the Palestinian Arabs and the bombs of their terrorists, the provocations of the Syrian hotheads and the taunts of others would never be permitted to force him into war prematurely. He alone would choose the time and the place, and the time was not yet.

In a way, he was a figure of pathos. The question so frequently put in Cairo by visiting Congressmen and others was the natural and inevitable one: Was he an Arab imperialist bent on adventure, or a patriot dedicated to the welfare of his people? And the inevitable answer was: Both. Under him, for the first time in centuries, Egypt was ruled by Egyptians, and he had done more than any other man in Egypt's history to educate his people and to improve their condition. When he said the greatest thing he had done for them was to give them dignity, he was voicing again the aspiration and motive that had animated the young army officer and had made him the leader of a national revolution. The great achievement of the Aswan Dam, the abolition of the land system of the pashas, the reclamation of desert areas, the new industry and the education of millions of Egyptian children had been his doing.

"He broke out of pattern. He felt hemmed in and he went for broke," the diplomat had said. In another sense, I thought, he had been true to the pattern throughout, and everything he had done had been in character. He expressed the discords of the Arab spirit; in him, the character of the Arab people was projected on a large screen, as at a spectacle, reinforced by his own bravura and his instinct for dramatic action. He seemed, to his people, to portray their character with the boldness of an actor whose native gifts and copious resources had destined him for the role. He expressed so well so many sides of their nature—their aspiration and their distress, their impatience and their need, their excesses and their obsessions.

The larger pathos lay there. Nasser's story epitomized the malaise of his people: the turbulent and misdirected, ever renewed and ever frustrated Arab search for identity. The excesses in word and action, the quest for glory, the need for triumph, the irrational fiction, the spirit of revenge and negation, the denial of Israel and the will for her destruction—these were not the wayward or flamboyant expression of one side of the Arab character. They, too, belonged to the pattern, and they epitomized the Arab predicament. They were part of the psychic heritage of a deeply unhappy people.

· 2 ·

Glory and Decline

TWELVE HUNDRED YEARS AGO the Arabs were the masters of the civilized world. They ruled over an empire that was breathtaking in its physical extent, ebullient in its social and intellectual activities, and radiant in the manifestations of its culture. Their dominion spanned the civilizations of East and West, rising on the banks of the Indus River and descending at the farthest limit of the known world, on the African shore of the Atlantic Ocean. In the East they held Bukhara and Samarkand; in the West, the Straits of Gibraltar, Morocco and nearly all of the Iberian Peninsula. Arabic was the world language spoken by the peoples of this diverse empire. They sprang from a multitude of races and religions. Throughout the empire, as it advanced toward its height, the spirit of enterprise prevailed, and a wide and varied cultural and commercial intercourse gave it both a cosmopolitan wealth and a consciousness of unity. Merchants traveled to India, Persia and Spain in search of the products of those lands, while men of learning and students set forth on equally long journeys, with like facility and sense of purpose, in search of knowledge.

The creation of this empire was accomplished in the century that followed the death of Mohammed. In his triple role as divinely inspired Prophet, administrator of the law and commander of the army, he had fulfilled with complete success his mission of unifying the undisciplined tribes of Arabia. He had given them one God where there had been many, and an Arabian nation where there had been none. Exactly one hundred years later, in 732, the westward advance of the Arab conquerors was halted and turned back, in central France, at the Battle of Tours. Reading the story of their conquests, one is still struck with wonder and astonishment.

In the mind, the image of those conquests is that of a conflagration, sudden and swift. They occurred at a time when Western Christendom was sunk in the dateless barbarism of the Dark Ages. Who can remember a single thing that happened in the Europe of the seventh century, or name a single man who lived in that anarchic time, or recall a single date? For us it is the lost century, when nothing happened worth remembering; and several more centuries were to pass before our ancestors began to re-emerge from the forest and build the cities where a new civilization was born. But for the Arabs it is an unforgettable time. While Europe slumbered, the Arabs were busy making history, recording one illustrious date after another in a succession of military victories. In 635, three years after the Prophet had died in Medina, his warriors captured Damascus. All of Syria was subdued in the following year and all of Iraq the year after that, and in 638, the invaders entered Jerusalem. Three years later they completed their invasion of Egypt and, the next year, their subjugation of Persia.

Already at this time, faction and violence had divided the ranks of the conquerors, and it was not long before their leaders had fallen to war among themselves. The Prophet's widow, the "Mother of the Faithful," was active in the fierce disputes that surrounded these events. The successor of the Prophet, the third caliph, Othman—in principle a holy man who held supreme temporal and spiritual power —was murdered; and in 656 the contenders for the succession met in battle near the Euphrates River, producing the great schism in the House of Islam that has endured to this day. What is surprising is that, in spite of these quarrels, the disciples of the Prophet found the energies to pursue their expansion. They extended their sway beyond the frontiers of Armenia and India, and meanwhile, in the West, overran the African provinces of the Roman Empire. Before the century ended they were in Carthage, in 697; soon thereafter they reached Gibraltar, and the mastery of the Mediterranean was theirs. In the second decade of the next century, with the help of the Berbers, whom they had made their allies, they carried their arms and their faith into Spain, where, with the help of the Jews who lived there, they were soon to create the most civilized society in Europe.

The rapidity of this expansion made a deep impression on the conquerors themselves. Not unnaturally, they attributed their success to the religious banner under which they fought. The banner of Islam was the symbol of invincibility, and the Revelation of Mohammed was the bond that united the new empire. The secret of victory lay in the single sentence of their Profession of Faith: "There is no god but God, and Mohammed is God's Prophet."

But rapidity was not the only remarkable aspect of these conquests. The almost total lack of serious destruction was another; and this was due, at least in part, to the lack of serious opposition. The raiders from Arabia, exploiting the mobility which their experience of the desert had given them, were able to outwit and outpace the cumbersome military machines of the two tired empires, the Byzantine and the Persian, which for so many centuries had been warring against each other. The desert tribesmen came not to destroy but to acquire. They did not devastate the cities or lay waste the countryside. They did not pillage the splendid buildings they found in Syria, the like of which they had never seen in their homeland. Unlike the barbarian invaders of the West, who destroyed the civilization of Rome but accepted its religion, the Arab conquerors kept their faith but surrendered to the civilizing influences they encountered. The ancient frontier forts of the Romans became the first palaces of their princes; the Christian churches were either left to the Christians or converted into mosques. The adaptation was a simple matter of altering the position of the doors, ignoring the Christian aisles and praying across them in the direction of Mecca. In similar manner, the sons of Islam acquired and converted entire civilizations. In Syria, they inherited and preserved what was left of the tradition of classic Greece, in a region that had lived within the orbit of Hellenistic culture for nearly a thousand years. To the east, they acquired and assimilated the civilization of Persia, which had been dominant for even longer. Their glory lay in an achievement more astonishing than all their conquests. By some process of cultural alchemy, they transmuted all they found into something new, with a luster and a color peculiarly their own. The empire they created was not a conglomerate but a cultural whole; not an exotic amalgam but a society that was specifically Arab.

The period of their political unity was extremely brief. In the eighth century, Spain asserted her independence and soon thereafter acclaimed her own caliph; then Tunisia broke away, and later, Egypt. In large parts of the empire, the military conquests were politically superficial, and in some, the rule of the Abbasside caliph in Baghdad was acknowledged only by the mention of his name in Friday prayers. By the end of the tenth century, three caliphs ruled over the three great regions of the empire, each claiming to be the rightful heir of Mohammed. Yet, even in this time of decadence, the cultural achievement remained. The Arabs and the peoples they conquered, first by their arms and later by their language, were one community, united in the pursuits of a single culture, contributing to its manifold growth and enjoying everywhere, from the Pyrenees to the borders of Chinese Turkestan, the stimulating effects of its radiation.

In that age, the Arabs were the modern world. The interests of their society extended in all directions, both in time and in space. The savants of Spain traveled to Transoxiana and China. The goods of Seville found their way to the markets of Baghdad. The expansion of learning, like the expansion of trade, proceeded with eager excitement. Christian and Jewish scholars in Syria were commissioned to translate into Arabic the works of Euclid and Aristotle while, at the same time, other learned men were busy translating books on trigonometry brought home from India. The philosophers of the new society, in general more remarkable for the range of their interests than the originality of their thought, compiled encyclopedias of the knowledge thus amassed and wrote lengthy commentaries on the works of the Greek philosophers that were thus revealed to them. Some attempted to reconcile the primacy of Greek reason with the primacy of the Islamic faith. Their ambition was to smuggle the rationalism of the Greeks into the closed world of Moslem theology. In this valiant effort they were defeated. Theology won the battle and barred the way to further speculation. But what the Arab world lost, the West in due time was to gain. Among the many things that the Arabs communicated to the Western world was a knowledge of the works of Aristotle, a discovery that marked the beginning of a new and momentous journey in European thought.

If the Arabs lacked the speculative gift that produces great philosophers, they were rich in the intellectual curiosity that produces mathematicians, geographers, historians, astrologers and alchemists. These, together with poets and merchants, were the type-figures of their culture. In the perspective of world history, the role of this culture was to be that of carrier and transmitter. The ideas of ancient Greece and the techniques of the contemporary world were gathered in by the Arab scholars and traders; and centuries later, principally by way of Spain, this vast accumulation was passed on to the West, where it helped to awaken the European mind and, later, to arouse its energies for the adventures of the Renaissance. The varied occupations of Arab society are suggested by the range of benefits that it transmitted, both in the realm of knowledge and in the refinements of living. We owe to the Arabs the Arabic numerals we use, which they themselves call "Hindi" because they discovered them in India. European mathematics began with the Arab gift of the decimal system and the concept of zero, originally, again, the gift of India. From the Greeks and Indians, the Arabs gained their knowledge of trigonometry, a science in which they made a number of improvements before retransmitting it. From the same sources, they acquired algebra; and in this case, the West acknowledged the debt by retaining the Arabic word *al-jabr* in its vocabulary. The languages of Western Europe owe to the Arab navies the words *admiral, corvette* and *cable,* among many others; to Arab alchemy *alkali;* to Arab medicine *soda* and *syrup;* to Arab chemistry *alcohol* and to Arab astronomers *zenith* and *nadir.* Arab navigators contributed the use of the compass, having learned of the magnetic needle in China; and Arab astrologers, in their endeavor to solve the mysteries of astral influence on earthly life, invented longitude and latitude. The Arabs revolutionized the dressing and eating habits of the backward and underdeveloped West. The aromatic spices of the East may have only a limited market, but pepper has been a necessity since the Arabs presented it to us eight centuries ago. They sweetened our food with the introduction of sugar (we had previously used honey for the purpose), and they refreshed our leisure with soft drinks. They brought silk to Europe, over the Central Asian trade route from China; and in Samarkand, from Chinese prisoners, they learned the art of making paper, which soon led to a notable expansion of the publishing industry and the multiplication of bookshops. They brought sericulture to Spain and, what was far more important for most of Western mankind, they introduced the planting of cotton in the same country, and again we demonstrated our gratitude by adopting the Arabic word (*kutun*).

All this was long ago. The time of decay and disorder had set in long before the Mongols came in the middle of the thirteenth century, slew the caliph, massacred the inhabitants of Baghdad and demolished the irrigation system that was the life of Mesopotamia. What came after that devastation was not so much decay as the irretrievable results of decay. The Arabs as a people disappeared from the stage of history. No Arab nation existed and none was to reappear until the twentieth century. The Ottoman Turks produced a remarkable work of statecraft, the last of the Islamic empires; but for the Arabs who lived under it, the centuries of Ottoman rule were a social and political Dark Age of unrelieved lethargy, until the West broke in on it. During those centuries, the map changed, trade and power moved westward, and the world passed the Arabs by, leaving them isolated along the southern and eastern shores of their inland sea or forgotten in their desert hinterland. The Sublime Porte, the imperial government in Constantinople, was indifferent to their needs and neglectful of their welfare, being chiefly concerned that its provincial governors maintain the minimum degree of public order they required in order to collect taxes for themselves and the Sultan.

The time of grandeur was long ago. But it has left its imprint on the minds of men. The memory of that time is cherished by the great majority of educated men who call themselves Arab. It is kept alive by their study of the Koran, their principal textbook for the learning of Arabic, and by their reading of those literary works of the classic age which they regard as the highest achievement of the Arab spirit. The Arab Empire, triumphant but short-lived, blazing but evanescent, is still for them the outstanding fact of history. Given the cultural circumstances of the Arab world, the outsider, searching to understand, is compelled to wonder. To what degree does memory inspire the Arabs? To what extent does the experience of a distant past still shape their imagination? How far does it reach into the depths of consciousness and return to find expression in a desire to recover the political unity they knew for so brief a time so long ago? No one can measure these imponderables. Arab grandeur, Arab discontent, Arab unity—the lines of connection are too fine and too obscure for anyone to trace them objectively. Everyone must make his own appraisal.

Yet in seeking an appraisal, there are certain striking facts about the Arab experience, some of which are historically unique. Islam alone among the world religions achieved instant victory. Unlike the Jews, the sons of Arabia did not know enslavement and exodus or have to contend with a righteous but wrathful God. Nor were they taken into bondage, to be exiled to a foreign land and denounced by their prophets for their wickedness. The experience of a thousand years did not go into the making of their faith; nor did they see the destruction of their Temple. Unlike the Christians, they did not carry the memory of a Savior's sacrifice or, in imitation of him, seek martyrdom in order to bear witness to their faith or suffer persecution to assure its triumph. Judaism was an ethical struggle within a people, Christianity a spiritual revolution from below. Islam was, rather, a conquest from without. The conquest was secular as well as religious, since the party of Mohammed was a political party, national and military, as well as a brotherhood of the faith. The spiritual and the temporal, the cult and the state, religion and politics were one in the world of Islam, and the triumph of the faith signified the triumph of the Arabian nation. The mark of the Arab experience was success—immediate, spectacular and commanding.

Equally striking to Western minds is the psychology of the Arab people. Their approach to reality seems inseparable from their feeling for language, and no other people in the world, it is said, is so deeply responsive to the power and magic of the word. So it was in pre-Islamic times and so it is today. From the age of the tribal poets in the century before Mohammed, the word—written, spoken or declaimed before enraptured multitudes, the word sonorous and rhetorical, sensual and rhythmic—has exercised an overmastering spell on Arab minds. The Koran itself is venerated as a marvel of language, and not only as the message of God on which all law and science are based. It is said that the verbal genius of Mohammed, an unlettered man who dictated his revelations to scribes so that his people, no less than the Jews and the Christians, might have a Book, is one of the most cogent proofs of his divine inspiration. The Arabic language, rich and beautiful, is the most treasured heritage of the people who speak it, the object of reverent enthusiasm. For the educated, it is a source of delight in the refinements of literary expression; for all, it is a source of enchantment and the medium of their most deeply felt experience.

The poems that are most highly admired were written many centuries ago. Classic Arabic is remote from the spoken language of today, but the recitation of these poems profoundly moves contemporary audiences that are unable to understand them fully. It is a form of oral experience without parallel in the Western world. A large body of this classic poetry belongs to the tenth century, the ripe middle age

of the Abbasside caliphs. But the poems that are honored as the finest
expression of Arab genius were composed in the warring age that preceded Mohammed. They were declaimed by their authors, remembered by their audiences and transmitted orally from generation to
generation until, centuries later, literary men assembled and edited
them in book form. Already in that tribal time, Arabic was a mature
language with its established literary forms, and these poems, we are
told, were written in the terse and vivid speech of the desert, unviti-
ated by the search for subtlety and addiction to ornament that pleased
a later and no doubt less heroic age. The young Arab student still
reads with excitement these Arabian odes, which tell of the tribal activities of fighting, hunting, raiding and cheating and celebrate the
tribal virtues of valor, virility and honor. The poet in those times was
as highly honored as the warrior and his services were as highly
prized; he was a public figure whose talents were of inestimable value
in the politics of tribal rivalry. In his *History of the Arabs* Philip K.
Hitti tells us that "as his office developed the poet acquired a variety
of functions. In battle his tongue was as effective as his people's brav-
ery. In peace he might prove a menace to public order by his fiery
harangues. His poems might arouse a tribe to action in the same way
as the tirade of a demagogue in a modern political campaign." Now as
then, the word has a talismanic power; and often, words are more real
and more compelling than deeds.

A further peculiarity of the Arab world, which in a past age was
synonymous with the world of Islam, lay in its conception of itself.
Islam was a pugnacious religion. The natural assumption of superiority which every self-confident culture seems to display toward every
other took a very particular form. The world view of the Moslems
divided mankind into two communities, the House of Islam (*Dar Islam*) and the House of War (*Dar Harb*) or the House of the Infidels.
The House of Islam was in a permanent state of war with the House
of the Infidels that lay beyond its borders, and it was by definition
invincible. Among the various types of infidels who inhabited that
outside world, the Islamic mind drew no particular distinctions. To
make peace with the House of War was impossible; and since it was
equally impossible to engage in perpetual warfare, the periods of
peace which the Moslems accepted were defined as periods of armistice. The honor of Islam as well as its theology helped to encourage
this concept of history.

For us it is sometimes difficult to reconcile this notion with other things we know about the Arabs and their empire. The caliphs for the most part showed a generous enlightenment in their treatment of the religious minorities who lived under them, at least to a degree that shamed the Christian rulers of the West. The terrors of bigotry and theological hatred that culminated in the Spanish Inquisition were generally unknown in Islam. No caliph or Moslem prince ordered a mass expulsion from his territory, as did a thirteenth-century king of England with the approval of the church. England, as a result, lived without Jews for three centuries. The practice of the Arab conquerors was to exact a tribute from their non-Moslem subjects, and in return they granted religious tolerance. It was at least a more genial bargain than anything offered by the Christians. Many Jews and Christians found it easier to sacrifice their faith and embrace the religion of their rulers than to sacrifice their money. They submitted to assimilation, and this process was greatly facilitated by the simplicity of a faith that carried no heavy cargo of complicated dogmas. The Christians and Jews who kept their faith suffered various social disabilities to remind them that they were second-class citizens, but the occasions on which they were compelled to wear black clothes and ride on donkeys or accept similar indignities were rare. One caliph of the Fatimid dynasty outraged Christian Europe by murdering Christians and destroying the Church of the Holy Sepulchre. He also destroyed the synagogues throughout his domain and burned the Jewish quarter of Cairo to the ground. All the scholars agree he was insane. And in Morocco a fanatical sect put to the sword those Jewish communities that refused to accept Islam. But such outbursts were the exception. No part of Islam ever knew the anti-Semitic crusades, the popular killings that became mass movements of plunder and massacre in the name of Christ, and in the end destroyed Jewish life in northern and central Europe and drove the survivors to Poland. In the age before that slaughter, Jews served in the highest positions, as ambassador, vizier or prime minister, at the princely courts of Moslem Spain, while Jews, Christians and Moslems alike shared in all the activities of Spanish society. The Arab masters, in those days, still sought the collaboration of their subjects. The great majority of the Jewish people and their most flourishing communities were then to be found in the Arab world.

But this age of tolerance died and soon gave way to an age of surly

fanaticism. As the Moslem society decayed, the social cleavages became wider and deeper. The transformation proceeded at various
paces in various parts of the fragmented empire. The Christians
helped to excite the fanaticism by their Crusades; they lost their asso-
ciate role in Moslem culture, while the Jews sank back to the status of
an unwelcome and despised minority. Moslems as well as Christians
and Jews were the victims of the general decline, becoming more hostile and exclusive as they became more miserable. The society of Islam, as it lost strength, became ever more deeply confirmed in its
sense of exclusivity with regard to the rest of the world.

Late in the seventeenth century, the House of War turned against
the last of the Islamic empires. The armies of the sultan were repelled
at the gates of Vienna and thrust back into the territory of their earlier
conquests. The Ottoman Turks had to bear the psychological shock of
this first reversal, and a few years later, for the first time, Islam was
forced to accept a peace treaty dictated by the infidels. The theological illusion of strength was shattered and the doctrine of invincibility
destroyed; and further humiliations were in store.

For the Arabs, the awakening came in 1798. General Bonaparte, at
the head of a French expeditionary army, landed in Egypt and swept
triumphantly to Cairo. The French departed less than two years later,
but the Arab Middle East is still living under the shock effect of the
new meeting with the West that began with that adventure. The significance of the French expedition, accomplished with such stunning
ease by an army that possessed the most advanced weapons in Europe, lay in its immediate involvement of other Western barbarians in
the affairs of the Middle East. The British were aroused to the pre-
eminent strategic importance of a region that lay astride their land
routes to India. A century and a half of Anglo-French rivalry followed, commercial as well as political, spurred by the great Egyptian
cotton boom of the 1860's, when the world source of cotton was eliminated by a civil war in the United States. One result of that rivalry
was the construction of a waterway, the Suez Canal, an undertaking
resolutely opposed by the British, who feared the establishment of a
French enclave at the crossroads of empire, but successfully brought
off by a French promoter of irresistible missionary zeal, Ferdinand de
Lesseps, who sold it to his countrymen as an investment in French
commerce and glory and to the Egyptians as a guarantee of their prosperity and independence. In 1882, thirteen years after the Canal was

opened, the British occupied Egypt in order to protect De Lesseps'
creation and their many related interests in the country; and in 1898,
to protect Egypt, they completed their occupation of the Sudan. Six
years later, Britain and France mutually sanctified each other's colonial rights, with an agreement that acknowledged British dominance
in Egypt and French dominance in Morocco.

Today in the Middle East we are still measuring the psychological
fallout from these events. After the first shock to Arab solitude came
a xenophobia that still hangs like a mist over Arab society. It was the
xenophobia of a world that had for so long been separated from reality by lonely and romantic memories, until invaded by infidels bringing a powerful technology and all the arrogant paraphernalia of a victorious alien culture. The irruption of that culture revealed to a proud
people the weakness of its own.

The idea of success, the magic of the word, the sense of exclusivity
—these are part of the psychic heritage that seems to have governed
so largely the Arabs' reaction to the West and their approach to the
political ideal of Arab unity. Other peoples have a common language,
common culture and common memories—the Spanish-speaking
peoples of Central and South America, the English-speaking nations
in various parts of the world. None like the Arabs have a common
hope and none like them are ruled by a common dream. The declared
goal of Arab nationalism is the achievement of pan-Arab unity. Even
more than a political goal, it is an emotional imperative.

Remembering their past greatness and treasuring that memory, the
Arabs ask themselves: Why, with our culture and our history, are we
no longer great? Why aren't we a success? It is a painful question and
a source of great internal suffering.

In seeking an answer to that question, the Arabs tend to externalize
the blame. It is easier for all of us to look outward than inward, and in
this fashion the Arabs seek to explain their dilemma to themselves. If
they are weak and unsuccessful, it is because they are politically divided. If they are quarreling, it is because unnatural borders have set
them against each other. If these borders were abolished, their internal problems soon would be resolved; and if political unity were secured, the Arab nation would again be a force in the world. Unity
seems the sovereign remedy not only for their political frustrations
within and without, but for the more intimate and profound anxieties
that disturb the Arab mind. The Arab intelligentsia are persuaded that

without this remedy there can be no Arab cultural revival, and the wounds of a humiliated Arabism will remain unhealed. In the achievement of unity, they see the image of regeneration.

If the quest for unity has thus far brought nothing more than a new series of frustrations, the failure seems to lie less in the difficulties and obstacles, real and formidable as they are, than in the nature of the dream and of the imagination that sustains it. Weak, poor and divided, the Arabs still pursue a politics of grandeur. Their struggle with the imperialist West is enacted as a heroic drama in which a messianic protagonist, like Nasser, performs extraordinary feats to the applause of the Arab masses. The poets of this drama are the ideologues and propagandists. They summon the Arab peoples to assert their strength by seizing the levers of power that the enemy has created among them. Oil is the first of these levers and the Suez Canal is another. By withholding the oil and by closing the Canal, the enemy will be humbled, his bank balances depleted and his vaunted naval power, the United States Sixth Fleet in the Mediterranean, reduced to a mess of floating scrap. In this drama the Arabs overestimate their strength and seek a role that is beyond their means in the modern world. Support for the Arab cause, in its political and economic boycott of Israel, is made the test of relations with powers far greater than either Israel or they. Even on their own people they impose their conception of honor. They do not permit the slightest move to resettle the Arab Palestinian refugees on Arab territory, no doubt because they believe it is politically opportune to preserve this living proof of a lasting grievance, but equally because Arab honor cannot accept an implicit acknowledgment of defeat at Israel's hands. The refugees are only temporarily refugees; tomorrow, with victory, they will return to their homes in their plundered motherland. Meanwhile, they are confined to their camps or, at best, to the meager prospect of seeking a livelihood in the barren kingdom of Jordan.

The disasters of the heroic imagination have been most costly in the sphere of inter-Arab politics and especially in the passionate quest for unity. In the Arab mind, this goal is to be reached not by the processes of integration but by a sudden breakthrough. It will be a heroic action, accomplished not through the development of political institutions or the tedious unfolding of an economic design, but with éclat— by a challenging exploit of arms or diplomacy. It will be achieved by intrigue, pressure and bargaining; the lion and the fox together will bring it about. It will be an affirmation of Arab honor. The hero demonstrated that he lacked the means to bring off such a coup; his first venture in pan-Arabism, the union of Egypt and Syria, was also his last, since he had overreached himself. The Arabs were disappointed in that performance, but they still aspired to complete political union, to be achieved by a stroke. In the idea of unity, they see the image of immediate and spectacular success.

With its assumption of cultural superiority, Arab society was psychologically ill-equipped for its encounter with the West. It was a society deeply disturbed in itself. The malaise lay within. The first thing that strikes one on a personal meeting with Arabs is the vivacity of their charm; the second, the ritual of their courtesy; and the third, their deeply instilled sense of hospitality. Next, one becomes aware of the solemn patriarchal organization of their families and, as a corollary, of the inferior and sometimes abject position of the women. One is not permitted to penetrate very far into these mysteries, and one's awareness of the subjection of women comes principally from the fact that one so seldom sees them in Moslem homes or, for that matter, anywhere in the company of men. They are busy elsewhere, while the men talk. One senses the bleakness of a social life from which the pleasures and consolations of feminine company are so uniformly absent. Only in the half-Westernized societies of Cairo, Alexandria and Beirut, and notably among the Christian families, which give quite another place to women, does one see exceptions to this general drear picture of nonmingling of the sexes, so firmly marked by masculine dominance and feminine dependency. The men, in their worldly pursuits, are forever on guard against the envy of their fellows. Whether they are desert Bedouins or city merchants, they are solitary individualists who make their way through life by a series of personal transactions. The sympathies and civic obligations of the wealthy seldom extend beyond the class into which they were born. They are fatalistically indifferent to the misery of the poor, the dispossessed, the derelicts, the refugees. It is the world at large that has brought into being these unfortunates and, specifically, the Western world that is responsible for the refugees and must succor them with its charity. For the destitute in general, there is little hope in the efficacy of action.

Last of all comes an impression of loneliness. The Arabs as a people feel themselves to be alone in the world; individually, they feel themselves to be alone in their own society. Beneath the graceful ritual, more deeply instilled than the sense of hospitality, is the sense of mistrust. Every man, one comes to feel in the end, lives by himself and for himself, trusting no other. Every man must plot to save himself, and deception is a rule of self-defense against the malice of one's brothers. Lacking the bonds of trust that normally give cohesion and stamina to a society and bring meaning to endeavor, men live in a moral atmosphere of loneliness and betrayal. These are, indeed, recurring themes in contemporary Arab poems and novels. It is a saddening condition. Collectively and individually, the ruling passion is the passion of honor. Son plots or fights for his honor against father and father against son, brother against brother, cousin against cousin, and family against family; the entire Arab nation, having lost its self-respect and self-confidence, craves to win back the respect of the West and fights for its honor against the outside world. The affirmation of honor is victory, prestige is the reputation for being victorious, and the shame of dishonor is the admission of defeat.

The idea of unity is also fostered by what Westerners see as a peculiar ambivalence toward facts in Arab minds, an ambivalence that seems forever tilting away from reality toward fiction. The Western mind in recent times has developed an unassailable esteem for facts: hard, concrete, observable facts with sharp and definite contours. We base our sciences on the collection and association of these dispersed but sharp-edged particles; in our untiring compilation of statistics, we flatter ourselves that we also base our public policies upon them; and we have amassed so many that we feed them into machines that handle them for us. We even look into ourselves to discover whether the facts of our emotional experience are really what they appear to us to be. Our children soon learn the distinction between subjective and objective. But in Arab culture, facts do not hold this exalted and secure position. They are infirm and fluid, of doubtful substance and uncertain color, their contours melting away into the world of imagination. The Arabs seem to have a faculty, unknown to us, of feeling, thinking and living comfortably on two disparate planes of reality. There is the plane of everyday fact, on which they go about their business and manage their affairs. Then there is the plane of the emotional or rhetorical image, which they enter when they sit down to read their newspapers, listen to their radios or engage in a discussion of political or communal affairs. Such a discussion is an invitation to Arab fantasy. In seeking to explain the profound meaning of developments, the Arabs look for the hidden hand; there must be a plot or conspiracy somewhere behind the carefully arranged façade of events. Islam has taught them that internal as well as external forces are at work in history. The world today is populated by these internal forces, portentous and powerful, screened from view but ceaselessly active. They bear such names as Western imperialism or international Zionism or, more prosaically, the oil interests. The Arab vision makes politics exciting and history entertaining and vivid. But the Western correspondent or diplomat, so persistently and dogmatically intent on ascertaining facts about the actions of men, feels adrift and apprehensive on these high seas of the imagination which grow more stormy and menacing in times of political crisis and emotional pressure. Every correspondent who has known such times in the Middle East is acquainted with the feeling of dizziness with which, at the end of the day, he surveys the information he has gathered during his rounds, not merely his hurried notes on the events that have publicly happened or have been officially announced by some spokesman to whom he can attribute them, but all he has been told, on this side and that, by people in various stations whom he calls his "news sources" and whom he has gone to see in search of enlightenment. He returns to his typewriter, begins to reassemble this material and sort it out in his mind, and then realizes that what he has is a vast, red-hot and amorphous ball of rumor. Before it can be of any use, he must consult his intuition of the dynamics of events; that is, use his common sense. Of each piece of "information" he has picked up, he must ask the same question: Is it a fact, a belief, a hope or a fear?

Every journalist who has worked there has his store of episodes illustrating this creative tendency of the Arab mind. They would indeed be merely episodes if they were not so representative: the story of the dummy shells and bullets with which Jordanian artillerymen and machine-gunners were treacherously provided during their defense of Jerusalem, which is why the city fell so rapidly; of the Egyptian officers who came across the lines in Sinai to betray to the Israelis the strategic plans of the Egyptian Command and the order of battle, which is why the battle was lost; of the capture of Gaza, in 1956, by British and French troops landing from the sea, since the Israelis could never have done it by themselves. These tales were not the product of official propaganda nor even of common everyday credulity. They sprang spontaneously from the popular mind—that is, from the popular capacity for belief—and they soon became common currency.

In the autumn of 1956, when the Israelis were occupying the Gaza Strip, the young colonel who was the Israeli Military Governor of the area was puzzled by such extravagances and by their general acceptance by the people of the town. He resolved to put the claims of Cairo Radio to a psychological test. One evening he invited to his office a group of city fathers, the notables and elder citizens of Gaza, the men of consequence. As they sat in a loose semicircle in front of him, in the manner that the etiquette of the East prescribes for these occasions, he offered them coffee and presented the following challenge.

"Gentlemen, you have all heard what Cairo Radio has been saying. It says that on the day after the Israeli Defense Forces entered Gaza, they massacred seven hundred men, women and children here in the town. You are aware that this is not true. . . .

"How can you put any trust in Cairo Radio? Can you ever believe them again?"

After a pause, one of the eldest notables, sitting closest to the colonel, felt it his duty to reply. He leaned forward and said: "Ah, but we *feared* it might be true. . . ." He then sat back, satisfied that he had explained his position.

In Baghdad a few years ago a Western correspondent had occasion to interview the Iraqi Prime Minister of the time. During the preceding months the Prime Minister had made a number of speeches announcing the imminent suppression of the Kurdish rebellion by the forces of the Iraqi Army. The Kurdish rebels, fighting a stubborn and resourceful guerrilla war in their mountains in northeastern Iraq, refused to be suppressed and still were active in their harassment of the government forces. The Prime Minister had just made another speech, promising their imminent destruction.

"Mr. Prime Minister," the correspondent asked, "why did you make your speech yesterday? The Kurdish tribes are still fighting hard. Won't your speech boomerang, especially after the others you have made, if the new offensive against the rebels fails?"

The Prime Minister was surprised and, it seemed, nonplused by the question. Gathering his wits, he replied that this time things would turn out very differently, since the Iraqi Army was in a strong position, with every prospect of bringing its mission to a successful conclusion. At the end of the interview, his *chef de cabinet* accompanied the correspondent to the stairs.

"Mr. Y.," he asked somewhat sharply, "how long have you been in the Middle East?"

"For two years."

"Then surely you should have known better than to ask the question about the Kurds. You should know that when the Prime Minister made his speech, he believed it and so did everyone who heard him. They would never think of calling him to account if, by mischance, the army campaign does not go according to plan."

In the summer of 1967, an English visitor stopped at one of the two large camps for Arab Palestinian refugees outside the town of Jericho, in the West Bank region occupied by the Israelis. The residents of the camp had fled to the East Bank of the Jordan River before the arrival of the Israeli troops, and only a few camp officials remained, among them the Arab camp manager and an Arab schoolteacher, a woman. The schoolteacher talked of her experiences during the war and told how the Israelis had lined up her children against a wall and shot them. "I don't believe that story," the visitor bluntly said. "Where did you get it?"

With vehement passion the woman replied, "I didn't get it from anyone! I lived it myself, I saw it happen!"

Later the visitor asked the camp manager about the story, reminding him that he himself had told her the entire camp population had fled in panic across the river and no one was left when the Israelis came.

"It didn't happen exactly as she says," the manager said. "It isn't exactly true. But for her it is a fact and she believes it, because she believes it could be true." It was enough that she believed the Israelis were capable of such a deed.

Even after long exposure one cannot cease to wonder at the facility with which the Arabs are able to rewrite history as it is being made, then to believe their version of it, and in some cases, to act on the basis of their belief. In times of stress, their imagination propels a hope or fear or suspicion across the line that we are trained to draw between lie and truth. It is a world of subjective truth, where belief may have the validity of fact for the purposes of action. For us it is another universe of discourse, often exasperating and nearly always disconcerting, since we can never be certain where to draw the line. Immediately we leave the world of humdrum everyday existence, we

begin to encounter this strange disparity that pervades so many regions of Arab thought and life: the disparity between fantasy and fact,
belief and reality, the image and the event, the word and the deed.
Myth takes over from history and rhetoric replaces action. It has been
remarked that the same ambiguity can sometimes be observed in the
operations of Arab armies or the practices of Arab governments. A
command may seem as good as its execution, and the announcement
of a plan or program may be taken as the guarantee of its fulfillment.

The power of the word plays its part in these mental processes. The
Arabs may know that the claims of Cairo Radio do not correspond to
the facts, yet these claims have an imaginative reality for them because they wish to believe at least a part of their message. When Cairo
Radio one day in 1956 told the Arabs of Israeli-occupied Gaza not to
send their children to school the following morning, because the Zionists had laid a plot to blow them up, they knew it was not necessarily
so. But they heard and they believed the inner message, the awful
warning that the Israelis were a treacherous people, supported by the
powerful and hidden forces of Zionism, dedicated to fighting the
Arabs everywhere by any and all means, and, therefore, the Arabs of
Gaza must never give them their trust or consent to collaborate with
them in any way.

So, too, the verbal image of the "Arab nation" so often evoked in
the speeches of Arab statesmen, with its flattering promise of rebirth
and glory, has a consoling and compensating power, and becomes an
image that Arabs nurture and live with. It commands the allegiance of
many Egyptians who with another part of their minds are convinced
that Egypt's place is on the Nile and that her supreme effort must be
made not in the tempting lands of Arab Asia but at home on Egyptian
soil. It sustains the hope of Palestinian refugees on the West Bank and
in Jordan, who feel they belong to no one and least of all to the Hashimites, and through the image of unity find escape from the ordeal of
daily living into the nonexistent world of a reunited Arab nation. In
that larger world they rediscover their identity. The Arabs, it seems,
must say and believe in order to survive. Their power to believe, together with their fatalism, is their resilience.

From all of this comes the lasting discrepancy that is the salient
fact of Arab political life. The talk is always of unity. The everyday
political reality is the clash of interests among established nation-
states. The goal of all political action is the achievement of pure pan-

Arabism. The reality is the recalcitrance of everyday political facts. The drama of inter-Arab politics lies in the tension between this homeless, wandering dream of a pan-Arab nation and the innumerable sources of division. Hydra-headed and at odds with itself, speaking with many tongues, the Arab East is still self-entangled and self-bound, haunted by the same proud hope and impelled by the same need. Political life reverberates with the continual interreaction of events and pressures. "I found nothing but echoes responding to one. An event may happen in Cairo today; it is repeated in Damascus, Beirut, Amman or any other place tomorrow. . . ." The words are Nasser's. With all their disputes and schisms, the Arabs are still a community. Their aspiration is genuine and the goal of unity is valid.

Their language and the culture of which it is the carrier are the source and spring of this yearning. It is strongest in the literate classes and especially among the intelligentsia, schooled in the literature of classic Arabia; and, through the very medium of language, it is preserved in the sensibility of all educated Arabs. Among the people at large, it has received a new stimulus from the processes of modern mass education, not to mention the incitements of modern propaganda. Another heady stimulant has been the gift of nationhood. It is impossible for the Jordanians, and difficult for the Syrians and the Iraqis (though considerably easier for the Egyptians), to find something resembling national identity within the borders the British and French drew for them. It is natural that the Arabs should seek a more convincing national character. They themselves argue that the imperialist powers dealt a particularly cruel blow to the Arab world. To the peoples of India and Indonesia, the British and Dutch left a large measure of unification; on the Arabs, the British and French imposed a political hodgepodge as they divided the spoils after the destruction of the Ottoman Empire. There is force in this argument. The British and French misused the Arabs, broke their solemn engagements to them and appropriated to themselves various sections of a region that was strewn with religious and ethnic minorities, Christian and Islamic, tribal and national. Beneath the level of Arab cultural unity, there was a host of subcultures that presented, and still presents, a picture of warring diversity.

The gift of modern nationhood had a further psychological consequence. It brought with it a new consciousness of history, and in a sense the achievement of nationhood was not a release and fulfillment but the source of another frustration, as the Arabs recalled their history and beheld their fallen state. Soon the enterprise and technology of the West brought a glittering promise of seemingly unlimited wealth that was the cause of a further schism. Oil divided the Arab states into the haves and have-nots. The discovery and exploitation of Middle East oil preceded the period of Arab independence; but the immense expansion of production that created the schism is a recent phenomenon that followed the national liberation of the major Arab states in the aftermath of the Second World War. A greater degree of economic and political union is a valid goal if only because of the benefits the Arab world might gain from it, if statesmanship could bring it about.

Once again the Arabs look outward and tend to externalize the blame. They are compulsively inclined to impute to the West the historic responsibility for their condition, and their sense of grievance is a collective obsession. To blame the Western imperialists for the weaknesses of their society, the impoverishment of millions of their people, the bad habits of their bureaucracy and the failures of their leadership is to deny their own history and to disregard the legacy of four hundred years of Turkish misrule. Measured against the centuries, the Western invasion of the Middle East was only a large-scale raid. The period of Western rule was much shorter than that experienced by many other colonial peoples: seventy years of British domination in Egypt, sixty in the Sudan, forty in Iraq, twenty-eight in Palestine; a hundred and thirty years of French suzerainty in Algeria, but less than half as many in Morocco and only one generation of French rule in Lebanon and a similar brief span in Syria. The oldest British holding in the Arab world was the port of Aden. In 1839, alarmed by the plunder of an Indian ship off the South Arabian coast, the British seized the fishing village of Aden in order to prevent such piracy and annexed it to India. Except for that port and its hinterland, the Arab Middle East never had to endure the burdens of colonialist rule in the classic form of direct imperial subjection. What the experience of the Arabs seems to show is that the indignities of indirect rule can often be as abrasive as the burdens of classic imperialism. Of these indignities the Arabs had a wide experience.

The British and French were imposing themselves in Egypt long before the British military occupation of 1882. Traders, bankers, contractors, speculators, political advisers and "diplomatic agents" with paramount economic powers were busy in Cairo and Alexandria long before British troops arrived there. After the occupation, British administrators—the finest their country could offer in the service of empire—managed every major department of an Egyptian government that was nominally headed by a khedive who owed allegiance to the Ottoman Sultan; and in the moralizing language of that day, which did not differ too greatly from that of our own, these British executives discharged with zeal their "duty of giving advice" so that "prosperity and stability" might be restored to a bankrupt country. For seventy years the British Army remained in the Nile valley and the Canal Zone, whether Egypt was considered a province of the Ottoman Empire, or designated a protectorate of the British crown, or proclaimed an independent nation enjoying special relations with the British government.

In Iraq, the requirements of indirect rule produced other arrangements. An Arab king reigned while a British High Commissioner ruled under a League of Nations mandate; and when Iraq was granted her independence, the High Commissioner departed but the British Army remained. There is probably no way to strike a balance between the affronts that are visited on a people by this manner of rule, erratically marked by strife and bloodshed, and the injuries openly administered in the name of a foreign sovereign, as in imperial India. The imperial power rules, the protecting power interferes—with force, when necessary—and the presumptions of a High Commissioner or Ambassador who has an army at his call are no doubt as mortifying as the commands of an imperial viceroy.

For the Arabs they were deeply mortifying, and the Arab people still bear the psychological scars of their colonial experience. It was, for them, the experience of a cultural defeat. It brought a loss of confidence in themselves and their culture and implanted both a sense of inferiority and a bitter conviction that the West had not only exploited their material wealth but had somehow stolen away their spiritual possessions and cultural heritage. Their sense of inferiority still expresses itself in a number of morbid ways—sometimes in exaggerated self-assertion, sometimes in escape into self-flattery and vainglory, sometimes in self-contempt, as they come to see themselves through Western eyes. Sometimes in all three. Resentment and rancor against the West are still the mark of Arab national self-consciousness, and the obsessions of injured pride are often most painfully pronounced among those modernizers and Westernizers who feel themselves to be the vanguard of the nationalist movement.

The man who more than any other made it his business to erase the political marks of the past was Nasser. As we look back over the full course of his career, we are caught by its dramatic consistency of pattern and the recurrence of certain arresting themes and features. The first is the motivation underlying his relations with the West. Very early in his career as head of Egypt's military regime, his rejection of Western tutelage in any form, real or suspected, and his insistence that Arabs be treated as equals and not as colonials, announced that a new kind of leader had arrived. The Western powers were slow to appreciate this fact and even slower to adjust themselves to it, a failure that was catastrophic for Britain and France and often costly for the United States. Second, we see that his extraordinary appeal to the Arabs, the secret of the victories that invested him with glamour, lay in his capacity to inflict humiliation on the hated imperialists. In the psychodrama of Arab politics, Nasser's conquests were invariably psychological conquests. Then, as we survey the history of his reputation, which is the history of a myth and an unexampled exercise in contemporary myth-making, we see that certain events stand out like the peaks of the pattern, sudden acts that rose above the others and lifted him to that succession of summits that were his moments of glory.

He reached the first of them in 1955 with an international coup. His unheralded arms agreement with the Russians by way of the Czechs was founded on his rejection of what he felt were the paternalistic pretensions of the United States. The American desire to ration arms shipments to Egypt in order to maintain a precarious Middle East balance, the insistence on sending a Military Aid Group to Cairo in order to advise on their use—these conditions, for Nasser, were an affront to Egyptian sovereignty and an attempt to reintroduce the insidious practices of indirect rule. He turned to the Russians, and the agreement he made was a watershed in the history of the region. In one bound the Russians scaled the barrier of Turkey and the warm-water moat of the Mediterranean, landed in Egypt (with their military advisers) and introduced themselves to the world as a Middle Eastern power. For Nasser the deal was an affirmation of "positive neutralism" and of the Arabs' right to dissociate themselves from Cold War interests and entanglements that were no concern of theirs, at a time when the United States and Britain were laboring to hold the region within the defense orbit of the West. The agreement had many other consequences that could not be foreseen or precisely calculated at the time. In the dynamics of Middle East tension, the rearming of Egypt speeded the rearming of Israel and led in the following year to that unwritten Israeli-French alliance that was to last for a decade. In Arab countries, which for the first time witnessed the humiliation of Western pride and power, the agreement carried Nasser to the heights. Even those Arabs who feared his ambitions admired this demonstration of Arab self-interest and enjoyed the skill with which the leader of Egypt engaged in the electrifying game of getting the best of both worlds. Even those who disapproved of the deal were compelled to join the circle of applauders. All the Arab countries felt the thrill of elation, and the acclaim Nasser received on this occasion marked his consecration as a hero.

The victory opened the way to a number of local successes. Nasser was encouraged to expand his propaganda and clandestine activities against Saudi Arabia and Jordan and, in the months that followed, to pull Jordan and Syria ever more tightly into the Egyptian ring. He became more aggressive toward Israel, increasing the scope and audacity, and murderous effect, of the *fedayeen* terrorist raids out of Gaza. Washington was disturbed by these developments. The Americans at that time were divided in their view of Nasser, uncertain whether he was a legitimate Arab nationalist or some new type of crypto-Communist. In spite of their doubts they decided to start again and, not without qualms but in a spirit of "let's see," opened negotiations for the financing of the Aswan Dam. Britain and the World Bank were also to be partners in this venture. Nasser as always was deeply suspicious of the "strings"; he balked at the fine-type conditions that are normally required in World Bank dealings of the kind. Negotiations stretched out and on, with long periods of silence on either side. In the end American mistrust ignited with anger when Nasser suddenly extended recognition to Communist China, having previously assured the United States he would not do so without giving notice, and with indignation when it was discovered he was simultaneously seeking better terms on the financing of the dam from the Russians, and even pretending he had gotten them. What for Nasser was a clever gambit in positive neutrality was for Washington the chicanery and blackmail of the oriental market. The Americans were confirmed in their suspicion that he was much too tricky a man to

assist without strings. John Foster Dulles canceled the American offer
on Aswan. His excuse was that the Egyptian economy was too weak
to support so great an enterprise—an explanation that was taken by
the Egyptians to be deliberately provocative. Nasser's resounding
riposte was the nationalization of the Suez Canal in July, 1956.

His handling of that crisis was his masterpiece. The physical take-
over of the Canal operation showed how much care and thought had
gone into the contingency planning. Nasser was firm but flexible under
the pressures of the outraged maritime powers. He stood his ground
under their threats, refused to be drawn by their provocations, and in
reply to the demands of the British and French, showered the two
powers with counterproposals that had every air of being reasonable.
His conduct throughout was that of the cool logician. Although the
nationalization had been brutally swift, it was perfectly legal; and
Nasser took care that nothing occurred that might be a pretext for
military intervention, no mishaps to British or French citizens in
Egypt, no delays to Western ships in their passage through the Canal.
In the event, it was not the Egyptians but the British and French who
were the irrational ones in this affair. The wrath of the British identified Nasser as an Arab Hitler who had to be stopped at all costs; and
the French, by one of those fanciful exercises in abstract reason of
which their genius sometimes makes them the victims, convinced
themselves that the elimination of Nasser was a prerequisite to the
suppression of the revolt in Algeria. Both deluded themselves that
they were still masters in a colonialist age; both assumed that the
United States would be able and willing to countenance their invasion
of Egypt in the fall of that year. The United States, through the
agency of the United Nations, compelled them to leave. For the Arab
people, the nationalization of the Canal was a brilliant demonstration
of the uses of Arab power; and the humiliation of Britain and France
was all the more crushing because they had inflicted it upon themselves. It was Nasser's second summit of glory.

He mounted to the third in February, 1958, when he entered Damascus as the President of the newly created United Arab Republic.
This seemed to the Arabs to be the cornerstone and foundation of the
pan-Arab structure of their dreams. In fact, the merger of Egypt and
Syria was a measure of last resort aimed at saving the Syrian Republic
from dissolution. The Syrian pan-Arab nationalists, at a moment of
frantic instability when a variety of Communist, pro-Soviet and pro-

Iraqi pressures threatened to overwhelm them, could think of no other solution than a *fuite en avant* into the embrace of a union with Egypt. They entreated Nasser to take them in. He agreed to undertake the rescue mission only after expressing many well-founded misgivings, but an outpouring of pan-Arab enthusiasm sanctified the new state. Only Nasser's name had made it possible. It was, once more, a psychological conquest.

Yet, viewed in retrospect, it was the highest peak in the series, in terms of his power and his pan-Arab reputation. In the months and years that followed, there were several fleeting moments of messianic promise. General Kassem's revolution in Iraq in 1958 seemed, at first, to swell the oncoming pan-Arab tide, but that strange dictator had other ideas and soon dominated and suppressed the Nasserists in his midst. Five years later, when the Kassem dictatorship was overturned and a regime led by the Baath, the party of pan-Arab nationalism, seized power in Baghdad, Nasser's credit soared again amid excited talk of an Egyptian-Syrian reunion and elaborate negotiations for a tripartite union including Egypt, Syria and Iraq. But the interests of sovereign states and the jealousies of political factions defeated these ambitious schemes. The moments of euphoria were short-lived.

Meanwhile there was the war in Yemen, with its bottomless commitment, and wherever Nasser turned he seemed to meet setback and frustration. But underneath all the frustrations in Yemen and elsewhere, and preceding them, lay the memory and heavy shock of two defeats. One was the defection of Syria and the demise of the United Arab Republic, after a life of three and a half years, in September, 1961. Seen in retrospect, it was the turning point of his career. When his name and his methods of rule lost their charm for his Syrian brothers, the Republic was finished. It was a defection which he denounced as treason to the Arab cause but which he could do nothing to reverse. From this blow, so easily administered to the hero of Arabism by a small band of counterrevolutionaries, he never fully recovered. It was a defeat that could not be redeemed unless someday some unforeseen opportunity or combination of international circumstance should point the way and urge him to step forth again as the protector of Syria.

The second reverse that had left its mark lay still deeper in the past. In the blinding light of his political victory over the British and French in the crisis of 1956, he had been able to conceal from his people the military defeat his army had suffered at that time, when the Israelis made their first sweep across Sinai to the Suez Canal. But his enemies in the Arab world never let him forget it, and the signs of that defeat were still visible. To get the Israelis out of Sinai and the Gaza Strip, he had accepted the presence of foreign troops, the United Nations Emergency Force that stood as a buffer on his side of the Egyptian-Israeli borders. The soldiers of the United Nations were an indispensable convenience which he freely accepted but, as he knew, a heavy propaganda liability for a leader who commanded the greatest of Arab armies and who had always insisted on the liquidation of foreign bases and the expulsion of foreign troops from Arab territory. A second sign of that defeat remained: As part of the general arrangements under which Israel had agreed to withdraw from Sinai and the Gaza Strip, Nasser had quietly acquiesced in another condition. Thenceforth, Israeli flagships and all other Israel-bound vessels enjoyed the internationally recognized right to pass freely through the Straits of Tiran and across the "Arab waters" of the Gulf of Aqaba to the port of Eilath, Israel's maritime gateway to Africa and Asia.

The Jews and the Arabs have had many extraordinary encounters in history, but none more extraordinary in its origins than that which has brought them into conflict today. The national aspiration of the Jews, like that of the Arabs, was a response to their meeting with the European world, and it was the political action of the West in this century that brought these two nationalist movements together and set them face to face. It is as though history had labored to arrange this appointment in the land of Palestine and when the time came, had chosen one of the Western intruders, Great Britain, to be its agent. The victory of British armies over the Turks in the First World War prepared the way for the new encounter, and the decisions of British statesmen in London did the rest. The victory made possible the national liberation of the Arabs and the fulfillment of the Jewish dream of a national homeland at the same time, in the same generation. The first steps in both directions were taken in the same year. On February 28, 1922, the British Government ended its protectorate over Egypt and declared that country to be an independent, sovereign state. Five months later, on July 24, the League of Nations approved a British mandate over Palestine. The terms of the Balfour Declaration, in which Britain had pledged she would "view with favor" the establishment in Palestine of a Jewish national home, were included in the preamble to the League's statement.

The Arabs today, still harboring their sense of injury, still ascribe their failures and frustrations to the West or, since the Western powers have nearly everywhere gone home, to what they regard as a final incarnation of Western imperialism, a last bastion, a last colonial establishment.

The Arab arguments against Israel are so unyielding in spirit and so deeply rooted in Arab emotion that they leave no choice but to state them in their own terms: The Israelis are usurpers in an Arab land. Neither the Seljuk Turks nor the Mongolians, the Christian crusaders, the Ottomans nor the British ever altered the character of a land that has now been Arab for more than thirteen hundred years. Israel is the successor state to the British Mandate. In issuing the Balfour Declaration, the British promised to give away what was not theirs to give. When, during the days of the mandate, the Jewish settlers in Palestine purchased land from Arab proprietors, they were employing a stratagem to displace the Arab natives and eventually to buy their way to majority status. When David Ben-Gurion, in 1942, set aside earlier proposals for a binational Palestine in which Jews and Arabs would find a common homeland, and called for the creation of a Jewish commonwealth, he at last revealed to the world the grand design toward which the Zionists had been advancing by guile and stealth. He addressed his appeal to an American audience in New York, since the new Zionist program required the political support of the United States and the financial support of the greatest of Jewish communities. The United Nations General Assembly, by its recommendation in 1947 to partition Palestine so as to permit the creation of the Jewish state, imposed foreign domination on the Arabs, a people whose demands for self-determination had never been heeded. In defending the new state against the Arab armies in 1948, the Israelis, therefore, were waging a war of aggression. Eight years later, in the Sinai campaign, they invaded Egypt in collusion with the French and the British, and thereby revealed to the world their country's function as an imperialist military base to be used against the Arab world. Israel remains an outpost of the West, an irritant deliberately left behind by the departing imperialists.

Neither the legacy of Jewish religious experience, nor the bond of the Jewish people with the land of Palestine, nor the drama and the claims of history, the memory, the unbroken link, nor the human reality, the unequaled horror they have known in our own time—none of this in any way modifies the Arab position. The death camps and the gas chambers were the work of Christian Europe, and the extermination of six million Jews lies on the conscience of the Christian nations. This point is central in the Arab argument. Auschwitz, Treblinka, Belsen—these things did not happen in the Arab world. The United States, the greatest of the Western countries, refused asylum to the hundreds of thousands of Jews who sought to leave Europe after the holocaust; and, to salve its conscience, gave them a state of their own in the land of a people who were in no way associated with the crime. Anti-Semitism in the experience of recent centuries has been the malady of the Christian but not of the Moslem community. Why then must the Arabs be asked to assuage the Christian sense of guilt? Why must they be compelled to pay the price for disburdening the conscience of Europe and America?

In the end, the Arabs make no specific claims against Israel. Their claim is against her very existence. They rejected the United Nations' 1947 Partition Resolution and fought a war to subvert it, while the Jews accepted the resolution and fought a successful war to uphold it. In winning their War of Independence the Jews extended their territory beyond the areas that had been awarded to them by the U. N. General Assembly; and thereupon the Arabs, reversing their stand, invoked the very resolution against which they had made war. They called for its implementation, not in order to make peace with Israel but as a means of reducing her national territory. Thus they never accepted the military defeat of 1948 and never acquiesced in its political consequences; they always remained at least one war behind the facts. Their goal was still Israel's liquidation as a state by force of arms. A military victory they were unable to achieve remained the only alternative to a compromise or adjustment they refused to accept. They were therefore unable and unwilling to redress any of the injustices done to their people in the violence of Israel's birth, since the only way to redress them was by negotiation with the victor. The refugees remained refugees, condemned by the double refusal of the Arab states to find homes for them on Arab land or, alternatively, to seek terms with the Israelis. Before the entire world, they maintained the giant disparity between speech and action. Their grievance, Nasser repeatedly said, was not the refugees; their boundless grievance was

Israel herself. They therefore denied her existence.

The attitudes of present-day Arab anti-Semitism, promoted by the conflict with Israel, reveal a curious split. The indoctrination courses of military schools, like the cartoons of magazines and newspapers, picture the Jews as contemptibly debased human beings, in the manner of Julius Streicher; and much of the anti-Semitic literature that is issued with official sanction reads like a catalogue of odium, with its fulsome piling on of adjectives. At the same time, the Israelis are feared as diabolically gifted adversaries, and their success in building a new society, with its fresh evidence each year of a culture so much stronger than their own, has strengthened this second image among the great majority of Arabs. At this point, ideology helps to fortify them in their sense of ultimate victory. An expanding literature in recent years, the work of ideologues and publicists, has identified Israel as a pure colonialist phenomenon. These studies review the entire course of Zionist and Israeli history to prove their case. The Jewish settlers who sought to occupy and dominate Arab Palestine, with the financial help of Jewish capitalists in the West, are placed in the same ideological compartment as the French colons of Algeria, the Italian colonists in the Libya of Mussolini and the Afrikaners of South Africa. Like other colonialists, they had their "home country" or capitalist base, represented not by a particular country but by world Jewry at large with its immense resources. The Jewish settlers gained a foothold in Palestine under the protection of an imperialist power, Britain, who for strategic reasons welcomed the establishment of a friendly community close to the corridor of empire and the way to India. Having entered by infiltration, the Jews imposed themselves by force and proceeded to establish a Western society. The grants of the United States Government, the donations of American Jewry and the conscience money paid as reparations by a repentant Germany, have made possible the growth of this intruding state. It is now a neocolonialist bridgehead in the Arab East, since its Western capitalist ties have automatically placed it in the imperialist camp against the peoples of the underdeveloped world.

In the calculations of the Arab ideologists, this creation is doomed to die, since we live in an age of decolonialization. The forces of history have fixed their cannon against Israel. The Arab cause is supported by the dynamics of a world conflict whose denouement is manifest; the Arab struggle is seen as part of the twentieth-century anticolonialist revolution of the emergent nations, and thereby acquires the dignity and inevitability that history confers. History, like the Arabs, will refuse to compromise. Many arguments are adduced to bolster this global vision. Israel is a small and unnatural state and, with her meager resources, inherently unviable; she is rocked by the disputes of her political parties, weakened within by the class conflict between her Western and oriental Jewish communities, and surrounded everywhere by peoples engaged in the liberating process of anti-imperialist revolt. There are more than sixty million people in the Arab Middle East. Israel, overwhelmed by numbers and historical determinism, will disappear. This vision and these arguments, so carefully garnered and developed by the Arab intelligentsia, evidently have a significant effect in hardening the Arab position. They bring a new rigor to passion and a new justification to violence.

But the gulf that divides the Arabs from the Jewish state in their midst is above all a gulf of passion. Israel is an offense not to any particular Arab nation but to Arabism itself. It is the universal focus of frustration, felt by groups and sects and classes far outside the circle of the intelligentsia. Within that circle, the conviction has taken hold that Arabism is disabled by the mere presence of Israel, that it cannot be whole again as long as Israel exists, and that there can be no cultural rebirth or genuine reconstruction of society until this offense is redeemed. The depth of this conviction, and the extremity of emotion that informs it, are reflected in the prose that is written on the subject. A professor of history at the University of Beirut, Q. Zurayq, has written as follows: "The forces which are at the disposal of Zionism all over the world will, if only they take root in Palestine, endanger the independence of all Arab countries and become an eternal standing threat to their very lives . . . will subject the Arab world to their will . . . stifle Arab vitality and prevent any progress and advance of their civilization, if the Arab world will be allowed to survive at all."

In the early years of the new state there were many, both in Israel and in the West, who hoped and believed that certain underlying factors would in time work toward a resolution of the conflict. A new Arab generation would grow to maturity, freed from the incubus of the recent past, pursuing new interests in a changing Arab world that would find ample scope for its energies. As this world advanced and developed, it would become more and more absorbed in its own multiplying tasks and in the search for solutions to its many problems. It would be less and less haunted by its grudge against Israel. The Arabs of the new generation would certainly continue to believe that their people had been the victims of a historic injustice. But Israel would become a fact; they would adjust themselves to it and would forget their obsession. Indeed, it was thought, by the time the Arab countries grew sufficiently strong to overwhelm Israel, they would no longer have the desire to do so. Perhaps at some happy time this prevision may still prove to have been valid, but the disappointment of these hopes until now has hurt not only the Israelis but the Arabs themselves, because so many to so great a degree have wasted their souls on a fixation. Since the assassination of King Abdullah of Jordan by a Palestinian fanatic in 1951, no political leader in the Arab Middle East has wished to make the attempt to set his people on any other course. The power of twentieth-century communications has been used to exploit the loneliness of homeless people and to excite the fears and hopes of the unhappy and the ignorant. The condition of these people is one of poignant distress.

The inability of the Arabs to recognize that the Jewish people have any human right or legitimate claim to establish a national home in Palestine seems, finally, to come from a deeper source than the mere intransigence of political passion. The barriers to understanding are the product of a cultural isolation. The unrelenting view that permits Arab intellectuals to reduce the drama of the Jewish return to Palestine to the dimensions of an ideological cliché seems to reflect a genuine lapse in human perception that is in turn a cultural failure. The humanist and liberal elements evolved by Western culture form no part of the tradition of Islam; there is nothing in the Arabs' own experience or education that enables them to surmount the passions of the day or to see beyond the stereotypes that ideology offers them. The experience of the Jews is *sui generis*. What are called in the lexicon of Zionism "the historic rights of the Jewish people" are not legally definable. The Jews of the Diaspora evidently had no juridical right to return and found a state in Palestine merely because they had once ruled over an independent Palestinian kingdom that was ended by the Romans more than two thousand years ago. Already for five hundred years and more before the coming of Rome, the majority of the Jewish people had been living elsewhere, outside the borders of their homeland. A juridical view of human affairs can find no place for their national claims, for the simple reason that their history has been unique.

If the Arabs are incapable of appreciating or acknowledging the human reality of Israel, their failure may be due in part to the rigidities of a religion that is so inalterably based on law and divorced from history. Judaism in a sense is no less rigid; it preserves a body of detailed prescriptions and a maze of minute legislation that not even Islam can rival. But unlike the Arabs, the Jews traveled throughout the world and shared in its cultural adventures and, through the centuries, had their unique experience of encounter and exodus, of change and mobility within the processes of history.

Throughout those centuries, they maintained the unbroken connection. What was remarkable in their story was not so much their awareness of origins as the continuity of their attachment. A small Jewish community continued to live in Palestine, and Jewish pilgrims and students never ceased to return there. But the bond for the Diaspora was a bond of the spirit, a type of historical consciousness that has had no parallel in the experience of other peoples. Fortifying and sustaining them through the centuries of dispersion, through all the adversities of exile—the rejections, the diverse wanderings, the rigors of persecution—binding them together and strengthened in turn by their trials, the bond with Palestine remained the central spiritual fact of their lives: the glory of Zion, the myth of the land, the promise of renewal, the certainty of ultimate salvation. In the center of those myths, recapitulating all the others, stood the city of the Jewish prophets, Jerusalem, Daughter of Zion, her Temple destroyed but still, in the dust of the ruined sanctuary, the city of deliverance, the goal of memory. No other people has had this experience of overwhelming identification. Parts of Jerusalem were sacred to the Moslems, parts were sacred to the Christians, but all of it was sacred to the Jews. Much of its history belonged to the Moslems, much belonged to the Christians, but there was no part of its history that did not belong to the scattered children of Zion.

Yet the movement of return to Palestine that had its beginnings a century ago was not a religious movement. Its impulse was nationalist and its aims were secular. A new wave of migrations and displacements had gathered the majority of the Jewish people in the ghettos of Eastern Europe, in the provinces of Russia and in the imperial Pale of Settlement that extended from the Baltic to the Black Sea. The pogroms and degradations of the 1880's gave the impetus to still another wave of emigration, in which tens and sometimes hundreds of thousands fled from Russia every year. The main stream of that exodus went to the United States. A much smaller stream of Zionist pioneers went to Palestine. They were spurred by the national liberation struggles of other European peoples and by what was then the distant hope of creating a state in which Jews would not be a minority. Their movement was a secular revolt against the immobile religious ghetto society of Eastern Europe. Although, of course, they did not renounce their Judaism, they received little support or encouragement from their rabbis. Through the centuries, three times daily, the Jews had prayed that a Messiah might gather them in and take them home; the Zionists were those who resolved not to wait for a Messiah but to act themselves. Zionism was the secular expression of an experience that had been religious, and the ideals that the pioneers carried with them to Palestine were the secular residuum of three thousand years of religious history. They took with them their sense of total identification. The myth of the land, which for centuries had been present in Jewish prayers and folklore, became the program of a national revival. The Hebrew language, which for centuries had been used only for the purposes of the cult and of scholarship, became the national language of the pioneers. Even in those early days of Jewish settlement in Palestine, the pioneers knew they had to defend themselves to survive. There was no question in their minds as to their right to be there.

In 1939, on the eve of the Second World War, the Jews in Palestine were a community of 450,000. Their numbers had nearly tripled in the previous six years as a result of the Nazi persecutions. Then, at the end of the drama, under the shadow of hatred and war, their feeling that they could never be at home among Gentiles, and would be secure only when they were masters in their own state, was given a traumatic dimension by the savagery of the twentieth century. It remained for this century to condemn an entire people as subhuman and consign it to liquidation. The surviving remnants fought their way by underground routes to the East, past the gantlet of the British Navy, and on arriving in Palestine, found that they still had to fight for their survival. Under the leadership of those who had preceded them, they fought, with hard skill and bitter knowledge.

They fought, they won, they survived. But they did not win peace. They fructified the land and they renewed their lives, but they did not win safety. A generation after that war, the two sides still confront each other with the legitimate claims and human rights that history has given them, unreconciled and in great part unreconcilable. If it were not a conflict of rights, it would not be a tragedy. It would be merely a predicament.

· 3 ·

Israeli Issues and Men

THE NIGHT WAS COLD and the road ahead was empty and untraveled as we drove southward through the rainswept countryside of the Gaza Strip. Glimpses of the landscape came to us whenever the road turned, a snatch of scrub desert or the corner of an orange grove and occasionally a one-story Arab house, blank and solitary, its door closed and its windows shuttered. The entire coastal area, for so many years the overcrowded place of confinement for ninety thousand Arab natives and more than two hundred thousand refugees, was under curfew until dawn. The night's operation had to be swift; it also had to be adroitly timed so as to avoid that interim of uncertainty and tension when the claustrophobic emotions of the Arabs might erupt in demonstrations or in acts of terrorism against the withdrawing troops.

We swung into the town of Gaza, drove past the railway station and an ascending row of mud-brown houses and quickly out again into flat country; and at a bend in the road a few miles farther on, we saw what we had come to meet. The bouncing lights of a long truck convoy advanced toward us, slowly and warily through the dark and unfamiliar country. The rain drove across the beams of the headlights as they came on. A white jeep was in the lead; the blond youngster at the wheel wore a blue helmet and a shoulder patch that said: Denmark. The trucks that came after him, heavily packed with canvas, bore a yellow cross on a blue field, the shield of Norway. The troops of the Danish-Norwegian battalion were the vanguard of the United Nations Emergency Force that was coming in from the Sinai Desert that night to occupy the four main towns of the Strip, place its guards on the refugee food depots that were the most likely targets for looting at these times of change-over, and post its soldiers along the thirty-five-mile border between Gaza and Israel. After the Danes and the Norwegians there would be other strangers—Swedes, Indians and Colombians—a peace-keeping force of twenty-four hundred men. They had no billets for the night and they would be sleeping under canvas.

It was March 6, 1957. After one hundred and twenty-five days of occupation, the army of Israel was surrendering control of the disputed area. Prime Minister David Ben-Gurion, seventy years old, yielding at last after a long diplomatic struggle with the United States, had agreed to the evacuation although he had failed to obtain the guarantee he had always insisted was Israel's minimum condition. His cabinet and his party were divided on what had become an overriding national issue; his General Staff was despondently skeptical of the ability of the United Nations troops to police the Strip or control its borders; the opposition in the Knesset, the Israeli Parliament, was pressing for a nonconfidence motion, which, if approved, would repudiate his decision; and public feeling throughout the country was instinctively and fiercely against unconditional withdrawal. Ben-Gurion had taken his decision alone. He gave the order to evacuate without waiting for a vote either in Parliament or in his cabinet, and on the following day went before the Knesset to defend his decision. For the first time since the War of Independence, the Israelis saw barbed-wire barriers around the little Knesset building in Jerusalem, with the adjoining streets blocked against demonstrators by an unprecedented concentration of police. Inside the building, tired and white-faced but speaking quietly, and waiting with folded arms whenever the catcalls of the opposition interrupted him, the Prime Minister dominated the assembly by his presence and his logic and won approval for his action. He said there was no assurance that Egyptian administrators, military and civilian, would not return to the area where the *fedayeen,* in the months before the Sinai campaign, had mounted their raids of havoc and murder into the Israeli border region. "My heart," he said, "is with the border settlements, who heard with anxiety of the decision to withdraw." But, measuring the future prospects of Israel, the material needs of her army and the place of the American relationship in the security of the country, he knew the time had finally come to draw back in the face of superior power. To support his hopes, he had received a personal message of reassurance from the President of the United States; and since he knew the President and respected him, he took the message as a commitment of honor.

In the Gaza Strip on that rainy night, Danish and Norwegian officers by late evening were alighting from their jeeps and having their first look at the place we called the downtown square of Gaza, a characterless and muddy intersection near the railway station. Israeli soldiers were there to welcome them and tell them where they were. The change-over was to be an unphased operation, all in one move, while Gaza slept; and by dawn or shortly thereafter all Israeli troops, police and civilian aides would be back on the Israeli side of the boundary, having left some three hundred *fedayeen* in the Gaza jails for the new administration to worry about. The rain was thinning out to a fitful drizzle when an Israeli army car drew up at one side of the square and an officer casually got out, unaccompanied, wearing a black patch over his left eye but no medals because the Israeli Army did not award any and no campaign ribbons because he evidently hadn't bothered. Relaxed and alert, with his attractive aura of debonair self-confidence and invulnerable natural poise, Major General Moshe Dayan, Chief of the General Staff and architect of the Sinai victory, stepped past the headlights and paused a moment to observe the scene, his one eye, serene but inquisitive, roving but sharp, easily performing the service of two. He managed to convey a sense of bravura without the slightest impression of effort or show. He was the enemy of ceremony and conventional routines and he was always likely to turn up anywhere in order to see for himself. It was clearly a matter of pride for him to be present at a time of withdrawal and transfer, no less than in the time of victory. He walked through the mud and into the crowd, asking the first Israeli soldier he saw how the hand-over was going. There was no exchange of salutes. He spotted the Danish colonel who was the commanding officer of the Scandinavian battalion, went up to him and shook hands. A good-natured question brought the reply that everything was in order. Dayan nodded.

"Good luck," he said, turned and walked back to his car, driving off a few seconds later to see how his own men were doing.

At forty-one, Dayan had emerged from the events of that year with a popular allure and a degree of public trust that were second only to those that surrounded the figure of his guide and master, the man who had appointed him, Ben-Gurion. Underneath the air of bravura, there were certain traits of personality and leadership that he seemed to share with the older man. He had a faculty of going straight to the point and of pulling clarity out of confusion. He was not a man who took partial responsibility; he took the whole of it, and what he did was on his head. He broke down complex issues to their essentials and made them look simple in one plain and succinct sentence. He did this in his own personal way, thinking and acting intuitively and never seeming to be particularly interested in things he did not intuitively understand. He took his decisions and held to them, often enough without consultation and apparently indifferent as to whether they were popular or not—always one of Ben-Gurion's salient points of strength; and like Ben-Gurion, it seemed, Dayan had a realist's respect for forces that were greater than himself. There was caution in his zeal and boldness in his moderation. The Israelis as much as other people like the dashing man to whom success comes easily, but Dayan's celebrated dash in his private life, his carelessness of his own safety, his love of speeding, his habit of plunging into archaeological digs without benefit of pit props—all of this was probably deceptive. When in command, he was not careless, and the risks he took were weighed against the possible consequences he foresaw in gain or loss. His daring strokes were based on calculation, and from the first he seemed to combine in a remarkable way the virtues of audacity and prudence. So it seemed, and time would tell.

There were at least two fields of knowledge he intuitively understood: farming and war. He was born and bred on a collective farm, the son of pioneers, and was completely at home in his first government post as Minister of Agriculture; but whether he was a minister or simply a member of the Knesset, in the government or in the opposition, the main and abiding interest of his life was the security of Israel and he never forgot it. Politically he was unclassifiable and wayward, never the party man, even after he entered politics; he always went his own way, kept his own counsel, with few close friends, disdaining party machinations with more than a touch of aloofness and grandeur. Elder politicians wondered about his ambitions, and some feared them. His delight in finding unorthodox solutions, so much admired by the general public, made him an iconoclast to the old guard; and his cavalier attitude toward such things as speed limits and the laws governing private excavation helped to make him suspect to various intellectuals. Others mistrusted his strong native disposition to identify himself with Israel and her destiny. His enemies said he was not a true democrat and cited, in evidence, his hatred of time-honored red tape, his dislike of round-table consultations, his love of short cuts, his failure to call meetings and his utter abhorrence of work in commissions. Well, observed one Israeli political commentator, if work in commissions was the test of democracy, Dayan was no democrat.

But the reason the down-to-earth and pragmatic youth of Israel were so strongly drawn to him was that he was so clearly one of them, in style, temperament and outlook, even though he belonged to the veteran generation that had fought the War of Independence in 1948. The style was above all a question of language. He was the foe not only of bureaucratic rules but of easy slogans of every sort and of rhetoric in general. He despised what he called "phraseology" and professed full confidence in Israeli youth even though so many had preferred the attractions of city life and no longer shared their fathers' enthusiasm for pioneering on the kibbutz. "They *are* idealists," he said. "They just don't want to buy words. . . . I know the people who were born here." His language was the only one that appealed to a generation impatient with the solemn and humorless grandiloquence of the old-time, Russian-style orators who had set the tone of political debate in Israel. Dayan's Hebrew prose, like his Hebrew speech, is said to be clear, crisp and economical, touching the key points but never troubling to spell everything out in pedantic explanations. If his Hebrew is anything like his spoken English, then the description is accurate. In a dozen words, he summed up the attitude of the majority of his countrymen when he said: "I never go to synagogue but I feel Jewish to my bones." He was a secular Judaist, like most Israelis, not an orthodox believer but a man with his "own kind of Judaism," as he called it; and in this, like most of the Israelis who had been born in that land and had given their indelible stamp to the national character, he was as self-conscious and deeply committed an heir of Jewish history as any orthodox believer. The springs of association were the same that touched the Israeli paratroopers, all nonbelievers, when they conquered the Old City of Jerusalem. After a hard fight outside the walls, in which eighty of their comrades had died, twenty-five of them because they had gone back to gather their dead and recover their wounded, they suddenly burst into a small open place and stopped, laid down their arms and stood in tears as they beheld the time-blackened stones of the Wailing Wall of the Temple: so intense was the encounter with the past and, in the moment of recognition, so powerful the bond with Jewish history.

It was not by chance that a man like Dayan, whose bent and interests were not scholarly, was so fascinated by archaeology. His digging for ancient Palestinian artifacts was not a quixotic hobby, since the fascination and the passion were national. It was a characteristic but less-than-Orthodox pursuit, and its significance was underlined by the special disfavor in which it was held by the Orthodox rabbinate. The rabbinate in Jerusalem, unlike the religious leadership of Jewry in the United States, Britain and elsewhere, was remote from any concept of the nature of modern society, and represented for most Israelis the ossification of the Jewish religion. It viewed with repugnance the archaeological explorations in the Holy City of Jerusalem, but grudgingly acknowledged they were proper if they did not become merely the expression of the idle curiosity of scholars.

This line of defense reflected a deep and instinctive antagonism to the role of the scholars in Israeli life. For them and others, archaeology was a means of deepening Israel's national consciousness and strengthening her identification with history; for the Orthodox, the road to such identification must be purely religious. The work of the scholars and of individual enthusiasts like Dayan was a rival to religion in promoting an association with the past. The "church" in Israel, the Orthodox establishment, had never really reconciled itself to a state whose creation owed so little to the help or guidance of a Messiah. The rabbinate extended to the state a kind of *de facto* recognition, and the state in return imposed a number of religious restrictions on the life of the nation. The result was an extraordinary degree of religious governance in a secular-minded country, over such matters as marriage, diet and the public services on the Sabbath. On all these matters Dayan made known his representative views as a layman. Public services such as transport, he felt, should be available to everybody on the Sabbath, and those who wanted civil marriage or civil divorce should be able to have it. The youth of Israel generally resented the taboos as an imposition of bigotry, but no one in the nation proposed to make a divisive political issue of them or to ask for a referendum. The ensemble of arrangements between church and state represented one of those anomalous compromises that are philosophically accepted in the life of nations as the foundation of communal coexistence and peace in the family.

"The people who were born here." It was they, the native-born, the sabras, who had been the determining archetypes in the moral life of the country, and another veteran of 1948 who represented them, a man of equal stature and of a very different range of gifts, was Yigal Allon, soldier, politician, student and author. With a field of intellectual interests much wider than Dayan's, he had, like him, the easy gift of communication and that quality of presence which the Israelis admired. Allon made an immediate impression of physical and mental vitality. He was three years younger than Dayan but even so was regarded, with reason, as Israel's elder soldier. His military experience, like that of so many others, began in his late teens with the defense of Jewish military settlements against the Arabs during the riots of 1936. Five years later he helped to found the Palmach, the striking force of the Haganah, the underground army which the Jews had formed for their defense since they had no intention of relying on the British. Late in 1941 he was fighting with the British, as Dayan was fighting, behind the enemy lines in Vichy-held Syria, where the Jews' knowledge of the country made them invaluable as saboteurs, guides and collectors of information. At the end of the war, at twenty-six, Allon became commander of the Palmach and for the next three years directed those operations against the British authority that enabled nearly a hundred thousand Jews, the survivors of Nazi Europe, to land safely on the shores of Palestine despite the vigilance of British naval power, and to find haven in illegal Jewish settlements despite the strong mobile forces which the British maintained in the mandate. At twenty-nine, with the creation of the Jewish state, he was a Brigadier General and in the campaigns of the War of Independence proved himself one of Israel's most brilliant military minds and the first of her field commanders.

He started in the north in the spring of 1948. At the head of the Yeftah Brigade of the Palmach commandos, he swept the Arab forces out of northern Galilee and secured the region for Israel. Two months later, moving to the central front, he directed the uphill fight to secure a corridor to Jerusalem and the short, sharp campaigns that lifted the threat to Tel-Aviv with the capture of Lydda and Ramla. In the fall of the year, as commander of the southern front, he planned and led the offensive that expelled the Egyptians from most of Palestine. Ashdod fell, Ashkelon and Kiriat Gat, and then the whole of the northern Negev Desert, including its capital, Beersheba. In the last week of the year he launched his pursuit of the routed Egyptians. It carried the Palmach across the international boundary into Sinai, where a mobile task unit got to within forty miles of the Suez Canal while Allon led the main body in a rapid thrust to the outskirts of El Arish, the Mediterranean town that was the hinge of the Egyptian line. His object was to take the town, attack the Egyptians from the rear and proceed to the final destruction of their forces in the Gaza Strip. His plan was never fulfilled. Suitably incensed by his trespassing on Egyptian territory, the British made representations to the Americans who made representations to the Israelis; and Ben-Gurion, on the insistence of the United States, halted the advance and ordered the withdrawal of all Israeli troops from Egypt. Allon flew back to Tel-Aviv; he protested and obeyed. The dismay and anger that he repressed at that hour could be felt in the tight sentence which he wrote years later, with set teeth, in comment on the decision: "The order was resented by the troops, but accepted, thanks to their discipline."

He did not give up. He regrouped the Palmach on the other side and made a lunge into Gaza across the sand dunes from Israel, putting a wedge into the slender coastal band and blocking the main road. The entire region was again cut off. The Egyptians at this point agreed to armistice negotiations, but only on condition that Allon's wedge be removed. This condition was accepted by Israel: "mistakenly," Allon later wrote—mistakenly, because Israel thereby relinquished her bargaining position, and in the armistice agreement that was signed in February, 1949, the Gaza Strip, a part of Palestine, was left in Egyptian hands.

The campaigns were not over. With Egypt out of the war, Allon turned south into the granite wilderness of the Negev, a wasteland of canyons and craters. By March 16 his three brigades had overrun the region, reached the Gulf of Aqaba and won for Israel her tiny foothold on an Asian sea. The village of Eilath was then a collection of huts along the arching sand shore at the head of the Gulf.

In the autumn of the previous year, following the Egyptian rout, one body of Egyptian troops had remained behind. They belonged to what Allon later described as "one gallant Egyptian brigade," which had been hopelessly surrounded in the Faluja pocket in the northern

Negev. He had tried to negotiate their surrender at the time. Together with an aide, Major Yeruham Cohen, he drove to the enemy lines to seek out the commander of the trapped brigade. On his arrival, an officer who had been standing in the dugout of the Egyptian command post emerged and stepped forward. He was Major Abdel Nasser. His commander was "a brave man named Colonel Tahal Bey," but it was the younger man who directed and controlled the discussions on the Egyptian side. The four men arranged for a formal meeting the next day. The question of language arose, with the Israelis offering to speak Arabic but with the Egyptians, who did not know Hebrew, proudly refusing to share their language and insisting that the talks be conducted on the neutral ground of English. "You are fighting the wrong people," Allon said. "You should be fighting the British." But the Egyptians would not surrender. Since at that time he did not feel sufficiently secure in his English to take part in negotiations, Allon sent Major Cohen back alone for the many talks that took place in the following days. The younger Egyptian officer, who, as it turned out, was born in the same year as Allon, questioned Major Cohen at length about the Israelis, their labor movement, their kibbutzim, their medical care program, their plans for land reclamation and, most closely of all, about their organization of underground resistance against the British and their success in mobilizing world opinion behind them. "This man Nasser," Cohen reported to Allon, "has a lot on his mind. One day we will hear of him." The Egyptian brigade never gave up and remained in its pocket until after the signing of the armistice, when it marched out with colors flying.

After the capture of Eilath, a large, populous and strategically critical area of Palestine was still held by the Transjordanians. This was the West Bank region with the Old City of Jerusalem; and, as the fortunes of battle had willed it, the Arab line bulged westward into Israeli-held territory to a point where the soldiers of Transjordan, looking down on the coastal plain, were only nine miles from the Mediterranean. For Allon, it was now Transjordan's turn. He went straight to the Prime Minister with his well-laid operational plan for the liberation of the area. He was in a hurry, since armistice negotiations already were under way with Transjordan and were soon to enter their final phase. He urged the Prime Minister not to sign. Ben-Gurion rejected his request. The matter, he said, had been put to a vote in the cabinet and he himself had been in the minority. It was another mistake, another missed chance, Allon later said, and added, "Ben-Gurion was glad to have gone on record before history as voting in favor of action, and was also glad to have been in the minority." Allon was able to repeat this to others without malice, since he had said it to Ben-Gurion himself at the time. "A Prime Minister," he remarked, "can always create a majority, by urging his view, calling in his military to support him and so on." Allon's military verdict on the War of Independence was that Israel had achieved much less than it was in her power to achieve, and much less than what she needed for her future security.

But Allon did not brood over missed chances and recalled them, mainly, in order to point conclusions for the future. He was to suffer other disappointments; he knew how to take them gracefully. On the order of Ben-Gurion, who wished to assert the authority of the new state and the nonpolitical character of its army, the Palmach was disbanded after the War of Independence. Since it had been led and manned predominantly by members of left-wing kibbutzim, Allon saw its dissolution as a political move aimed at altering the ideological tilt of the army, and he resigned in protest. He moved on to other interests: politics, the trade unions, socialism. In 1954 he was one of the founders of the Achdut Ha-Avoda, a party of socialist labor; the next year he was elected to Parliament; and in 1957, to extend his experience of the world and his knowledge, he took a two-year leave from politics and from Israel and went to St. Antony's College at Oxford University to immerse himself in political science.

He was a hard-liner on questions of national security, but a humanist in his sympathies and preoccupations. Unlike some exponents of Israel's hard-line school, he could not accept the implications of perpetual belligerence and he knew the spiritual as well as the material cost to Israel of an indefinitely prolonged conflict. He realized the great need of Israel's youth for peace and growth. He did not, like some hard-liners, reject or simply ignore the human claims of the Arabs because it was convenient to do so. Being themselves totally rejected by their enemies, the Israelis were tempted to dismiss or belittle the Arab grievance against them and to regard the Arab Palestinian refugees as more or less interchangeable human parts that could be resettled in the more or less interchangeable geographical parts of the Arab world. The very condition of Israel's existence tended to foster an insensitivity to the predicament of the refugees. It was fruitless to offer practical solutions for a problem on which the Arab states refused to compromise, maintaining the refugees in their misery as a permanent challenge to Israel's presence in an Arab land. It was impossible to discharge a moral obligation by taking back some of the refugees when the Arabs insisted on the principle of Israel's nonexistence. Among the victims of this condition were the quarter of a million Arabs who lived in Israel itself, second-class citizens permanently estranged and ill at ease in the Israeli society. They lived in a gray purgatory of their own, seen by the two sides with varying degrees of suspicion, by the Arabs generally as the accomplices of "Israelism" and by the Israelis as a people physically present but spiritually elsewhere and as potential fifth-columnists in the event of war.

The Zionist pioneers of the early generations went to Palestine in quest of salvation. They tended to forget that it was the salvation of the Jews that they sought and not of the Arabs. They were insensitive to the rights of the Arabs or, more exactly, they were ethically unpreoccupied with them: they showed concern for the Arabs' welfare but did not deeply consider the problem of their rights. The pioneers who with dedication and sacrifice went out to build Jewish settlements in an Arab country did not intend or wish to dominate or expel the Arabs who lived there. They assumed that Palestine would be large enough to sustain and accommodate two communities. But, in the dialectics of antagonism and then in the shock of war, the Jews did in the end replace the Arabs; and in the struggle that created the new state, hundreds of thousands had to encamp themselves along its borders or wander elsewhere for a place to live. The Arabs of Palestine had never had a nation in the thirteen hundred years they had lived there; history had never granted them one; they belonged in that sense to a prepolitical age. They had had no representative leadership, and the Palestinian leaders they had in the days of the mandate, the men of wealth and influence on the Arab Higher Committee, were violent, corrupt and self-seeking. But with all these political deficiencies, the attachment of the people to their Palestinian lands was nonetheless intimate and deep. This was their tragedy. It was idle to think there could ever be a just solution for everyone, illusory to hope that all wrongs could somehow be repaired, and impossible to envisage a settlement that could redeem the rights of all those who, through the toils of history, had inherited an ancient claim to live in Palestine.

The finest of Israel's statesmen and scholars were sensitive to the ethical problem that her very existence had posed. They did not forget the claims of those whom Israel had displaced. Allon was one of these, and as a man who was ethically involved, he represented more finely the range of Israeli awareness than did the standard and conventional hard-liner. He remembered that the Jews had founded their state, in violence, on the expulsion of hundreds of thousands of others. He remembered that his parents and their parents before them, as pioneers in the remote hills of Galilee, had been a lonely Jewish minority among the Arab natives. Now, with the balance reversed, the Jews were a confident majority in their own state, but now and always they would continue to be a numerically overwhelmed few in the Arab world in which they must find their way and, one day, gain their peace. To live in an abnormal state of semisiege, as Israel was compelled to do, surrounded by people who demanded her annihilation; to accept belligerence as a way of life, as she had to in a region where belligerence was indigenous; to be always on guard, always alert, always ready to meet challenge with challenge and militance with militance—this was not a life propitious for the flowering of humanistic attitudes. It was easier no doubt in the protected world of the universities; far more difficult in the practical world of statesmen, politicians, generals who must make daily decisions in response to events. There were times, during Allon's many years as Minister of Labor, when the visitor to his office in Jerusalem was unable to find him or to learn from his staff where he was or when eventually he might be seen. These were the times, one later discovered, when he had left the capital and returned to his kibbutz at Ginossar on the Sea of Galilee, to be alone, to reassemble his thoughts and to refresh his vision.

The kibbutz, the army and the labor movement had been the three formative influences of his life; and to these he added a fourth, the interesting people he had known from whom he had learned something. But what was the kibbutz, this legendary institution of which one heard so much but which evidently had long since passed its great and florid days? In the history of the Jewish people, the kibbutz was the meeting of two myths. The first generation of Jewish pioneers in the 1880's had made the decision that in order to build a home the Jews must settle on the land; the second generation in the early 1900's, when Ben-Gurion had come as an immigrant from Poland, had decided the Jews must work the land themselves. Their motive was not to discriminate against Arab labor, which was cheaper, but to avoid the creation of a Jewish planter class exploiting the Arab workers. Mismanagement and labor disputes beset the first cooperative farms, and their economic failure led to a third decision. One of the cooperatives was handed over to the workers themselves. Thus, in 1910, the first kibbutz was founded, at Degania near the Sea of Galilee, where five years later Dayan was born. The settlers were fully ready for this communal experiment. They had brought from Eastern Europe the revolutionary socialism of that time and a determination to break with the ghetto occupations of their fathers; they aspired to make their new life on the land, where they would be no longer middlemen but creators. So the myth of Jewish prayers and folklore, the myth of the promised land with its ideal of spiritual rejuvenation, met the socialist myth of collective living, with its goal of a new society based on justice and equality. Membership in the kibbutzim was voluntary, wages were equal regardless of output, and the exploitation of class by class was banished. The ideal of classlessness was Marxist, while the concept of simple living and work on the soil owed some of its inspiration to Tolstoy. At the outset, the kibbutzim had to rely on themselves and their own armed watchmen for defense; later, voluntary military groups developed that were ready to help them on a countrywide basis. The force that later became the Haganah, and then the army of Israel, had its origins in the small units of volunteers who went out to join the farmers in the defense of their isolated settlements.

The time of greatest expansion for the kibbutzim began with the Arab uprising of 1936 and ended with the War of Independence. In the expectation that Palestine would be partitioned, the pioneers set forth, some voluntarily, some on instructions from the national agency, to found settlements and "establish facts"; that is, to establish their homeland deep in the Arab interior and often as close as possible to the borders of the mandate. Both military and political strategy dictated the choice of the sites, and the ideal units for the task were the self-dependent and collectively organized kibbutzim. They became the spearhead of Jewish settlement, in the farthest hills of Upper Galilee, in the valley of the Jordan River and in the semiarid zones of the Negev. As new settlements were subject to instant Arab attack, they had to go up in a single day, prefabricated wooden villages with huts, communal kitchen and dining hall, a double-walled stockade filled with rubble and fitted with firing slits, and an outlying ring of barbed

wire and mine strips. In the center of the compound stood the watch-
tower with its searchlight. It was the heroic age of the kibbutz; the
soldier-pioneers were the shock troops of the Jewish homeland and
their farms were its military outposts.

One decade after the founding of the state, the position of the kibbutz had changed. Israel in the late 1950's was a radically different
place, no longer the homogeneous and compact society of pioneer days
but complex and various, with sharp pulls and stresses, transformed
from a community of European settlers into a social agglomerate
whose population, after the flood of new immigrants from Arab countries, was preponderantly of oriental origin. Almost any newspaper
any day of the week would tell the story of the change: on the front
page, the political news of Israel and the highlights from abroad, and
on the inside pages, the assorted items that fill the press of any democratic country, trade union disputes, charges of malgovernment, the
bickers of the political parties and the normal quota of petty crimes,
black-marketeering and bank scandals. Seen from these pages, Israel
was a normal modern society of politicians, farmers, scholars, scientists and thieves; and evidently not always exemplary. There was the
familiar population trend toward the cities, particularly toward Tel-
Aviv, and the capitalistic pursuits of urban life offered the lure of new
excitements, new vocations and higher wages to the youth of the country. The generation that grew up in this decade was not attracted by
the challenge of collective living and not moved by ideology. The capitalist cityward drift brought a number of crises to the kibbutz, both
material and spiritual.

It cost the kibbutzniks a hard struggle to recruit new members and
often to keep the members they had, and thus to maintain the ratio of
barely 4 percent that they represented in the population of the country. In the new era, they were no longer the revered members of a
dedicated elite performing an arduous and indispensable role in the
service of the nation. It cost many of them an ever harder struggle to
hold their own economically. Inside their idealistic compounds, they
faced a crisis of conscience as the need to increase their earnings impelled them into many fields of industry, which meant the hiring of
workers, the exploitation of labor and the admission of the profit motive into their communal world. They had, as well, with the shifting
climate of the times, to recognize and provide for the human need
for privacy. There were many members who, with all the idealism in

the world, had difficulty in adapting themselves to the living habits of collectivism and to what was for them the psychic strain of having to meet the same people every hour of the day, in the dining hall, in the fields or at the repair shop, in the communal shower in the afternoon, at a lecture in the evening and at the cowshed in the morning. They hankered after a life of their own. Sensibly, the kibbutzim effected a number of bourgeois-leaning changes to meet the nagging needs of the individual; and the advance from a one-room hut to a two-room bungalow with its own kitchenette, toilet and shower marked the beginning of a revolution in the style of kibbutz life. In time, it gained a new variety and sophistication; the kibbutzim acquired their own libraries, museums, movie halls and beauty parlors and even, on occasion, their own music festivals; and their members were provided with the means to travel abroad. Jewish individualism, so important and so striking a component of Israeli democracy, won out in the kibbutz as it was bound to. The pioneers had brought a strong anti-intellectual bias to their back-to-the-earth adventure, with its cult of the farmer's life and its exaltation of manual work. But the great majority of them were middle-class intellectuals after all, and through the years, in the kibbutz schools, they continued to maintain the highest educational standard in the country, for the simple reason that they had the best teachers.

The kibbutz was a mold that set its lasting mark on national life and on the Israeli personality. The very basis of its society was a sense of collective responsibility, but it managed to develop its communal life without resort to the pressures of regimentation. In that sense it was an intense mirror of Israeli society at large. More than any other institution, it helped produce that representative type of Israeli humanism which the Israelis themselves were most inclined to venerate: the individual who had a touch of the Renaissance man, the soldier-scholar, the farmer-intellectual, the man of contrasting skills and ranging interests who might be called to service in the most varied capacities, as a specialized delegate to an international conference, as a political adviser in an embassy abroad or as a technical expert to build an irrigation system or triple the output of some particular crop in some struggling country in the underdeveloped world. If Israel was an exceptionally determined and persistent society, a large measure of the credit went to the kibbutzniks, who, by their own persistence, kept alive the memory of the idealistic vision and spirit of endeavor that had brought the Zionists to Israel. Their way of life was a reminder that the ultimate role and mission of Israel, which would always remain a small country with limited resources, would be in the realm of intellectual effort, in the art of making much of little and in its success in meeting the ethical tests of a modern society.

The kibbutzniks were still the leaders in the tradition and practice of volunteerism. In the armed forces, they continued to contribute far more than their share of volunteers to the tougher and more hazardous services, the air force and the parachutists, the armored corps and the frogmen; and always far more than their share of the casualties. They kept their identity within the army through such bodies as Nahal, the soldier-pioneering youth group on which the country still relied for the founding of settlements. They continued to provide the state with ministers and generals, members of the Knesset and senior officials, as a kind of farming aristocracy with a vocation of public service. Of this farming society, Allon was an accomplished representative, and what could be said of him could be said, in suitably adapted terms, of countless others: he was equally at home at his kibbutz mess, at a labor meeting, as a speaker before a New York audience, as a student at Oxford or guest lecturer at the Hebrew University in Jerusalem, or as a government emissary in India, Canada and the Soviet Union.

The individualism of Jewish democracy created the Haganah and through the years shaped the distinctive character of the Israeli Army. No other army in the world made so few concessions to the normal forms of military discipline. In prestate days, the Haganah had learned how to mobilize and train civilians, and the state of Israel retained this unparalleled capacity to arm an entire population, improving on its Haganah experience with the mandatory addition of women. Unmarried women between the ages of eighteen and twenty-six were subject to conscription for twenty months' service; the creation of the Women's Corps would have been an awkward and probably aberrant experiment in a society any less fully and freely emancipated than Israel's. The I.D.F., the Israel Defense Forces, were in the broadest sense an armed people or a citizens' army. It consisted of a small nucleus of regular officers, commissioned and noncommissioned, a standing contingent of men and women called up for service, and then the wide mass, the Reserve, from generals to privates, embracing the great portion of the able-bodied civilian population of military age.

The individualism that was the mark of this army was first of all a military fact, in the sense that every soldier was trained to operate in small units as well as large, in platoon formation, on patrol or completely on his own. But even more notably it was a social fact that expressed itself in the relationship between officers and men. One could spend days in their company, at a base or in the field, without encountering any of the familiar forms of discipline, an allusion to rank, a word of deference, a peremptory order, a simple salute. The men as often as not addressed their officers by their first names. In the upper echelons one looked in vain for some evidence of military swank or caste, whether in dress, manner or speech; and still more vainly for some sign of militarist mystique. Since neither the army itself, nor the Knesset nor the President nor anyone else in the Republic bestowed military honors, there was a total absence of bemedaled chic, and the highest recognition to which anyone in the armed forces could aspire was mention in an order of the day or individual citation by the Chief of Staff. There was, as far as the outsider could observe, no bucking for position in the higher ranks. Israel was full of colonels fully qualified to be generals. But, of course, there was only so much room at the top. The army was not in the business of creating brass, and few were chosen for the top field commands or the General Staff. The colonels who failed to make it seemed perfectly content to remain colonels.

Israel proved it was somehow possible to build a military machine without resort to militarism on any level, but an outsider still could only wonder how an army could get along with so much democracy. There were some, like Allon, who thought it might be a good idea to "tighten up discipline a bit"; the soldiers might look smarter, the boots shinier and the ensemble of dress, footgear, trousers and shirt, more of one piece, like a uniform. The Israelis learned a great deal from the British, fighting with them or against them, but among the things they did not keep were the British conception of battle drill, which they dismissed as an artificial way of acquiring combat habits in the field, and the British reverence for leather, for which they felt no inclination. They evidently had something better than such marks of barracks discipline. They had the moral cohesion of their society, of which their army was the expression, and its purposefulness; and these were apparently enough. On the battlefield or in the rigorous field exercises of his thirty months' service, the soldier obeyed the orders of authority because he knew, among other things, that when and if the time came for him and his comrades to advance into enemy fire, the lead man in the assault would be his commanding officer.

The army performed a further role in the development of Israeli society. It ran schools, both primary and secondary according to the need, with courses in Hebrew, reading, writing, history, the Bible, current events, mathematics, physics, geography and the land of Israel. Since every young person went into the army, everyone also had occasion to go to school, if he had happened to miss it elsewhere. During the period of mass immigration in the fifties, when people came from more than eighty countries, thousands from Arab lands who had the most meager primary education, the majority ignorant of Hebrew and many illiterate—in that time the army was the ethical school of the nation, the body that was chiefly responsible for absorbing this new population and making it part of the Israeli citizenry. The army did not reject the illiterate; it took them in and educated them, in accordance with the central principle of Israeli life that every last human resource, like every last material resource, must if possible be saved and made productive. In this process the army became the integrating social force of the country and the cradle of the new generation.

Everybody in the army, it seemed, went to school and not only the new immigrants. It was the habit of the senior commanders—Dayan, Yitzhak Rabin, Yeshaya Gavish and numerous others—to attend courses at military schools in foreign countries, chiefly Britain, France and the United States, not because they needed instruction as generals but in order to study modern warfare methods, keep abreast of advances in tactics and technology and explore their uses for Israel. It was also their habit to shed their uniforms when occasion offered and go to university in Israel or abroad, to pursue their nonmilitary interests, in the law or business administration or some field of the liberal arts. The highest echelon of the army was, by and large, a cross section of the best of Israel's managerial class, and in opening a conversation with a senior officer one never knew how far it would range by the time it was ended. Brigadier General Gavish was a Master of Arts in political science, and Israel Tal, commander of the armored force in the 1967 war, was a Ph.D. in political science and philosophy. In the crisis of May of that year, when the Chief of Staff needed Haim Bar-Lev to be his deputy, he had to summon him home from Paris, where he was completing a course in political science at the Sorbonne.

The younger generation to whom Dayan and Allon appealed were practical in their interests, straightforward in their address and informal in their manners. At political meetings they were plain-spoken; they wanted facts and logic, not grandiloquence and catchwords; and being sharply critical, they gave the speakers little peace. But like their elders they were not obstreperous or rowdy and still less riotous, because the political leader who was addressing them was after all one of them. In Israel, they said, every man was Prime Minister. The sabras of the new generation looked at you with open faces and clear, unflinching eyes that told you they were proud to be Jews but did not in the slightest care whether you were Jewish or not. They had no taste for fine formalities; their country had not had the time to develop a fastidious tradition of manners and courtesy. In general, their manners were as unadorned and unpretentious and as lacking in surface embellishments as was the domestic architecture of a country that was still a work in progress, still seeking to make much of little, still unformed and unfinished. The youth of Israel had no knowledge and no experience of anti-Semitism in their own country; they were free of the defensive attitudes of anti-anti-Semitism that were part of the experience of an older generation that had lived in Europe. They had lost some of the talents and refinements of the Jews of the European Diaspora, and some of their sensibility: the gift for languages, the restive probing, the ethical discontent, the spiritual neurasthenia; they had also lost the mental habits of soft treading and accommodation. They had won the new gifts of naturalness and self-reliance, spontaneity and freedom. They had little appreciation of the human meaning of the holocaust and little understanding for its victims. This was something that had happened in an alien, incomprehensible world, in the era of their fathers. They rejected it because they could not conceive it; they had no experience of submission; they did not after all have it in their character or their senses to be passive Jews. They harbored no hatred of the Germans; and while some Israelis thought the young had been too quick to forget, it was yet a sign of vitality and resilience. The impulse was to live with the present and look to the future, not to brood or look back. With regard to the Arabs, there was a tendency among hard-line nationalists to assert the historical precedence and superior moral rights of the Jews in Palestine, and this could lead to complacent scorn for Arab failings and an easy assumption that whatever Israel did in her defense was right because of an accepted superiority in her moral position. But such tendencies were recognized, criticized and combated. By and large, hatred of the Arabs was nonexistent. Among Israeli youth, there was no inclination to yield to hatred and no tendency to entertain it. It was another sign of vitality.

A representative attitude of the young was lack of interest in political developments outside Israel. They were disdainfully indifferent to proceedings at the United Nations Security Council or General Assembly during Arab-Israeli disputes. They had no faith in the efficacy of United Nations action, nor in the will or capacity of that body to maintain peace in the Middle East or defend the integrity of Israel; nor did they or their elders for a moment believe that Israel could ever entrust her security to anyone else. They were a people alone; no matter how important their friends were to them, they put their trust in themselves for their survival. Israel needed the support of powerful friends, but it was her own self-reliant strength that induced those friends not to abandon her. Self-reliance was not only an attitude of mind but also a policy of state, and how many times through the years it had been publicly affirmed by Israel's leaders. "Our future," Ben-Gurion had said in a speech to the armed forces, "depends not on what non-Jews say, but on what Jews do." Years later, in June, 1967, two days before the outbreak of war, at a time when many of Israel's friends in the outside world feared she could not withstand the combined strength of her enemies, Dayan struck the same proud chord and rallied the confidence of his people. "If somehow it comes to real fighting," he said, "I would not like American or British men killed here and I do not think we need them. . . . I do not expect or want any people to fight or get killed for us. That is very clear."

Self-reliance had been a watchword in the days of the British Mandate, during the Arab assaults on the Jewish community; and after the experience of the Nazi holocaust, it became the life and premise of Israel's military doctrine. "There are two faces or aspects of the Jewish character that are alive in Jewish memory," Yigal Allon said to me, in a discussion of these attitudes. "There was the Jewish community that depended for its livelihood or its very existence on the will of someone else, landlord or tyrant, and made its accommodations accordingly. There was the Jew who was the stubborn resister, the fighter who held out against insuperable odds or miraculously saved a desperate situation, Judas Maccabeus and the partisans behind the

German lines in Russia and Poland in the last war. There were the
Jews of Spain who chose the *auto-da-fé* rather than renounce their
faith, and the fighters in the Warsaw ghetto; and there were those who
went, together with thousands of Gentiles, to the extermination
camp."

The Jews who went to Palestine and later to their own state in
Israel did not make the journey in order to be led to the gas chamber,
or to be shot at, or to get down on their knees and ask for favors, or to
argue their right to a national existence. They were antidefeatists in
spirit and in principle, since defeat would mean annihilation. Their
representative leaders were unintimidated men. "You must remember," Allon said, his blue eyes leveling, "there are two fundamental
facts that are deep in our national psychology. The first is that Israel
is the only country in the world that cannot lose a war . . . and
survive. It is the motive of 'no alternative' that everyone felt so
strongly in 1948, when the Arabs invaded. The second fact is that
Israel is a country whose disappearance the world would tolerate
. . . deeply regretting the tragedy but permitting it to happen."

A bitter thought, but one that was engraved in the minds of those
who were responsible for Israel's security.

Israel was ultimately dependent on her own strength: this was the
conclusion that Israeli statesmen and strategists, no less than the Israeli people at large, drew from their experience. But this hard proposition, both practical and moral, was never as simple as it seemed.
Israel in another sense was a dependent country who at every moment
in her history had to search out and establish new lifelines of strength.
The character and direction of these lifelines changed, since the international political scene around her was continually changing. The
spheres of big-power influence in the Middle East shifted unrecogniz-
ably, as the Americans and Russians eclipsed the British and French,
and Israel was immediately caught up in the new circle of tension
between East and West. Since she was surrounded by enemies who
refused to acknowledge her existence and tried to wear her out with
siege and attrition, she needed to multiply her ties with the outside
world and gain the widest possible recognition by the major powers.
But specifically and urgently, there was something she needed even
more than political recognition and acceptance. She needed arms. On
Middle Eastern seas, not even the stoutest lifeline of military strength

could be regarded as permanent, and the quest for new sources of arms was fundamental to her strategy for survival. This had always been true, even in the days before the founding of the state, and from the very beginning, knowing she could depend on herself alone, she had sent her most resourceful and sure-footed men into the quest.

On an afternoon in the last week of November, 1947, Ehud Avriel, twenty-nine years old, Vienna-born, came back from the fields of the kibbutz he had helped to found in Upper Galilee and saw a familiar black sedan waiting in the compound. Ben-Gurion's political secretary had come, unannounced, to take him to Jerusalem. Three hours later Avriel learned from Ben-Gurion that the United Nations General Assembly would be voting within a few hours on a resolution to partition Palestine between the Jews and the Arabs. It was uncertain whether the resolution would win the required two-thirds majority but, Ben-Gurion said, if there was partition, there would be war; and if there was no partition, there would also be war. On both the Jews and the Arabs, the United States had placed an arms embargo, and the Jewish defense forces needed a large amount of arms very quickly: 10,000 rifles, 4,500 submachine guns and several million rounds of ammunition. Members of the Haganah General Staff had prepared a procurement list, consisting largely of spare parts and replacements for a heterogeneous armory of old British weapons. Ben-Gurion realized that Avriel had only recently come back to home and family, and he regretted the short notice, but he would have to leave for Europe immediately. Avriel was delighted; it was the assignment he had been hoping for. Two days later he was in Paris.

Behind him were five and a half years' experience with the political and intelligence underground of Nazi-occupied and postwar Europe. In Istanbul in 1942, he had set up shop for Aliyah Beth, "Immigration B," the illegal smuggling of Jewish refugees into Palestine, as distinguished from "Immigration A," the tightly restricted quota that was officially permitted by the British. Aliyah Beth was the business of rescuing Jews, and Avriel's task as emissary of the Haganah was less to get the Jews to Palestine than to salvage Jewish life in the Nazi-held territories. Through contacts in Turkey and by telephone with third parties in Bucharest, Sofia and Budapest, he organized the hiring of ships, the assembling of the refugee parties in Rumania and Bulgaria and their embarkation from the Black Sea ports of Costanza and Varna. The crucial point in their passage was Istanbul itself. The

Turks did not want to keep this mass of displaced people; the British did not want them to move on to Palestine. The practical effect of British policy was to collaborate with the Nazis in the trapping of East European Jewry. Early in 1942 an overloaded refugee ship, the S.S. *Struma,* was detained in the Dardanelles; unwanted by anyone, it was ordered to sail back to its port of embarkation, and the next day seven hundred persons died when an explosion sank it.

The outcry of shock and protest in the United States and elsewhere that followed this disaster opened a small loophole in British policy. The British Embassy in Ankara was advised by London that those refugees who arrived in Turkey "under their own steam" should be allowed to pass, but since the Embassy failed to inform the Turkish Government of these new orders, many months passed before they had effect. Avriel by then had contrived his own means of breaking the system. Every boatload of Jews that came down the Bosporus from the Black Sea and every trainload that arrived in Istanbul from Budapest, which at that time was still a haven for fugitives from Nazi Europe, brought with it quantities of valuable information. British military intelligence officers in Istanbul were interested not in keeping Jews out of Palestine but in securing information and in winning the war, and on this basis Avriel won their collaboration in what became a common conspiracy against the policy of Whitehall. In time, the Jewish underground was organizing prisoner-of-war breaks from Nazi camps in the Balkans and helping Allied airmen through Hungary to the Titoist lines in Yugoslavia. Farther south, thousands of Jewish refugees from Eastern Europe had meanwhile reached the end of their road in Athens and Piraeus. To rescue them, Avriel and his friends secured the help of Ellas, the Greek underground, which brought them out to the Turkish port of Smyrna by caïque across the Aegean, at five gold sovereigns a head. Since Ellas had an agreement to work for British intelligence only, the caïque operation had to be concealed from Avriel's British friends and confederates in Istanbul; it was a side enterprise, a conspiracy within a conspiracy.

In the three years to the end of the war, some 120,000 Jews escaped from Nazi-held Eastern Europe by the underground routes and devices that Haganah had established.

Already, toward the end of 1944, Avriel was on the other side of the continent in Paris, preparing for the next phase of Aliyah Beth. Paris after the war became headquarters for the illegal Haganah com-

mand in Europe, with Avriel again in charge of saving the survivors of
the Nazi destruction of Jewry. It was a vast undertaking—the mass
movement of refugees from D.P. camps to Mediterranean ports, the
hiring of crews, the chartering of more or less seaworthy ships, the
enlistment of diplomatic connivance, the eastward journey—a movement across international borders and international seas in defiance of
British intelligence, British air reconnaissance and British naval control of the Mediterranean. It was in Paris, on the frequent trips he
made to the Haganah headquarters during those years, that Ben-
Gurion first met Avriel, and it was Avriel who convinced him that
Aliyah Beth should use big boats, not small, to present to the world a
bolder affirmation of the Jewish cause and a more dramatic exposure
of the brutalities of British policy. Ben-Gurion had a keen eye for
human value and character, especially in the younger people about
him. He was impressed by the talent of this purposeful young man
whose forthright and winning manners had opened so many doors to
his artifice and ingenuity. Avriel was a man whose senses were mobilized and present for all occasions, with all his capacities at his command and with an end in view. He was not a man who could be easily
stopped.

By September, 1947, his job was largely done and he was told he
could come back to his kibbutz. Since he had been blacklisted ten
times over by the British in Palestine, he stopped in Marseilles on his
way to pick up a false British passport at the document factory which
the Haganah maintained there. At home in the fields of the kibbutz,
he wondered impatiently when his next call would come.

In Paris again at the end of November, he was visited by many
people at the Haganah headquarters on the first day of his return
there. Each of them had arms to offer, or professed to; all were large
in promise, tall in price and hazy in commitment. None was convincing. At the end of these talks, Avriel's old secretary, still at the headquarters, told him of a man-about-Paris who had insisted on seeing
him, an entrepreneur of some sort who was also a balletomane and
who had shown his friendliness by providing the staff of the Jewish
underground with one of the priceless items of that year, box seats for
the ballet during a brilliant season of which Serge Lifar was the lion.
Nothing more was really known of him. "Why must I see him?" Avriel asked. "He knows no more about arms than I do about ballet."
But he agreed to see him anyway.

The man came in, elegantly dressed and carrying a briefcase. He announced, as he took his seat, that there was nothing easier than to purchase arms. He produced an arms catalogue and, not waiting for either questions or comments, went down the list with pertinent explanations and quoted the prices. From the manner, the idiom, the pointed remarks, the professional concreteness, Avriel knew that this was it. The man inspired confidence both in what he was saying and, more importantly, in himself. The rifles were $47.25, far from cheap but notably cheaper than the other prices Avriel had been hearing earlier in the day. But who was this gentleman of trust? The question brought a rapid synopsis of a lifetime. He was Robert Adam, Jewish, from Rumania. For several years before the war he had been the Bucharest representative of Czeskoslovenska Sbrozovska, the Skoda arms concern at Brno in Czechoslovakia. He had left Rumania soon after the arrival of the Germans in 1940 and then, intercepted by the British on his way to Palestine, was interned in a camp in Cyprus, where he spent the remaining four years of the war. He then became an Aliyah Beth immigrant to Palestine. He was an epicure and a boulevardier and he recognized that Palestine was not for him; and so, following the line of his tastes, he forsook the pioneering life and came to Paris. He had always entertained feelings of compunction and guilt about this act of desertion, and had maintained contact with his former associates at Skoda in the thought that one day he might be in a position to discharge his debt of conscience. This was why he had come. He would accompany Avriel to Skoda the next day; they would be expected; the air tickets were in his pocket. He had bought them on the way to the hotel.

On his earlier Paris assignment, Avriel had acquired one hundred sheets of the official stationery of an African Consulate General, through the complaisance of a member of its staff. They had cost him one thousand dollars, which he had presented in the form of a jeweled ring to the consular gentleman in question. But the sheets had been well worth the price and had served admirably in the procurement of transit visas and other facilities for various displaced and roaming persons. In the drawer at the Haganah office, three sheets of this store remained, unsoiled and unfrayed. Avriel slipped them into his bag before leaving with Robert Adam the next morning.

The first Israeli-Czech arms contract was concluded at the office of Czeskoslovenska Sbrozovska that day: the 10,000 rifles, 4,500 submachine guns, the ammunition and various other key items on Avriel's shopping list. They were German weapons, manufactured for the Wehrmacht; they represented leftover stock that Skoda was delighted to dispose of, since the armed forces of Czechoslovakia were already in the process of conversion to Soviet armament. Avriel learned that the Skoda people would also be able to provide some surplus Messerschmitts and even some British Spitfires that had come their way. As for the present contract, there was only one rather delicate point of protocol. It would be awkward for the company to sign a contract with an underground army that was clearly illegal under the terms of a League of Nations mandate. What would Avriel suggest? The answer was at hand. Two copies of the contract were drawn up and executed on the stationery of the African Consulate General. It was, indeed, a most fortunate coincidence, since Skoda had only recently sent its representatives on an arms-selling mission to the capital of that particular African country. Avriel assumed for the occasion the power of attorney and signed, so to speak, on behalf of the sovereign state in Africa.

Robert Adam personally met all the expenses of this fruitful trip. He declined his agent's commission from Haganah but accepted his commission from Skoda and handed it over to Avriel.

It was a long way from Prague to Palestine and the most difficult part of the task lay ahead. Avriel went from Prague to Belgrade, hoping that his wartime relationship with the partisans would now serve him well. He was not disappointed. The Yugoslav military intelligence gave its blessing and protection to the transport of the Skoda weapons to Bakar, a small port on the Dalmatian coast. Avriel moved on to Italy, to look up an old acquaintance from Haifa, a Jewish businessman who was versed in the dodges of commercial smuggling, knew the language and hieroglyph of the ports and had a cohort of friends along the Italian waterfronts. A suitable ship was hired in Venice, the 500-ton *Nora,* and on the instructions of the man from Haifa, her hold was filled with Italian onions. With this plausible cargo, she set sail for Bakar, where she off-loaded the vegetables and on-loaded the crates of Czech weapons, onto which the onions were piled to a depth of several feet. The *Nora* sailed for Tel-Aviv with an Italian captain, an Italian crew and a Haganah ship's commander, a young man who "knew every wave of the Mediterranean," since he had performed the same service countless times for Aliyah Beth. When British soldiers boarded the *Nora* for the inspection in the ways at Tel-Aviv, they drove their bayonets several times into the mound of onions without striking wood or metal until, discouraged by the smart in their eyes from making a deeper exploration, they gave up and passed the cargo. The time was mid-April, 1948. Israel did not proclaim her independence until the following month, but the War of Independence was already engaged on many fronts, and the Czech guns, fresh with their factory grease, were hurried to the Jewish forces that were fighting to relieve a number of besieged places in the corridor to Jerusalem.

Ben-Gurion for many weeks had been calling for an immediate delivery of arms. Avriel had arranged for the use of intermediate landing fields in Corsica and Italy and had already managed to airlift some rifles out of Czechoslovakia. These first air shipments had been flown to areas in Palestine from which the British had withdrawn in the first stage of their phased pull-out, to small hidden valleys in Galilee and desert strips in the Negev. Until May 14, the day the British Mandate ended and the state of Israel was born, the sea-borne shipments traveled with onions; after the 14th, with the expiration of British power, they went without them. The following month, a first shipload of Skoda heavy machine guns, 37-millimeter, were unloaded at Tel-Aviv, and these weapons, mounted on jeeps, were the nearest thing the Israelis had to mobile artillery for their mechanized battalions. They were first used in the renewed fighting of July, at the end of a United Nations truce, when one such battalion in a daring and gambling raid, scattered the superior forces of the Arab Legion from the area around Lydda, a half-hour's drive from Tel-Aviv. The international airport at Lydda also fell to the Israelis. The author of the raid and commander of the battalion was Moshe Dayan.

By a curious stroke of fortune, the *Nora* had not been the first vessel to carry Czech arms to Tel-Aviv. Much earlier in the game, Yugoslav intelligence had alerted Avriel to a large consignment of Skoda weapons that was being transported across Yugoslavia for shipment to Syria. The Czechs had been doing a lucrative business on both sides of the street. While the Yugoslavs could not deny passage to a cargo that was destined for a friendly Arab state, they could and did invent appropriate bureaucratic hurdles to delay its departure. To keep an eye on this operation, Avriel went to Rome, using his forged British passport to obtain a *permis de séjour*. The Italian police at that moment were examining foreign documents with more than their usual care, because they were alarmed by the possibility of Communist agents filtering into the country during the great electoral contest that was then in progress between the Communist-led bloc and the parties of the democratic center. In Rome, Avriel had the assistance of a number of old and valued Haganah hands. There was Aliyah Beth's man in Italy, Yehuda Arazi; there were four Haganah pilots who by courtesy of the Italian Air Force were using the Ciampino military air base near Rome to overhaul and retune some Spitfires they had recently acquired; and a young naval officer from Palestine whose services Avriel had requested for the singular and challenging enterprise that was now at hand. He was Yochai Ben-Nun, who later became the Commanding Officer of the Israeli Navy. The four pilots shadowed the Syrian arms ship as it steamed south through the Adriatic, but they lost all trace of it during a violent storm and the game was apparently up. Later in the day it was learned that the ship had found sanctuary from the storm in a small bay a few miles from Bari. Ben-Nun, who was a frogman, set out for the scene, and the next day the scuttled ship and its cargo were lying on the sandy shore of the bay. At this point the Czechoslovak insurance company, as the party financially responsible for safe delivery, intervened energetically; the weapons were salvaged and transported to a nearby warehouse where they were placed under guard.

Czechoslovakia had just succumbed to a Communist coup, and in the excitement of those pre-election days in Rome, it was not difficult for Arazi and his friends to launch the report that the arms from Skoda had been earmarked for Communist agents in Italy. The Italian authorities gallantly espoused this interpretation of the incident. The Syrians, as a result, were unable to find anyone in Rome willing to offer a ship for their suspect and probably subversive cargo. A deep-draft Egyptian vessel tried to come to the rescue but was unable to enter the shallow waters of the inlet. However, after a few days, the Syrians came across a hitherto unheard-of shipper who was ready and able to cooperate. This helpful individual was Yehuda Arazi. With an Italian crew, a precious cargo of salvaged arms, and a pseudonymous Haganah ship's commander, the ship provided by Arazi was soon able to set sail from the little bay for its destination in the Levant. En route on the high sea, a larger vessel crossed its bow and announced its piratical intentions over a loudspeaker. The weapons were transshipped at gunpoint. The purpose of this artistry was to enable the

Italian captain, on his return home, to report in all honesty that his cargo had been highjacked by persons unknown.

On May 19, five days after the proclamation of the new state, Avriel was named Israel's first Ambassador. Soon thereafter he moved with ease into the diplomatic world of Prague, to assume a post for which his great native urbanity and warmth, no less than his bold skill, so eminently equipped him. Later he doubled as Ambassador to Hungary and later still he was accredited to Rumania as well. The Israeli-Czech arms relationship, which had been approved by Foreign Minister Jan Masaryk, was honored and extended by his Communist successors, having meanwhile won the blessing of Moscow. It continued for two years and brought to Czechoslovakia $12 million of badly needed foreign exchange. To be sure, it was clear that political as well as financial considerations had helped to sustain the arrangement. The Russians in those days, unlike the Russians of a later time, formed the opinion that Israel was an anticolonialist phenomenon and were prepared to assist her in order to hasten the expulsion of the British from the Middle East. The Russian origin of so many Israelis and the turn-of-the-century Marxist inspiration of so many of their political leaders no doubt helped to foster the hope, in Moscow as in Prague, that Israel in time might take her place among the people's democracies. Avriel was careful not to discourage these illusions. He remained on good terms with the Communist Foreign Minister, Vladimir Clementis, until the day Clementis was purged.

But the lasting debt that Israel owed—and there are occasions when this term may be plausibly used in international politics—was less to the Czechs than to the Yugoslavs of Marshal Tito. Without the ready help of the Yugoslav intelligence the arms that Avriel had bought in Prague could not have reached the Jewish forces in time, and Israel's War of Independence might today be remembered by another name.

Five years after Avriel's initial contract in Prague, there was a further sequel to the story. The new revolutionary regime in Egypt condemned to death the Egyptian who had been one of the Syrians' chief agents in negotiating their contract with Skoda. The unfortunate man was accused of selling arms to the Zionists. Ben-Gurion wrote a personal appeal to General Mohammed Nagib, the Egyptian President, assuring him that the condemned man had never been guilty of such traffic and expressing the earnest hope that he would not be made the victim of a struggle that had already cost so many lives. General Nagib, a good and kindly man, replied in the most gracious terms. He thanked Ben-Gurion for his intervention and the motive that had inspired it, and accepted his assurance; the accusation would be withdrawn; but, he said, the sentence of death by hanging would be carried out since the man had been guilty of other crimes against the state. The Egyptian Revolution had been warmly greeted in Jerusalem, with many sanguine speeches in the Knesset, where it was generally predicted that Egypt's republican leaders would seek to achieve a new and sensible relationship with Israel. The cordial and lofty tone of General Nagib's reply to the Prime Minister seemed yet another reason to hope for better days.

As the man who had carried supreme responsibility for the establishment of the state and the development of its armed forces, Prime Minister Ben-Gurion remained his own Minister of Defense throughout the years of his leadership, on the principle that the two posts must be one for as long as Israel lived in a state of emergency. The quest for arms, never relaxed, became a matter of urgency once again in the late summer of 1955. In the previous year, Israel had watched with anxiety the American attempts to create a Middle Eastern defense system that would be based on Egypt with the collaboration of Nasser. She now grew alarmed when the Russians countered the Americans and rewarded Nasser for his neutralism by agreeing to equip his army. The Israelis turned to Washington. Secretary Dulles was then at that point in the seesaw where the advices he received were almost evenly balanced; while experts in Washington feared that Nasser had fallen irretrievably into the clutches of Moscow, the American Ambassador in Cairo, Henry Byroade, was convinced it was not too late to save him. The Ambassador argued that Nasser's resort to Soviet help had been a one-shot remedy at a moment of desperate need, and Dulles decided to take five or six months to test this theory, using the negotiations on the Aswan Dam as his vehicle. Duly preoccupied with this experiment, he was not eager to upset it by selling American planes to Israel. Pressed by the Israelis, he sought to reassure them they were in no immediate peril; pressed again, he agreed to intercede with third parties; and by May, 1956, with American approval, the Israelis were close to a final agreement on the supply of forty-eight jet fighter-bombers from France and Canada. But they still had no firm commitment on their early delivery. The months were passing, and the tempo of Egypt's absorption of her new Soviet arms was increasing.

Ben-Gurion was not unprepared for the difficulties he encountered in Washington. Indeed, having foreseen them, he had taken precautions. Months earlier, soon after the announcement of the Egyptian-Soviet arms deal, he had sent one of his ablest young lieutenants to Paris as his personal envoy to search for arms.

At thirty-two, Shimon Peres, as Director-General of the Ministry of Defense, was Ben-Gurion's second-in-command in the field of national security. He was a man of widely inquiring mind and strong executive gift, who had come with his family to Palestine at the age of ten from his native village in White Russia. A boyhood of practical pioneering and kibbutz-building with other new immigrants, and then of mobilization work that had carried him up the ladder to Haganah headquarters in Tel-Aviv, had made him a complete Israeli of the new generation and one of its most vigorous exponents. He was as impatient as any sabra with what he felt were the tired symbols and fossilized ideologies of the traditional political parties. Ben-Gurion had sent him abroad once before as head of an arms-purchasing mission to Washington, and Peres, intellectually restless, had taken time out to study at Harvard University. He had other personal endowments that made him an ideal emissary to Paris. Genial, witty and coolheaded, Peres possessed the quality of grace and inborn sophistication.

On the high official level, the atmosphere in Paris was unfavorable to his mission. The French Foreign Office was hesitant. It was mindful of France's residual ties in the Arab world, its interests in Syria and Lebanon, and its host of educational institutions in Egypt. Like most Western foreign offices, the Quai d'Orsay at the time was of two minds about the Middle East. With one mind, it imagined that a heating-up of the Mideast situation, through active opposition to Nasser, would in some way profit the French in their struggle with the Algerian rebellion; with its other mind, it believed that a calm approach to Nasser would attain the same goal at less cost. The balance between hawks and doves was uncertain. But on the popular level, the Parisian climate beamed with favor. French politicians of all colors were courting the Israelis; to be pro-Israel was chic and to be pro-Jewish was part of the vibrant heritage of the Resistance in which the Jews had so proudly fought. Peres in these circumstances elected to move at large through the political society of the capital, making friends. He made them on the right as well as on the left and in the ranks of the opposition parties no less than in the offices of the government. In particular, he established warm personal ties with a number of leading Socialists, Guy Mollet, Christian Pineau, Maurice Bourgès-Maunoury and others, who were then out of power and entertained only the faintest hope of getting in. In February, 1956, the time came for general elections and, to the surprise of Western Europe, the Socialists won; and the three party leaders who were Peres' closest and most important friends became, respectively, the Prime Minister, Foreign Minister and Defense Minister of France.

French governmental processes in 1956 bore little resemblance to what they later became under the reorganization carried out by a Presidential regime. The government ministries were not yet the precision instruments of a Presidential will; they were, on the contrary, the makers and movers of policy, of independent mind, not always in close touch or consonance with one another. The relationship with France which Peres achieved was informal and unconventional; in a way, the arms agreement he concluded was even stranger than the one Avriel had made with the Czechs eight years earlier. Like the Avriel-Skoda accord, the Peres arrangements were based on no political pact; unlike Avriel's, they were based on no contract. No documents record the story of the Israeli-French relationship, no written engagements spell out or confirm its secret terms, and no signatures remain to attest the good faith that underlay it. It was based on a series of personal and private understandings that were reached orally across the table at the French Ministry of Defense. More remarkably still, the French were apparently content to embark on this relationship with no precise profit-and-loss account in their minds; they were moved by no particular or demonstrable French national interest but rather by the reflexes of a lively sympathy for the Israelis and an instinctive desire to maintain French *présence* somewhere in the eastern Mediterranean. The unwritten alliance was the product of personal diplomacy and not of defined policy or doctrine; and though at a later date arms contracts were duly drawn up and signed, it remained an alliance of convenience. It was not theoretical or formulated, but practical and popular.

To be sure, the alliance with Israel soon acquired what the French conceived to be a solid basis in national interest and, as a result, Peres' negotiations with his friends at the Ministry of Defense received an unexpected boost from Foreign Minister Pineau, who changed French policy at the top for reasons unrelated to the matter of arms for Israel. Pineau imagined that Nasser was the power behind the revolt in Algeria and that France would be in a position to master the revolt if only she could manage to break him. This revelation seems to have come quite suddenly. On a tour of the East, Pineau had met Nehru in New Delhi and Nasser in Cairo, and the Egyptian leader, it appeared, had given him his word as a soldier that Egypt would provide no military assistance to the Front de la Libération Nationale in Algeria. A few days after Pineau's return to Paris, the French fleet intercepted an Egyptian arms ship on its way to the Algerian rebels, and from that moment the anti-Nasser struggle and the anti-F.L.N. struggle were inseparable in the French imagination. The humbling of Nasser became an imperative of French policy. If the issue for Britain in her confrontation with Nasser was the Suez Canal, the issue for France was Algeria; and Peres, benefiting as a diplomat by the passionate complications of French logic, but not losing his detachment as a philosophic observer, reflected on the pre-eminent role that imagination plays at crucial moments in human affairs.

Thanks to his arrangements, Israel received her first Mystère fighter-bombers in the spring of 1956. The existence of the French arms deal became known in the summer, although the rate and manner of delivery were successfully kept secret. For two months before Israel launched her invasion of Sinai on October 29, the French arms, in a series of one-hour turnabout operations, were unloaded offshore and picked up by the Israelis. During those two months, Nasser and his pan-Arab partisans were driving to close the ring around Israel. Elections produced a pro-Nasser government in Jordan; pro-Nasser forces were aiming to unseat King Hussein; Iraqi troops were poised to enter his kingdom, and a tripartite defense agreement proclaimed the unity of Jordanian and Syrian forces under Egyptian command.

The nationalization of the Canal in July, 1956 was the precipitating event in the creation of the undercover *de facto* alliance that ranged Britain, France and Israel against Nasser in the following autumn. The war aims of Britain and France were mainly punitive—to administer a crushing blow to the leader whose revolutionary pan-Arabism was imperiling their positions in the Arab world and who had just rocked their prestige by nationalizing the Canal company in which they were the majority stockholders. The war aims of Israel were mainly preventive—to demolish Nasser's new and expanding military potential while there was still time, and to break the threatened ring of Arab military strength under his captaincy. Israel had urgent immediate objectives as well—to end the lethal incursions of the Egyptian *fedayeen* commandos and to open the blockaded Straits of Tiran, and if possible the Canal itself, to Israeli shipping. Israel went to war primarily to achieve a new settlement of her existence, as a state under siege, by routing the most dangerous of her besiegers; and the Suez crisis that agitated the two Western powers was, for her, an advantageous occasion to achieve this objective, since it offered the assurance of their political collaboration and, to a degree, of their military support.

On October 28 Ben-Gurion informed his cabinet of the invasion that was to begin at five o'clock the following morning. Only his Foreign Minister, Golda Meir, and a few department heads had been privy to the decision. When his ministers asked whether Israel intended to keep the territory she expected to conquer, Ben-Gurion warned that everyone would be against her—the United States, the Soviet Union, the United Nations and Nehru. But, he said, of all these there was only one whom he feared. Only the United States, by invoking sanctions and stopping the flow of dollars, could impose her will on Israel without sending one soldier to the scene. His reading of the situation was even more accurate than he knew.

Ben-Gurion went from his cabinet meeting to his home, to receive Edward Lawson, the American Ambassador. Washington had been alarmed by the news of the Israeli mobilization but Ben-Gurion was even more alarmed by the danger that an advance leak of the Israeli plans might bring international intervention to block them. Lawson brought a personal message from President Eisenhower requesting Israel to take no aggressive action that might jeopardize peace or the growing friendship between the two countries. The Prime Minister, caught between his desire not to deceive the President and his fear of last-minute intervention, told his aide, Ya'acov Herzog, to draft a reply that would emphasize the perils to Israel's existence but would give no undertaking to refrain from action.

The reply was not yet ready when, early the next morning, a second personal message arrived from the President, repeating his request in sharper terms. By early afternoon Ben-Gurion, in bed with a fever, had approved the final draft of his reply. "It would be a betrayal of my government's main duty," he told the President, "if it did not take every possible step to ensure that the declared policy of the Arab leaders to liquidate Israel by force is thwarted. . . . I am certain that with your wealth of military experience you will be able to appreciate the grave and fateful danger in which we now find ourselves."

Secretary Dulles the previous day had put a similar stern request for nonaction to Abba Eban, the Israeli Ambassador in Washington, who was not among the restricted number of Israeli officials who knew of the invasion plans. After this interview, Eban sent an energetic query to Jerusalem demanding to know what was going to happen. He received no reply. He returned to the State Department the next day to stress the dimensions of the Arab threat, and as he and his interlocutor were engaged in this discussion, an agency bulletin was brought in announcing the invasion of Sinai. The conversation was abruptly ended.

Israel had greatly misappraised the international repercussions of her action and was unprepared for the storm of alarmed hostility that now gathered around her. What she had envisioned as a local war within the ambit of Middle Eastern tensions was seen in New York, and even more apprehensively in Washington, in the awesome perspective of East-West conflict and big-power confrontation. The forceful crossing of borders in the prevailing international atmosphere, Dulles said, could ignite global war. The White House and the State Department were stung to anger; they felt they had been egregiously misled by Israel, and communications with the Israelis in Washington were practically severed. Several days passed before Ben-Gurion and his ministers appreciated the intensity of this reaction or its implications. In a speech to the Knesset on November 7 Ben-Gurion announced that Israel, whose military victory was now complete, was ready for direct negotiations with Egypt and would not withdraw without a peace settlement. The events of the next few hours were to overwhelm that statement, and Ben-Gurion the next day was forced to reverse his stand.

On the morning of that day, November 8, he heard the news of the General Assembly's resolution demanding unconditional withdrawal and calling for the establishment of a United Nations Emergency Force to supervise the evacuation. The vote was in effect unanimous, with sixty-five nations for, only Israel against and ten others abstaining. Secretary-General Dag Hammarskjold, the Americans, the Russians and the Afro-Asians under Khrishna Menon were agreed that Israel was the single factor threatening world peace. A few hours later, at 8:30 that morning, by telephone from the Israeli Embassy in Washington, Ben-Gurion received the text of a third message from the White House, of a severity without precedent in Israeli-American relations. Eisenhower said it would be a cause of regret to all his people "if Israeli policy on so grave a matter as world peace should in any way affect the friendly cooperation between our two countries." At a meeting at the State Department, American officials underlined the threat of sanctions that was implicit in that sentence, with a firm hint that since Israel was jeopardizing the peace, the United States might halt all official and private aid. Three days earlier Ben-Gurion had received a message from Moscow; a note from Soviet Premier Bulganin had accused the Israeli Government of "criminally and irresponsibly toying with the fate of the world and its own people" and of sowing such hatred as must "bring into question the actual existence of Israel as a state." Rumors flew in the Middle East of Soviet bombers landing at bases in Syria and of the prospect of Soviet missiles as well and Soviet Moslem "volunteers" to fight for Egypt. Ben-Gurion had not budged under the thunderbolt from Moscow and was apparently unimpressed by the flash of alarmist rumors, but the threat of American action could not be so easily denied or outfaced.

Israel found herself on unfamiliar and uncharted ground, at the verge of a precipice, and on the afternoon of November 8 the Israeli cabinet in emergency session voted to obey the Assembly's call for withdrawal. Even in obeying, Ben-Gurion sought to hold fast. He did not himself believe the great powers were at the brink of war. He urgently inquired of Eban whether a personal meeting with Eisenhower was possible; he was told it was not, in view of the totally hostile atmosphere in Washington. He then asked the Ambassador whether in his judgment it would be possible to tie Israel's withdrawal to the arrangements she would eventually make with the United Nations Emergency Force, and Eban asked for time to make his soundings. Ben-Gurion hoped that by means of gradual withdrawal Israel might force recognition of her claims, and reckoned that if he could delay compliance with the Assembly's order, the world in time would recover from its eve-of-war fever and Israel in time would be able to argue her case and set her conditions. He waited several hours for Eban's answer, with the text of a radio speech already in hand. The answer that finally came was yes, and when Ben-Gurion at half-past midnight on November 9 went to the microphone to announce to a saddened nation his decision to withdraw, he was able to add a qualifying phrase that left a loophole for negotiation.

Only the day before he had told the Knesset that Israel would "never humble herself before the great forces of the world." There was sorrow and bitterness in Israel when he changed his mind, but there was no recrimination. Much of the sadness that Israelis felt was for the man himself; from the subdued tone of his weary voice, from the slow dignity of his phrasing, they knew he had only one choice and had taken his decision because the risks of any other course were too great.

But in the event, he had not lost. While Britain and France obeyed the United Nations order and withdrew their forces from the Suez Canal Zone, Israel accepted the order in principle and defied it in fact. Ben-Gurion fought for time and gambled on a change of heart. His main conditions for withdrawal were a guarantee of free navigation through the Straits of Tiran and the demilitarization of Sinai and the Gaza Strip, with UNEF alone to be stationed in the Strip and made responsible for its administration. Hammarskjold, armed with the resolutions of the Assembly, stood like a granite monument in resistance to these demands; and the State Department, muffled in grave displeasure, was inaccessible. The Secretary-General insisted on swift and unconditional withdrawal, on the principle that aggression did not deserve a reward; and the United States refused to negotiate, on the principle that it was Hammarskjold's affair. The Israelis, ostracized in Washington and isolated at the United Nations, were obliged to make the first concession: in December they announced that by January 23 they would withdraw all their troops to the north of El Arish and retain only the Gaza Strip and their outpost at Sharm el Sheikh overlooking the Straits of Tiran. On January 17, another General Assembly resolution, the fifth in the series, called for immediate and total withdrawal; the State Department spoke of the possibility of sanctions; and early in February a sixth Assembly resolution was followed by a further message from Eisenhower demanding Israeli compliance. The President said that "continued disregard of world opinion would almost certainly produce further United Nations action liable to harm Israel's relations with United Nations members, including the United States."

The room for maneuver between the threat of sanctions and the hope for guarantees was desperately narrow, but Ben-Gurion did not believe it was yet the time to yield. He rejected the sixth resolution and said in his reply to Eisenhower: "It is inconceivable, now that we have renewed independence in this ancient land, that we should submit to discrimination. Together with us, the world will not accept this, be the price what it may." On February 20, Eisenhower sent a fifth message, asking for an immediate reply on the question of withdrawal and again hinting at sanctions, and then broadcast to the nation the reasons for his stand.

Ya'acov Herzog, who had been delegated by the Israeli Foreign Office to be Ben-Gurion's political adjutant during the months of crisis, has related the events of that night in Jerusalem. Herzog awoke the Prime Minister at midnight to give him the news of Eisenhower's broadcast, and Ben-Gurion in his dressing gown paced the room in agitation, talking of the President, recalling the "great humanity" that had so impressed him at their first meeting in Frankfurt in 1945, and expressing his distress and amazement at the lack of understanding. He was profoundly irritated by the moralizing criticism of Israel that was now issuing from Washington. He had always enjoined his people not to worry about what outsiders said; but this precept did not stand alone, and he also held it to be axiomatic that Israel must always worry about what outsiders did. If the big powers were prepared to act against her, he once observed to me with a keen, reflective smile as he looked back over these events, then Israel could not resist them; there was nothing she could do. Nevertheless, on that night, he did not believe that Eisenhower's broadcast was his last word, and he resolved not to move without guarantees.

"Be the price what it may . . ." Partial sanctions, as he knew, would mean a deep cut, across the board, in the living standard of all classes in Israel, and total sanctions would bring the country's economy to a stop. Already the mere hint of sanctions, together with the actual withholding of American food surpluses and financial aid, had brought a number of stringent measures, and plans were under way to reduce the national budget by $55 million, 12 percent of the total, for the coming year. Sanctions would mean higher prices and taxes, further government cutbacks, almost certainly a general freeze of wages, severe fuel rationing and less food. But more important than all of these was oil: at least 95 percent of the oil that produced Israel's electricity, ran her transport and her factories and generated power

for the pumps that carried water across thousands of acres of irrigated farmland and up the Judean hills to Jerusalem, came from abroad. So did 60 percent of her foodstuffs. Total sanctions would be overpowering, but Israeli strategists did not think they could ever be total, in view of Israel's prowess in the craft of international smuggling and of the help that friends had promised her in the event of a siege. The port of Marseilles would be a major hole in a sanctions blockade, and Israel had many men on whom she could call in order to revive her underground routes around and across the Mediterranean, trafficking not in arms or in people but in food and oil. If Israel in the end should have to yield, Ben-Gurion thought, it must be only to irresistible pressure; but before he could make a final decision, he had to know whether her current stocks of food and reserves of oil were sufficient to meet the challenge. To get the answer he summoned Levi Eshkol, his Minister of Finance. He was the master of the nation's economic facts and the man most qualified to form a judgment.

An immigrant from the Ukraine at the age of eighteen, Eshkol had started out in Palestine as a farm worker and watchman at Petah Tikva, the oldest of the Jewish settlements, and then had moved north to help form a new one on the southern shore of the Sea of Galilee. One day they came to him at this settlement and said: "Shkolnik"— for that was his name then—"we need you to make a company to bring water to the land"; and he organized the national water-supply company that over the years transformed the gritty wasteland of Palestine into the green and bountiful countryside of Israel. Soon they needed him for many other things and he became the director of twenty companies engaged in the building of Eretz Y'Israel; then Ben-Gurion called him and began changing his jobs depending on where he was most badly needed and, as his friend and leader, even changed his name from Shkolnik to Eshkol. They wanted someone to take in hand the settlement of new immigrants, and he became the best absorption man the Jewish Agency ever had, organizing the structure of fund-raising and the methods of financial support for the new settlements. Then Ben-Gurion wanted him in the government as Minister of Agriculture, and finally, when he sought a man to oversee the whole edifice of the Israeli national economy, he took him out of agriculture and made him Minister of Finance. Eshkol did not have an electric presence and he lacked the gift of the word; he was a patient and adept mediator and trouble shooter in the back-room wrangles of the party

factions, but a gray and ponderous public speaker; and his socialism
was the sentimental socialism of the *shtetl* from which he came, the
European Jewish community where the important people were the
Rabbi, the most learned Talmudic scholar and the richest man, and
where everybody looked after everybody else in the spirit of Jewish
fraternity. His background was parochial but his sympathies and his
understandings were warm and wide. He was, as Ben-Gurion knew,
the kind of man one could go to when one had a problem.

The Prime Minister asked him if Israel had enough stocks to con-
template a siege. The answer was a single sentence. "You tell me for
how long you want it and I will arrange it."

So the decision was taken. In Washington on the same day it was
reported that the State Department felt United Nations sanctions were
inevitable unless Israel modified her stand. Nevertheless, the barome-
ter was falling and the ground was beginning to shift in the American
Republic. Israel's arguments were now being heard, and at this critical
moment they received encouragement from a powerful quarter. Secretary Dulles had received a letter expressing the strongest opposition to
sanctions in any form, and arguing that it did not become the United
States to act against the Israelis when she had not dared to act against
the Russians at the time of their invasion of Hungary. "Two wrongs
do not make a right," Eisenhower had said in his broadcast; but the
fact remained that the letter was signed by the majority leader of the
Senate, Lyndon B. Johnson, with the full support of the minority
leader, William Knowland. Moreover, as Ben-Gurion had anticipated,
the crisis in the Middle East had ceased to be a world crisis, since
Britain and France were both well out of it; and a week earlier, in a
memorandum to Eban that had remained secret at the time, Dulles
had made a gigantic half-turn in the American position. He had accepted the view that the Straits of Tiran were an international waterway and that no nation had the right to bar free and innocent passage
unless the World Court determined otherwise; furthermore, he had
said, the United States itself would undertake to uphold the principle
of free passage by sailing one of its own ships through the Straits to
Eilath. Ben-Gurion leaped at this opening. He summoned Eban to
Jerusalem and then sent him back to Washington to formulate a final
question: If Egypt again barred free passage, to commercial vessels or
warships, would the United States recognize Israel's right of self-
defense? The question was crucial, since the dispute had centered on

the charge that Israel had been guilty of aggression.

At this point, Israel's loyal friends, Mollet and Pineau, arrived in Washington to see the Secretary of State, on their first visit since the humiliations of the Suez War. With their timely collaboration, a formula was found and agreement was finally reached on the circuitous and artful arrangements by which the crisis was resolved.

It was Eban who personally negotiated the details of these arrangements with Dulles. Since it was impossible to win a two-thirds majority in the Assembly in Israel's favor, the Americans and the French had devised an alternative scenario, in which the British as well were to play a principal role. It was agreed that the Israeli Foreign Minister, Mrs. Meir, would announce to the Assembly Israel's agreement to prompt and full withdrawal, subject to certain assumptions and expectations. Her major assumptions would be that UNEF would move into the Tiran zone to prevent the renewal of the Egyptian blockade, and would take over exclusive control of the Gaza Strip. She would reserve Israel's right of self-defense to make good these assumptions. The representatives of the three Western powers would then make sympathetic speeches in support of the Israeli expectations so that Israel, in effect, would carry out her withdrawal on the basis of these public assurances. Eban and Dulles together scrutinized every paragraph of Mrs. Meir's text, and it was Dulles, as Eban later recalled, who took the pen and wrote in a phrase to reinforce her statement that any armed interference with Israeli shipping would be regarded as an attack entitling Israel to exercise her "inherent right of self-defense" and to "take all measures that are necessary." On March 1, Mrs. Meir delivered in the Assembly the speech that had been thus edited and thus approved by the American Secretary of State, but she heard with dismay the speech of Henry Cabot Lodge that followed. The American Ambassador endorsed her assumptions regarding the Straits of Tiran, but with respect to Gaza he sided with Hammarskjold and affirmed the right of the Egyptians to return to the area together with UNEF. Lodge added the hope that UNEF's role would continue until a final settlement was reached on the future of the Strip or an over-all settlement between Israel and Egypt.

On receiving the text of this speech, Ben-Gurion ordered Eban to seek immediate clarification from Dulles. Israel found herself without the guarantee on the basis of which she had agreed to evacuate Gaza. While the Prime Minister was breaking this news to a special meeting of his cabinet, his Ambassador was conferring with Dulles and the French; and the upshot of these talks was a sixth personal message from the American President to the Israeli Prime Minister. It was the last of the series.

Eisenhower expressed his deep gratification at the Israeli decision to withdraw, and said: "I know that this decision was not an easy one. I believe, however, that Israel will have no cause to regret having thus conformed to the strong sentiment of the world community as expressed in the various United Nations Resolutions relating to withdrawal."

The final words of the message referred to the expectations that Mrs. Meir had voiced in her speech: "I believe that it is reasonable to entertain such hopes and expectations and I want you to know that the United States, as a friend of all the countries of the area and as a loyal member of the United Nations, will seek that such hopes prove not to be in vain."

Eisenhower's letter represented the final document in the settlement of March, 1957, and, as a Presidential assurance, it remained its centerpiece. The settlement was indirect and imprecise. It was proclaimed outside any agreement between Israel and Egypt, the parties directly involved, and it did not bind the Egyptian Government in any way. The Egyptian Foreign Minister, Mahmoud Fawzi, had indeed rejected it; he had told the Assembly on March 1 that in Egypt's view the United Nations had been unanimous in expecting "immediate and unconditional withdrawals." On March 11, as the Israelis had expected, the Egyptians announced the appointment of a military governor for Gaza. Nevertheless, Israel had the word of a President, supported by the pledges of Britain and France. The Western powers were committed to uphold the right of free passage and they recognized Israel's right to use force to defend it. Two months earlier, in January, at the height of the diplomatic contest, Ben-Gurion had sought the intercession of General Walter Bedell Smith, the President's wartime Chief of Staff, and Smith now wrote to him to say that in his opinion Eisenhower and the United States had accepted a moral undertaking that would be honored. Knowing the loyalty of the President and the mettle of his Secretary of State, for whom a commitment once given was always and unalterably a commitment, Ben-Gurion could with good reason believe that the two authors of the undertaking saw it in exactly the same light.

Striking the balance of war and diplomacy, the Israelis could be well satisfied with their many gains. Foremost among them was freedom of passage to and from Eilath, for which they would have paid even with sanctions. Ben-Gurion had ordered the final evacuation from Gaza precisely for Eilath's sake, so as not to jeopardize the greatest political gain of the Israeli military victory. In the months and years that followed, even Gaza was quiet and the Israelis were free from *fedayeen* raids; they had expected the worst but they reaped the best, since UNEF performed its buffer role well; and though Egyptian administrators returned to the Strip, Nasser had learned his lesson and the *fedayeen* did not. A further gain was a new arms alliance with France that had been tested in war and gave promise of longevity. Finally, when the last Israeli soldier left Gaza on the morning of March 7, Dayan as well as Ben-Gurion knew that Israel had established herself in the region with a new sense of strength. Before the Sinai campaign, both the army and the nation had needed new confidence; and with Sinai, they had won it.

Seen from a somewhat higher angle, the implications for Israel's future were of a different order. The settlement of 1957 was based on indirection; it avoided the concept of contractual peace and acquiesced in the state of war. The peace-keeping role of the United Nations Emergency Force depended to an unusual degree on the personal authority of its creator, Hammarskjold, who intended that it continue to perform its function until some kind of political settlement was reached. Israel's condition remained anomalous and indeterminate, with no secure or final boundaries, no explicit engagement on the part of her enemies, no acknowledgment of her statehood, no recognition of her identity and no acceptance of her existence. The Sinai war and its aftermath brought a decade of nonwar but they perpetuated the state of siege. They confirmed the Israelis in their acceptance of a long conflict and they hardened the Israelis' reliance on their own deterrent strength as the only means of preserving the peace and the gains they had made.

With the Suez crisis, the spheres of power changed and the United States moved into the vacuum that the British and French had left; and when the next crisis came, in June, 1958, the Marines were landing on the shores of Lebanon to save that country from the threat of Nasserist upheaval while a British military airlift, with American support, was performing a similar service for King Hussein. The strategy of big-power competition now dictated American arms policy in the region. Since the Americans had to combat the ascendancy of the Russians in various parts of the Arab world, they did not wish to be Israel's only powerful protector and strove to avoid what the language of geopolitics calls a "polarization" between East and West. They were not only pleased but eager to have other powers undertake to arm Israel, and nothing was more convenient for their purposes than to have France act as the main supplier of Israel and Britain see to the arming of Jordan while the United States Sixth Fleet cruised in international waters, an offshore and unseen presence.

One idea that was considered in the late 1950's was that Israel should aim for a formal defense pact with the United States, and the reasons why this proposal never got off the ground either in Washington or Jerusalem were revealing. Both the Americans and Israelis eschewed too final an identification. Both feared that an American commitment to the Israelis might provoke a Soviet countercommitment to the Arabs, and in any case, the Israelis realized, commitments were two-way streets. If the United States were formally bound to Israel, Israel would be similarly bound to the United States and would lose her freedom of action. She had other good reasons to look askance on the proposal. The issue of East-West alignment raised worrisome questions for a country whose national interests were in a peculiar sense world-wide. A central ambition of the state of Israel was to ingather the Jewish people to their homeland, and the greatest reservoir of potential immigrants was in the Soviet Union. This ambition evidently counseled nonalignment. To take sides in the Cold War would jeopardize immigration from the Soviet bloc and would be, in the words of Allon, "an irresponsible act with regard to Soviet Jewry."

In May, 1960, Ben-Gurion went to the United States on his first visit since the Sinai war and discussed arms for Israel at a cordial meeting with Eisenhower. As Ben-Gurion later recounted their conversation, the President advised him not to worry, since the United States would be ready to help at once if Israel were attacked. The Prime Minister objected. Before the United States could come to Israel's aid, he said, the President would have to consult the Senate, and no doubt the State Department and Pentagon as well, and for Israel it would be too late. "We don't want American boys to die for us," Ben-Gurion said. When Eisenhower protested that the Israelis by themselves were "not enough," Ben-Gurion assured him that "we can handle it"; if the United States supplied the arms, the Israelis would take care of themselves. Eisenhower agreed, and American arms were sent to Israel on conditions that accorded with the precept of nonpolarization. It was understood that the United States would not become a major supplier and that she would provide defensive weapons only, such as Hawk ground-to-air missiles and recoilless rifles, and then only if Israel was unable to obtain them from any other source.

A month after his meeting with Eisenhower, Ben-Gurion went to Paris, and the conversation he had at the Elysée Palace was not unlike the one he had had at the White House. President de Gaulle asked him why he was worrying, since France in case of need would come to Israel's aid and would not let her down. Gratified as he was by this assurance, which confirmed the spirit of the Israeli-French alliance, Ben-Gurion again demurred. French military aid would be too late, he said; and if France provided the arms, Israel would do the fighting. The President agreed and kept his word. On the occasion of their next meeting at the Elysée, De Gaulle sanctified the alliance with a toast which, coming from a master of deliberate and precise language, could only be taken as a solemnly weighted political utterance. "It is well," he said, "that friends and men of good will meet again. I raise my glass to Israel, who is our friend and ally."

The years passed and in September, 1963, the President of France showed a reawakened interest in the Arab Middle East. He invited King Hussein to Paris and, again raising his glass at a state banquet, expressed the desire to "end misunderstandings between the Kingdom of the Hashimites and the French Republic which were inspired from abroad." Remembering the disservice which the British had done to France by ejecting her from Syria in the closing days of World War II, De Gaulle was evidently content to pick up this Jordanian pearl from the old imperial crown. *Le petit roi* was to return to the Elysée on three further visits in each of the three subsequent years. The Israelis noted that De Gaulle's courtship of the Arabs grew more determined as their own relations with Washington gained new cordiality under President Johnson. In October, 1965, De Gaulle broke the ice with Egypt by welcoming, at the Elysée, Nasser's Deputy Supreme Commander, Field Marshal Amer, while Nasser signaled his eager satisfaction with the visit by pardoning four French diplomats whom he had imprisoned three years earlier on charges of espionage and complicity in a plot to overthrow his government. In the following March, De Gaulle sent his Minister of Culture, André Malraux, on a goodwill visit to Egypt that was made memorable by the high tide of his eloquence. "I believe in the soul of nations," Malraux declared in Cairo as he exhorted Egypt to seek salvation "by integrating her immense heritage with her present reality" and to find her soul "by laying claim to her amazing millennial past." In Paris meanwhile, the incisive and skeptical mind of Couve de Murville, the brilliant technician of the Quai d'Orsay, was beginning to question the merits of an alliance that was based less on interest than on sentiment. Couve did not believe that France should be *cavalier seul* in supplying arms to Israel. The alliance was still honored and it was still proving a profitable commercial transaction for the French, but it was, perhaps, growing somewhat complacent and fat.

Israel's campaigns for new sources of arms led her down many devious and unexpected passageways. The fact that Jordan was usually seeking arms in the same places presented a vexing complication. The Israelis at one point sought tanks and destroyers from Britain, who granted the destroyers but refused the tanks. "Why?" the Israelis asked. "Because," replied Selwyn Lloyd, the British Minister of Defense at the time, "you have no sea frontier with Jordan." In due time the United States became Jordan's principal protector and had to take over the job of arming the Jordan Legion; the British then relented and sold Centurions to Israel. But the acquisition of American Patton tanks by Jordan posed a new security problem on Israel's eastern frontier and Peres, as Deputy Minister of Defense, was soon knocking at Washington's door. He was assured that Jordan had obtained her Pattons on the understanding that she would use them only in self-defense, and on the further condition that the advanced models, the M-48's, would not be deployed west of the Jordan River. Since all weapons become weapons of self-defense in wartime, Peres was unconvinced and requested Pattons for Israel. The political art of arms-juggling then produced an ingenious solution, negotiated by Peres, the Pentagon and the West German Ministry of Defense, whereby the West Germans agreed to supply the Pattons from their own national store. A certain number of these Pattons, together with West German radar-controlled artillery and other electronic equipment, were already in the pipelines and some items were already delivered when news of the three-cornered deal leaked out to the world. The prompt anger of Nasser mobilized the Arab states and confronted the West Germans with a pan-Arab diplomatic boycott. The Germans pulled back, the deal collapsed and the United States had to pick up and fulfill the rest of the German commitment. Thus, in 1966, the first Pattons direct from the United States were delivered to Israel.

On the political front as well, Israel's efforts to surmount her isolation led her far afield. Shut off by a wall of noncontact from her Arab neighbors, she sought the most variegated contacts in the world beyond. Most remarkable as a feat of statesmanship was her campaign to make friends in the uncommitted world which, during the crack-up of colonialism in the post-Suez years, created so many new states with delegates and voting power in the General Assembly. The spirited pathfinder in this campaign was Avriel. In 1958 he arrived in Accra on an assignment for which he had both the zest and the aptitude. Officially he was Ambassador to the newly independent state of Ghana, which combined British Togoland with the old Gold Coast; unofficially he was envoy-at-large to nationalist Africa, of which Ghana's President, Kwame Nkrumah, was the idolized spokesman. Avriel won the friendship and confidence of the Ghanaian leader, and their warm personal association soon burgeoned in a political relationship of unique intimacy. Avriel initiated a program of Israeli technical assistance in Ghana, and to the Africans in general, as they faced the challenges of nation-building, he offered the skills and services of Israeli experts. As an undeveloped country that had developed herself, Israel was familiar with the problems of the new African states; and as a nation with no colonialist record who had won her independence after a struggle with the British, her political position was beyond reproach. Avriel promoted the attractions of a country that was sufficiently developed to be of help and sufficiently small and undeveloped to involve no political commitment and no threat of officious interference. The Ghanaian capital in that year was the Mecca of anticolonialist liberation movements on both sides of the continent, and the All-Africa People's Unity Congress provided a timely and useful occasion for the nationalist leaders to see Nkrumah walking down the streets of Accra, arm in arm with the Israeli Ambassador.

This was the beginning of Israel's foreign aid program, known as the Program of International Cooperation, which in the next nine years sent 1,700 Israeli technicians to work on development projects in sixty-two countries of Africa, Asia, Latin America and the Medi-

terranean region. Israeli pioneers organized new settlements with
dairy farms and fruit plantations in Venezuela; Israeli hydraulic engineers helped set up the reservoirs and pumping stations for water-
supply systems in Nigeria; Israeli rural planners directed the construction of model villages on land reclaimed from a malarial jungle in
Nepal. To complement the work of the experts, students from these
and other lands, from Brazil and Tchad, Kenya, Thailand and the
Philippines, went to Israel for training in the specialized techniques
that concerned them. The Israeli specialists knew how to find quick
answers with little money; their assistance was modest in scope but
suited to the needs of countries with limited means; and, since it involved few men and a minimum of overhead, it was equally suited to
Israel's own budget. She offered her technical aid impartially, without
regard for the political postures of governments. At an average cost of
$5 million a year, she presented herself as a country ready to share
her knowledge with the people who most needed it, and established
her presence throughout a region of Africa which Nasser was jeal-
ously disposed to regard as his political backyard.

For the Israelis, the world's most important capital was always
Washington, not only for reasons of power but because of the multiplicity of human ties. Whether seen from Washington or Jerusalem,
the character of the nexus between the United States and Israel was
unique in the world spectrum of relations between great and small
powers. Israel could not be adequately defined by any of the standard
terms or criteria available in the political glossaries of our time. By
any conventional test, she was a political client and, for many years,
an economic dependent of the United States, but she stubbornly defied
this narrow definition. The relationship with the United States was
paramount in Israeli diplomacy, in terms of power; but this American
predominance was tempered and qualified by the psychology of the
connection. On the American side, there were the cultural and religious bonds between Israel and American Jewry, which in the plural-
istic American society were felt to be a natural expression of the
American social character, entailing no problems of double allegiance
such as those that had arisen in the society of prewar Europe. The
American commitment was not strategic or visibly bound to a national interest; it was moral and for one part of the American community it was intimate. On the Israeli side, the history and instinct of the
nation forbade her to be a client. Had she been merely a client, she

would not have come into existence. She was a small power determined to be master of her own fate; she had always lived dangerously and she was forced to continue to do so. Without that determination, there would not have been an Israel. She needed American financial aid, and this had been decisive in the years of her take-off; but to be eligible for help she had to be able to prove herself and save herself. The American Sixth Fleet roamed the Mediterranean, affirming the credibility of American commitments in the area; but if the United States was a protecting power, it was not in Israel's nature to be a protectorate. This dualism in the Israeli-American relationship had been there from the beginning; indeed, it had antedated the birth of the state. There had been many political and military misgivings in Washington before President Truman took his decision to extend *de facto* recognition to Israel; and George Marshall, the Secretary of State, sharing some of those misgivings and deeply apprehensive as to the military capacity of the Jews, had entreated Ben-Gurion's representative, Moshe Shertok, not to proclaim the state of Israel because he believed it would be overwhelmed. But the Israelis were their own masters and made their own choice.

Statistically, by the per capita yardstick, Israel was the most heavily subsidized nation of any that the American people had undertaken to assist. In her first eighteen years, she received more than $1.1 billion in grants, loans and other forms of aid from the American Government, and hundreds of millions more in private contributions from the American Jewish community. After 1961 she no longer needed government grants of any kind, but she continued to depend on American private donations which, in the balance of national bookkeeping, were roughly equivalent to her trade deficit; in 1966, the deficit was $335 million, the total of private gifts and grants, $306 million. But in the moral bookkeeping of the nation, in which there was no place or rubric for feelings of dependency, these statistics were balanced by a record of remarkable achievement. In those eighteen years Western capital and Israeli technology had built a new society in which hundreds of thousands of immigrants were settled in what had been largely a desert and which now, through the skill of farmers and water engineers, was providing an expanding population with a range of foodstuffs nearly as wide as that of any European market. At the beginning of that period, Israel's exports had paid for only eleven percent of her imports; at the end, after an uninterrupted rise, they paid for approximately seventy percent: and her population had mean-while quadrupled.

The lesson of 1957 for Israeli policy-makers was clear and they took it to heart. Never again must Israel provoke a situation in which the two great powers acted in concert against her; never again must she invite or permit a breakdown in communications with the United States. In the interplay of East-West rivalry that now encompassed the Middle East, her vital link was with Washington; under no cir-cumstances must it be broken and least of all in times of trouble. Israel after the Sinai campaign had faced a blank wall at the United Nations, and had been able to win a hearing only after she had moved the scene of negotiations from the office of Hammarskjold to that of Dulles. When the crisis was over, an American official had said, "If you want us to be with you on the landings, you should advise us about the take-offs"; and his chaffing recommendation became a pol-icy byword both at the State Department and the Foreign Ministry in Jerusalem. It was an apt summation; it made sense and it was fair enough. Nevertheless, the process of week-by-week and day-by-day decision-making in Jerusalem was never simple; major decisions in-volving national security regularly felt the strain of contrasting views and pressures. The members of the Israeli Government, like the Is-raeli people, were rarely if ever the compact and indivisible body that they appeared to the outside world. Among the ministers and their senior advisers, there were those whose chief concern was Israel's po-litical posture on the other side of the Atlantic, and those for whom her immediate security interests in the home region had incontestable priority. At moments of crisis, some gave their first thoughts to Wash-ington and others, in the national spirit of self-reliance, to the threats or challenges that they saw on Israel's borders. This disparity of offi-cial outlooks was a source of tension on the decision-making level, and the attitude of particular officials was likely to depend on the particular desks at which they sat. Symbolically and often in fact, the two attitudes were represented by two branches that had different worries because they looked in opposite directions; the Foreign Minis-try and, under the Ministry of Defense, the General Staff.

On the American side as well, the Sinai crisis was a turning point; it clarified and deepened the Israeli relationship. The Americans discov-ered there were limits to the pressure a great power could effectively exert on a small power that was determined to defend its interests and prepared for great sacrifice. In some circumstances the United States could impose its will and in 1957 it had done so, but only by the overwhelming threat of sanctions and then only up to a point, just as the Israelis had yielded only to a degree and not without saving concessions at the end. Indeed, in that contest of wills, Israel had wrested a new commitment from the country that had proved, at the last, to be still her greatest friend. The Americans learned they could not dictate to a nation that was ready ultimately to stand alone and if necessary to fight alone for its survival, and might one day be called upon to do so. The United States could counsel the Israelis; it could try to guide or restrain them; it could bring pressure on them; but there were some issues on which it could only try to persuade them. It could not tell them what to do.

Israel remained a country that still had to establish herself in the region in which she lived. She was a recognized fact for the United Nations and the United States and for a widening circle of friends, but she was not a fact for the people with whom in the end she would have to live. She remained a foreign enclave closed in by a wall of denial, and as a nation under siege and quarantine she was hypersensitive to any threat of curtailment. Any compromise with enemies who denied her would carry a threat to her survival; any challenge by such enemies was a challenge to her right to exist. In the psychology of survival that shaped the ethos of the nation, she could suffer no abridgment of her sovereignty and no contraction of her national life. To the terrorist raids that in later years came with increasing intensity across the borders from Syria and Jordan, the Israelis responded with a fierce will, sometimes overreacting in the facile conviction that "the only thing the Arabs understand is force." The strategic intent of their retaliation was warning and prevention, but behind the large-scale reprisals for the deaths of three, four or five Israeli soldiers lay a motive psychology that was peculiar to Israel. The Israeli kibbutzim in the plain of the upper Jordan valley, shelled by Syrian artillery mounted above them on the Golan Heights; the farmer shot in the field; the lone border policeman killed at night; the deaths of three soldiers blown up in their half-track by the mine of an Arab infiltrator —these were not matters of national pride but of individual compassion. In the small, fraternal, close-textured Israeli society, they were events of instant and intimate concern that brought their sorrow and imposed their strain on the entire community. When the raids con-

tinued, the pain of harassment became exasperation; when they persisted still, exasperation became ferocity. When the strain grew too
great, Israel reacted powerfully, hoping that a punitive counterraid
would break the cycle.

Behind their seeming intransigence in their dealings with the Arabs
was the simple human fact of their refusal to comply with the eternal
Arab wish that the state of Israel liquidate itself and that its people go
away. No other people has had to face this kind of political and moral
dilemma. It was precisely defined by the Israeli scholar who had explored more patiently and more sensitively than any other the attitudes of both Israelis and Arabs in their confrontation: Yeosaphat
Harkabi, a former director of Israeli military intelligence. "Israel, by
the nature of her position," Harkabi wrote, "will prefer existing dangerously to offering a concession incurring the danger of non-existence. Any concession which may weaken Israel is too big for her; for
the Arabs, it is too small if it leaves the existence of Israel intact."

No place on the map of Israel was more clearly the focus and symbol of her self-affirmation than the place named Eilath; no right
touched more closely the nerve of national sovereignty than the hardly
won right for Israeli ships to pass without hindrance through the
Straits of Tiran. Eilath in 1957 had one pier and one jetty. It was a
pioneer outpost at the edge of a desert amphitheater, between the
fretted mountains of Sinai to the west, the Red Sea waters of the Gulf
of Aqaba and, eastward, the spiked hills and red and yellow crags of
Arab Jordan. After the opening of the Straits in the month of March,
the outpost by the sea was engulfed by a new construction camp, busy
with engineers and surveyors, cement-mixers, bulldozers and directo-
rial jeeps. By day the Israeli prospectors traveled in convoy, under
armed escort, as they explored the desert; by night Israeli soldiers
patrolled the open border against Arab marauders. The six and a half
miles of desert shoreline that Israel held at the top of the Gulf were
the outlet to the East that made her a two-sea nation; and the development of Eilath—wharf, warehouses, oil storage tanks and pipeline
—was her answer to Egypt's closure of the Suez Canal to Israel-
bound ships. The port was important in several ways. It exported pot-
ash and phosphates from the Negev interior, and it received more
than ninety percent of the country's imported oil, brought from Iran
in Liberian tankers and sent through the pipe the length of the country
to the refineries at Haifa. With the Gulf unblockaded, freighters from

East Africa brought cargoes of meat and oil seed and hide, and sailed away with Israeli fertilizer and cement. Eilath was the future; the hope of exploiting the mineral wealth of the Negev, the empty half of Israel; the promise of commercial expansion; the vision of dynamic advance in a country which, if it lost its dynamism, lost its will and its reason for being. Yet all of this was not enough to explain the meaning of Eilath in the mind of the Israelis. Economically, Israel could survive without Eilath just as she could survive without Haifa, and the United States could survive without New Orleans. It was not the exports; not the commercial artery, the new sea route, the short cut to Asia east of Suez; not even the oil cargoes or the pioneer cry of the new frontier: it was the fact of recognition. Israel lived by her faith in herself and her access to the future; and the future demanded recognition of her undivided sovereignty and of her flagships. The denial of her flagships was an attack on her existence. Invariably in the statements that Israeli diplomats prepared on the issue of free passage through the Suez Canal, the key sentences were those that insisted that Israel receive the same treatment as all other nations; and so, on the same issue as it affected the Straits of Tiran, the name of Eilath expressed the overwhelming psychological need for acceptance. Without Eilath, Israel would be worse than a truncated nation, she would be a nation in moral decline; any relinquishment of sovereignty, any compromise on the issue of free navigation presented a mortal challenge to the state and incurred, in Harkabi's phrase, the "danger of non-existence." Repeatedly, the government made known that a renewal of the blockade would be a *casus belli*.

As Ben-Gurion had told two Western Presidents, the Israeli General Staff wanted arms and not soldiers. Its choice of arms was determined by its military doctrine, and its doctrine was a response to two ineluctable facts of geography and world politics. Israel was nine miles wide at the waist, with her greatest population and communications center lying close to this north-south corridor; and there was no place in the country that was farther than twenty-five miles from the nearest hostile frontier. She had no defense in depth, no hinterland, no room for strategic or tactical retreat. Confined in space, she was equally circumscribed in time, since the powers would intervene in order to bring any Arab-Israeli war to a quick end. The physical impossibility of retreat and the political certainty of international intervention dictated the first precept of Israeli strategy: the war must be carried as deep as possible into enemy territory in the allotted time. This meant that Israel must have the capacity to conquer the Sinai Peninsula, a region which through the years had the dual function of being a buffer of empty space in peacetime and a battleground of convenience in war.

The doctrine of offensive defense imposed a number of decisions regarding the structure of the Israeli defense forces and a system of priorities with respect to arms. Mobile forces and offensive arms had the highest priority—tanks, mechanized infantry, masses of paratroops and a tactical air force. Other components of a modern national force such as naval power and strategic bombers were beyond Israel's means and she sacrificed them. Her midget navy was wholly inadequate to protect her merchant fleet or to shield her open coast against marine invasion. In all the measurable categories of military strength, she was inferior to the Arabs, outmanned and outgunned; but the immeasurable factor, the qualitative superiority of the individual soldier, was no doubt the most vital one in the light of her strategic doctrine.

Since she must be prepared to fight on at least three fronts, the Egyptian, the Jordanian and the Syrian, and could not take the offensive on all three at once, she had to devise a system of interim or provisional defense while the army and air force pivoted from one to another. This system was based on the chain of paramilitary settlements she had established along her borders. With her ability to mobilize an entire people, she could reinforce the settlements in time of war with underage "reservists," boys and girls who could replace the military-age workers in the fields, and overage reservists from the cities, veterans who had completed their term of military service and, no longer liable to call-up, still wanted to fight. The role of the settlements was to hold the enemy for a few days—three, four or five—while the army completed its main task elsewhere.

But Israel's most vulnerable frontier, infinitely more vulnerable than her six hundred miles of land border, was in the air; and her first line of defense was her air force. All her cities, Tel-Aviv, Haifa, Jerusalem, were less than fifteen minutes' jet-flying time from airfields in Egypt. Conceivably, Israel could lose her air force and still win a war, but at a fearful and unacceptable cost in human lives. The immediate task of the Mystères and Mirages was to save the people of Israel by destroying the enemy's offensive air power in the first hours of conflict.

These and other aspects of Israeli military strategy were discussed in official publications, analyzed in newspaper articles and expounded in books. The Israelis could never attain arms parity with the Arabs but they could realistically aim to achieve what they called an "arms balance," and to this end the General Staff ceaselessly refined the implementation of its doctrine in the light of the information that its military intelligence gathered on the structure of the Arab armies and the Soviet-inculcated doctrine of the Egyptian and Syrian commanders. Yigal Allon, though he had retired from the army, always kept abreast of these developments, and in 1959 he published his book *Curtain of Sand,* a vigorous summing-up of the Israeli official doctrine to which, characteristically, he added some bold flourishes and original concepts of his own. Like so many of his pronouncements on other occasions, his *obiter dicta* provoked a rustle of protest and were soon the subject of high-level and behind-doors controversy. Allon argued that in view of her extreme vulnerability and of the tight limitations of time and space, Israel must regard any massive concentration of offensive forces on her borders as an aggressive threat to which she was entitled to respond with force before the enemy took the initiative against her. A concentration of Egyptian forces on the Sinai frontier was the obvious example of such a threat, and Allon gave the name of "anticipatory counter-attack" to the pre-emptive response that he recommended. He rejected the conventional "reactive counter-attack," in which the enemy is allowed the advantage of the first strike, and the "parallel counter-attack," in which the two sides strike simultaneously, as inappropriate for Israel, since both involved prohibitive risks.

He wrote: "Since the enemy may set himself as a first objective the liquidation on the ground of the Israeli Air Force, Israel must maintain the moral and political right as well as her operational capacity to take the initiative before the enemy's planes take off; if not, Israel's fate will be sealed at the outset." It was part of his thesis that by maintaining this political right, Israel would greatly enhance the credibility of her deterrent strength. He acknowledged there was an apparent contradiction in terms: how could an operation be called a counterattack if no attack had yet taken place? He evidently believed that a country in Israel's position could not afford to base her military doctrine on the niceties of nomenclature. In any future war with the Arabs, he said, "the historical mistake of the War of Independence and the Sinai campaign must not be repeated. The war must not be interrupted before full victory is achieved, which means territorial integrity and a peace treaty that will ensure normal relations between Israel and her neighbours."

Allon's book was translated into Arabic and diligently read in Cairo, where, however, the published reviews seemed to indicate the Egyptians had not fully grasped the message. In the course of his long exposition, Allon had said that the Arabs were superior to Israel by all the standard measurements of military resource and power, in the categories of manpower, geographical position, economic potential and so on—except one. The exception was Israel's "social structure." He explained: "An army is generally a reflection of the social and political regime under which it functions. Its properties and weaknesses are a function of the society that creates it." With Israel enjoying this lone advantage, the Egyptian reviewers read his analysis as an admission of her inferiority.

Allon's doctrine of the anticipatory counterattack drew the reproachful criticism of the political left, of which he was a member, and the firm disapproval of Ben-Gurion, who saw it as a subterfuge and linguistic gimmick for preventive war that was certain to be recognized as such and would bring down on Israel the right-minded and vehement censure of her friends and the eager indignation of her enemies. On other issues of strategy, the two men were in agreement, including the matter of nuclear deterrents. A minority school of opinion in Israel held that possession of a nuclear deterrent by both sides in the Middle East would create a local balance comparable to the global one and would impose a peace of mutual terror on the area. Allon and Ben-Gurion rejected this line of thought as reckless intellectual humbug that took no heed of the political instabilities of the region. As insurance against the nuclear risks of the time, Israel maintained her own atomic establishment, including an advanced reactor at a desert site in the Negev; but Ben-Gurion, Allon and the majority school of military thought chose to bear the risks of the conventional deterrents that they had rather than fly to others that they knew not of. If Israel produced the nuclear bomb secretly, Allon argued, it would be ineffectual as a deterrent; if she announced acquisition of the bomb or carried out tests, the great powers would step in and take it away from her; or if, rashly, they decided to arm the other side, the bomb would then be in the possession of both responsible and non-responsible powers, "a situation," Allon remarked, "of immense and unequal hazards."

The stir of dissent that his doctrine provoked could be ascribed, perhaps, to a fault in presentation. As a politician seeking to justify a presumed right of first strike, he had tried to give moral color to a precept of military strategy; as a military analyst, he had merely defined the inescapable necessity that certain circumstances might lay upon Israel. After Dayan's departure from the government in 1964, Allon was the only military authority of first rank among the ministers; and as a member of the Cabinet Committee on Defense under Prime Minister Eshkol, he was the most important link between the government and the General Staff. He was Israel's elder soldier not only by virtue of his record and knowledge, but because he had trained so many of her finest commanders and had been their mentor. As a young officer at a Haganah training camp, he had held and guided the hand of a new recruit, four years younger than himself, as he threw his first grenade. The recruit was Yitshak Rabin, who ended his military career nearly thirty years later after serving as Chief of Staff during the third Israeli war with the Arabs. As Commander of the Palmach, Allon had chosen Rabin to be his Chief of Operations, and among those who had served under him as battalion commanders were a young immigrant from Yugoslavia, Haim Bar-Lev, who in time was to succeed Rabin as Chief of Staff; Yeshaya Gavish, who commanded the Sinai front in the war of 1967; and David Elazar, who, in that war, led the troops that captured the Golan Heights and pressed on into Syria. Among the first pilots in those early days, flying the Palmach's Piper Cubs on reconnaissance, was Mordechai Hod, who as Commander of the Israeli Air Force in 1967 was responsible for the three-hour operation that destroyed the air force of Egypt. The men of 1948 remained a close-knit company, and Allon's controversial doctrine, disavowed by Ben-Gurion and unacknowledged by any one else, was nevertheless a stimulus that influenced staff thinking, not directly by formal adoption, but indirectly and by inference, in discussions back and forth between him and his friends. He enjoyed the arguments: he had never had any taste for yes-men.

Nor did he ever amend his views. In a lecture early in 1967, he propounded them once again and added some sharpening touches.

There was no need, he observed, "to say in advance how much time is required for an Israeli attack anticipating an Arab offensive. It would be best to allow the enemy to gather most of his forces in Sinai and to strike before his preparations are complete." The anticipatory counterattack was vital as a "major or sole means of securing Israel's existence." Its aim must be to gain immediate air superiority and to seize "vital security objectives deep in enemy territory" so as to assure to Israel a "bargaining position in negotiations for the future of peace and the demarcation of boundaries."

In this lecture Allon enumerated Israel's *casi belli*. What he called a threatening "offensive concentration of forces" headed his list; the remaining causes of war, however, were the traditional ones so often enunciated by Israeli spokesmen. Among them were an air attack on Israel's nuclear reactors and science institutes, and the association of Jordan in a military alliance that would permit the forces of another Arab state to mass in Jordan or to cross to the West Bank of the Jordan River. Last on the list was a renewal of the Egyptian blockade of the Straits of Tiran. In any of these circumstances, Israel would be entitled to respond with a war of defense which "she would wage in a way, in an arena and at a time of her choosing."

Allon delivered this lecture on February 22, 1967. Exactly three months later, the Straits of Tiran were blockaded by Egypt. Allon, however, had not been prescient. He had not foreseen or suspected that any of the *casi belli* he mentioned would confront Israel in the month of May. His lecture had been not a prognosis but a recapitulation.

Considered again at a somewhat higher angle both in time and in space, Israel's military position was paradoxical and the political gains she could expect from victory were uncertain and problematic. The Israelis by their own calculation could destroy the military machine of Egypt and overwhelm the Jordanians and Syrians as well. Their weaponry, their fighting units, their staff planning were all keyed to the objectives of their military doctrine. Yet they could not defeat their enemies and subdue them as Germany defeated France in 1870 or as the Allied Powers defeated Germany in 1918 and again in 1945. They were too few against too many. They could invade the territories of their enemies but they could not finally disarm them; they could defeat them but not vanquish them; they could conquer and occupy, but they could not exact capitulation. Even if they pressed on to

Cairo, a city of four and a half million, they could not remain there; it would be a show and an incursion only. Even if at tremendous cost they overran and held the entire land of Jordan, there would still be Syria and Iraq, unreconciled and beyond them. In the wide spaces of the Arab world, the most spectacular Israeli victory could bring only a tactical advantage. In the end, in the term of years, there was no hope for peace through belligerence.

The Arabs could refuse peace because they could get along without it more easily than the Israelis. They could continue to place their hope in belligerence. They were the many against the few. They could suffer the crushing defeat of their armies in the field, retreat into their space and rely on time and their numbers to redress the balance. They could look forward to the day when their re-established and reunited armies might achieve in war the political settlement they hoped for, the liquidation of the state of Israel. Every defeat was an incitement to fight again. Every battle lost remobilized their passion and rearmed their intransigence. For the Arabs, every war was only a single battle; and after it they could withdraw, wait and prepare for the battle to come.

For Israel, the position was the reverse. Every war that she fought had to be devastating, conclusive and short. Any war that she lost would be her last.

• 4 •

A Damascus Affair

AT DAWN on February 23, 1966, the sound of scattered but persistent machine-gun fire in and around Damascus and the sudden deployment of tanks and armored cars along the main thoroughfares announced to the people of the capital that they were experiencing the eighth military coup d'état in the twenty-one years since the foundation of the Syrian Arab Republic. The action followed a tactical pattern that was standard and familiar. Tanks took up their assigned positions at public buildings and commanding intersections; troops occupied the international airport, seized the broadcasting station and telephone central, and broke into the homes of government leaders and ministers. The insurgents struck fast and hard. An untold number of loyal army officers were shot down in brief but brutal encounters, but of the incumbent political leaders only one, Lieutenant General Amin Hafiz, the President of Syria, was able to offer a brave but futile resistance. Surrounded at his home near the American Embassy, the General and the hundred and twenty men of his Bedouin guard held out for four hours under the shelling and machine-gunning of their besiegers until, their ammunition spent, they were overcome in the fired and ruined house and Hafiz was taken prisoner. By nightfall several hundred persons associated with him and his government were in jail. As always in such upheavals, the whole of Syria was placed under curfew and sealed off until further notice, her telephone communications cut and her frontiers sullenly closed to the outside world. Businessmen in the modern quarter of Damascus locked their show rooms, and in the covered bazaar inside the old walled city the shops and booths of merchants and artisans were shut and bolted along the "Street Called Straight." Damascus was implausibly calm; the victory of the conspirators was stunningly complete.

In her twenty-one years of independence, Syria had sampled the benefits of six different constitutions, while her army officers and politicians had made and unmade twenty-three governments. No other Arab country could rival this record of political impermanence. The kaleidoscope of Syrian politics and Syrian plotting was in perpetual motion, unseizable and unpredictable, to the despair of foreign diplomats, the bewilderment of correspondents and the exasperated discomfiture of all the country's neighbors. But more disturbing than this internal confusion was the flagrant incongruity between word and deed that had made the Syrians the notoriously untrustworthy *enfants terribles* of the Middle East. Damascus and not Cairo was the birthplace of the pan-Arab idea and the firebed of the Arab nationalist movement; nowhere in the Arab world did the flame of pan-Arabism burn more fiercely and nowhere was the disparity between the dream of an Arab nation and the reality of modern statehood more frustrating and rankling.

Through all their history the Syrians had never been a nation. Egypt had enjoyed a sense of conscious nationhood for some four thousand years, but Syria had been only a name for a vaguely delimited region that had belonged to a succession of foreign empires. Modern Syria, the invention of European map-makers, was a remnant of that region. In times past, as a geographical term, Syria included Jordan, which the British had bequeathed to one of their Hashimite protégés; Palestine, which they had kept for themselves as a mandate and then left to the Israelis; Lebanon, which the French had carved away; and the northern port and district of Alexandretta, which France, as the mandatory power, had generously ceded to the Turks. Toward all these lands, the Syrians looked with resentful and unrequited longing. What they had left for themselves was difficult to distinguish as a nation. It was, rather, a miscellany of races and religions, a country of sects and schisms in which the dominant orthodox community of Sunni Moslems was beset by an assemblage of rival minorities—Alawis, Druses, Ismailis, Christians, Armenians and Kurds. Nevertheless, the Syrians as a people esteemed themselves as more especially and intensely Arab than any other, and were animated by a belief in their historic mission as the agents and carriers of Arabism.

Damascus, the oasis city at the edge of the great Syrian desert, had indeed kept much more of its Arab character than had the cosmopolitan capital of Egypt, corrupted by its long exposure to so many alien ruling castes, Mameluke and Circassian, Turkish, Albanian and British; and it was they, the Syrians, who had discovered political Arabism and first raised its banner against the oppression of the Ottoman Turks. The banner waved still. On the political level, the extremist passion of the Syrian pan-Arabists reflected a frantically unstable nation's quest for stability; on the emotional level, in the pathology of the Arab search for identity, it expressed a turbulent escapism; and in the particular neurosis of the Syrian nation, struggling with the painful discrepancy between dream and fact, it seems to have owed at least some of its extravagance to the goad of self-hate.

The Syrian pan-Arabists never recovered from the intense frustration that followed the collapse of the United Arab Republic. Except for a minority of Nasserist zealots, they were agreed that Syria had done well to bring that experiment to an end. Nasser had done his worst in the name of unity, and for three and a half years his one-party system and his security police had held the Syrians in colonial subjection. He had brought a measure of order to the country at a humiliating price to Syrian liberty and Syrian self-regard. In his political union the Syrian leaders, bedecked with titles, were seldom seen and never heard, and in his economic union Syria was cast in the role of an agricultural supplier and used as a market for the products of Egyptian factories. The arrogant ubiquity of Egyptian bureaucrats in the Syrian province, with an Egyptian high commissioner in the person of Field Marshal Amer; the invasion of Syrian universities by Egyptian professors, of Syrian courts by Egyptian magistrates and of the Syrian Army by Egyptian officers in command positions down to the brigade and battalion levels, stoked the anger of a prideful people. The mechanics of power in Syria were primitive, and a one-day military coup was sufficient to demolish the entire structure of Nasser's monolithic rule. The great majority of Syrians felt the action had been forced upon them by the insolence of Egyptian imperialism.

Yet even so, the dissolution of the United Arab Republic was the shattering of a passionate dream, and even as they broke with Egypt, the men in Damascus felt impelled to hail the "sacred union" they had just destroyed. When Nasser capitulated to the revolt and publicly accepted the restoration of an independent Syria, even Syrians who mistrusted him listened in tears to his broadcast speech of renunciation, so masterfully conceived and movingly delivered. For Arab unity's sake he renounced the struggle and pledged there would be no civil war in Syria to force the issue. He accepted his impotence with statesmanlike grace and invested it with heroism by his eloquence. "It does not matter to me whether I remain the President of Syria. What matters to me is that Syria, herself, remain." But the shock of parting was felt as keenly in Damascus as in Cairo. If the end of the United Arab Republic was traumatic for Nasser, it was no less so for the nationalist leaders of the Syrian Baath, the messianic party of the pan-Arab revolution, who had sacrificed their country's independence in a desperate search for political stability. Syria was the one country that had been able to achieve political union with Egypt, and she had been obliged to repudiate it. To the other compulsive emotions of Syrian nationalism, there was added the emotion of guilt.

Between Nasser and the Syrian Baath, the Arab Socialist Renaissance Party, the feelings of contemptuous mistrust were mutual. Nasser counted it a great treachery in the Syrians that they had wearied of his rule. He scorned them for their faithlessness and exhausted his vocabulary of political abuse when he spoke of the leaders of the Baath; they were traitors, fascists and windbags who bandied slogans "without philosophy or sense." He was infuriated by their big words and their troublemaking. His vehement dislike was fully reciprocated. The Syrians in general contemned the vulgarly bossy Egyptians; the leftist intellectuals of the Baath viewed with disdain the "bourgeois" leader of Egypt and despised his pretensions as a pan-Arab socialist; and whoever was in power in Damascus feared him. Whether Nasser liked it or not, the Baath, despite its political ineptness, had caught the floating explosive mood of the Arab world. With its nebulous but militant socialist ideology and its pan-Arab fervor, it expressed the radicalism of Arab youth more fully than any other group or party, with the notable exception of certain revolutionary movements that were more or less permanently underground.

Prompted by history, the Syrian nationalists were forever seeking a dominant role in Arab politics and a position of influence that was beyond their capacities. Their permanent mood was one of hot-tempered self-assertion. Their permanent dilemma was reflected in the ambivalence of their feelings toward Nasser. Syria, distracted and un-sure of herself, was an obsessively messianic country without a mes-siah and had to look beyond her borders for a champion who could bless and sanctify her "progressive" and "revolutionary" Arabism. Only Nasser had such luster and authority. The aim of successive Syrian regimes was to stay within his orbit but well outside his power. The Syrian leaders knew from experience it was impossible to have him as a partner, but they still sought the protection of his name. At the same time, they were in the most jealous competition with him. With their guilty memory of the Syrian breakaway, they felt com-pelled to justify their action and their ideology and so were driven to be more absurdly nationalist, more preposterously pan-Arab and more fanatically anti-Israeli than anyone else, in order to carry high the standard of pan-Arab revolution and still maintain their independ-ence of Nasser. In this auction, Israel was placed on the pan-Arab block. The Syrians were determined to outbid all others, and chiefly Nasser, for political leadership in the war to liberate the despoiled Arab land of Palestine. They indulged their fanaticism freely and to their risk, and assumed responsibility for the most highly organized Palestinian terrorist group that had appeared since the days of Nas-ser's *fedayeen*. Hatred of Israel was their most febrile passion, and militance in the anti-Israeli war was made both the test of dedication to the Arab cause and the instrument of blackmail between Arab and Arab.

The coup that ended Nasser's dominion in Syria in September, 1961, was directed by half a dozen army officers and supported by the conservative classes, merchants, industrialists and landowners, who had been hurt or threatened by the taxes, trade controls and nationali-zations of Egyptian socialism. The new Syrian regime proposed to turn the clock back to pre-Egyptian days and still was engaged in this process when a countercoup, on March 8, 1963, again elevated the Baath to power on the shoulders of the army. The party of socialism and pan-Arab revolution imposed itself on the country from above, with the argument of tanks and helmets; ultimate power resided in a pro-Baath military junta, which, with its civilian friends, established a National Council of the Revolutionary Command. Lieutenant Gen-eral Hafiz returned from exile in Argentina to join this high-sounding body. For a few weeks the Baathists ruled in coalition with a Nasserist group that had participated in their coup, but Hafiz, suspecting that this power clique was up to no good, soon expelled it from his government and proceeded to a purge of Nasserist officers in the army. These actions provoked a violent but abortive Nasserist rebellion in Damascus on July 18. The General used tanks and jet fighters to crush the uprising, and executed twenty-seven of its leaders, civilian as well as military, in the three days that followed it. The manner of the repression startled the Arab world. Such political savagery was common enough in Baghdad but was generally foreign to the more civilized mores of Damascus. From that moment, the Baath ruled alone and General Hafiz was master.

Within the Baath, however, there were abundant grounds for discord and faction, with rival political and ethnic groups maneuvering for power. There was a widening rift between the party's right and left wings. Hafiz together with Salah Bitar, the elder statesman of the Baath, represented the right; the Chief of Staff, Major General Salah Jedid, a member of the country's largest minority, the Alawi tribe of schismatic Moslems, was the leading military figure on the left. In 1965, Hafiz cashiered Jedid as Chief of Staff and thereafter set in motion further plans for a rejuggling of the Baath which, had they been fulfilled, would have sealed his triumph with the final elimination of his rivals. In the coup of February 23, 1966, his moves were anticipated and the game was reversed. Hafiz was imprisoned and Bitar was exiled. Of the old political class that at one time or another had ruled Syria since independence, not a single representative remained; the men who now took power were completely new.

They were young, they were impatient and they were doctrinaire. Their position as ministers in the new government rested on Jedid's control of various key army commands, many of them occupied by members of his own Alawi sect and some allotted to officers of the smaller Druse minority. Jedid himself became Secretary-General of the new rump edition of the Baath which he now presented to the country, and took control of the party's extensive organizational network. As an Alawi, he preferred the obscurity of back-room control and raised two youthful members of the country's orthodox Sunni majority to the highest offices of government: Nureddin Atassi, thirty-six, became President and Youssef Zayen, thirty-five, was named Prime Minister. An extreme left-wing faction of the army thus allied itself with an equally extreme and schismatic faction of Baath civilians. The young men around Jedid, who was himself in his early forties, were the most militant and intemperate politicians whom Syria had ever beheld in government; and the new regime, in which an ethnic and religious minority in the army ruled through a political minority of the party, was the most unrepresentative body of men that had yet fastened itself on the nation.

For one week after Jedid's coup, Syria remained muffled in conspiracy. On March 1 the new leaders announced the formation of a nineteen-member government and the next day they reopened the country's frontiers. While the names of the government ministers were largely unfamiliar, the list nevertheless contained a helpful and broadly demonstrative hint: the Ministers of Economy and Commerce were Communists. Understandably, the overriding concern of a government so narrowly based was purely pragmatic. Its first aim was to save itself, and like many Syrian governments in the past, it was driven by a fearful sense of insecurity to look outside Syria for support and protection. There was ample room for conjecture as to what the Soviet response would be. True, Syria had always been of peculiar concern to the Soviet Union, as Moscow's quick reactions at various times had shown. True, Jedid might offer the first political opportunity the Russians had had to make headway in Damascus since Nasser had pulled the carpet out from under them with the creation of the United Arab Republic. But intimacy with this particular regime could only mean trouble. The Russians were as familiar as anyone with the pathological unreliability of Syrian governments. Both in the Middle East and in Africa and as far away as Cuba, they had known the costs and the hazards of committing themselves to irresponsible or ungovernable clients. They knew the mercurial shifts and violent broils of Syrian politics. All in all, in the judgment of most Western diplomats, they seemed unlikely to place any large bets on the Jedid regime.

The Americans and the Israelis were equally unprepared for a new Soviet initiative in Damascus. The Israelis had always fixed their eye on Nasser as their one genuine adversary and had inclined to look on the Syrians as merely a stormy nuisance in terms of their over-all security. The Americans in their Middle Eastern policy had concentrated through the years on Egypt as the one country of predominant weight in the area. Syria as a country of subordinate rank occupied a marginal place in American worries; and the higher policy-making echelons at the State Department gave scant attention to events in Damascus. In the regional contest between the Americans and Russians, Cairo was the central and engrossing arena. All of this was natural enough. Yet in years past the Russians had given warning of a hypersensitive regard for Syria and had demonstrated that the vicissitudes of Syrian politics, of secondary interest in Washington, were of lively concern to Moscow. They had grasped the opportunity to reequip the Syrian Army and Air Force during the period of political flirtation that had preceded the merger with Egypt. Their political association was cut short but their military collaboration was maintained. In the fall of 1957, at the height of a sharp but ephemeral crisis over the massing of Turkish troops on Syria's northern frontier, the Soviet response had been immediate and emphatic. Foreign Minister Andrei Gromyko had led the parade of orators in support of a United Nations resolution denouncing Turkey's presumed aggressive designs, Soviet troops had mobilized near the eastern Turkish border, and even Israel had been warned to keep hands off Syria.

Looking out from Moscow toward the borders of the intercontinental mass that they controlled, the Kremlin leaders in the mid-1960's saw a striking variety of pattern in their strategic situation. Between their western borders and Atlantic Europe they had an ample *cordon sanitaire,* a belt of buffer states that included not only the countries of the Communist bloc, whose status of political subjection they were prepared to maintain by force of arms, but neutral or effectively neutralized states like Austria and Finland. Their longest and most exposed frontier was in the East, where they confronted China with no buffer whatever. To their south they had had considerable success in gaining the political neutralization of India and Pakistan, and had intervened with authority to quiet the Indo-Pakistani conflict when this had threatened to embroil other major powers in the region. Prime Minister Alexei Kosygin on that occasion had reminded the world of the Soviet Union's national interest in an area that was "in the vicinity of Soviet borders." Closer to home, the Russians had achieved the total neutralization of Afghanistan.

But in the Middle East the situation was ambiguous. Turkey, an ancient enemy now allied to Western Europe and the United States, stood athwart the Russian way to the south like a gigantic bolt. The Russians, of course, could leapfrog over Turkey to new positions in the Arab Middle East, and they could seek a rapprochement with the

Turks by diplomatic wangle and blandishment. They did both, but neither resolved their problem. Their most obvious and reliable means of neutralizing the Atlantic base on their border and of circumventing a Turkish threat to their security was to outflank Turkey by establishing a Soviet political and military base to her south. Syria was the pivotal country in the creation of such an outlying buffer zone. She offered advantages in several directions. She held a focal position in inter-Arab politics and was strategically placed to influence the course of events in Iraq and Jordan. Upstream in water, she controlled the Euphrates River; downstream in oil, she was astride the pipelines from the Iraqi fields at Kirkuk and controlled the transit fees to the Lebanese port of Tripoli. Politically she was in a comparable trouble-making and blackmailing position, in view of the tight balance of the Iraq regime and the pressure of the Iraqi Baath Party; while in Jordan she could wage a remorseless cold war against King Hussein by arousing his Palestinian subjects and inciting the Palestinian liberation groups in their marauding raids against Israel.

The French concept of the *cordon* still had meaning and validity even in an age of intercontinental ballistic missiles. Short of a nuclear confrontation of the great powers, in which the deepest buffers could be overflown, there was still a wide, imprecise, variable range of possibility for local military pressure or local armed intervention or the waging of local wars with conventional or semiconventional weapons. In this realm, unaffected by the nuclear standoff, buffers played their role by insulating the Soviet Union against its dangers and advancing the frontiers of the Soviet sphere of interest.

There was an essential difference between the Russians' interest in Egypt and their concern with Syria. Their investment in Egypt was much larger, with their financial and technical help in the building of the Aswan Dam and their creation of a solidly Soviet military establishment. Egypt for the Russians meant association with the one Arab leader of international stature and the possibility of asserting their authority and influence throughout the Arab world. It meant political access to Africa and the opportunity to push south toward the Indian Ocean, not by direct domination of the Arab land mass but by the extension of Soviet footholds along and around its shores. There were several premonitory signs of a new strategic design in the area, although at the outset they were largely political demonstrations—the establishment of a Soviet naval presence along the waterways of the region, at Hodeida in Yemen and at Mogadiscio in Somalia; the intensified interest in the litoral states of the Persian Gulf, and the naval challenge to the Sixth Fleet, undertaken, as Soviet leaders proudly said, in order to demonstrate to the people of three continents that the Mediterranean was "no longer an American lake." The Russians' interest in Egypt was global; their special stake in Syria was national and, in this sense, more peculiarly immediate and pressing. Whenever their diplomats saw or professed to see imminent threats to Syria's security, they spoke in accents of solicitous alarm. With their paramount and fearful concern for the security of their borders, the Russians chose to regard the southern flank of Turkey as within their area of vital interest; and in the doctrine of Soviet political and military strategists, the southern security frontiers of the Soviet Union ran through the Republic of Syria.

In the winter of 1965–1966, the Middle East began to attract a new and keener interest in Moscow. A number of costly setbacks in other parts of the noncommitted world had caught the attention of the strategists. Three eminent leaders had been toppled from their anti-imperialist bastions: Ben Bella had disappeared without a trace in Algeria, Nkrumah had been banished from Ghana and, the last and most serious cut of all, Sukarno had been routed from office in Indonesia in an anti-Communist counterrevolution that had erased whatever political gains the Russians may have made from a $2 billion program of aid. Soviet diplomacy at this stage was busy cultivating friendlier ties with the non-Arab states of the Middle East, Turkey herself, Iran and, ironically, perhaps, in view of the radical turn that was about to take place, Israel. The Israeli Government proposed to make every effort to improve its relations with Moscow after a long period of drought and doldrums.

Several recent developments had encouraged the Israelis to believe that a rapprochement was in the making. A cultural agreement had brought Soviet artists to Israel and taken Israeli artists, lecturers and scientists to the Soviet Union. The Soviet Ambassador in Tel-Aviv had received a delegation of the World Jewish Congress and later, appearing before the Israeli chapter of the Congress, had spoken of the common cause that history had given the Jews and Russians in their fight for survival against Nazi barbarism. More remarkable still as a portent of policy, in the month of January, 1966, the number of Soviet Jews permitted to emigrate to Israel had exceeded the total for the previous year; it was a matter of several hundred persons only, but still more than Moscow had released in the whole of 1965. These signposts were duly noted by the Israeli Foreign Minister, Mrs. Meir, and by the leaders of the small Israeli Communist Party, which by then had been split into two independent parties by the stress of the Arab-Israeli conflict. This breach in Communist ranks had occurred the previous summer. The pro-Israel Communist Party was entirely Jewish; the pro-Arab dissident group, the "New Communists," was heavily Arab but counted some Israeli Jews in its membership. The two parties vied for votes in the general election of November, 1965. Together they polled 3.4 percent of the national total, with the pro-Israel party electing one deputy to the Knesset and the pro-Arabs, three. But if the Communists were a political fraction with only a small forum in the nation, the ideological issue that their polemic had raised was critical. Was the Arab-Israeli dispute essentially a conflict between neighbor nations, as the pro-Israel party asserted, or was it, as the pro-Arabs said, an ideological struggle between the imperialist-colonialist state of Israel and its oppressed colonial victims? What was involved in the ideological garb of these opposing theories was, in fact, the survival of Israel. The first article of faith of the pro-Israel party was stated by Moshe Sneh, one of its two principal leaders and its most vigorous spokesman. "Communism," Sneh said, "is inseparable from national independence, and a threat against Israel's independence is a threat against the Israeli Communist Party." Since this was the issue and since it had irreparably ruptured the party organization, it was natural to assume that sooner or later the question posed by the Israeli Communists would have to be answered, authoritatively, in Moscow.

Sneh was a prominent figure on the historical landscape of Israel. All the veteran officers of Haganah knew him. For six years he had been Chief of the Haganah High Command and for two years a member of the Jewish Agency Executive, the shadow government of the still unproclaimed Jewish state. His long career, first in Zionism and then in Communism, had had no parallel in Israeli politics and very few parallels elsewhere. It was remarkable for the direction it had taken, since Sneh had made the complete journey from right to left. He had been a leader in the Zionist movement since his student-and-journalist days in Warsaw, where he had headed the Jewish Students' Association and later the General Zionist Organization of Poland.

The outbreak of war in 1939 found him in London on a Zionist mission. He took the last plane back to Warsaw to report for service, fought on the eastern front, escaped to neutral Lithuania, waited for his wife and daughter to join him and flew with them to Paris. In March, 1940, they went to Palestine and three months later, at thirty-one, Sneh was appointed to the highest post of Haganah. Late in 1946 he became the Jewish Agency's ambassador-at-large to Europe, as head of its political department in Paris, with the primary assignment of winning international support for the partition of Palestine and the establishment of the Jewish state. In this work he canvassed the whole of diplomatic Europe, meeting Russians, Poles, Czechoslovaks and Rumanians as well as French and Italians, but the diplomat who won his warmest admiration was the papal nuncio to Paris, Archbishop Angelo Roncalli. The Latin Americans were ready to endorse the Jewish cause at the United Nations provided there was no prohibition or objection by the Holy See. Sneh sought an assurance of Vatican neutrality and the future Pope John procured it for him.

Another man he met in Paris, who was staying at the same hotel as he and Ben-Gurion and who gave a new direction and impulse to his thought, was Ho Chi Minh. They had many conversations. Sneh at this time began to see the Jewish contest with the British in Palestine as part of a universal struggle against Western imperialism, and his break with the Jewish Agency came late in 1947. The Agency, acquiescing in a demand by Foreign Secretary Ernest Bevin that had been relayed through Secretary Marshall, canceled its plan to bring two ships with fifteen thousand illegal immigrants from Rumania. Sneh resigned in protest and quit the General Zionist Party. Early the next year he helped to found a new socialist party named Mapam; six years later he led a left-wing faction out of Mapam and into the Israeli Communist Party. No longer a Zionist, he was still an Israeli—a Communist wrestling with the "national problem" and hoping that the internal conflict on the highest levels of Soviet Communism would eventually be resolved in favor of a democratization and greater autonomy for the national Communist parties. Sneh continued through the years of his leftward march to command the personal loyalty of those who had been with him in Haganah, however strongly they might disagree with his opinions. He was a widely read man of great brio and wit, keen in debate and formidable in dialectics. His absence was immediately felt when he lost his parliamentary seat in the election of 1965. The Knesset was a duller place without him. The deputies missed the combative and agile parliamentarian who had so often enlivened their plodding debates and brought to them a grateful element of intellectual surprise and fire.

The Israeli Communist Party, Sneh said in his argument with the pro-Arab faction, "should not turn its negation of Zionism into negation of Israeli statehood, or its defense of Arab rights into support of the Arab states and Arab nationalism." It was a position he was prepared to defend not only against the pro-Arabs but against the leadership of the Soviet Communist Party, if necessary, and in the fall of 1965 he was summoned to Moscow to do so.

In the Soviet capital on November 21, Sneh and Shmuel Mikunis for the pro-Israel Communists, and Meir Wilner and Emile Habibi for the pro-Arabs, appeared before Mikhail Suslov, the ranking ideologue of Soviet Communism, and Boris Ponamarev, who was then in charge of relations with parties in the non-Communist world. The Israeli representatives were invited to present their views. Their Soviet interlocutors were courteous to both sides and gave to both their full attention. In presenting the "pro-Israel" case, Sneh cited Lenin to demonstrate that while nationalist revolutions against imperialism must be supported, they must not be endorsed without discrimination. Their progressive features should be encouraged but their inevitable regressive features, the legacy of feudal and imperialistic rule, must be condemned and combated. On this basis, he argued, the Communist movement must condemn and combat Arab chauvinism. At the end the Soviet judges, tactfully disclaiming any wish or intention to interfere in the affairs of the Israeli party, presented their own views. They substantially upheld the "pro-Israel" position. They offered some criticism of the Sneh-Mikunis party on peripheral matters, but vindicated its reasoning on the main doctrinal issue. They defined the Arab-Israeli conflict not as an ideological struggle but as a "dispute between nations" that should be settled by peaceful means so that both sides could live in "good neighborliness."

Four months later, on March 25, 1966, two delegations from the two camps of Israeli Communism, departing by separate planes, flew once again to Moscow. The occasion of their visit was the Twenty-third Congress of the Soviet Communist Party. Before leaving Israel, Mikunis had a meeting with Foreign Minister Meir, who spoke of the prospect of better relations with the Soviet Union and of Israel's lively desire for such an improvement. At the Congress the most significant event on the ideological front was a sharp downgrading of "peaceful coexistence," which had so recently been recommended to the Israeli Communists. Ever since the Twentieth Congress in 1956, Nikita Khrushchev's "peaceful coexistence" had been proclaimed the "general line of Soviet policy" and had kept its hold on first place in the enumeration of Communist objectives. Now the "anti-imperialist struggle" displaced it at the head of the list while, after a number of other general aims, "peaceful coexistence" appeared in seventh place in the policy line-up, not as an end in itself but as a means of "building Socialism." This eclectic formulation represented a compromise in the internal conflict of the Soviet party; the specter of Mao Tse-tung had finally intimidated the ghost of Khrushchev, whose party colleagues had removed him, partly because they had found him guilty of "losing China without winning the United States." For the Israelis, however, there were more intimate signs of a change that directly affected them. Outwardly everything was as before; the Sneh-Mikunis party still received precedence over its pro-Arab rivals in the official lists and fraternal greetings. But in the corridors of the Congress, the Israeli delegates soon were made aware that a new attitude prevailed; from private contacts they gathered hints and admonitions to this effect, and they left Moscow with the realization that, in the interval since their last visit, there had been an abrupt realignment of Soviet positions in the Middle East.

A startling reversal had indeed occurred. Three developments in the intervening months had prepared the way and precipitated the change. In December, 1965, after a meeting with Shah Reza Pahlavi of Iran, King Feisal of Saudi Arabia had floated the notion of a general conference of the Islamic nations which, though it never took shape, was to haunt the Middle Eastern scene with dreamlike tenacity for months to come. The idea of such a conference, associated with two monarchs unalterably opposed to Nasser and determined to defend their hegemony over the region of the Persian Gulf, excited immediate speculation about the creation of a pan-Islamic front which, on the face of it, might include not only the Islamically inspired Arab states but many key nations outside the Arab sphere, such as Turkey, Pakistan and even distant Indonesia. Nasser conceived the proposal for an "Islamic Conference" to be a plot to form an "Islamic Pact" and responded with instant fury. The pan-Islam idea was vague and

all-embracing; it aroused the hostility of the Arab "revolutionary" re-
publics that it challenged and the profound misgivings of many of the
Islamic monarchs to whom it was addressed; and since it was obviously Feisal's answer to the Russians' equally insubstantial notion of
a common front of the Arab "progressive democracies," it invited the
worst suspicions of the Kremlin. The Russians imagined that this imperialist design had the blessing and covert patronage of the United
States. In fact, the Americans shrank in fright and distaste from a
project that was to cause them infinite nightmare in Cairo; in their
view an Islamic alignment, by provoking a Soviet counteralignment,
would violate the cardinal maxim of nonpolarization and would be a
certain recipe for trouble. It would enhance the fishing prospects of
the Russians and set the stage for Nasserist subversion by enraging
Nasser; and making Nasser mad was thought to be bad policy. These
American fears, in the event, turned out to be woefully well justified.

The first response of the Russians was to renew their call for a
common front of the Arab "revolutionary and progressive" states to
disrupt the threatened union of Islam. Algeria, Egypt, Syria and Iraq
were the four countries prominently mentioned in Moscow as the can-
didates for this venture. But if the Islamic alignment was tenuous and
watery, this "progressive" alignment was not much better. Both were
very thin soup. It was clear to the Kremlin leaders that the quartet of
Arab states was too dispersed geographically to make a credible coun-
terbloc; and politically, their professed socialism was too wavering in
its revolutionary purpose, too ill-defined in its objectives, too weak in
its institutions and too opportunistic in theory and practice to be a
solid base for anything. The Soviet ideologists had always recognized
this fact and had abstained from bestowing the Marxist title of "socialist" on any of the one-party, anticapitalist Arab regimes; indeed
the Marxist vocabulary had been hard put to find a name for them and
had finally settled on the label of "revolutionary democracies." It was
a complimentary sobriquet for countries that were nationalist, anti-
imperialist and in varying degrees susceptible to Soviet influence but
which, at the test, lacked the ideological cement for a binding political
alignment. The Russians realized soon enough that ideology was an
inadequate basis for the unity of Arab nations under their sponsorship, and they would have to find something better.

In the same winter months they were increasingly alarmed by the
inroads that Maoist thought and Maoist arms had been making in the

Arab world. The Chinese Communists were gaining an ideological beachhead in the Arab country that Soviet strategy had firmly placed in the southern defense area of the Soviet Union. The Arabs, looking for a way and needing ideological consolation and guidance in their Palestine struggle, were busy translating the works of Mao and Che Guevara; the *Thoughts* of the Chinese leader were a best-seller in the political bookshops of Damascus. Mao's theory of inevitable conflict all at once in all parts of the globe fascinated the Syrian and Palestinian ideologues; they were fired by his doctrine of popular liberation war and his concept of implacable collisions, which offered a rationale for their own predicament and a justification for their extremist program against Israel. Emotionally, the marriage of Maoism and Arab chauvinism was an ideal union; ideologically, the Maoist principle of continuous revolution everywhere endowed the Arab cause with the ardor and dignity of a universal faith. What the Chinese could actually do for the Arabs, as a power, was extremely limited; they could not of course begin to match the economic or military investment the Russians were in a position to make in the countries of their choice. But precisely because they were far away and had no great-power responsibilities in the region, they could send arms and encouragement anywhere, to any firebrand Palestinian group and any terrorist organization, without setting conditions and without asking questions. Mao had received with honor in Peking a man whom the Russians had refused to welcome in Moscow notwithstanding his eagerness to go there: Achmed Shukheiry, Nasser's nominee as head of the Egyptian-controlled Palestine Liberation Organization. Chinese machine guns, mortars and bazookas were soon reaching Shukheiry's Palestine Liberation Army while other Chinese shipments were being gratefully received by El Fatah, the rival Palestinian commando-and-liberation group sponsored by Syria. Shukheiry was a specialist in the noisome demagogy of hatred and he had brought home an incendiary message from Peking. "You [the Arabs] are one hundred million," Mao was quoted as telling him, "and they [the Jews] are two million, so what are you waiting for? Sacrifices? I also said to the Algerians: What is a million sacrifices? After independence the birth rate will increase." But the volume of Chinese assistance to the Arabs was, for the Russians, irrelevant; the mere fact of Mao's aid and ideological presence in Syria was intolerable. The door to China had to be closed, the specter of Maoist influence exorcised, and a political strategy urgently devised that would exclude the Chinese from the Arab world.

The third precipitating event of that winter occurred on the morning of February 23 in Damascus. Whatever Western diplomats may have thought of Jedid and his band of young men, the Russians saw the advent of the new regime as a windfall. It was evidently a providential chance to restore an intimate relationship with the rulers of Syria after a hiatus of nine years. In March, *Pravda* and *Izvestia* spoke wooingly of the new government; they assured the regime that in its march toward socialism it would have the support of the entire socialist camp and of progressive forces everywhere. Advices from the diplomatic front disclosed that Moscow looked with special favor on the new and abridged edition of the Baath, approached it with attentive care and nurtured it with a kind of motherly solicitude. Overtures were soon completed and on April 18 Prime Minister Zayen and a party of twenty-eight ministers and economic advisers of the regime took off from Damascus for a six-day sojourn in Moscow. At a lunch at the Kremlin the day after their arrival, Kosygin said that plans for the creation of an Islamic Pact disregarded the lessons of history, and he pledged his government's support for the "strengthening of the political and economic independence of the Arab countries."

The moment was opportune for a major political commitment in the area. The goal of consolidating the Arab progressive states under Soviet leadership assumed new significance in the light of Britain's decision to pull out and fade out as a Middle Eastern power. The British in January had announced they would withdraw from their South Arabian Protectorate within two years and close down their last major Arabian base at Aden. The United States was wholly embogged in Southeast Asia and probably too involved with the war in Vietnam to make her full power felt on the opposite side of the world. The new Syrian regime was an unstable political weapon that would have to be mastered, but it held several immediate attractions. It was militantly and compactly left. It was radically socialist and dedicated to the proposition that all major sectors of the Syrian economy should be brought under state control. It was not anti-Communist like the previous Baath government; and though not pro-Communist, it was pro-Soviet. It presented no ideological block to close political collaboration. It was more decidedly left in its pattern and structure of power than any other Arab state and looked, in this respect, like a caricature of a Communist People's Democracy. All these properties made it an instrument well suited to Soviet ends. However, the main fact about it was its inherent instability. The Russians' chief and urgent concern was to preserve and strengthen a regime that had given them the opportunity to lay a new stake in Syria.

They fully appreciated that they were dealing with a political clique that was based mainly on a combination of minorities and they accepted the hazards. By their own strategic support and by means of a rapprochement with Nasser, they hoped to assure its survival. For Syria's sake, and in order to forge a common Arab front with Cairo-Damascus as its axis, they reversed their ideology. Their fundamental political decision was to discard Arab socialism and embrace anti-Israeli chauvinism as the instrument of Arab union. Henceforth the anti-Israeli cause was the way to bring the Arab states together and anti-Israeli nationalism was the binding force of the projected alignment. In the past the Russians had upheld what they called "the lawful and indivisible rights" of the Arab Palestinians; as the new patrons and protectors of Syria, they espoused the Arab struggle as a popular campaign to liquidate the traces of colonialism and liberate a subject people. The fight against Israel became an anti-imperialist fight under Soviet sponsorship. The new strategy required that Israel be condemned as a Zionist-imperialist-expansionist phenomenon, the stooge and agent of Western imperialist interests.

But the process of consolidation and advance in Syria and elsewhere could not be headlong and adventuresome in the Arab fashion. It would take time. The Russians perceived the pitfalls; they were committed to riding the convulsive forces of Arab nationalism in Damascus but at the same time they would have to control them. The most obvious danger was that the "war of liberation" the Syrians were waging against Israel, training and arming the commando-raiders of El Fatah and glorifying their exploits on Damascus Radio, would provoke the Israelis to a large-scale military reprisal; and the Russians did not expect the Jedid regime would be able to survive such a punitive expedition into Syrian territory. The exacerbated nationalism of Syria and the crusading fervor of her free-wheeling leaders were a threat to their central and consistent purpose. Their design was long-term and they wished to proceed with caution. They aspired gradually to tighten the Syrian relationship and convert the country by degrees into a Soviet base, so that in time they could confront the West with an accomplished fact: We are now established in Syria and Syria is established within our sphere of national interest. The Chinese would be effectively expelled, and Syria would be the springboard for a wider initiative to create a bloc of Soviet-aligned states and challenge American authority in the region. The Russians' interest was to restrain their Syrian friends and prevent them from upsetting this design.

Within two months after the formation of the new government, they were running into trouble. The Jedid regime insisted on receiving Soviet financial and organizational support for the El Fatah crusade. This was the last thing the Russians wanted. The Syrians spiced their request with gentle hints that they might have to turn to Peking if they failed to find satisfaction in Moscow. The Russians, on the spot, replied: Yes, you have Soviet support for the war to liberate Palestine, but not *now*. The first political prerequisite for the war of liberation, they explained, was for the Syrian Government to "gain the broad support of the masses." In the graphic short cut of Marxist jargon, this phrase had a very precise meaning for the Russians; translated into everyday English, the sense of their injunction was that the first thing the Syrians must do was to stabilize and consolidate their new regime. Unversed in such semantics, the young Baathists of Damascus misunderstood the message, accepted it literally and went ahead mobilizing the enthusiasm of the masses behind the guerrilla and sabotage campaign of the El Fatah warriors. This confusion of purpose between patron and client illustrated the equivocal nature of the Soviet involvement with Syria which a year later, in an ascending cycle of raid and counterraid, was to lead to the specific Soviet responsibility for a Middle Eastern war. The Russians could not control the Syrians, but they committed themselves to support them, diplomatically and publicly, in whatever they chose to do. Mindful of their client's waywardness, Soviet Middle Eastern experts came in time to the conclusion that desirable as it was to curb the terrorism of El Fatah and others, the Soviet Government could not press Syria too hard without undermining and perhaps jeopardizing its own position in Damascus.

The Syrian problem the Russians were now taking on, as the price for their new foothold in the country, was the same that had exasperated Nasser throughout the years of Egyptian-Syrian competition at the Israeli auction. To deal with the problem, he had executed one of those sudden political transformations with which it was his wont to present an entirely new face to an inexpectant Arab world. This exercise had been consummated in January, 1964, when at his invitation the Arab heads of state, "reactionary" monarchs and "progressive" presidents alike, had joined him at a conference table in Cairo to frame a common policy on the question of Palestine. Thus was inaugurated the era of Arab summitry that brought to an end the Nasserist era of revolutionary pan-Arab socialism that had begun soon after the dissolution of the United Arab Republic. From that smarting defeat Nasser had drawn the conclusion that his principal enemies were the Arab reactionary classes, capitalist and feudal, and that the road to Arab unity lay across the battleground of social revolution. The loose, empirical creed of Arab socialism became the rallying cry of the new order. A series of sequestrations in Egypt dispossessed the propertied classes so thoroughly that they had little left to be sequestered; and a series of nationalizations with equal thoroughness left little of importance in industry to be nationalized. In a revolutionary mood as the champion of the Arab proletariat, the mass leader appealed to the Arab people above the heads of their rulers and continued to exert his popular magnetism in the Arab world. According to his new political doctrine, there could be no unity of the Arab nations without a greater uniformity of their social systems and without social uniformity there could be no political cooperation.

This proselytizing course was abandoned with Nasser's call for a meeting of the Arab heads of state. Popular among the masses but hemmed in and hard-pressed in the arena of inter-Arab politics, the statesman came forward, dismissed the internationalist mass leader, put the doctrine of pan-Arab revolution on the shelf and substituted the tactic of inter-Arab cooperation in the form of summitry. The statesman's calculations were sober and astute. Thwarted in the war in Yemen, where Saudi Arabia was stubbornly arming and abetting his royalist adversaries, he hoped to create a "unity atmosphere" on the holy issue of Palestine in which King Feisal would find it difficult to be intransigent. It was a subtle application of the blackmailing virtue that was implicit in the Palestinian cause. Challenged also by the Syrians, who were threatening to plunge him into war over Israel's diversion of the "Arab" waters of the Jordan River, he planned to counterattack with the unifying cry of "Palestine, Palestine." Cunningly he appraised and exploited the paradox of the Arab position. Whenever the Arab states got together on a common Palestine policy, provocation of Israel was abated; whenever they flew apart, provocation was intensified. They were forced to seek a lowest common denominator when they acted in concert, and realism tended to make the denominator moderate. The course of moderation was the only one that Nasser was politically or militarily prepared to follow at this juncture. The unruly Syrians and those perfidious characters, the Baathists, were forever shouting for war, but if war came it would be Egypt and not Syria who would have to fight it. The Syrian diatribes had badly damaged his position. He was the deliverer of Palestine in Arab eyes and Arab hopes because only he could unite the Arab world and only the united Arab armies could annihilate Israel. The Syrians had accused him not only of holding back but of reneging on the Arab cause and pulling out of the fight in pursuit of his own interests.

He was obliged to act. Nothing the Israelis had done since the Sinai war had more fiercely shamed the Arabs or more plainly exposed their impotence than the diversion of the Jordan waters. The Israelis already had constructed their underwater pumping station on the west shore of the Sea of Galilee, in full view of Syrian army posts along the Golan Heights on the opposite bank. Canals and pipes were being built and laid for the national carrier system that was to channel the northern waters across Israel to the Negev Desert. These were acts which the Arab states had always said would be met by war. The Israeli Government had accepted but the Arab states had spurned a unified plan of water allocation that had been worked out in 1955 by Eisenhower's envoy, Eric Johnston. The Israelis proposed to divert only that share of the waters that had been assigned to them under this Solomon-like and evenhanded plan. Since the headwaters of the Jordan rose on Arab territory in Syria and Lebanon, the denial of diversion rights to Israel was a matter of Arab honor; but since under the Johnston plan, the water allocated to Israel would constitute one-third of her national supply, the project for the Israelis was a matter not of honor but of life and death, and any military interference with her carrier system would be a *casus belli*. The Syrians had always threatened an immediate showdown on the issue. Ingloriously shown up, they went to the Cairo Summit parading their bravado and advertising their grievance against the leader who did nothing.

Nasser aspired at the Summit to establish an Arab consensus for his position and, in so doing, to isolate the Syrians. He easily achieved both aims. The heads of state, settling on a compromise formula, ruled that war with Israel was inevitable, but not *now*. They agreed that the Arab states should coordinate their military programs in preparation for that war but in the meantime should refrain from doing anything that might provoke it prematurely; and they therefore placed a formal ban on sabotage raids and terrorist activities. Nasser knew from experience where these could lead; in 1956 he had sought to spread alarm and despair in Israel with his *fedayeen* murder squads and had paid for it in Sinai. A number of positive decisions were also taken. A United Arab Command was created, with Egypt as the paramount member and an Egyptian general as the commander-in-chief. The Arab states did not relinquish any of their sovereign rights to this body. It was granted no legal authority to transfer troops from one country to another or to impose its orders. The United Arab Command was designed as an instrument of coordination in operational planning, and in surveying the training programs, standardization of arms and general state of military preparedness of the member countries. A Joint Staff was established and a yearly budget of 15 million pounds, or 42 million dollars, was announced to encourage the build-ups of Jordan, Syria and Lebanon. In addition the Summit created the Palestine Liberation Organization, to preserve a sense of Palestinian entity without which the Arab Palestinians might be absorbed into the Arab states and the Palestinian cause itself might wither away; and as its military arm, the Palestine Liberation Army, the standard-bearer and spearhead of the eventual war. This body was to be organized as a regular fighting force and not as a massive *fedayeen* adventure in disguise. With a Palestinian army in the vanguard when war came, it would not appear that the Arab states were leading the attack from the outside. Finally, to silence the Syrian clamor over the Jordan River, Nasser produced a counterscheme for the counterdiversion of the Jordan headwaters, with the ultimate objective of depriving Israel of her Arab sources by a system of canals and pipes on Arab territory upstream. All of this was conceived as an interim program of preparation until D-day; the consensus of the heads of state was that the inevitable war was still several years away, and a minimum of five years was mentioned as the period the Arab countries would need in order to attain a credible offensive power.

The Cairo Summit was a victory for Nasser, and the Syrians went home rebuffed and resentful. When the Syrian President, General Hafiz, again raised the cry of immediate war at the second Summit, held in Alexandria in September, 1964, his appeal was drowned in derision. But the initiation of summitry was nonetheless a turning point in Nasser's policies toward Israel. He won his point; he had sought to contain the pressure of the Syrians and for a while he contained it; but he paid a price for his respite. He formally accepted the Syrian war doctrine that the Palestine question must be settled by arms and not at the conference table. In so doing, he pushed the clock forward. The morbid and destructive fixation of the Arabs, riveted on the concept of inevitable war and haunted by dreams of Israel's cataclysmic disappearance, was enshrined in the program of the Arab states and, most importantly, in the policy of Egypt. Moreover, with the creation of a united command and of a Palestinian army, Nasser institutionalized the doctrine. In May, 1964, he chose Shukheiry to carry the banner of the new Palestinian organization, a man who placed the facile violence of a political hack and the scourge of his tongue at the service of the cause. Egyptian military analysts, retired officers and others, pondered in newspaper articles over the strategic shape of the war to come, the operational alternatives, the problems of terrain, the structure of forces. Some of their cogitations were fanciful, many were sober enough. In general they held that the preponderance of the Arab armies must be such as to anticipate foreign intervention with an all-out drive that would achieve at least their main objectives; they were concerned to create circumstances in which Israel would be seen as the aggressor; they often developed the thought that concurrent crises in various parts of the world would help the Arabs by discouraging international intervention and permitting the East to neutralize the West under the lid of the balance of terror. Shukheiry assigned to his Liberation Army a detonating role in the conflict; his scenario for the opening of hostilities called for marauding actions by *fedayeen* in order to provoke Israeli reprisal, after which the Palestinian Army would invade Israel with the Arab national armies following. While Shukheiry spoke exuberantly of Israel's obliteration, Nasser couched the objective in less brutal but nonetheless fatalistic terms. The Arab war aim of eliminating a state was not, after all, calculated to win sympathy. "There have been attempts," Nasser said on March 26, 1964, "to separate the issues and present them in an imaginary way, as if the question of Israel is just the refugees, and that once this problem is solved the Palestine question would be solved and no trace would be left of it. The Israeli danger lies in the very existence of Israel and in what this state represents."

Overruled at the two Summits, chastised but unrepentant, the Syrian Government honored their decisions for a time and then defied them. The heads of state had to deal once again with the Syrian problem at their third meeting at Casablanca in September, 1965. By this time a new situation had arisen. The new commando group, El Fatah, impatient with the supine wait-and-prepare policy of the Palestine Liberation Army, had entered the lists in the previous January with a few raids from Syria and Jordan. These were followed by three minor sabotage actions from Egyptian-administered territory in the Gaza Strip. Nasser immediately squelched the dissident saboteurs in Gaza, rounding them up in the refugee camps of the Strip, and they turned to Syria for support and patronage. The Syrians welcomed this opportunity to outbid their competitor. The tempo of El Fatah activity from Syrian bases increased sharply in May and June and, during the summer, the organization was placed under the operational control of Syrian Army Intelligence. Thenceforth, the El Fatah commandos were paid by the Syrian Second Bureau, trained and equipped by Syrian army echelons and based inside Syrian army camps.

Nasser was then at his nadir and his country was adrift on a sea of expanding insolvency. The endless and unwinnable war in Yemen; the total suspension of the American wheat shipments that for three years had relieved him of his greatest problem, that of feeding his people; the national penury, the shortages in sugar, oil, rice, fish—the crisis was spreading and tentacular, and the people of Egypt were feeling its grip. The dead in Yemen were no longer brought home for burial; the private obituary notices on the war dead in the Egyptian press were forbidden. The cry of Arab socialism had lost its élan, and economic crisis had generated a political challenge of the kind that Nasser dreaded most. The Moslem Brothers, the outlawed party of violent Islamic reaction, were profiting by the general unrest to gain new support among the intelligentsia, beyond their traditional recruiting grounds among the peasantry and proletariat. Nasser had no time for the Palestine problem or the tiresome Syrians. On May 30, he unburdened himself in a speech to the annual conference of the Palestine Liberation Organization. "The road to the liberation of Palestine," he said, "is strewn not with roses but with blood; there can be no liberation of the plundered fatherland now, when we are riven by internal disputes, strife and even inter-Arab war in Yemen." The projects for the counterdiversion of the Jordan waters? They should be postponed

"until we are strong enough to protect them. . . . Let us face reality
and stop deluding ourselves." Israel? "How can we attack Israel when
fifty thousand Egyptian troops are stationed in Yemen? Our aims can
be achieved only by a united Arab people and revolutionary regimes."
Planes to protect Syria against Israeli retaliation? "Without our own
air bases in Syria, guarded by Egyptian forces, I will not send planes
to Syria." The Baathists? "We shake hands and embrace each other
like Arab brothers, but underneath lurks a deep mutual mistrust."

All the while, by the most plausible estimates that foreign econo-
mists could make in the labyrinth of Egyptian financing, the war in
Yemen was costing $180 million a year, not all of it in dollars, but
some of it, yes. Egyptian cotton helped defray the cost of Soviet arms;
the Russians apparently were picking up the bill for various activities
of the Egyptian intelligence establishment in Yemen; but the shipping
costs for basic imports, at a time when Egyptian vessels were being
commandeered as military transports, had to be met with hard currency. Nasser had no choice and in August he went to Jiddah in Saudi
Arabia to seek a Yemen peace pact with King Feisal. It was his Ca-
nossa; he went as a petitioner; he was in no position to summon Feisal
to Cairo. Although the terms of the Yemen pact were never fulfilled
and never brought peace, the negotiations led to a lull in the warfare,
and to that extent he was able to gain by them. At the end of the
month he went to Moscow for his first meeting with Leonid Brezhnev
and Kosygin. He was anxious to sound out the new Soviet leaders on
their Middle East intentions. On August 29, in a speech to a mixed
group of Egyptian and Syrian students in the Soviet capital, he returned to the theme of Syrian fecklessness and treachery. "Every time
the Jews fire a couple of artillery rounds," he said, "the Baath come
running to us. They said the Israelis had shelled a tractor and Egypt
had kept quiet; that she must attack and destroy Israel. If in fact we
are capable today of destroying Israel, why wait until tomorrow? I told
them inside the Summit conference [at Alexandria]: If you are today
capable, if all we Arabs are today capable of destroying Israel, why
then wait? But let us see what Israel is. Israel consists of itself and of
those who are behind it . . . combines itself and its supporters. This
is the situation we discussed frankly. Consequently in confronting Israel we must act in stages. The first stage is to increase our defense
power. This will deter Israel from attacking any Arab country and at
the same time will provide us with a deterrent [sic] force that will tac-

kle Israel once it tries to penetrate the defense of any Arab country. This is the immediate objective. Later on is the liberation of Palestine, for which we must be fully prepared; and there must be propitious international circumstances. Those who today bargain and say that Israel has attacked them and that Egypt must attack Israel are joking and talking nonsense and cannot be talking responsibly. What the Baathists are actually trying to do is to create embarrassing situations of various kinds. If things go on in this way, the Arab states cannot possibly cooperate with each other. . . . [The Baathists] serve nothing but the imperialists and Zionists and they will destroy the spirit of the Summit conferences."

The last sentence was a warning. Nasser told the students he would go to the Summit meeting that was to open on September 13 but would announce his withdrawal if this unsatisfactory state of affairs continued. There was no confidence between the Egyptian and Syrian governments, and as long as there was no confidence, there could be no active United Arab Command, since the two countries occupied so great a portion of the Israeli front. Nasser's visit to Moscow produced a Soviet-Egyptian communiqué that was relatively subdued. The Russians proclaimed their ritual support of the "indivisible rights" of the Palestinian Arabs, but the communiqué mentioned Israel only once and in passing, with a dig at the West Germans for their Israeli arms commitment. Unlike the Khrushchev-Nasser communiqué in the spring of the previous year, it ignored the irksome question of the Jordan waters. Nasser was no doubt content to let that issue sleep. He had learned from his water engineers how vulnerable the counterdiversion was to Israeli attack along the Syrian border, and from his political advisers how queasy the Lebanese were about sharing the risks of this venture. Washington, moreover, had been firm. In a letter to Senator Robert Keating, the State Department had said the United States would oppose any "Middle Eastern attempts to frustrate the Israeli [diversion] plan by other counter-diversion projects" that were in excess of the Johnston allocation. Such attempts would be regarded as aggressive acts.

Nasser again won a favorable consensus from the Arab heads of state at Casablanca. The conference made two noteworthy decisions. It concluded a "solidarity pact" in the form of a noninterference agreement: each of the Arab countries was free to choose whether to permit the Palestine Liberation Army to station forces on its territory.

Neither Lebanon nor Jordan wanted to open its doors to Shukheiry; but the decision was obviously of special interest to King Hussein. The creation of the Liberation Army spelled trouble for the monarch, who counted more than a million Palestinians among his subjects; a Palestinian army on Jordanian soil would be a Nasserist fifth column against the Hashimite throne; and in principle Hussein was now free to reject it. The Summit's second decision was directed at the Syrians and was not publicly announced. The conference declared a moratorium on commando activity and approved a general no-terrorism agreement; it was arranged that the Arab members of the various Mixed Armistice Commissions, concerned with border problems under the armistice accords of 1949, would convene and decide, on the Summit's instructions, to desist from all terrorist action.

The commando groups of El Fatah had now been espoused as paramilitary units by the Syrian Army. They had their home bases at three army camps in the environs of Damascus and at a fourth near the Lebanese border. The Syrians adopted them as the vehicle for their war of liberation; and as matters stood in the fall of 1965, it appeared that the danger of escalating border conflict, or at least of igniting sparks, would come from Syria. However, in the months immediately following the Casablanca Summit, the Syrians honored the no-terrorism agreement after their fashion, reluctantly in the observance and then more and more frequently in the breach. At least for a time there was an over-all scaling down of El Fatah activity. For all her fantasy as an Arab power, Syria retained her instinct of self-preservation. The Syrian leaders were torn between their desire to force the pace of events toward a war which the Summits had relegated to an indefinite future, and their fear of tripping themselves into war alone. Though intoxicated, they were not blind, and though obsessed, they were not suicidal. They entertained a well-founded suspicion that their Arab brothers might let them down and desert them if the Israelis struck back in force.

Nevertheless, in the winter of 1965–1966, the compulsions of the anti-Israel crusade kept pace with these calculations of prudence. The Syrian mood on the Palestine issue became ever more radical, rigorous and ideologically imbued. Palestinian ideologues began to discuss the El Fatah phenomenon in global terms and they found a receptive ear in Damascus. Among others, Salah Shibl, in articles for the Lebanese press and pamphlets for the Institute of Palestine Studies in

Beirut, cited the examples of Algeria and Vietnam to show that a primitive guerrilla army could defeat or in any case hamstring a large, powerfully equipped and technologically superior force. These encouraging models were recommended for Palestine with little thought for the geographical limitations or the balance of strength, popular as well as military, on the terrain of modern Israel. The Arabs, Shibl urged, should not be discouraged by the formidable Israeli deterrent. Furthermore, the Vietcong were successful because they had a national supporting base in North Vietnam and, by analogy, El Fatah needed a permanent base in Jordan. This line of reasoning had been anticipated to some degree by events, since El Fatah already was operating extensively from Jordanian territory. But El Fatah was in Jordan under sufferance and not because Hussein had welcomed it. From the Vietnamese experience Shibl extracted the lesson that the main road to Tel-Aviv led through the King's capital, Amman, and that consequently Hussein, the archlaggard in the liberation cause, must go.

Like the sorrows of another king, in *Hamlet,* troubles in the Arab world come not as single spies but in battalions. At this point on the inter-Arab scene, a new rift was threatening the foundations of summitry and was soon to have fateful consequences in Damascus. By midwinter it was clear that the Nasser-Feisal pact for peace in Yemen had come to nothing; a follow-up meeting between Yemeni republicans and royalists had aborted; and Nasser's bid to gain something more than a truce in the Yemen war had misfired. In the spring of the new year he surprised the Arab world with yet another of his lightning reversals. Turning in rage, he pilloried Feisal, the king with the beard and the money, in a succession of speeches whose vehemence announced the imminent end of Summit collaboration. Nasser employed a number of sophisticated rhetorical devices on these occasions. He foretold that his enemies would be "seized by the beard" and he evoked that grisly scene in which the other Feisal—the last Hashimite king of Iraq—had been assassinated in his palace courtyard in Baghdad in 1958. He spoke of amputating the legs of the "merchants of religion" who used Islam for their own egotistical purposes; and no doubt Feisal's untiring efforts to drum up support for an Islamic conference, as he traveled to Guinea and Mali, Turkey and Pakistan, and solicited the interest of the Emirs of Kuwait and Bahrein, were a major goad to Nasser's wrath. The pan-Islam idea competed with summitry and was designed to weaken it. But this by itself hardly seemed sufficient reason to throw summitry overboard and accept an indefinite prolongation of the Yemen war. To some it had seemed that by going to Jiddah, Nasser had shown his readiness to pull out of southern Arabia, but no one really knew and no one knows. He was ready, perhaps, to pull out on his own terms, and his terms changed as time went on. Some believed that if it had not been for Feisal's Islamic fancy, the spirit of Jiddah might have prevailed. This seems unlikely. No one outside the Presidential circle in Cairo can say what was in the master's mind and those outside it can only judge by events. An event to conjure with was the British evacuation of southern Arabia, officially set for 1968; and in February, 1966, in order to deal with the terrorist movements that were then under the direction of Egyptian Army Intelligence in Yemen, the British imposed emergency rule on the Aden Protectorate. Their move infuriated Nasser and brought an instant retort. "I will stay as long as the British stay." So always he reacted to the stimulus of events. The temptation to hold on in Yemen for two more years and, having expelled the British from the northern end of the Red Sea, at the Suez Canal, to replace them at the other end, at Aden, had evidently overborne such considerations as the costs and miseries, the disease and death, of the dubious battle in the hills of Yemen. At any rate, he vowed he would hold on. The decisive factor was probably the political lure, the challenge, magnified and aggravated by Feisal's globe-trotting conspiracy against his leadership. Moreover, he had found to his alarm that it *was* a conspiracy. In the summer of 1965, his police had informed him that gunmen of the Moslem Brotherhood had made three attempts on his life, some of which, it later appeared, had narrowly missed. In the autumn he discovered that Feisal had been subsidizing the Moslem Brothers in disturbingly prodigal amounts. A few months later, on February 22, 1966, in a speech on the eighth anniversary of the defunct United Arab Republic, a date still celebrated and revered, he accused Feisal of contributing 200 million pounds sterling to finance the overthrow of the Egyptian Government by the Moslem Brothers. "Don't be afraid of the Brotherhood," he said. "They are all behind bars." The size of the subsidy was immaterial; it was another of those rhetorical figures. The menace lay in the presumed association between Saudi Arabian money and the bullets of the Brotherhood.

Thus the prosecution of the war in Yemen, or at least the maintenance of a military stalemate in what had now become a severed and almost partitioned country, appeared again in Nasser's political imagination as part of a global contest against imperialism, represented by the United States in the local guise of an Arab king. He was at this time unable to meet the interest payments on the loans Egypt had contracted with half a dozen nations; on the other hand he could hope that a *de facto* cease-fire in Yemen might reduce the costs of the ordeal and even permit him to retire some of his troops. It was bankruptcy brinkmanship, as a correspondent in Cairo remarked. Whatever his calculations, he was, at any rate, in pattern and in character. The breach with Feisal was a fulminating action in which, as so often in hours of challenge, he put politics first. He put his Arab prestige above the interests of his defaultant nation, and the claims of grandeur above the needs of his people.

In Damascus the Jedid regime came to power in the midst of these developments and was quick to grasp their significance. It saw that the castigation of Feisal meant the certain end of summitry and eagerly drew its own conclusions. On March 19 on Damascus Radio, Prime Minister Zayen said his government no longer felt committed to the solidarity decisions of Casablanca. If summitry was dead and buried, so was its policy, and Syria was no longer bound by its noninterference principles or its no-terrorism agreement. The Summits, after all, had been Nasser's instrument for bringing pressure on the Syrians and the instrument was jettisoned. The Baathists needed no better excuse to break away from the Arab consensus and go it alone. Nasser's renunciation of summitry was the signal for the regime to call out El Fatah; and the pursuit of the Syrian chimera—the Palestine War of Liberation—was the restored order of the day. To be sure, the Syrians anticipated somewhat the official funeral of summitry, but their prognosis was perfectly correct. Nasser's speeches followed the expected crescendo. On May 1 he threatened an invasion strike from Yemen at the royalist bases in Najran and Jizan in Saudi Arabia; on June 15 he declared an end to pan-Arab cooperation, accusing his foes of using summitry as a cover for their faithless plotting against him, "pretending to join us for the sake of Palestine" and then grabbing daggers to await an opportunity "to stab us in the back." He revived the pan-Arab revolutionary call: "In order to liberate Palestine, we must first of all liquidate Arab reaction, reactionary regimes and reactionary leaders." Finally on July 22 came the formal repudiation: he would not attend the summit conference that had been planned for Algiers in September. He could not "sit together with the reactionaries" because this would mean reinstating them. On July 26 he rehearsed his grievances in one of his long and brooding reconstructions of history: "We called for the Summit conference [of 1964] . . . because there was one thing that concerned us, Palestine. We sat with reaction. We forgot all that and for the sake of Palestine, we decided to sit with reaction. It was not an emotional or hasty decision. We tried to purify the atmosphere . . . to bring everyone together. I went to Jiddah to liquidate the problem [of Yemen] with Saudi Arabia. We found that Arab reaction hated us more than Israel."

The Syrians, the Egyptians and the Russians all embarked on new political ventures in the uncertain spring of 1966; and with the easy clairvoyance of hindsight, the historian or political student can now say that the interescalation of these ventures, and of the fears and frustrations they gave rise to, created the conditions that in the spring of the following year were to let loose an avalanche of crisis on the unprepared and unsuspecting capitals of the Western world. At the time, however, no one took particular note of the altered tone and accent of events; no one saw the new combination of circumstances as particularly menacing; and no one in the responsible echelons of the United States Government appears to have seen any special need to confront them by a special effort of policy. For Washington, it was business as usual in a perennially disturbed and neurotic part of the world that continued to send in signals of trouble from time to time. No doubt some of the signals were disregarded and some of the portents were unread, both in Washington and Jerusalem. But it is an easy game to read the portents after the catastrophe has happened and to conclude, from the sheltered perch of hindsight and with the unearned sense of wisdom it bestows, that the professional readers of signs and portents were all napping. Some of them were wide awake and deeply worried. Others went about their job of applying the usual dampeners to the usual combustible elements. None of them, by any twirl of the crystal ball, could possibly have foreseen the denouement of May, 1967—the particular shape and size of the avalanche—that threw both Washington and Jerusalem into a state of total mental disarray. It was only by the floodlight of later events that the responsible professional men were able to see so clearly what so very few had seen at the time, namely, the potential for trouble that was implicit in the fact that one of the combustible elements, the Soviet element, was new. The novelty in the situation was the Soviet stake in the government of Syria.

In the ring of tension that was beginning to close around Israel in the spring and summer of 1966, there were three levels of rivalry, in ascending order. On the lowest level, in the contest between "liberation" groups, the Cairo-sponsored Palestine Liberation Army competed for Arab favor with El Fatah, the child of Damascus and the instrument of its immediate-action program. On the intermediate level, Cairo vied with Damascus for mastery of the anti-Israeli crusade. And on the level of big-power rivalry in the cockpit of Syria, the Russians contended with the others. There were two such "others," the Chinese and the Americans. The Russians with their superior resources could dispose of the Chinese without great difficulty. But the Americans were another matter. Although not paying too much attention at the time, they were the ultimate adversaries. The Russians were as fearful for the security of their new Syrian clients as were the clients themselves.

Syria's new band of leaders made an early estimate of the threats to their survival. They believed that sooner or later the United States would seek to overturn their leftist "popular" democracy and replace it with a regime closer to American tastes and more responsive to American interests. Putting four and four together, they conceived that the American instrument in this attempt would be Israel; the United States would order or incite the Israelis to attack in order to bring down the Damascus Government. This assessment was accepted by the Russians. They were probably encouraged to accept it by the nature of their ambitions in the country. They had no foolish ideas about creating a People's Democracy in the Middle East; they wanted to form an alignment of Arab "progressive" states that would work in close union with Moscow toward the final objective of expelling American power from the area. The Syrian-Soviet diagnosis of an American-Israeli threat was based on strategic calculations, not on the findings of Soviet intelligence. From first to last, it was a political estimate and not an intelligence conclusion.

The Soviet Government on May 28 made its first diplomatic commitment to the Syrian regime. Katriel Katz, the Israeli Ambassador in Moscow, was summoned to the Soviet Foreign Ministry. The Director of the Department for Middle East Affairs handed him a note that accused Israel of acting as the agent of other powers in a conspiracy against Syria. The note, exceptionally harsh, was based on a Tass Agency statement that was published in *Pravda* the same day. After mentioning the appearance of the Sixth Fleet in the waters of Lebanon and a meeting of American ambassadors in Beirut, the Tass statement said: "The peoples of the Arab states understand full well the dangers to peace and to their independent development lurking in the new intrigues of the imperialist powers, of their reactionary agents in the Near East and of the ruling circles of Israel—in particular, their attempts to intervene in the internal affairs of the Syrian Arab Republic." It added that the Soviet Union could not and would not be indifferent to "the attempts to disturb peace in a region that is situated in the immediate vicinity of the borders of the Soviet Union."

The Israelis had already been aware of a cold wind blowing from Moscow. There had been many small but unmistakable signs. Two weeks earlier the Russians had sent only lower-echelon officials to the Israelis' Independence Day festivities at their Embassy in Moscow—a show of deliberate displeasure in the iconography of Soviet protocol. The Israelis had done nothing to provoke the Syrians although the Syrians had more than provoked them. On May 16 a land mine planted by saboteurs in a dirt track a thousand yards from the Syrian border had blown up an Israeli farm vehicle and killed its two occupants. The incident had occurred at Almagor, a farming settlement on high ground just north of the Sea of Galilee, overlooking the fields in the valley where the Jordan River enters the sea. Immediately the other side of the river was a Syrian army position, and investigation by United Nations observers had indicated that the saboteurs had crossed to the Israeli side at a point directly opposite that post.

The Russians had reason to remember the name of Almagor. A few years earlier, in August, 1963, two young Israeli farmers had been ambushed and murdered on their way back to the village from their fields. On that occasion also, the evidence gathered by a United Nations team had indicated that the infiltrators, a party of eight men, had crossed the river in the area of the Syrian post and had departed in the same direction. The Israelis had complained to the Security Council; a majority of the Council had voted for a resolution condemning the act and calling the Syrian Government's attention to the evidence, and the Soviet Union had vetoed it. Now two more farmers had been killed, about two hundred yards from the scene of that ambush. Israel had taken no reprisal action but had received, instead, the sharpest demarche that had come from Moscow since Bulganin's note to Ben-Gurion in November, 1956.

Why were the Russians so alarmed? The answer was partly topographical. For years the Israelis had known and the Syrians had known that small-scale reprisals were impossible on Israel's northeastern frontier. This was the premise of any raid-and-retaliation action on the Syrian border. Along its entire forty-eight-mile length, the Syrians in their dugouts and pillboxes on the crests and shoulders of the Golan Heights commanded the Israeli countryside that lay like a map below them. Soviet military engineers had instructed the Syrians in the fortification of those hills; Syrian artillery posts held the towns and villages of upper Galilee within their fixed fields of fire. Across the lake, the Sea of Galilee, the Syrians looked toward Tiberias on the western shore and could follow the ribbon of road that skirts the fishermen's sea, traversing the Plain of Gennesareth, passing the Mount of Beatitudes, winding across brown hills, then straightening and heading due north toward Lebanon, through softer landscapes, tilled and cultivated, busy with tractors, closely settled with towns and kibbutzim among green fields. If Israel wished to retaliate after a succession of border provocations, there was no easy way; a limited lightning strike by ground troops against the Syrian positions was excluded; the topography of dominating hills and open valley imposed an operation in strength, with artillery and aerial support, into and across the Golan Heights and onto the plateau beyond toward a worthwhile military objective—possibly as far as the Syrian Army's southern headquarters at Kuneitra. The Russian fear in this respect was genuine. A spiraling series of border incidents could culminate in a large-scale punitive incursion into Syria; and it could reasonably be supposed that the Syrian regime would stagger and fall under the blow.

The new Syrian leaders were unresponsive to whatever restraints the Russians may have urged upon them. They announced they had chosen armed struggle as their means of delivering Palestine. An interim phase of guerrilla and sabotage warfare, designed, the Syrian Chief of Staff said, to bring "fear and alarm" to "every house in Israel," would pave the way for the War of Liberation that had been formally denied to Syria by three Arab Summits. The ideological yearnings of the new regime gave to this campaign the exalted name of "People's War." Its military strategy, insofar as it had one, was inspired by the meditations of the Palestinian theorizers, and its objectives were proclaimed by the Baathist leaders with uninhibited vehemence. The War of Liberation, President Atassi said in March, was the "keystone of the revolution," and on May 22 he continued: "We yearn to open the battle. We raise the banner of the People's War of Liberation. . . . We want total war—a war that knows no bounds and that will destroy the Zionist base . . . this will be total war, the first aim of which will be a scorched-earth policy." Scorched earth as a strategy of defense in an invaded country was understandable; as a strategy of liberation it was new and evidently reflected no more than the fancy of an unwary orator caught in an ambush of rhetoric. However, General Achmed Sweidani, a former Director of Military Intelligence who was now Chief of Staff, did no better. Speaking on the same day to Syrian soldiers at the front, he left some confusion as to the role they would play in the People's War. "If we build our strategy on the purchase of tanks and planes," he said, "this theory is false and unfounded. The correct principle is to be found in the party's pronouncement: this is the principle of the War of Liberation that is not based on the classic methods. The traditional war that is based on superiority in the quantity of arms will lead us nowhere. Therefore we have no choice but to launch a war of liberation. Algeria will serve as our model, and Vietnam also is an example that proves our argument sound." The knot of passion and borrowed ideology was inextricable. It became known, at any rate, from these and other statements, that Syria had embraced a policy of unremitting belligerence and that the Russians had found her leaders as intractable as had others who had sought to deal with them.

Heroically emblazoned as a national doctrine, the People's War was less than heroic in practice. The El Fatah "spearhead" seldom penetrated farther than an easy walking distance into Israel. Squads of saboteurs infiltrating at night, laying their antitank mines along roads and tracks, or planting their demolition charges under a village house or farm building, a bridge or water pump, then vanishing before the time-fused charges went off and recrossing the border well before dawn—the Israelis reported fifty-three of these incidents in the eighteen months ending July 25, 1966. On ninety-three occasions during this period, Syrian artillery fired on Israeli farmers in the fields, fish-

ermen on the lake and vehicles on the roads. Many times the infiltrators came from Jordan and Lebanon, topographically convenient because of their more open borders and politically opportune because
they made the Syrian origin of the raids less obvious. The government-
controlled Syrian press and government-operated Damascus Radio
reported and celebrated these deeds in the fulsome war communiqués
of El Fatah's "General Command." The Syrians reckoned that by re-
stricting El Fatah to small-scale actions close to the border, they
could have their People's War and still escape retaliation. Israel
warned that its citizens "look to their government to adopt such measures as are in its judgment essential for the security of the state, its
territory and its citizens." In practice, Israel did not retaliate for prop-
erty damaged, equipment destroyed or citizens wounded. It retaliated
only for deaths. Two, three or four Israelis killed—this represented
the limit of aggression that Israel would tolerate without response;
and when, on July 14, six and a half weeks after the delivery of the
Soviet note in Moscow, two Israeli farmers were killed and a third
was maimed by a land mine that wrecked their vehicle, at the village
of Almagor, the Israeli Air Force replied by bombing tractors and
bulldozers engaged on Syria's counterdiversion project twelve miles
inside her territory. A Syrian Mig was shot down in the course of the
operation.

The Soviet demarche of May 28 startled and dismayed Jerusalem.
Prime Minister Eshkol denied the Tass allegations. Foreign Minister
Eban called in Dmitri Chuvakhin, the Soviet Ambassador, to reject
the charge that Israel was acting as an agent or was in any way involved in an imperialist conspiracy. Eban caught and read the signal:
Soviet policy had veered in its course and had staked out a claim in
Syria. Through the American Ambassador, Walworth Barbour, he
urged the United States to come up with a riposte. He felt that failure
by the Americans to say anything about insinuations that touched
them would be taken as evidence of slow reflexes and evasion of commitment, and would encourage the Russians along their new line. The
State Department, undisposed to assume definitive positions, preferred to treat the Israeli-Syrian border situation with the familiar palliatives of United Nations procedure.

The Soviet note was the first of a series in which the Russians built
up their case against Israel. Three of these notes, in connection with
the raid-and-reprisal cycle that began in the fall of the year, were

delivered to the Foreign Ministry in Jerusalem, the others to Ambassador Katz in Moscow. Their main thrust was to accuse the Israelis of military collusion in a plot against Syria. The Israelis' unvarying reply was to deny such complicity and at the same time to make clear they were determined to respond with force to the Syrian El Fatah actions, at a time and in a manner of their choosing. The submission of the notes was always followed by an informal exchange, and both the notes and the oral exchanges varied in tone. But whether they were harsh in language, or sober and moderate, they carried the same message and monotonously repeated the same two themes. The Russians clearly feared the political consequences of escalation on the Syrian border. They realized their inability to restrain the Syrians and, understandably, took alarm. Their alternative was to try to restrain the Israelis. Whenever they were pressed to use their persuasive powers to induce the Syrians to call off El Fatah, they replied that there was nothing they could do about that; El Fatah was the creature of the Central Intelligence Agency and the imperialist oil interests. The second leitmotiv of notes and conversations was a firm reminder that Israel was "in the close vicinity of Soviet borders." This refrain came so persistently that the Israelis could only translate the phrase as a warning whose full significance the Russians were anxiously concerned to put across. They apparently were saying: You are in our backyard, in our area of paramount interest. They apparently were also saying: We will be your ultimate masters, and you would do well to conduct yourselves accordingly. *Don't* touch Syria.

Chuvakhin, the Russian man in Israel, was a former member of the Soviet political intelligence and an industrious diplomat. He was a full-bodied man, physically and mentally active, sly, intelligent, with a quick sense of humor; he could be rude and charming by turns. He was a bona fide member of the Soviet foreign service, which used him on special assignments in view of his previous experience. He had served in Canada and Zanzibar before coming to Israel. He applied himself with energy to his new special task and cultivated an unusually wide range of contacts among the Israeli political parties. On the left he knew Moshe Sneh and at the opposite pole Menachem Begin, the leader of Herut, the party of the extreme, mystical and nationalist right and the political heir of the pre-independence terrorist organization, Irgun Zvai Leumi, which Begin had headed. Chuvakhin's twofold assignment was to deter Israel from taking action against Syria and to make an evaluation of what Israel would in fact do. To the Israeli Foreign Office professionals who at one time and another spent hours talking to him, it appeared that Israel nonplused him. He found it difficult to sort out the democratic hubbub of Israeli political opinion and the apparent divergences among men of authority. He was often frankly bewildered. "How," he would ask, "can I make an evaluation of this country?" He complained that Eshkol, who was a sensible man, would make a provocative statement while Dayan, who was a militant, would say something conciliatory and Allon would say something else. Even the "militarist clique" disagreed with itself. Eshkol, on one occasion, sought to explain this phenomenon to him. Communication between the two men was easy; they had not only their language in common but their memories of prerevolutionary Russia. There was no fuss or fluster over protocol; tea was served and they conversed alone. Eshkol, using the human approach that was his natural vein, recalled his youthful experiences in the Zionist movement in the old days in the Ukraine. As for Israeli diversity, he offered a simple antithesis. "In the Soviet Union," he said, "you have a thousand minds but you speak with only one voice. Here in Israel, we speak with a thousand voices but we are of one mind in a showdown." Chuvakhin waved this aside as a tricky sophistry. He was interested in the Marxist contradictions of Israeli society, if that indeed was what they were—the discontents expressed by Western European immigrants for whom life was hard and strange in the new country, and the re-emigration from Israel of people who failed to find the opportunities they had expected to find there. He saw that Israel in 1966 was knee-deep in an economic swamp and that unemployment figures were at their highest level in the history of the state. He heard the political dissonance of the various parties, and weighing all these symptoms on his own scale, the Marxist dialectic of capitalist decline, he found they pointed toward inevitable disintegration. As for the critical matter at hand—Israel's determination to protect the lives of her citizens against Syria—he may well have suspected Israeli motives and almost certainly he missed the psychological point, given the negligible physical dimensions of the problem. In Russian terms, the casualties that Israel sustained were trifling. The deaths of hundreds of Soviet soldiers on the China frontier might go unnoticed and unmourned in the Soviet Union if Moscow decided not to notice or to mourn them. Israel was a riddle for the Russian official mind, and a

Soviet diplomat probably could not take Israeli protestations about El Fatah raiding at face value.

On October 12 Eshkol called Chuvakhin to his office in Jerusalem. On the same day he summoned the ambassadors of the United States, Britain and France, for separate interviews. Three days earlier, at Sha'ar Hegolan in the north, four Israeli border policemen had been killed by the blast of a saboteur's mine. On October 10, in an article entitled "General Rabin Rattles His Saber," *Pravda* reported a "partial mobilization" of Israeli reserves and a menacing concentration on the Syrian frontier, and accused Israel of plotting the invasion of Syria. It was, of course, a coincidence that the terrorist mine had killed the four Israelis and *Pravda* had published its accusations within a few hours of each other. The sabotage warfare across the border and the anti-Israeli press barrage in Moscow had reached a peak at the same time, and the conjunction of the two events prompted Eshkol to see the four ambassadors. On the day after the mine blast, in a speech to the paratroopers, he had warned that Israel would deliver a "proper response . . . at a time and place of our choosing"; and an answering voice from Damascus, that of Prime Minister Zayen, had said that Syria would "never retreat from the popular liberation war to recover Palestine." "We are not sentinels over Israel's security," Zayen said, "and are not the leash that restrains the revolution of the displaced and persecuted Arab Palestinian people."

For more than five months *Pravda* and other Soviet publications had been arraigning Israel as a stooge of American imperialism. Sometimes they spoke of troop concentrations, sometimes of the "aggressive plans" of Israeli "extremist circles," sometimes of Israeli partnership with the imperialist powers in an anti-Syrian conspiracy. Usually these charges were broadly wrapped in innuendo. The *Pravda* accusations of October 10 were more explicit. "It appears," the Communist Party newspaper said, "that Israeli reactionary militarist circles, no longer content with provoking border incidents, are harboring plans for a deep armed invasion of Syrian territory to overthrow the government which exists in that country."

Eshkol expressed his concern over these allegations in his talks with the three Western ambassadors. He asked the Western powers to use their influence, which was small, to restrain the Syrian Government. He said that "Israel cannot but see the Arab rulers of Syria and

Jordan as responsible" for the border troubles. Thus he blamed not only the Syrian instigators but those through whose territory the saboteurs passed. At his meeting with Chuvakhin, after denying the Soviet charges and citing official statements in which Syria had taken full responsibility for the terrorist raids, he requested that the Soviet Government exert itself to bring moderation in Damascus. He never received an answer to this request. The next communication from Moscow was a note that reached the Israeli Foreign Ministry the following day. "According to the information in our possession," it said, "a concentration of Israeli troops can again be discerned along the Syrian frontier, and preparations are being made for an air attack on the areas bordering the Syrian frontier, so that in its wake Israeli troops may penetrate deep into Syria. The Chief of Staff of the Israeli Defense Forces recently announced in public that Israel's military preparations 'will be directed first and foremost against the present regime in Syria.' These acts bear witness to the ceaseless attempts of extremist circles in Israel to increase their operations against neighboring Arab states with independent policies, and particularly against the Syrian Arab Republic. . . ." On the same day, October 13, Chuvakhin asked for a return interview with Eshkol.

His first task at that meeting was to check Israel. As the party who had requested the interview on the instructions of his government, he led with the attack. He protested against the mobilization of *twelve* Israeli brigades along the Syrian frontier. The central exhibit in his case was the statement by the Chief of Staff that had been highlighted in the Soviet note: Rabin had issued his warning to the Syrians in an interview the previous month with an Israeli military affairs correspondent. This was incriminating evidence of Israel's evil designs. Chuvakhin hammered away at it; he was anxious, under the cover of accusation, to probe Israel's real intentions. At the same time the best way to deter the Israelis from a major retaliation was to accuse them of planning an invasion. The other main counts in Chuvakhin's indictment were drawn from the twilight abstract world of Marxist projecting; they concerned the hidden hand of imperialism; they were shadowy, melodramatic and unanswerable. The reactionary militarist clique in Israel was plotting the downfall of the Syrian Government, instigated by the Western oil interests, evidently those in Iraq and Saudi Arabia whose pipelines to the Mediterranean passed through Syrian territory. The C.I.A. was the master link in this conspiracy and the Israeli armed forces were its instrument. The Israeli activists, thus, were continually seeking a provocation that would serve as a pretext for massive military intervention in Syria. This was the meaning of the twelve brigades. These were the conclusions on which the Russians based their facts.

Eshkol, denying the troop concentrations, assured Chuvakhin that everything was normal on the Israeli side of the frontier. Appropriately unmollified and unconvinced, Chuvakhin kept to his brief. Eshkol invited him to visit the border region to see for himself. "Let's go immediately," he said, and offered to accompany the Ambassador on a tour of the area in the Prime Ministerial car. Chuvakhin replied: "We know better in Moscow. When my government sends me information, I don't check on it or question it."

Chuvakhin, of course, had no choice but to decline the invitation with ill grace. At any rate, if his reply was curt, it was forthright in its cynicism. He must be credited with knowing perfectly well what he was saying and doing. The report of the twelve brigades he had received from Moscow was political and not military information; it was an unverifiable figure of speech, a kind of sign language, a manner of speaking. Chuvakhin knew very well there was no such thing as a standing Israeli concentration on the border. He knew that a massing against Syria, if it came, would come overnight; and given the structure of the Israeli armed forces, even partial mobilization entailed a disruption of civilian life, and all Tel-Aviv would know about it the moment it happened. Israeli brigades did not mobilize, mass and sit on the Syrian or any other border in the manner of a World War I disposition; if there was to be a strike, it would occur suddenly, in hours. If there were troop movements in the form of a feint in some other part of the country, these too could be hidden from no one. Cognizant of these circumstances, Chuvakhin knew, as Eshkol knew, that his information did not come from Soviet military intelligence; the military men could not possibly be so horribly wrong about facts that were so easy to check. When he talked of troop concentrations, he was shouting protectively; the twelve brigades were merely the paraphrase of a Soviet fear.

There is no way of knowing what the Soviet leaders really thought and believed at this moment. They certainly were not shamming their alarm over Syria. But whether they believed their own tale of conspiracy is a very different matter. Their haste in taking the new Syrian regime under their wing and their zeal in protecting it had no doubt been heightened by their suspicions of the United States at a time when Sukarno and others in the nonaligned world had fared so badly. They had accepted the Syrians' own estimate of their situation, and the two paranoias had probably fed each other. Perhaps they really believed in an American plot with Israel as the military proxy. Perhaps the enormous notion of a C.I.A.–Rabin–oil magnate conspiracy, so obdurately rooted in the fancy of Soviet diplomats in Israel, was merely another metaphor, a vivid image for the Soviet fear of an eventual American push to unseat the new men in Damascus. The second guess is probably closer to the mark. The Russians were proceeding throughout on the basis of a political assessment and not of any facts they had received from their intelligence services.

They were working without facts, but they were using "information." The recurrent alarms, the alleged troop concentrations, the warnings of imminent invasion on this or that date, at the end of the month or the beginning of the next, were something more than an elaborate yarn for Arab mass consumption. They became an instrument of policy, not only a cautionary weapon against the Israelis but a means of political incitement to the Arabs. Invented in Damascus and patented in Moscow, the twelve brigades became a device of the Soviet intelligence in Damascus and soon found their way, in modified form, to Cairo. It was irrelevant whether the Russians had first heard the story of the Israeli border massings in the Damascus bazaar, or had picked it up from Syrian intelligence or had thought of it themselves. Two days after Chuvakhin's meeting with Eshkol, it achieved international currency when Nikolai Federenko, the Soviet delegate, reported at the United Nations: ". . . we know that, of late, Israel has been concentrating large military forces on the Syrian border. In areas adjacent to Syria, military maneuvers are being staged. A large number of landing troops, equipped with artillery and mine-sweepers, have been thrown in. There has been a partial mobilization of reserves in Israel. In addition, there is information that an air attack is being prepared in Israel against neighboring Syrian territory in preparation for an intrusion of Israeli forces deep in Syrian territory." The phantom brigades, swelling sometimes to sixteen or eighteen, sometimes retreating to thirteen and occasionally dropping to eleven or nine, as they passed back and forth between Soviet, Syrian and Egyptian intelligence, were destined to have a lively career in the seven months that followed their first appearance in Eshkol's office. On the high political plane, the plane of Nasser, the reports in due course were recognized for what they were—a conventional signal, a manner of speaking, a political prompting, when they came from the Russians; and simply another impatient goad when they came from the Syrians. The Russians were dealing in misinformation both as propaganda and as sign language; and in the Arab society, so naturally permeated by misinformation on so many levels and so receptive to it, so easily and warmly seized with fantasy, Chuvakhin's figure of speech was to have many remarkable uses.

Israel did not retaliate for the deaths of her four men. In a speech to the Knesset on October 18, Eshkol regretted that "a world power with which Israel desires to have sincere friendship" was circulating the "foolish charge" that Israel was planning to attack Syria as part of an international conspiracy. To the Soviet Union he said: "The defense of the lives and rights of its citizens is one of the primary duties of any government. To describe the matter as part of an international conspiracy is a flagrant distortion of the truth." Two days later he observed: "It takes courage not to make war immediately on being attacked. It is necessary to wait and see—that is not a sign of weakness." By then, a team of United Nations military observers had reported there was no build-up in the Israeli-Syrian border area, after inspecting it along its whole length to a depth of ten kilometers on either side. The Israelis received another Soviet note of protest and reproof within the week, and a third was to follow fifteen days later. The warnings from Moscow seemed to become more turbid each time they were replayed. The note of November 9, after accusing "foreign imperialist forces" of "trying to interfere in the internal affairs of the Syrian state [and] organize conspiracies against her," declared: "The timing of the incidents which, according to the Israeli Government's memorandum, recently occurred on Israeli soil, and which resulted in loss of life, and are aforementioned devices of the said powers, can only lead one to wonder to what extent it is possible that this type of incident was organized expressly by well-known services, or by agencies of these services, for provocation purposes. History has examples of such provocations. Can they be accepted lightly by the nations?"

Among those who were curious to explore the recesses of the Soviet mind at this time was Moshe Sneh and, knowing Chuvakhin, he found more than one occasion to do so. He, the Ambassador and others at the Soviet Embassy in Tel-Aviv had several far-ranging discussions in which they argued the issue down to the ground. Their talks would begin with the immediate issue of the border raids. Sneh would argue that even if the Russians disapproved of the Israeli policy of reprisal, they could not ignore the raids by El Fatah that had provoked them. Chuvakhin and his colleagues said they did not know just who or what the El Fatah bands really were; and in any case, the Syrian Government was not responsible for them. But, Sneh protested, the bands were operating from Syrian soil and the government should be urged to control them. Why wasn't this done? Chuvakhin replied that the Syrians were too weak and unsure of themselves to attempt it. But, Sneh persisted, even admitting this was true, why did the government-controlled radio put itself at El Fatah's service, broadcasting its communiqués and applauding its deeds? And even supposing it was too weak to withhold this radio privilege, why did the President of Syria, among others, publicly extol the stirring feats of the saboteurs? At this point the Russians tacked sideways and admitted that, in fact, they did try to abate the heat of Syrian belligerence. Well then, said Sneh, pursuing them on this new course, why, if this is true, do you support Syria in all your public statements? Surely there must be some consistency between what you advise the Syrians in private and what you publicly tell the world. The Russian argument tacked again and headed toward an entirely new horizon. Don't you understand, Chuvakhin said, that these El Fatah bands are most probably imperialist agents, provocateurs hired and organized by the C.I.A.? That Israel is using them in order to play her part? That the American and British oil companies want to overthrow the Syrian Government? And that the whole plot is being abetted by the militarist clique in Tel-Aviv? Sneh, a strong logician, set out in pursuit again. What rot and nonsense, he declared. What would be more certain to unite the Arab world behind Syria, and isolate Israel, and condemn the United States in the eyes of all Arabs, than an American-Israeli coup in Damascus? Or rather an attempt to provoke such a coup by military intervention? What would be more certain to bolster the Syrian regime? And Sneh went on for a further point. When we staged a reprisal action against Jordan, he said, you accused us of reinforcing King Hussein; you can't have it both ways; our raids cannot strengthen a regime in one country and topple it in another.

But the argument shed no light; it was a grapple in the dark. Like

Eshkol, Sneh offered his car and proposed that Chuvakhin and he visit
the border zone together. The Ambassador declined. Sneh and Mikunis, however, left the obscurity of their discussions at the Soviet Embassy with one firm impression. The talks convinced them of the in-
sincerity of the Soviet case. Chuvakhin's arguments, they felt, were
the cover for Soviet collusion with Damascus in a larger affair, and
the twelve brigades were a gambit in a political maneuver that had
other ends in view.

Early in November, Soviet diplomacy achieved a notable success.
Since the spring of the year, it had been the Russians' fixed purpose
to bring Egypt and Syria together again after their long estrangement.
The goal of re-establishing the Cairo-Damascus axis commended itself for many practical immediate reasons, quite apart from their
more distant aims in the region. The Syrians needed a shot in the arm.
They were fearfully alone, both at home and in the Arab world. A
renewal of the Egyptian bond and association with the one effective
Arab leader would brace them in their isolation. Nasser himself badly
needed a boost. Something had to be done to rescue him from his
morass of troubles—the stalemated mess in Yemen, the disaffection
at home, the deflation of the revolutionary mood, the slough of crisis.
On the inter-Arab scene as well, his policies were insolvent. Many
Arab states were ignoring or sabotaging his will and beginning to
boggle at summitry even before he interred it. If the Syrians needed
political reinsurance, Nasser needed inter-Arab rehabilitation. The
Russians' main preoccupation was to promote Arab unity in a way
that would strengthen the regimes of both Damascus and Cairo. Their
second ambition was to bring them together under Nasser's leadership. They were persuaded, as all the great powers were persuaded,
that he was the Arabs' only first-rank statesman and only possible
protagonist. He was the Deliverer; the Russians accepted the messianic image and fostered it. Most urgently of all, they wanted his help
in Damascus. They needed a more stable leader with whom they
could work and whom they could more reasonably hope to control,
and who in turn had every interest in controlling the Syrians.

They sought to persuade Nasser to adopt a bolder policy of protection, to give self-confidence to the Damascus regime or at least relieve
it of some of its phobic insecurity. At the same time, they sought to
sell the attractions of a bilateral defense pact to the Syrians. This
could not have been an easy undertaking. The Syrians cherished no

fond memories of Egyptian rule, while Nasser held the recalcitrant young men of the Baath in utter opprobrium. The first visible sign of tentative rapprochement was a trip to Damascus by the Egyptian Foreign Minister, Mahmoud Riad, in July, the first visit any Egyptian Minister had deigned to make there since the end of the United Arab Republic. The fact was that both the Syrians and Nasser wanted and did not want a mutual defense pact. The Syrians wanted Nasser's name and glory but not his authority or his hold; they wanted to tie him to them and not vice versa. Nasser aspired as always to regain a foothold in the Arab capital that had expelled him, but he recoiled from any commitment to the men who ruled there. In the event, the Russians had an easier job in Damascus than in Cairo. They overcame Syrian reticence and misgiving, and then rallied Syrian support for the project.

Nasser's reluctances and resistances went much deeper. The Soviet proposal raked the coals of ancient and abiding mistrust. He knew his Syrians; no one was more sagaciously alert than he to the dangers of a Syrian involvement. He did not want to assume responsibility for the *enfants terribles*. If he were tied to them, he argued, he would be tied to their adventures; *they* would ignite the catastrophe and he would pay the price. He could not possibly give Syria a formal guarantee against any and all attack by Israel, and it is extremely improbable that the Russians wanted him to do so. What was an attack? A border raid? A local air strike? The object was not to put Nasser at the mercy of the Syrians and El Fatah, but to strengthen his hand in curbing them. It was the old, wearisome story and Nasser had been through it time and again. He had always said he would never return to Damascus except with full authority. His negotiations with the Baath for the revival of the Egyptian-Syrian union had broken down on this point in the spring of 1963. He had wanted a restoration pure and simple, under his personal hegemony as President, with no nonsense about multiparty democracy and with the Baath, therefore, graciously dissolving itself. The Baath did not acquiesce in these terms and the talk of reunion evaporated.

The defense pact, nonetheless, was a temptation. There was the tug of memory, the old shock of the Syrian breakaway, the nostalgic ambition of the pan-Arab leader to get back again into Arab Asia. Nasser was being offered his former title of Protector of Syria and, after all, it was the Russians who were offering it to him. We have no means of knowing to what extent the Soviet promptings influenced him; he played his own wary game with the Russians and kept his cards covered; but still, they were powerful sponsors. Early in autumn the converted Syrians began pressing him hard. They reported that *nine* Israeli brigades were massed in Israel's northeastern corner opposite the Syrian frontier, and it appears that for a week or so he believed it. He took the obvious precaution of sending his intelligence officers to Syria to check out the story and they reported it was not true. On October 31 Zayen went to Cairo. On November 5 the Egyptian-Syrian Defense Pact was signed there. Whatever brought Nasser to his final and perhaps reluctant decision, he did not decide on the basis of military misinformation.

Did the Egyptians or the Syrians get the better of the bargain? As a military agreement, it was fraudulent hocus-pocus, as both sides recognized. Neither committed itself to anything. Egypt and Syria already were joined in a United Arab Command, and Egypt already was bound to go to the aid of Syria against Israeli "attack." The defense pact added nothing to these vague understandings. Nasser had said the United Arab Command would never be effective as long as Egyptians and Syrians eyed each other with "lurking" mistrust. His judgment was sound, and the new pact did nothing to appease the mistrust. The Syrians refused to permit the stationing of Egyptian troops or Egyptian air force units on their territory, and declined to give Nasser any manner of control over their forces. Nasser gave no guarantee and assumed no new responsibility for Syria's defense. Both sides agreed they would not go to war without consulting the other—a clear avowal of mistrust; but this provision was of little help or relevance under the circumstances. It was not a question of the Egyptians or Syrians going to war in impetuous folly without consultation, but of El Fatah's flipping them into one. On this point the defense pact was silent.

Precisely because the pact was an empty bag, people at the time tended to assume it concealed a special meaning somewhere. Supererogatory as a military agreement, it must have a political purpose. In this, indeed, they were right. The general assumption, however, was that Nasser had agreed to sign in order to keep the Syrians from ensnaring him in a general war with Israel. Since he was known to want to restrain the Syrians, even some Israeli professionals concluded that he would now be in a stronger position to restrain them. But in the end it was the Syrians who got the better of the deal. They had exposed Nasser—on paper—to new military risks but had accorded him no powers with which to face them; they had granted him no military positions on the ground. He was Syria's Protector now, and by virtue of his signature more vulnerable to the slings and arrows of recrimination. All in all, the Syrians had improved their blackmailing position. Already, they had turned Nasser's flank on the lowest level of rivalry between El Fatah and the Palestine Liberation Army. In that contest, El Fatah was the winning group, the organization that was increasingly popular not only in Syria but generally in the Arab countries. Nasser himself had acknowledged this check by reversing his line, rhetorically and for the Arab record. He had spoken with favor of those who bravely took the destiny of Palestine into their own hands. As early as July 27, he had struck the note: "Our new road lies through cooperation with Arab revolutionaries and fighters who work toward the liberation of Palestine by deeds and not by words." It was the Damascus line. Before the summer was over, the Palestine Liberation Army was suiting the action to the tune, with a sabotage raid on the railway station near Jerusalem. Shukheiry's men had the foresight to prepare suitable leaflets, which they scattered at the scene, declaring the deed to be their work and identifying themselves as "the heroes of the return."

Nasser had no delusions as to his power to control the Syrians. He knew them better than the Russians did and he recognized the indeterminate risks of the Syrian compact. He soon made explicit reservations about it. On November 24, he told the Egyptian National Assembly: "The road of return [to Palestine] is long and difficult. The biggest obstacle along the way is the alliance of Zionist racism with imperialism supported by [Arab] reaction. The United Arab Republic [Egypt] therefore reserves to itself absolute freedom of action in harmony and cooperation with the Arab revolutionary forces which alone are capable of action. In view of this, it authorizes those forces to make the final decision regarding the date and place of any battle." The gnarled phrasing of Egyptian revolutionary prose needs to be transcribed. Nasser was saying that he alone would decide when to start the battle for Palestine, since Syria was the junior partner in the revolutionary alliance, and command of the alliance lay with Egypt. He could not control Syria or El Fatah, but he could and would reserve the sole right to determine what kind of "attack" brought into operation the terms of the agreement. He alone would determine when he was bound and when he was not bound. He would honor his obligations at his discretion. He would not challenge Israel to war simply because the escalation of border raids and reprisals produced some more local clashes. The position was exactly what it had been before the pact of Cairo was signed. Nasser would not go to war for Syrian tractors or bulldozers or even for any Syrian Migs shot down.

His doctrine of the eventual Palestine war had not changed an iota. As he had patiently repeated, in a number of public speeches as well as at the secret councils of the Arab heads of state, the war must await the fulfillment of three essential conditions. The first prerequisite was military readiness, the development of an offensive power capable of reversing the balance of deterrents between the Arab states and Israel. The second was the achievement of Arab unity, the effective unity of the combatant states. The third condition was political: the inevitable war must wait for propitious international circumstances. Each of these conditions was indispensable and all were uncertain visionary goals in the autumn of 1966. At Casablanca the previous year, it had been agreed that Arab preparations would proceed in two phases. The object of the first would be to consolidate inter-Arab military defenses and to win "freedom of action"; freedom, for example, to carry out the counterdiversion of the Jordan headwaters, unhampered and undaunted by the prospect of Israeli intervention. With Jordan, Syria and Lebanon made defensively secure in phase one, the armed forces of Egypt would be the kingpin in the offensive preparations of phase two. No precise dates were set at Casablanca. It was thought that the defensive phase would be completed sometime in 1967 or 1968, but this was one of those dates. In the absence of a precise target for a precise operational program, it is necessary to invent one, against which to measure one's hopes of progress.

As for Arab unity, this was as ever a pious and problematic goal. In setting unity as a condition, Nasser did not of course mean political union. He meant the real and credible coordination of inter-Arab military strength. The collective strength of the Arab armies already was superior to that of Israel. Deployed on paper, they had more planes, more tanks, more guns, more missiles, more everything, and it was high-caliber modern armament. But in fact, Arab "collective" strength did not exist. It was purely notional. The United Arab Command was a shadow, or at best an exercise in lip service. The Arab states were so obsessed by mutual mistrust that Israel was yet another cause of division among them, not a source of unity.

The political condition for war, the "propitious international circumstances," was missing and probably still far from fulfillment. Nasser envisaged a set of hypothetical circumstances that would neutralize the power that stood behind Israel and discourage it from effective intervention. He constantly reminded his audiences that Israel was not merely Israel; she was herself and the Western power who supported her. Usually he defined the enemy as Israel plus imperialism; when he was angry with the Americans, he defined it as Israel plus the United States. The American problem puzzled and worried the Egyptian military thinkers, who were anxious to devise a clever sequence of events in which Egypt would not appear as the aggressor: the United States must be given no manifest pretext for going to Israel's defense. In any case, the only power that could neutralize the United States in the event of war was the Soviet Union, and the Soviet leadership was in no mood for confrontations. The Russians had their hands full in Syria; their immediate task was to consolidate and not expand their commitments. They had taken on all they wanted. Their watchword was caution, not adventure, and the worst thing that could happen would be to draw the United States into the picture.

The Russians could congratulate themselves on the Cairo defense agreement. They had managed to conciliate the fears and suspicions of both sides and had brought off a nominal rapprochement. They had involved Nasser with the Syrians, which was one of their main objectives. At least formally, he had accepted a broad policy of protection over his lost northern province. The Russians had tempted him to take a first step in the direction of Damascus and in due time he might be persuaded to take others.

On the day the pact of Cairo was signed, they made another move in public support of their Syrian friends. After the killing of the four border policemen on October 9, the Israelis had consulted the State Department as to their next step. As on an earlier occasion, they urged the United States to take a definitive stand, especially in view of the Soviet imputations. The State Department countered by proposing recourse to the United Nations Security Council. Eshkol told the Knesset on October 19 that Israel hoped for international condemnation of Syria notwithstanding the Soviet position. The Israelis had as near to an open-and-closed case as it was physically possible to get, on the basis of evidence gathered by United Nations observers. The framing of a resolution was entrusted to six nonpermanent members of the Council—Argentina, Nigeria, Uganda, Holland, New Zealand and Japan, a representative group from four continents. The possibility of a Soviet veto hung like a sword above them, and in the usual manner, anticipating the blow but hoping to ward it off, the six members carefully diluted their draft and presented to the Council a statement of gentle rebuke, inviting Syria to take stronger measures to prevent such incidents. On November 5 the Soviet Union vetoed the resolution that was approved by ten other nations.

It was the fifth veto the Russians had cast in Arab-Israeli disputes at the Council, but the double-edged cut of the sword on this occasion was disastrous. If it did not set the course of events for the following months, it at least sharpened their pace. The Syrians took the veto as a green light, a political victory that shielded them from international censure and encouraged them in their El Fatah warfare. The Israelis saw it as a final demonstration that there was nothing they could hope for from the United Nations. In the absence of international pressure, they would have to rely on their own "deterrent" of reprisal action. In the weeks following the veto, Soviet diplomats at the United Nations and elsewhere spread the word that their colleagues in Damascus were busy trying to moderate the Syrians. There is every reason to suppose that they were, but this does not tell us very much. They probably exerted as much pressure as they thought they prudently could; and how much this was, it is impossible to know. In talks with the Israelis, they sometimes complained about the "Syrian hotheads," and their laments seemed a genuine reflection of worry. Perhaps it was a question of their not knowing how to deal with the Arabs. More probably it was a case of the Kremlin leaders deciding that the Soviet position in the Arab world required them to give unqualified support to the Arabs at every juncture. In any case, the veto did its work, and its practical political effect was to unleash the Syrian extremists. It was also a warning to the interested powers at the United Nations. No resolution to which an Arab state was opposed could possibly win approval, and no matter how far the Arabs might go, the Russians would go with them. They became the voluntary captives of their clients.

Seven days after the veto, a patroling Israeli army half-track hit a mine in the upper Negev desert close to the Jordanian border. Three soldiers were killed and six wounded. At dawn on November 13 a force of nearly four hundred Israeli paratroopers, mounted on armored half-tracks behind a spearhead of eight tanks, struck across the border in a reprisal raid against the Jordanian town of Samua, which was said to harbor the terrorists. The Israeli General Staff had given careful thought to the tactical aspects of the raid and the selection of the target. It had examined a number of alternatives in the light of the varying risks of "reasonable" and "escalated" response. The list of alternates included targets in Syria, and these were excluded because of the danger of escalation. The Syrian response could not be measured. Syrian shelling of Tiberias or Safed in upper Galilee would require a counterresponse that might quickly escalate into general conflict. Syria was the base of El Fatah activity, but the marauders had recently operated more or less freely from Jordan and had carried out thirteen acts of sabotage from her territory. Jordan had been warned. Eshkol had said: "We cannot exempt and we will not excuse the countries from whose territory the saboteurs come, to which they return and in which they are sheltered." Apart from this principle, Jordan was evidently chosen for reasons of military expediency. The Israelis proposed to control the factor of irrational escalation and thereby limit the possible casualties on either side. The government of King Hussein was relatively sensible and sober; the government of the Baath most certainly was not. The Israeli planners took pains that the raid should be clearly seen to be a raid, a local and restricted action, a reprisal and not an invasion; and this consideration dictated the operational scheme as well as the choice of Samua. Towns or villages that were too close to major centers were excluded, so that Jordan would not take fright and wrongly conclude that this was the start of a major expedition. An area was chosen where Jordan was known to have only light units, so as to avoid the risk of a clash with armor. The paratroopers struck crosswise into Jordan from south to north, so it would not be imagined they were heading toward the Jordanian tank camp at Hebron. Finally, they went in daylight, so as to finish their work quickly and be home again in Israel before tanks from Hebron could reach the scene. Above all, in daylight everything would be perfectly clear to everybody on the Jordanian side, and there would be no occasion for excited nocturnal fears.

It was a well-laid plan, but most of its more or less reasonable assumptions were falsified. Militarily the raid was a success; politically, a fiasco. The paratroopers completed their mission without difficulty. They evacuated the people of Samua from the houses that had been selected for demolition, and Israeli sappers blew up forty of them, according to the Israelis; a hundred and twenty-five, according to United Nations observers. But before they had finished their work, chance had contrived an unexpected encounter. What the Israeli General Staff had not foreseen was that the Jordan Legion's radio communications would break down on that morning; that because of the breakdown, a message would never reach the small Arab units in the area, telling them of an Israeli armored force on the approaches to Samua; that a particularly bold Jordanian officer, with precipitate courage, would lead two companies of the Legion in twenty trucks on a rescue dash toward the town; and that, unwarned and unaware, his men would drive headlong into a roadblock of covering tanks. The Jordanians were mowed down in their vehicles. Their appearance on the Samua road was against all the counsels of military logic and all the provisions of foresight. Still greater foresight might have made provision for the arrangements of chance. The United Nations reported eighteen Jordanian soldiers and civilians killed and fifty-four wounded.

The political backfire from the Samua raid was beyond anything Israel had expected. Intended as a prod to Hussein to control the saboteur bands on his territory, it had the opposite effect. The Palestinians on Jordan's West Bank clamored for arms to defend themselves; Hussein had to call on both police and troops to suppress a tumult of riots; and, drawing the wrong conclusion, the King was incurably confirmed in his delusion that Israel's aim was to dislodge him from his throne and proceed to the conquest of the West Bank region. At the United Nations the Israeli action was described as "inexcusable" by the United States and as "wholly disproportionate" by Britain. A raid of any kind against Jordan could not be countenanced when everybody's attention was fixed on Syria. Jordan sought redress, and the Security Council acted with high-minded speed. With New Zealand alone abstaining, it censured Israel for this "large-scale military action" and warned "that actions of military reprisal cannot be tolerated and that if they are repeated, the Security Council will have to consider further and more effective steps as envisaged in the Charter to ensure against the repetition of such acts." Many Israelis found the raid to be ill-judged and said so with asperity; but this did not alter their opinion of the United Nations, which had acted with concerted zeal on behalf of Jordan and, saying little about Arab provocations in its debate, had said nothing at all about them in its resolution. The Samua raid, it was realized, had been futile as a deterrent against Syria. The strong censure that followed it was a constraint on Israel's use of the reprisal deterrent thereafter. To the extent that it limited Israel's freedom to react, it augmented Syria's freedom to provoke.

Conflict along the Israeli-Syrian frontier changed its character and quickened both in pace and temper at the turn of the New Year. Regular forces were more and more frequently engaged. Syrian artillery from the Golan Heights fired on Israeli farms in the demilitarized areas along the border; Israeli artillery responded; tanks and aircraft joined in the exchanges. Most of these incidents revolved around Israel's claim to establish and maintain civilian life in the demilitarized zones—farms with patrols to guard them—and Syria's sporadic resolve to deny the claim with gunfire. The rule and practice of Israeli "response" on the Syrian border was to use artillery and aircraft only against Syrian regular forces and never in reprisal against irregular guerrilla action. On April 7, 1967, the Israelis followed their rule. Israeli Mirages appeared over the border heights after Syrian tanks had opened fire; Syrian Migs came up to meet them; and in the ensuing combat, the Mirages pursued the Migs into Syria as far as the outskirts of Damascus. The score in that encounter was a humiliation for Syria. Six Migs were shot down, with no losses for Israel.

"Large military forces have been concentrated on the northern frontier. . . ." So *Izvestia* had reported in February, adding a flourish or two about the call-up of additional Israeli reservists and the cancelation of leave for all military personnel. In March the Egyptians were again informed by the Syrian intelligence that Israel was massing on her northeastern border, a periodic report that now came with greater urgency. Again Egyptian officers were dispatched to Damascus to check on the report. On this occasion they argued it out with the Syrians, after ascertaining that the Israeli brigades were imaginary. The Syrians contended that the absence of visible evidence was not the point. Given the way the Israeli armed forces were organized, they *could* mobilize overnight in the border zone, and even this was not the point. The United States could order Israel to attack and intended to do so. The Syrians urged that Egypt come to their aid with a demonstration of strength that would prevent this from happening and would guarantee the security of her sister—and allied—Arab nation.

The tide of events was running persistently against the Russians in the early spring of 1967. We have no way of knowing exactly how they understood and assessed the dangers of the situation. But after a year's experience in Damascus, they had clearly been unable to contain Syria for the kind of slow and careful evolution they envisioned. They wished to consolidate the regime's hold on the country and then their own hold on the regime so that in time they might hope to extend their influence to Iraq and build a fairly impressive *cordon sanitaire* to the south of Turkey and west of Iran. The larger design was in jeopardy as long as their Syrian base was exposed and unstable. Until the spring of the year, they had relied on their powers of diplomatic manipulation to resolve their dilemma. They had failed on two fronts. They could not be certain of deterring Israel from a major retaliation, and they had definitely failed to moderate Syria in her intoxicated challenge to Israel. It seemed an inescapable quandary. The three political conditions that made possible an Arab-Israeli confrontation and a war that nobody expected, nobody intended and nobody was thinking of in the early spring were already present. Each was a prerequisite condition. Together they created the circumstances that cleared the way and gave the push to the avalanche. The first of the three was the political stake which the Russians had recently acquired in Syria and which they were determined to guard and preserve. The second was the accelerated violence that sprang from Syria's decision to defy the consensus of the Arab states. The third was Nasser's traumatic tie to the Syrian Arab Republic, where he had once been master and had borne the palm alone. Regarded separately, none of these peculiar conditions seemed treacherous or threatening. The danger that they represented in combination was unperceived. But the convergence of these circumstances and their exploitation were responsible for the crisis that led to war. If the Russians had not taken the Syrian regime under their wing with a purposefulness inspired by their concept of their vital interests in the region; if the Syrians, bewitched by the doctrine of a continuous "People's War," had not broken with the decisions of the Arab Summit; and if Nasser, once the Protector of Syria in fact as well as name, had not been incited by his desperate frustrations on other fronts to respond to the shocks and promptings of the past—if any of these conditions had been missing, the events of May and June, 1967, would not have taken place. All of this is perfectly clear today. It was barely suspected by a few prescient people at the time.

· 5 ·

The Road Back to Sinai

THROUGHOUT THE FIRST FIFTEEN YEARS of the
Egyptian military regime until the Arab-Israeli war of 1967,
American diplomats struggled with the problem of getting along
with Nasser. It was a singularly tantalizing problem. The chart of
American relations with him showed a series of erratic up-and-down
curves, with some happy peaks, several precipitous falls and many
gloomy periods at the bottom. The great watershed of those years was
the Suez crisis of 1956. The United States thereafter was the leading
Western power in the area, Soviet Russia was the leading challenger,
and the hero who had nationalized the Canal became the champion of
Arab rights against the imperialist powers who were everywhere opposing the march of Arab nationalism. The Americans' first response
to this new situation was to enunciate a policy, later known as the
Eisenhower Doctrine, requiring the Middle Eastern countries to stand
up and be counted, for the United States or against it, for the Communists or against them. The Doctrine was a summons to the Arab states
to abandon the crooked path of neutralism and join the Western
camp. It was a false start, and in the psychological war for Arab
favor, it was soon discredited. Both Nasser and the Russians had an
easy time demonstrating to Arab opinion that it was merely a pretext
for imperialist intervention, with the Americans taking over the
odious role of the British and French.

Enlightened by its errors, the United States discarded the rigidities of the Cold War and devised a more sophisticated approach. The Russians were in the Middle East to stay and the Americans recognized they would have to find a better way of adapting themselves to this irreversible fact. The Eisenhower Doctrine was quietly hidden away in the policy cupboard and the doctrine of nonpolarization was produced in its stead. This was a policy not so much of live-and-let-live as of competition by all means short of a divisive East-West alignment. Nobody should be compelled to make a final choice; the Russians must not be allowed to corner any part of the market; and it was better to share Arab favor with them than to let them become the only popular great power in the area.

Another undeniable fact was the preponderant importance of Egypt. Politically and strategically, Egypt was the gateway to the region, and of all the Arab countries it had the greatest potential for development, notwithstanding its ancient poverty and its meager natural resources. The dilemma of the Americans was basic and acute. How could they come to terms with Nasser, the nationalist leader who wanted to modernize his country and prosecute a pan-Arab revolution at the same time? To achieve the modernization of Egypt, he needed the friendship and assistance of the United States, but to establish Egyptian hegemony in the Arab world in pursuit of his revolutionary mission, he was continually attacking its interests and subverting its friends in the area. He shared with the Russians the general aim of expelling the United States from its positions of authority and influence. Nevertheless, the Americans reckoned, it was not too late to find some middle road of give-and-take collaboration. It was still possible to develop a sensible working relationship, if the problem of Israel could be kept in the icebox. Nasser, a redoubtable figure, was also there to stay, and Egypt was too important to be left to the Russians.

This was the American outlook and philosophy when, in 1962, on the decision of President Kennedy and under his personal direction, the United States launched a supreme effort to get along with Nasser. The new course was ambitiously conceived and carefully plotted; its grand goal was to achieve a *modus vivendi*. The United States undertook to feed the Egyptian people and thereby sustain the Egyptian regime for a period of three years. Egypt would receive nearly half a billion dollars' worth of wheat, for most of which she would pay with her own currency. The wheat would release her foreign exchange, and with the long-term provisions of the contract, leaping over the usual American procedures requiring year-by-year renegotiation, she would be able to plan her imports and purchase the industrial equipment and other goods she needed for her development program. These arrangements converted a food program into a subsidy of the Egyptian economy. American wheat became the financial base for Egyptian industrial advancement.

The first wheat under the new contract was delivered in July, 1962. Three months later Nasser set in motion a train of events that in the end were to cost him his American subsidy, bring his country to bankruptcy, isolate him in the Arab world and destroy his relationship with the United States. These events revolved around the war in Yemen. Their background and origin were something of a mystery at the time. Some diplomats insisted that Nasser had had no plans for a Yemeni adventure and must have been prompted by an accident of history: the Yemeni Free Officers had revolted on September 27, the first anniversary of the breakup of the union with Syria. Nasser, it was thought, had acted impulsively, urged by the black memories of the wrong that had been done him in Damascus on that day. Others believed he himself had engineered the Yemeni coup. An Egyptian military mission had been in Yemen for two years; it had recruited and encouraged the band of republican Free Officers in the Yemeni Army; and after their uprising, Yemeni political exiles in Cairo and Aden immediately flew home to join the new revolutionary government. Strange to tell, the archaic kingdom of Yemen had enjoyed a treaty of friendship with the Soviet Union since 1928, and after renewing that treaty the old Imam, Achmed, the fiercest of Arabia's feudal despots, had been persuaded in 1956 to follow Nasser's example and seek arms from the Eastern bloc. His ragtag army had thus come into possession of Czechoslovak and Soviet weapons. His son, Prince Mohammed Badr, had visited Moscow and Warsaw and had even journeyed to Peking to sign a ten-year trade and assistance agreement with the Chinese Communists. On his visits to Cairo, Badr had professed his pan-Arab faith and his devotion to the ideal of Arab unity. As a result of his travels, hundreds of Communist road-builders, technicians and engineers from both China and Europe had invaded his father's timeless domain, a decayed but exotic relic of medieval Islam, firmly planted in the fourteenth century and fanatically closed to strangers.

Achmed and Badr were not guileless men and their positive neutralism was not as naïve as it seemed. It was political insurance in changing times, hopefully intended to protect them from the onslaughts of propaganda and subversion that Nasser usually reserved for Arabian monarchs. Early in September, 1962, the old Imam died. His son and successor had every reason to believe he was fully in step with the times and with Nasser. Instead, on September 27, the Free Officers of the revolution shelled his palace—a tall, cramped structure on a narrow street in the capital city of Sana—and executed all members of the royal family whom they caught. Such is the grim custom of Yemen. The rebels, however, bungled their job by failing to capture and execute Badr. The new Imam escaped with his bodyguard over the garden wall, fled to the north, rallied the mountain tribes and appealed to the Saudi Arabians for help. His leap over the garden wall was historic. He established his home and his headquarters in a cave and lived to fight for many another day.

Neither of the two theories as to Nasser's role in these events was correct. He did not mastermind or direct the Yemeni revolution. Neither did he go into Yemen on the spur of the moment. The truth lay at a curious point midway between the two conjectures. The Egyptians in Yemen were fully aware that the revolution was coming. They told the Yemeni Free Officers: Go ahead, and if you need help, you will have it. It was not Nasser's choice but the old Imam's death that determined the timing. Nasser, as usual, intended to exploit events, in this case an event that he expected. He had no contingency plan for the revolution and no considered program when he rushed to its aid. He anticipated a short revolt. If the Free Officers ran into trouble, he would send some Egyptian troops to rescue them. He would tip the scales for republican victory with very few men. He did not take the plunge impulsively; he merely took it improvidently, thoughtlessly and in complete ignorance of the land and people of Yemen.

As far as anyone could judge at the beginning, the coup in Sana was a great success. The leader of the revolution and Prime Minister of the new republic, Colonel Abdullah Sallal, was in tranquil command of the capital. After a few days, however, the northern tribes were rising against him, and he was asking for help. Nasser sent a few planeloads of troops and a few bombers to quell the dissident tribesmen and thought this would be enough. In answer to a further call, he sent three thousand commandos and believed this would be enough. By the end of the year some thirteen thousand Egyptian soldiers were stationed in Yemen; more than twenty thousand by the spring of the next; a year later, twice as many, and in time, an expeditionary force of seventy thousand men.

The Egyptians knew in a general way that Yemen was a tropical country. Beyond that they apparently did not bother to inform themselves about the climate or topography of the land or the character of the society they would find there. They were unprepared for the seasonal rains that come twice a year, in the early spring and again in the autumn; unequipped for the heavy winter snows and ten-degree Fahrenheit cold in the Yemeni mountains; unaware that for centuries those mountains had bred stubborn rebellion among tribes whose spirit of martial independence was nurtured by the rude fanaticism of Moslem sects. Had he consulted the Turks, Nasser might have learned that Yemen had been the cemetery of thousands of their soldiers. The tribes in the mountain interior of northern Yemen had never submitted to the Ottoman armies. The Turks had fought them and settled with them, and then withdrawn to their strongpoints in the coastal plain, to confine their rule to the maritime rim of the country. In more civilized parts of the Arab world, control of the army meant supremacy in the nation; not so in Yemen, where every man was a warrior. The Egyptians sent their troops in summer khaki to endure the hardships of mountain warfare during their first winter.

Nasser received the usual flattering reports of decisive victories in the months and years that followed. The victories were not fictitious. Whenever the Egyptian Army concentrated enough troops in one sector, it was victorious. But its victories were never decisive and its gains could never be held. After a few months, as the Egyptian troops thinned out, the tribesmen would come back again, with arms supplied by Saudi Arabia and, later, by Jordan, Iran and Pakistan. This recurring pattern of dissipated military gains set the trap for political disaster. The greater their military frustrations, the more troops the Egyptians sent in; the more troops they sent, the more political support they lost as the tribes gathered against them. To maintain their army in the field and to continue a war they could not win, they proceeded to impose their dominion on Yemen. Republican ardor waned and republican support faded away. Hundreds of Egyptian administrators, advisers and teachers descended on Sana; Egyptian bureaucrats directed the Yemeni ministries; revulsion against the occupying power spread on all levels of the republican government. Republican ranks were split between those who despised the colonizer and those who were too committed to survive without him. Nasser's small band of military jackals was intransigent for war; the majority of republican politicians wanted to make common cause with the royalists to get the Egyptians out, conciliate the tribes and bring peace to the country.

The Egyptian Army went into Yemen to "defend the revolution" at the request of Colonel Sallal's government. After two and a half years of civil war, a representative republican government, had such existed, would have withdrawn the request and invited the Egyptians to go home. Nasser by then had only two reliable jackals left, Major General Hassan Amri, a diehard of the war party, and the ever faithful Sallal, who as President of the Republic had conferred on himself the rank of Field Marshal. Sallal in 1965 rejected Nasser's peace agreement with Feisal and refused to attend the meeting of Yemeni republicans and royalists that was supposed to implement it. Nasser summoned him to Cairo and detained him for nine months, and chose Amri as Prime Minister and Acting President during the interregnum. In March, 1966, the Egyptian Army began evacuating its last strongholds in northern and eastern Yemen. The local tribes again took over, and the Egyptians thereafter sought to keep them quiet with monthly handouts of food and arms. Even Amri, however, began to fret under Egyptian tutelage. He sought greater authority for the Yemeni Republic; he wanted the republican army to be paid by the Yemeni Treasury rather than directly by Egypt; and he stoutly opposed the suggestion that Sallal return to Sana. His loyalty became suspect in Cairo. He was showing too much independence; there was even the danger that his government might formally request the withdrawal of Egyptian troops from the country. In August, 1966, Nasser decided to get rid of him and ordered Sallal to fly home to Sana to reassume command as President.

The Sana airport was a scene of boisterous contention in the hours before his arrival. Yemeni troops at Amri's order occupied the field, intending apparently either to prevent Sallal's plane from landing or arrest him on arrival or redispatch him to Cairo. Egyptian Army units hastened to the airport, evicted the Yemenis and assured the Field Marshal's safe conduct into the capital. His return was the signal for violent anti-Egyptian demonstrations in the main towns. More Ministers defected and more tribes deserted the republican camp. Egyptian troops quelled the demonstrations, Egyptian planes bombed the rebellious tribes, and the Egyptian Army Commander, joining Sallal's new National Defense Council, in which the Egyptians formed the majority, took charge of purges and appointments. Amri, nevertheless, held his ground and insisted that Sallal be recalled to Cairo. On September 8, with a delegation of forty-one colleagues that included eight Ministers and twenty-eight senior officers, he flew to Cairo to present his case. Neither Amri nor any member of his party succeeded in seeing Nasser. The Egyptian police escorted him and his principal associates to various villas about Cairo and placed them under house arrest.

Thus began the final stage of Egyptian rule in Yemen. With Amri boxed away in Cairo, Sallal produced a new government, purged the army and police, arrested thousands and, after a two-hour trial, executed seven of Amri's chief adherents, among them a Minister and a former Deputy Chief of Staff. They were charged with a number of heinous transgressions against the Republic: they had plotted against Sallal, they had bombed the Presidential palace and they had received Saudi Arabian and British money. Egyptian troops thereafter stood guard at Sallal's residence and all other government buildings in Sana. The colonial power ruled alone; republican Yemen was an occupied country. When, in December, several tribes south of Sana rebelled, the Egyptian Air Force bombed, with gas, their mountain villages and the caves where their families had taken refuge.

Nasser would have called off his profitless war if his ambitions had not extended beyond the borders of Yemen. He had many opportunities to reach a settlement. He could have honored his agreement with Feisal, withdrawn his army, accepted a referendum and permitted Yemen to go back to the tribes. He would have done so if greater temptations had not urged him to stay on. The enemy was not Badr but Feisal. Yemen was of no interest to him in itself, but from his Yemeni base, he could aspire to dispute with Feisal the political future of southern Arabia. He could strike in two ways—directly at the Saudi Arabians by some combination of military harassment and internal subversion, and indirectly at Feisal's feudal confederates, the sheikhs and sultans of the Aden Protectorate who were soon to be forsaken by their British patrons. At Taiz in southern Yemen, the terrorist undergrounds of the Protectorate received arms, ammunition, cash and training from the Egyptian Army Intelligence, and thence made their way to Aden to blow up British army vehicles, murder British servicemen and hasten the retreat of British power. Nasser probably believed he could count on a swift victory as soon as the British left. A national liberation front directed by Cairo would then seize power in Aden, and if necessary the Egyptian Army would move in from Yemen at the invitation of the revolutionary government. The Egyptians would have an easy time sweeping up the enfeebled remnants of feudalism.

The Americans' overriding concern was to prevent the war in Yemen from spreading to Saudi Arabia. Feisal's single purpose was to get Egyptian troops out of Yemen and eliminate the Nasserist menace at his doorstep. In answer to Badr's appeal, he supplied arms to the royalist tribes from two Saudi Arabian bases, at Najran and Jizan, near the Yemeni border, and so exposed these desert camps to the imminent threat of Egyptian bombing. In the summer of 1963, invoking commitments under the Mutual Security Act that went back to the Administration of President Truman, he sent out his first call for air protection, and the Americans responded by flying F-104 Starfighters to Saudi Arabia as a warning to Nasser. He caught the warning and respected it.

The Russians' interest in the war in Yemen was simply to keep it going. It was a joint Soviet-Egyptian venture. The Russians' next objective was Aden, in their southward push toward the Indian Ocean; they provided the weapons and the financial means while Nasser fought the war that enabled them to keep and consolidate their Yemeni bridgehead. When Nasser reneged on his peace agreement in 1965, Feisal drew his own conclusions and took his own initiatives. Immediately after signing the agreement in Jiddah, Nasser went to Moscow for his meeting with Brezhnev and Kosygin, and it was clear soon after his return to Cairo that he had lost all interest in a settlement. Feisal deduced that the Russians had changed his mind, by assuring him of the required flow of arms and financial aid to sustain his army in the field. Feisal may well have been right. A few months later a large mission of Soviet military experts, headed by Marshal Andrei Grechko, the Deputy Minister of Defense, arrived in Cairo for consultations. Feisal turned to his American and British friends for further insurance against the Egyptian Air Force. From the United States he bought ground-to-air missiles and from Britain the other components of a complete air defense system. At this juncture, rallying to the Nasserist challenge, he conceived his grandiose scheme for a political counterattack and presented himself to the Arab world as the apostle of Islamic union.

Caught between the two contenders and deeply involved with both, the Americans were placed in an anomalous predicament. They were paying Nasser's domestic bill while he and the Russians were having their foreign adventure in Yemen. This was a great convenience for the Russians, who were in no position to subsidize Egypt's failing economy and were happy to have a wealthier power assume the burden. The American wheat was essential in the balance of Nasser's national accounts. The Egyptians had no stomach for war; they lacked the stamina for their leader's interminable anti-imperialist crusade; and they would have liked nothing better than to have him forget his pan-Arab argosy, bring his ships home and settle down on the Nile. The wheat made the war in Yemen palatable. The mass of Egyptians ate better than ever before during the three years of the wheat contract, roughly coinciding with the first three years of the war; and as long as the wheat kept coming, Nasser was able to get the best of both worlds, relying on the Russians for his Yemeni expedition and on the Americans for his domestic subsidy. He was convinced he was in a unique position to play this game. His messianic role in the global contest with imperialism enjoined him to espouse liberation movements everywhere, not only in Arab countries but throughout Africa, the second "vital sphere" of Egyptian interest, and he was persuaded that these international exploits were good politics for Egypt and a profitable investment. They enhanced Egypt's status on the world scene and brought her international leverage by attracting the interest and concern of the major powers. Her strength lay in her strategic position, which enabled her to manipulate the powers on a wide stage of international action; the wider the stage, the greater the opportunities for manipulation. Such was the rationale of Nasser's inflated foreign policy.

The breaking point in American-Egyptian relations came in the autumn of 1964. Strained by the war in Yemen, they cracked on the issue of the Congo. Cairo at the time was a haven for African political exiles and an international open house for African students. Nasser was infuriated by an American suggestion that he desist from his active support of Gizenga's dissident pro-Soviet regime in the Congo's eastern province. When, in November, the Americans provided the transport planes for the evacuation of European hostages from Stanleyville, a crowd of Africans in Cairo marched on the library of the

United States Information Service and, shouting death to imperialism, invaded the building and put it to the torch. They left it a smoking and nearly irrecoverable ruin. This festive riot occurred on Thanksgiving Day, and the Egyptian Minister of Supply, ineptly, chose this moment to visit the American Embassy and inquire about the next delivery of wheat under the three-year contract. What, he was asked, about a Minister to apologize for the wanton destruction of the library? The Egyptian Government, which had always asserted that no unapproved demonstrations took place in Egypt, disclaimed responsibility for this one: the assault on the library was an act of spontaneous arson by Africans. In a speech the next month, Nasser invited the United States to "go drink the Mediterranean." The American Congress, which does not suffer abuse gladly, did not forget this invitation for a long time. It was an expensive gibe. Washington's answer was to announce the termination of wheat deliveries to Egypt upon the expiry of its contract on June 30 of the following year.

This decision was not for all time. Matters were mended, and in November, 1965, President Johnson approved a renewal of wheat deliveries for six months beginning in January, 1966. Looking further ahead, Nasser in February requested a full year's contract for the fiscal period 1966–1967. The Embassy in Cairo, again considering the pre-eminent importance of Egypt in the balance of Middle East affairs, recommended that the request be granted. Getting along with Nasser was still worth another try. Several times in the following months the $150 million barrel of wheat was shouldered up the Sisyphean hill in Washington, through and past the four agencies whose concurrence was required—the State Department, the Department of Agriculture, the Treasury and the Agency for International Development; but each time the contract was cleared and ready for final approval by the White House, Nasser made another speech and the barrel went tumbling to the bottom. The arduous climb began again. The Americans in Cairo sought to explain matters as delicately as they could. They urged the Egyptians to consider that Nasser was making things very difficult in Washington; they reminded them that the American Congress was sensitive to vilification; and they suggested that if Nasser could be induced to suspend his marathon of unfriendly oratory, the Embassy would still manage to produce the wheat. This advice was received with suspicion and was evidently regarded as political blackmail.

Nasser never obtained the wheat but neither did he obtain a rejection of his request. The Administration could neither produce the barrel nor bring itself to say he could not have it. The Egyptians in Washington were told that for reasons beyond the control of policy-makers, the Administration could not deliver the wheat at the moment, but was continuing to do its best. In Cairo, on instructions from the State Department, the Embassy was saying: Please be patient; there are unavoidable delays, but the shipments will be coming along soon. These assurances soon lost their credibility and the Egyptians concluded they were being strung along. Without the American deliveries, they were living from hand to mouth, they were unable to plan their basic imports, and they had to seek their wheat month by month and pay higher prices for it. All of this fortified their darkest suspicions of the United States. The withholding of the wheat was obviously an imperialist plot intended to sabotage the Egyptian economy and starve the Egyptian people.

Late in 1966 David Nes, the Deputy Chief of Mission at the Embassy in Cairo, recommended that the United States drop its quibbles and tell Nasser the facts. This seemed the only way out of the thickening maze of mistrust. The Embassy should tell Nasser that his request was rejected and inform him frankly of the reasons: the war in Yemen, the political realities in the United States, and the American undertaking in that year to send millions of tons of wheat to the drought-stricken regions of India. Having made known its decision, the United States might offer its services in helping Egypt to procure the wheat from Canada or Australia. In any case, Nes urged, the Egyptians should not be kept hanging, in the absence of any definite prospect of fulfilling their request; prevarication was the worst policy and plain speaking the best. The State Department was loath to take so bold a course. It shrank from the risks of confronting Nasser with a firm and final cutoff, and Nes's proposal was turned down.

The Americans were in an invidious position. They had granted the wheat to Egypt for reasons that were ostensibly humanitarian and were now denying it for reasons that were clearly political. On the one hand, the Egyptian people were underfed; on the other, Nasser was waging war in Yemen. He was not only making ceaseless trouble for the friends of the United States but he was prosecuting his inter-Arab war by the gas-bombing of Yemeni villages. Nevertheless, hungry people should eat. The American aid was in the form of food, not dollars; and from the point of view of the Egyptians' understanding of the agreement, its termination was a malicious act. They had come to expect the wheat as the bedrock of American support; they now saw it as a blackmail payment to help them to survive only as long as the United States was content with their behavior. The Americans in Egyptian eyes had switched from a policy of normal relations and limited friendship to one of systematic hostility. They had declined to help Nasser in his hour of bankruptcy. In the summer of 1966, with his reserves of foreign exchange nearly exhausted, he had sent missions abroad to half a dozen of his creditors to persuade them to refinance the payments on his debts. France, Britain, Japan and the others agreed; the United States alone refused. The Treasury vetoed the suggestion. As for the wheat, the Americans had changed the rules of the game; they had cheated, in an evident policy plot against the Egyptian regime.

Harried and hemmed in, trapped in Yemen, seeing his pan-Arab fortunes in disorderly decline and Feisal leading the muster of his enemies, Nasser in 1966 imagined he was under assault by the combined forces of imperialism. What had become of the pan-Arab revolution of which he was the predestined leader? The embattled hero was the victim of imperialist sabotage. In the threatened "Islamic Pact" he saw an insufferable affront to his authority. His three principal adversaries—Feisal, Hussein and the Shah of Iran—were mobilizing against him; and the Islamic menace was above all internal, since under cover of a religious alignment, Feisal could abet insurgency by the Moslem Brotherhood. In the downfall of Nkrumah and Sukarno, he saw the pattern of a larger conspiracy. The C.I.A. was the prime mover of an imperialist counteroffensive against the revolutionaries of the nonaligned world; and of these revolutionary leaders, he was the chief one left. Just as the forces of imperialism had contrived to thwart the Arab people in their historic advance toward unity, so they were now plotting with their reactionary Arab agents to defeat the revolution and destroy its base in Egypt. The major instrument in this design was the "Islamic Alliance" fathered by Feisal.

The Russians, operating an active misinformation service in Cairo, fostered this conspiratorial vision of events: in the background, the image of an activist American President who had demonstrated his adventurism in Vietnam, Santo Domingo and the Congo; in the foreground but under cover, the bogy of a C.I.A.-directed counterrevolution aimed at progressive regimes everywhere and those of Egypt and

Syria in particular. The phobia took hold and became dogma in Cairo. Nasser believed that an unholy trinity was plotting to overthrow his regime; the reactionary monarchs were fomenting subversion by the Moslem Brothers with the encouragement and money of the C.I.A. The conspiracy took various shapes as various reports circulated in Egyptian government circles. When, in October, 1966, the story came to the Americans in a particularly vicious form, they straightway carried it back to the Egyptians. They denied the story and expressed their extreme apprehension over rumors which, if permitted to gain currency and credence, would be certain to poison relations between the United States and Egypt. They proposed that Washington and Cairo each appoint an intelligence officer of the highest rank to conduct a thoroughgoing investigation of the report. Confronted with the offer, the Egyptians declined.

But the mistrust persisted, and in January, 1967, the State Department sent an emissary to Cairo. His double task was to prevent Nasser from fulfilling a threat to bomb Saudi Arabia and to assure him that the Administration was still seeking in good faith to deliver the wheat. The uses of trouble-shooting diplomacy were unavailing. The Egyptian Air Force bombed Najran and Jizan in the middle of his visit, and Egyptian officials listened incredulously as he sought to explain the complexities of the American Congressional and administrative system. Doesn't the Democratic Party, they asked, have a majority in both houses of Congress? The American-Egyptian relationship, beset with suspicions and perplexed by phobias, was apparently corroded past recall.

Sometime in 1967, it seemed certain, Nasser would strike back. Besieged by frustrations on every front, he would seek to redress his fortunes by some impetuous counteraction. Such was the forecast of the American Embassy early in the year. The leader was at bay and in a mood to break out; his isolation in the Arab world would impel him to find the means and the occasion to seize the initiative. In every arena, the trend of events was working against him. His Arab opponents were profiting by the chaotic impasse of the war in Yemen to strengthen their alignment and improve their positions. At home in Egypt the socialist revolution had foundered in insolvency; already in the summer of the previous year, with the depletion of the country's foreign exchange, the development program had come to a dead stop. More treacherously, as he supposed, his enemies were carrying their counteroffensive to the territory of Egypt and threatening his regime. Even in the arena of the Cold War, the scene of his prestigious success in playing off the big powers, he had overreached himself. He had exhausted Egypt's possibilities of international leverage. The Americans had halted their aid and the Russians were showing no eagerness to move in and replace it.

The political officers at the Embassy anticipated trouble. The prognosis which they sent to the State Department at the beginning of the year was based largely on their estimate and understanding of the political personality of the man they had watched and studied for so long. "I do not act; I react." The hero felt the unquenchable need to respond to challenge and was searching for a role in which he might again command the applause of the Arab world. The springs of his behavior were obsessional, but his tactics as a politician were astute and meditated. He was a master of psychology in the play of power and he needed a quick psychological victory to restore his luster. But a victory over whom? What adversary would he choose? To the men at the Embassy, the answer was plain enough. American-Egyptian relations had disintegrated, and Nasser had irrevocably identified the United States as the archplotter against him. In keeping with the imperatives of the Arab imagination, which require that politics be conducted in the manner of a heroic drama, he would strike at American interests somewhere in the region. A drama in the heroic mood requires an antagonist of giant stature, and Nasser therefore would strike not at David but at Goliath in order to magnify his victory. He would seek a confrontation with the United States.

The Embassy officers in their report scanned the spectrum of possibilities and saw five areas of potential trouble. The farthest afield was perhaps the most obvious. Southern Arabia held the center of the stage in the Arab struggle for power, and Feisal, the guardian of Islam, the man with the oil, obdurate and crafty, enduring as a monument, was the foremost pillar of American imperialism. Nasser possessed two weapons he had not yet fully exploited against him. The Saudi Arabian Free Officers at his instigation could foment sedition in the King's armed forces; and the Egyptian Air Force could carry out that massive attack on Saudi military bases of which he had often and angrily warned. His bombers could easily demonstrate the ineffectiveness of the Saudi Air Force and the weakness of the American-supported ground-to-air defense system, whose personnel were not yet adequately trained and organized.

Closer to home ground and, perhaps, equally inviting as a target was the Kingdom of Libya. The Americans had substantial interests there, commercial and strategic, in the booming development of Libyan oil and the extensive air force facilities at the Wheelus Base near Tripoli; and Nasser had the apparatus to raise the anti-imperialist crowds. As a minimum objective, the Embassy reckoned, he might seek to force an American withdrawal from Wheelus; more ambitiously, he might aim for the overthrow of the Libyan monarchy. A third locus of trouble was Lebanon, always a tempting field for communal agitation and intrigue; and a fourth was the West Bank of Jordan, whose turbulent Palestinians might be called to full-scale insurrection against the last of the Hashimite kings.

The fifth and final possibility on the Embassy's list was a mobilization of the Egyptian Army in the Sinai Desert. Such a deployment, the Embassy assumed, would be of limited scope and purpose; it would be intended not as a military challenge to Israel but as a political demonstration to impress the Arab gallery. It would not involve the massing of Egyptian troops on the border with Israel or the removal of the United Nations Emergency Force that stood guard there. Nasser was militarily unprepared to take a step from which there could be no retreat. At the same time, the Arab gallery had been crying for Egyptian action ever since the Israeli raid at Samua. Nasser had had to swallow the abuse and ridicule of the Jordanians for his failure to stir on that occasion. He, the supreme leader, the founder of the United Arab Command that was supposed to protect the Arab states against Israel, had sat on his hands while the Israelis mounted the largest military action since the Sinai campaign in 1956. Where were the Egyptians on the morning of that raid? Where, asked the Prime Minister of Jordan, was their promised air support? Why didn't Nasser call his troops home from Yemen and move them into Sinai to face the Israelis? King Hussein himself had taunted him. If sending *fedayeen* into Israel was the proclaimed policy of Egypt, Hussein asked, why didn't she send them from her own territory? Above all, why did Nasser cower behind the shield of the United Nations Emergency Force on the Sinai frontier?

These were standard recriminations; the Jordanian radio had been broadcasting them for years. As for Samua, Nasser had a perfectly sound answer and he gave it. By the time he had heard of the raid, it was all over, the Israelis were safely home and there was nothing he could do about it. But in December, 1966, his enemies upbraided him again for hiding behind the skirts of the U. N. Emergency Force and shirking his part in the confrontation with Israel. Field Marshal Amer at that time proposed that Egypt silence her critics by requesting the withdrawal of the U. N. Force and redeploying her army in the Sinai Desert. Nasser refused. He had no intention of throwing away the U.N.'s protective cordon and exposing his army to Israel before it was ready. Sometime in 1967, the Embassy suggested in its report, he might send his troops across the Suez Canal into Sinai in an ostentatious political maneuver, but he would be careful to stop short of the United Nations trip wire along the border. He would not choose suicide.

The U.N. troops had come to Egypt and the Gaza Strip as an "Emergency Force" and had remained for ten years to become the symbol and witness of the United Nations' commitment to the arrangements of 1957. They were the conventional mechanism for ensuring that these arrangements would be maintained. They were a "peace-keeping" force that operated on Egyptian soil only with the consent of the Egyptian Government. They had no powers of coercion and no authority to open fire except in the extremity of self-defense; but as long as they remained as a buffer along the Gaza boundary and the Sinai border, the Egyptians and Israelis would not fire at each other. Hammarskjold had intended that they remain at their posts until they "completed their task"; that is, until the achievement of a general Egyptian-Israeli settlement. Nasser had never acquiesced in this interpretation and had simply abstained from committing himself to anything. He accepted the U.N. troops as insurance against a confrontation with Israel, for as long as he believed he needed them. When the time came, he might renew the war in a variety of ways, by a blockade of the Straits of Tiran or a revival of *fedayeen* raiding or a large-scale mobilization of the Egyptian Army in Sinai; and in each case a demand for the removal of the United Nations buffer would be the danger signal, a declaration of Egypt's readiness for war.

To the American Embassy in Cairo and to everyone else who knew the relative strengths of the two sides, it was perfectly clear that Egypt was not ready. The Embassy's survey of the risks and limits of the year ahead therefore excluded the possibility of a request for the withdrawal of UNEF. Nasser had always impressed the Americans with his sober appraisal of the balance of forces. In talks with American Ambassadors in previous years he had made great sense whenever he discussed the military picture. He was fully aware of Egypt's vulnerability. He recognized the strength of the Israeli deterrent; he indicated that Egypt had a long way to go before she would close the gap; above all, many times, he stressed the weakness of Egyptian air defenses. Egyptian cities, he said, were wide-open to attack, and Israeli planes, spurning the ineffectual Egyptian air-warning system, could fly at will over Egyptian territory. This had been demonstrated again in recent months. Israeli planes continued to overfly Egypt as freely as ever, and none had been shot down in the few encounters that had taken place. Egyptian radar operators and fighter pilots were too unskilled in the techniques of ground-to-air coordination to stop them. On those occasions when Israeli planes had been intercepted and pursued near the Sinai border, it was the intercepting Egyptian Migs that had been shot down, because the Israeli Air Force was in expert command of its ground-to-air communications. Nasser presumably was in possession of the military facts and knew he could not possibly challenge Israel to war.

All the professional estimates were agreed on this point. The American assessment had been unchanged for more than a decade, through all the years of the Russians' prodigal re-equipping of the Egyptian Army and Air Force. Year after year, ever since the original Soviet arms deal in 1955, the conclusion of the American Joint Chiefs of Staff had been the same: Israel's deterrent power was decisive. To be sure, along the way toward their assessment, some American generals occasionally had their doubts. The Egyptians had a formidable array of modern arms. The Russians did not saddle them with Soviet discards; they endowed the Egyptian forces liberally with their most advanced equipment, until in time Nasser's war machine represented their greatest military investment outside the Soviet bloc, superior to the Israelis in every category of armament, from tanks and artillery to naval units, jet fighters and bomber component. Bemused by inventories, the American generals sometimes hesitated and studied the line-up again. They then put aside the tables of manpower and weaponry and weighed the human and social factors which denote organizational mastery of the technology of war. Always in the end, in spite of the inventories, the Joint Chiefs came up with the same judgment and set the year 1970 as the earliest possible confrontation date. The estimate of Israeli military intelligence was the same; the British assessment largely concurred; and if Nasser measured the odds as realistically as he always had in the past, his conclusion should not have been far different.

As the sequel showed, both the Americans and Israelis misassessed his assessment. What both left out of their calculations was the possibility that he would miscalculate. This was a mistake, but it was beyond the reach of military logic or prevision. By making the unforeseen choice and ordering UNEF out of Egypt, Nasser amazed the Israelis, flouted the judgment of the Joint Chiefs and overturned what they had every reason to believe was his own best estimate. Both the Israelis and Americans assumed he would continue to compute the risks as they did and reach the same conclusion. Neither had any means of knowing that he would compute them in his own fashion and then make his own calculated wager; or that, more remarkably still, so would the Russians.

Yet the American Embassy's monitory forecast for 1967, in political essence if not in fact, was sharp and accurate. Nasser chose Goliath as his adversary. In the sustained harangue of his speeches and public statements beginning in February, 1967, the enemy was no longer Hussein or the Shah or Habib Bourghiba, nor even the Israelis or Feisal, although he threatened to form and equip an army to defend southern Arabia against the encroachments of the desert king; these were the mere hollow men of imperialism, of no account or substance, a conjuration of traitorous rogues, unable to stand by themselves. The real adversary was international imperialism, led by the United States. In these speeches, the United States was cast as the main enemy of the Egyptian revolution, indeed the only veritable one, and the entire Arab world was engaged in a portentous struggle between the forces of national liberation and the agents of imperialist enslavement. Feisal and the others were the attendant demons of the counterrevolution; the United States was the malign deity who guided and inspired them. In February Nasser abruptly canceled his request for wheat and terminated negotiations with a flourish intended to demonstrate that he rejected the servitude of American aid and American pressure. Resuming his philippic in a May Day oration, he announced he would not sell a grain of Egypt's soil for a hundred million dollars. "Our main battle," he said, "is with international imperialism and not with its stooges, such as Feisal, Bourghiba and Hussein; they are all instruments used by the Americans and these instruments have no value."

To this line of attack, Mohammed Hassanein Heikal, the editor of *Al Ahram,* gave oracular finality. As the acknowledged pundit of the regime and the confidant and intellectual mouthpiece of its leader, Heikal delivered a series of sermons on American-Egyptian relations from the editorial pulpit of his newspaper. His weekly articles, appearing in March and April, expounded the doctrine of inevitable collision. The American interest in Arab oil required the preservation of complaisant reactionary regimes, and the preservation of these regimes required the prop of American power; and from this it followed that the United States was unalterably opposed to the modernization of Arab society. American and Egyptian interests were too antipathetic to permit a settlement or reconciliation, and, Heikal concluded, this antipathy would lead inescapably to a confrontation between the United States and Egypt. In subsequent articles, less philosophical but more picturesque, he described the obliquitous machinations of the C.I.A., forever toiling to wreck the Egyptian Army in Yemen and forever hatching plots in collusion with Zionism and reaction in order to preserve American domination over the oil lands of Arabia. The theme of American malevolence haunted the refrains of Nasser's May Day speech. "Imperialism," he said, "never forgives us the fact that we stood against it and against its pacts, the Baghdad Pact, Eden and the Eisenhower Doctrine. . . . Imperialism will never forgive us that we stood against its stooges. . . . Imperialism will not forgive our call for social freedom, which is bound to political freedom, since this threatens its interests. Imperialism never forgives us our call for nonalignment and our efforts to save the colonized peoples. The imperialist stooges and reactionaries do not forgive us and Israel does not forgive us. The battle is continuing and is growing fiercer as Arab development goes forward."

In Moscow on April 21, Ambassador Katz was summoned to the office of Jacob Malik, Soviet Deputy Foreign Minister, who handed him a note for his government. As *Izvestia* later reported, the note concerned "the continuing aggressive actions on the part of Israel toward neighboring Arab states." Specifically, it dealt with the Israeli "aggression" of April 7, the aerial reprisal in the course of which six Syrian Migs were shot down, and accused the Israelis of embarking on "ventures constituting a grave danger to the peace" in an area which, as they were again reminded, was "in direct proximity to the frontiers of the Soviet Union." It was clear, the note said, that Israel was seeking to resolve Israeli-Arab controversies by military means, since Major General Rabin, the Chief of Staff, had stated that the attack of April 7 was not the last and that the forms, methods and timing of further actions of the kind would be chosen by Israel. The note ended with a caution: "As regards the Israeli attack of April 7, the Soviet Government sees the necessity to repeat its warning to Israel that her risk-laden policies implemented for the past few years against her neighbors are pregnant with dangers, and she must bear full responsibility for them. The Soviet Government expects the Israeli Government to weigh the existing situation carefully and hopes that she will avoid being used by those circles whose political impatience makes them willing to turn their country into a puppet of foreign enemy forces, thus endangering the essential interests of the state."

Unable to restrain Syria in her sponsorship of El Fatah, and knowing that Israel was determined to reply with force if the guerrilla raids continued, the Russians were seeking another way out of their dilemma by the time they consigned this familiar message to Katz. Beginning in March and continuing through April and the first two weeks of May, the Soviet military intelligence in Cairo repeatedly warned the Egyptians of Israeli troop massings in preparation for an attack on Syria. We do not know how carefully nuanced these reports were, or whether they distinguished between an Israeli invasion and a large-scale punitive raid, but the distinction was of only relative importance, since in either case it was believed the Syrian regime would be in jeopardy. Nasser was not so naïve as to accept these reports without checking; he had ample opportunity to do so and he did. But the truth of the reports was also a matter of secondary interest, since the Israelis could mobilize for an attack very quickly. The question was not so much "Are they mobilizing?" as "What are their intentions?" The Russians feared that any massive Israeli reprisal would have disastrous consequences in Damascus. The alleged troop movements and invasion preparations were, again, a figure of speech that advised Nasser of Moscow's serious concern. The importance of the Soviet reports lay not in their military information, which was dubious, but in their message of political incitement.

The Russians had both a problem and an opportunity. Their problem was to rescue their Syrian protégés and their opportunity was to parlay a difficult situation into a major political victory. The man who held the key was Nasser, if he could be induced to ensure the survival of the Syrian regime with a dramatic demonstration of his readiness to act. The Syrians, of course, had never wearied of crying wolf. Their story of threatening Israeli massings was a way of provoking conflict and of plunging Nasser into it, and it was precisely in this light that he had always mistrusted it. The same story told by the Russians had very different connotations. It was a spur to action and a signal of Soviet support. In the code language of these exchanges, the tale of the phantom brigades was both an encouragement to take the initiative on behalf of the imperiled regime in Damascus, and an assurance of Soviet protection. The brigades were a political metaphor and it did not greatly matter whether they really existed. At the very time the Russians were prodding him on, Nasser could ascertain for himself that the Israeli troop movements had not taken place, but he also knew he had the Russians' blessing for the return of the Egyptian Army to Sinai.

In reconstructing the Soviet role in this period, we are working in a field of assessment and deduction. The precise course of Soviet-Egyptian dealings during the pre-crisis weeks is known only to the Russians and Egyptians, and they are unlikely ever to gratify our curiosity on the subject. The general thrust and purpose of the Russians' promptings to Nasser is clear; the exact nature of the advice they gave him is uncertain. In the absence of conclusive facts, we have to rely on more or less reasonable surmises. We know—because Nasser himself has told us so—that the promptings came not only from Soviet intelligence but from the highest echelon of Soviet leadership. At the end of April an Egyptian parliamentary delegation, led by Anwar Sadat, Speaker of the National Assembly, a Free Officer of the first hour and one of Nasser's earliest revolutionary associates, visited Moscow at the invitation of the Soviet Communist Party. Sadat and his companions talked with Brezhnev, Kosygin and Gromyko, among others. After the Egyptian defeat, Nasser twice referred to this meeting in Moscow and gave two versions of what was said. He presented the following version in his resignation speech on the night of June 9:

"We all know how the crisis began in the first half of May. The enemy was devising a plan to invade Syria, and the statements by his politicians and his military commanders declared that frankly. The evidence was ample. The sources of our Syrian brothers and our own reliable information were categorical on this. Even our friends in the Soviet Union informed the parliamentary delegation which was visiting Moscow early last month that Israel had a calculated intention against Syria. We deemed it our duty not to remain with hands folded. It was a duty of Arab solidarity, and also a guarantee for our national security."

Egyptian government sources later revealed that the Soviet friend who transmitted this warning was Kosygin. On July 23, 1967, the fifteenth anniversary of the Egyptian Revolution, Nasser returned to the subject of his Soviet information and lifted the curtain a bit higher. Kosygin's warning was explicit:

"The first point that should be clear to us all is that we were not the first to create the Middle East crisis. We all know that this crisis started with Israel's attempt to invade Syria. It is certain that Israel in this attempt was not working for its interest alone; it was rather working for the interests of the powers which could not countenance the Arab revolutionary movement any longer.

"The information we had about the invasion of Syria came from different sources. We had information from our Syrian brothers to the effect that Israel had mobilized eighteen brigades. We investigated this information and were assured that Israel was mobilizing no less than thirteen brigades on the Syrian border.

"Our parliamentary delegation which was headed by Anwar Sadat and which was visiting Moscow at the time was informed by our Soviet friends that the invasion of Syria was about to take place. But what could we do? We could have maintained silence; we could have waited; we could have only issued verbal statements and cables of support. But if this country had accepted to handle the situation in that way, it would have renounced its mission, role and personality."

The Russians, thus, believed or professed to believe there was a clear and present danger of an Israeli attack on Syria. This was their line and official rationale throughout—in Moscow, Damascus, Cairo and Jerusalem, and, when the war was over, at the United Nations in New York. On June 19, in a speech calling for the unconditional withdrawal of Israeli troops from the conquered Arab territories, Kosygin repeated to the General Assembly what he had told the Egyptian parliamentarians in Moscow—and improved on it with an added touch. "In those days," he said, "the Soviet Government, and I believe others, too, began receiving information to the effect that the

Israeli Government had timed for the end of May a swift strike at
Syria in order to crush it and then carry the fighting over into the
territory of the United Arab Republic."

How did the Russians esteem and evaluate the situation in the
Middle East in the spring of 1967? Was it their purpose to open a
"second front" while the Americans were distracted in Vietnam? The
professional analysts at the State Department whose job it was to
search the future and divine Soviet intentions asked themselves this
question at the time. Just as the Americans on their side could construe
Soviet actions in the area as the successive steps in an established
master plan, so the Russians could—and did—build up a compelling
picture of sinister American designs. Their fear of an American-
Israeli push to topple the new men in Damascus was probably
genuine, and they may well have believed in an American-engineered
plot to consign Nasser to the limbo of revolutionary castoffs. Pursuing
these cogitations, the analysts in Washington tried to evaluate the
Russians' evaluation of the Middle Eastern picture in the light of the
larger drama of Vietnam.

How did Soviet strategists estimate American intentions in the
area? They might suppose the Americans had conceived a Middle
Eastern plot as a diversion from the frustrations of Southeast Asia. At
the same time, they might think that a Soviet adventure in the area
would divert the United States from the Vietnam war and would offer
some relief to their own allies in Hanoi—if, indeed, the Americans
were willing to become militarily involved in the Middle East. The
Russians in any case would create a second front only through their
Arab proxies; they would take care to avoid a confrontation with the
United States. This imperative of Soviet policy transcended all political gains that might be achieved, locally, in various key regions of the
world. The Soviet staff thinkers might argue that the United States,
embroiled in Vietnam, would exert maximum pressure to restrain Israel, in order to escape further trouble at all costs; but, taking into
account the political influence of the American Jewish community,
they could not be certain. They must have beheld an extremely complex picture of interacting calculations. The global mind readers in
Washington, trying to take the measure of Soviet strategic thinking,
concluded that even a local conflict in the Middle East would involve
incalculable risks for Moscow. The danger of such a conflict leading
to a big-power confrontation was too great, and, on this reading, they

discounted and in the end discarded the possibility of a second front. Their judgment was correct. The Arab-Israeli war in June was not part of the Soviet design. It was largely the result of Soviet miscalculations.

What the Russians had in view, as we can now deduce after the event, was neither a conflict nor a dramatic confrontation but a clever maneuver—an operation that promised high political returns with minimal risks. They believed they had found a peaceful solution for their Syrian problem. They had done a great deal for Nasser and his army; it was now his turn to do something for them. They decided to place in his hands the initiative for a diversion. He would redeploy his armed forces in the Sinai Desert, and in order to make this move militarily credible, he would demand and secure the withdrawal of UNEF. He would do this without firing a shot. The U.N. troops were on the sovereign territory of Egypt; he could order them out and no power on earth could compel him to keep them. The purpose of the diversion was to shift the locale and transform the nature of the crisis. The Egyptian mobilization would oblige Israel to concentrate the main body of her forces on the Sinai frontier, it would deter her from any bold retaliatory action elsewhere, and it would save the Syrians. The dangers of raid and reprisal on the Syrian border would be erased by the confrontation between national armies in Sinai, and Israel would be immobilized by Nasser's demonstration of his resolve to guarantee the security of his Syrian ally. Both Nasser and the Russians could expect a handsome political reward, he as the savior of the Syrians and they as the sponsors of a resounding political victory for the Arab revolutionary states. The Russians had worked patiently to bring Cairo and Damascus together in a common front under their auspices; they would now bring them together triumphantly, in a manner that would confirm and strengthen their own positions in the Arab world.

The Soviet strategic assessment was that there would not be a conflict. There would not be a major international crisis directly engaging the big powers. The United States could not intervene against an Egyptian mobilization on Egyptian territory, and it had no legal handle or pretext for challenging Nasser's sovereign right to dismiss UNEF. The resulting crisis would be local and limited. Israel would have to accept the new military situation on her southern flank. Fearful and isolated, she would not go to war without the guaranteed support of a foreign power. She would have no such guarantee. Britain and France, her allies of 1956, had long since departed from the Middle East; the United States was occupied elsewhere. Domestically, the Israelis were in bad shape. Nasser had a standing army of one hundred thousand men; Israel a tiny regular force. She would be compelled to mobilize all her citizens of military age and would be unable to sustain that effort for long in her economic distress. The Americans, involved in Vietnam, would strive to avoid a second involvement. If internal pressures for war mounted in Israel, the Americans could be counted on to restrain her. There would thus be time to work out a compromise, if compromise were needed to resolve the dispute and stabilize the situation on the Egyptian-Israeli border. Nasser would have his victory thanks to American pressure on the Israelis.

In the Soviet mind, this was a sober and cautious assessment. The Russians were not making a rash gamble, in the circumstances as they saw them; and their errors lay not in the broad picture but in details. The errors arose partly from the Russians' own overriding preoccupation and partly from an infixed habit of mind that esteems big things and disdains little things. They saw the crisis in the light of Soviet-American relations and in terms of big-power preponderance. On their world map, there were only two powers, with a third one in the wings; and in the Middle East it was the clear interest of the two big powers to maintain the peace. The Soviet strategists were guided by their reverence for what the Russians call "the law of large figures"; it is the large figure that talks and commands—and Israel was a minute figure indeed. Thus they were led to their two major political miscalculations. They overestimated the capacity and will of the United States to dictate to Israel, and they underestimated the political will of Israel to act alone.

To be sure, there were risks and they had to consider them. Nasser was going into Sinai on his own account and with his own objectives; there was always the danger that the gambler's appetite might grow too big. He might even be tempted to turn the clock back to 1956 by reimposing the blockade against Israel at the Straits of Tiran—a *casus belli,* as everyone knew. Oddly, if the Russians foresaw this possibility, they took no effective precautions against it. They accepted the risk of handing the crisis over to Nasser for him to conduct in his own way. There was the danger, too, that the Israelis with their backs to the wall might decide to fight, whatever the Americans said; and the

Russians must have recognized the risks that were inherent in Nasser's very first move. The massive deployment on the Sinai border was itself an act of war; Israeli spokesmen had always said such a mobilization would be a direct threat to Israeli security. A third risk the Russians must have seen lay in the all-important but uncontrollable factor of surprise in the kind of military situation they were promoting. As the two armies faced each other on an open frontier and as pressures intensified, each would be tempted to seize the decisive advantages that go to the one who moves first.

From the moment of the Egyptian deployment, the danger of war was present. The Russians accepted the risk, and it was the greatest of their miscalculations. They were prepared to stake the prestige of their arms and their military patronage on the performance of the Egyptian Army. In Washington, where the Joint Chiefs' unswerving estimate was gospel, it was axiomatic that the Russians knew Egypt could not fight Israel and unbelievable that they could possibly think otherwise. But the unbelievable was true. The Russians did not, of course, expect an Egyptian triumph in the event of war. They expected a standoff. Their basic assumption was that the Egyptians would be able to stop and hold the invader in the desert. The Israelis certainly would score some initial victories; but the Egyptian defenses in depth would absorb the blows, and the stalemated line would be drawn somewhere in eastern Sinai. The Egyptian bomber force, meanwhile, might be able to inflict severe punishment on Israeli cities, and in that case the cities of Egypt would probably be bombed as well. The war would be a small-scale affair of limited liability in the world picture, because the big powers would be able to circumscribe the risks. Just as the Americans could be relied on to bring strong pressure on Israel to avert a war, so they could be counted on to end a war as quickly as possible. The Egyptians would be able to maintain a stalemate at least for several days, time enough for the Russians and Americans to intervene at the United Nations and impose a cease-fire. The compromise that would then be found would evidently be in Nasser's favor, since the war had been started by Israel. His political victory would be preserved when the shooting was over; all the more reason, then, for Israel to accept a compromise in peace without facing the fearful risks of a conflict. It was even conceivable that the Egyptian Army might make some tactical gains that could be presented to the Arab world as a victory. If it actually succeeded in pene-

trating the Negev Desert with an armored thrust toward Eilath or
Beersheba, all the better. The Russians would then have the option of
saying to the Americans: Don't intervene; if you stay out, we will
persuade the Egyptians to accept a cease-fire. All that was required
for the Soviet strategy to work was that the Egyptian Army stand and
fight. The one contingency that was not provided for in the Soviet
position papers was that of a swift and decisive Israeli victory that
would rob Soviet diplomats of all their options in the space of a few
hours—so swift that it gave no time for international intervention and
so decisive that the new military facts it established on the Middle
Eastern map could no longer be undone.

The Soviet professionals should have known better. Where and how
did they go wrong? The trite explanations may be the most plausible
ones. After more than a decade of sedulous attention to the Egyptian
armed forces, equipped with the best the Soviet Union could provide,
developed under Soviet military guidance and trained in accordance
with Soviet tactical and strategic doctrine, no Soviet army or intelligence man was likely to submit an appreciation that admitted that all
this panoply of arms and expense of specialized effort had gone down
the drain. The professional men were probably impressed by the military machine they had created. It is the universal failing of military
missions to overrate the work they have done in the field. The Egyptian Army, the Russians believed, would give a good account of itself;
it would at least defend Sinai. This, perhaps, was an understandable
misjudgment, but it represented only half—the less critical half—of
the Soviet intelligence failure. The Egyptian intelligence net was probably able to obtain by itself most of the pertinent data about the Israeli armed forces—the number of tanks, the types of artillery, the
disposition of planes and the eventual deployment of troops. Such
facts and figures were not difficult to pull in. But for a final and comprehensive estimate of Israel's operational capability, the Egyptians
had to rely on the Russians. Only the Soviet intelligence could weigh
up the unweighables that were not to be found in the inventories, the
social factors that play so large a part in such evaluations—the rap-
port between officers and men, the lines of responsibility, the qualities
of leadership from the General Staff down to the commanders of pla-
toons where, in the army of Israel, every man knew intimately every
other man who was fighting by his side. Without knowing how an
Israeli platoon operated, one did not know the Israeli Army. The

Egyptians could not know these things and the Russians evidently overlooked them in their summing-up. They went by the law of large figures; they may have been blinkered by prejudice or ideology; perhaps they were intellectually unequipped to measure the relative strengths of two foreign, un-Marxist societies. Militarily as well as politically, they missed the point in their appraisal of Israel. The failure of their intelligence services seems to have been mainly an astigmatic failure of vision.

Nasser went along with their errors. During the year before the June war, he had left military matters to his military men, reading the reports of his generals in Yemen and probably believing them. He could assume that the performance of his troops in Yemen, a large force hamstrung by guerrillas as the Americans were hamstrung in Vietnam, was no measure of what they could do in a straight fight in the field. He, too, believed that his army could hold, since his generals told him they were ready; he, too, was certain that if war came the great powers would step in and halt it as fast as they could. His second calculation proved to be right. The great powers did step in, but the Israelis stepped even faster. He probably had the liquidation of UNEF under consideration for some time; Amer had proposed the move the previous winter and a contingency plan undoubtedly existed. At some time in the spring he formed a new assessment of his situation and decided to put the plan into effect. How many Arab politicians had been urging or inciting him to take this action on behalf of Syria and Jordan, and what an irritant their incitements had been! The new factor in the situation was that the Russians were inciting him as well. What had been a vexation and a challenge was now an opportunity.

The Soviet promptings were the decisive impetus—the shift in the international balance that made the difference. Nasser had always insisted that a direct confrontation with Israel must await the fruition of propitious international circumstances. This cardinal condition was fulfilled by the signals he received from Moscow. What he owed to the Russians was not the melodramatic information they fed him about Israeli troop massings but the assurance of their political support and their strategic judgment of the political and military odds. With their connivance and collaboration, the international moment was propitious.

After the affair of April 7, in which the Israelis had so signally clobbered the Syrian Air Force, Nasser's relations with Syria pursued their usual course of irascible mistrust. The Syrians sneered at his failure to come to their aid and advertised his delinquency to the Arab nations. They clamored for Egyptian air protection against such Israeli attacks. Nasser was vulnerable to their harpings, and on April 10 he sent General Sidki Mahmoud, the Commander of the Egyptian Air Force, to Damascus to explain that the operational plans of the United Arab Command were not complete and that Egypt could not and would not be responsible for countering Israel's retaliatory raids. Next he sent his Prime Minister, Sidki Suliman, to Damascus for talks on April 19 with President Atassi and Prime Minister Zayen. Suliman reminded them that Nasser would implement his defense pact only in the event of "total conflict"; that he was not responsible for El Fatah's guerrilla bands or for the trouble they might procure for Syria; and in any case, Egyptian planes and pilots would be placed at Syria's service only if they were based on Syrian soil under Egyptian protection. It was the old quarrel. The Syrians were too mistrustful to permit such an Egyptian military presence and Nasser too suspicious to agree to anything less. Continuing the argument in his May Day speech, he said he had offered to send any number of planes and pilots to fight side by side with the Syrians; but it was well known that jet fighters had a limited range and could not fly from Egypt to the frontiers of Syria and return. The Syrians could expect no help from him as long as they rejected his proposal to station air force units on their territory. Nasser's first concern as always was to prevent the Syrians from tumbling him into war and to reserve to himself any initiative under the terms of the defense pact.

On the problem of UNEF, he was a cautious gambler. Of the 3,393 soldiers in the Emergency Force at the end of April, 580 were Yugoslavs and 978 were Indians. Together they were the backbone of the force. The Indians were the largest of the national contingents and the Yugoslav battalion was responsible not only for keeping watch along the entire Sinai border but for holding the gate at Sharm el Sheikh, the isolated outpost overlooking the Straits of Tiran at the southern tip of the Sinai Peninsula. Nasser made informal inquiries in Belgrade and New Delhi as to the attitude of his two neutralist friends in the event that the issue of UNEF's total evacuation should be put to the test. Both the Yugoslav and Indian governments, it was learned at a later date, counseled prudence. They advised the Egyptians not to tamper with the Emergency Force but at the same time they made it clear that they would not maintain their contingents on the sovereign territory of Egypt if they were unwanted.

Soon after April 7 El Fatah opened its spring campaign. Coming from Syria and Lebanon, the saboteur bands widened the range of their operations, sometimes penetrating deep into Israel, laying mines along main roads in Galilee, on one occasion mortaring a border village, and in general demonstrating a proficiency in demolition that bespoke a conspicuously higher level of specialized training. The Israeli retaliation in early April had punished but not deterred. At the United Nations on May 11, Secretary-General U Thant deplored the renewed wave of El Fatah raiding, "a type of activity [that] is insidious, is contrary to the letter and spirit of the Armistice Agreements and menaces the peace of the area"; and added that it was the obligation of all governments in the area, under the United Nations Charter, "to take every measure within their means to put an end to these activities."

In a speech in Tel-Aviv on the same day, Eshkol said that Israel "may have to adopt measures no less drastic than those of April 7," in view of the fourteen acts of sabotage and infiltration that had taken place in the previous month. The next day in a newspaper interview Rabin was quoted as saying that there would be no cessation of El Fatah's terror campaign as long as the regime in Syria lasted. On May 13, in a radio interview, Eshkol said he would make the Israeli defense forces powerful enough to deter aggression, to repel it and to strike a decisive blow at enemy territory. "It is quite clear to the Israeli Government," he said, "that the focal point of the terrorists is Syria, but we have laid down the principle that we shall choose the time, the place and the means to counter the aggression." U Thant thereupon announced that his statement of May 11 "cannot be interpreted as condoning resort to force by any party"; and the State Department, on reading a news agency report of Eshkol's remarks, advised the Israeli Embassy that in its judgment such strong words were not conducive to stability. The Embassy replied that Eshkol's statement had been distorted by the punching prose of the agency reporter.

To these utterances of Eshkol and Rabin, and to the alleged concentration of thirteen Israeli brigades on the Syrian border, Nasser later attributed his decision to move into Sinai on May 14. The menacing speeches and the menacing troops were the two pegs for his action. Neither peg bears much weight. The ritual warnings of Israeli leaders may have alarmed the Syrians to whom they were addressed; alarmism was their permanent state of mind as well as their policy. The Israeli statements are unlikely to have stampeded Nasser. The warnings of retaliation were loud and clear, but in substance they were no more than Eshkol and Rabin had said on several previous occasions, to make the men in Damascus think again and to propitiate public feeling in Israel, and no more than the Israeli Foreign Ministry was telling Soviet representatives at the time. Earlier in the week the Israeli permanent delegate at the United Nations had given public notice that as long as Syria persisted in a policy of armed attacks, "the Government of Israel must hold it responsible for all the consequences and . . . regards itself as fully entitled to act in self-defense as circumstances warrant."

As for the massed Israeli brigades, the truce observers of the United Nations, once again visiting the scene and inspecting the entire border area, were unable to discover them. All was quiet on the northeastern front. The persistent reports of Israeli concentrations, U Thant told the General Assembly, had caused "anxiety and at times excitement," but the investigation of the truce observers had "confirmed the absence of troop concentrations and significant troop movements on both sides of the line."

Nasser exploited his two pegs, during his brief hour of apparent triumph, to persuade the Arab world that his response in Sinai had saved Syria from invasion. In a speech on May 22, he interpreted and paraphrased Rabin's remark after his fashion. "On May 12," he said, "a very important statement was made. . . . The statement said that Israeli commanders had announced they would carry out military operations against Syria in order to occupy Damascus and overthrow the Syrian Government." As for the invasion preparations, he later produced his own evidence: "Our planes reconnoitered the occupied land [Israel] to discover that the enemy had concentrated all its forces against Syria. There was not one single brigade in front of us. All the Israeli brigades were in front of Syria. This meant that their threats were not mere words, but constituted a plan that was about to be executed. So we decided to intervene."

The United Nations observers were not the only team of outside investigators to visit the border zone. American military representatives from the Embassy in Tel-Aviv also inspected the area and returned with the same report. To the Americans as to the Russians it was clear that a genuine danger existed—not of an Israeli invasion or attack on Damascus but of a punitive raid in strength against a designated target, a hit-and-run expedition possibly involving a deep incursion into Syrian territory. No Israelis had died in the recent El Fatah attacks, but the terrorist campaign was murderously systematic and no one could say when it would claim its first victims. Sooner or later, if the infiltrations continued, Israel would be certain to resort to the dissuasion of force. The United States, disturbed by the reports of Israeli massings which the Russians were now scattering far and wide, advised the Soviet Union through diplomatic channels that the circulation of such baseless rumors could only have a highly inflammatory effect in the prevailing state of tension. Soviet officials at this time were alerting not only the Syrians and Egyptians but even the Jordanians of mythical Israeli troop movements in preparation for an onslaught on Syria.

The chronicle of the last three days before Nasser moved is brief. On May 12, following a prolonged cold blast of polemical allegations in *Pravda,* Arye Levavi, the Director General of the Israeli Foreign Ministry, received Chuvakhin, who accused Israel of massing an invasion force opposite the Syrian border. Levavi renewed Eshkol's offer of the previous autumn and proposed that the Ambassador visit the area to see for himself. Chuvakhin, again loyal to the information he had received from Moscow, declined the invitation. On May 13 Soviet intelligence in Damascus informed the Syrians that Israel was mobilizing for an attack. The Syrians at once informed the Egyptians and the Egyptians at once reacted. On May 14 General Mohammed Fawzi, Chief of Staff of the Egyptian Armed Forces, flew to Damascus to advise the Syrians of Nasser's decision to implement the joint defense pact and of the military measures that Egypt was about to take.

On the morning of May 15, celebrating the nineteenth anniversary of the foundation of the state of Israel, the Israeli Defense Forces held their annual parade in Jerusalem. The Americans had urged the Israelis to make their show a small one, so as not to overexcite the Arabs; and the Israelis, complying, kept the parade within the arms and troops limitations prescribed by their armistice agreement with Jordan. But instead of quieting the Arabs, the modesty of the celebration aroused them: they promptly deduced that the Israeli Army, inconspicuous in Jerusalem, must be powerfully massed elsewhere. In the reviewing stand in the stadium of Hebrew University, President Zalman Shazar, Eshkol and Rabin took the salute as the marchpast began, and it was there that the Chief of Staff informed the Prime Minister that Egyptian Army units during the previous night had started moving toward the Suez Canal on their way to the Sinai Desert.

In Cairo on the same Monday morning, converging from army camps in the desert outskirts, following the grand concourse of the Nile corniche and at times turning in from the river for a demonstrative detour past the gates of the American Embassy, Egyptian Army trucks and armored cars traversed the city, south to north, in uninterrupted procession. Nasser paraded his troops in broad daylight through the surprised traffic of the capital. What was the meaning of this fanfare? Was it a show or a mobilization? A show, apparently, unannounced and unexplained but trumpeted and publicized for the edification of the Arab world. The army columns headed north for the tarmac road across the Delta and continued their journey eastward to Ismailia on the Suez Canal. The Egyptian staff work had been excellent. The operation was swift and smooth, carefully concerted, well planned and well executed—logistically perfect. By nightfall foreign military attachés knew it was more than a show. A substantial body of troops had reached the eastern bank of the Canal and proceeded on into the sand and gravel waste of Sinai.

The State Department had mismanaged its housekeeping and was caught without an Ambassador in Cairo at this critical moment. Ambassador Lucius Battle, who like many of his predecessors had been on familiar terms with Nasser, had returned to Washington in March to become Assistant Secretary for Near Eastern Affairs, and his successor had still not arrived. David Nes was chargé d'affaires. On May 16, while Cairo Radio was announcing that Egypt had placed her armed forces on an emergency alert because of "the tense situation on the Syrian-Israeli armistice lines, Israel's large military concentrations, its threats and its open demands for an attack on Damascus," Nes on instructions from the Department saw Achmed Hassan El Fekki, the Egyptian Undersecretary of Foreign Affairs. He assured El Fekki that the United States had excellent sources of information in Israel, virtually the equivalent of a military mission, which had been free to make an independent investigation, had traveled around the country as it wished, and had reported to Washington that there were no unusual Israeli troop movements and no preparations for an attack. El Fekki replied that Egypt had her own sources of information. However, he relayed Nes's assurance over the telex to Nasser's office. The President's aides received it less suavely than had the Undersecretary; their retort on the Foreign Office telex said the American message was "the assurance of an Israeli attack" and Nes's information was "the American cover."

Did Nasser's men believe what they said? Where was the line between fact and fantasy, reality and belief? In the fractured state of American-Egyptian relations, the lines of comprehension were severed and it was impossible to say. American credibility was gone; communication failed; and there was nothing the United States could further say to Nasser. Its information and above all its motives were suspect. Nasser and his circle were invincibly persuaded that the United States was plotting against them and, in the vortex of the Arab imagination, the intended Israeli attack was another step toward the consummation of the American grand design in the Middle East. If Syria fell, the Arab revolutionary front would be shattered, Nasser would stand alone, and Egypt, the protagonist of the anti-imperialist struggle, would be next on the C.I.A.'s list. Such was the vision; and in this state of exalted belief, the Egyptians had no time for Nes's information. The massed Israeli brigades were an article of faith. The Egyptians therefore chose to accept the word of the Russians and reject the word of the Americans. But this did not necessarily mean that the men at the other end of the telex, in the President's office, accepted the story of Israeli concentrations as literally true. Nor did it mean that Nasser himself was ignorant of the facts. He, at least, should have known them. Did he, in the end, act on the basis of misinformation? Did he send his troops to Sinai on the strength of a Soviet-Syrian false alarm which he accepted? What did he believe and not believe at that moment?

The Egyptians themselves have provided us with fleeting but fascinating testimony on this point. The witness is Shams Badran, the Minister of War who was brought to trial by a special tribunal on charges of complicity with Amer in a postwar conspiracy to overthrow Nasser. Badran defended himself with spirit, loquacity and skill. He was a clever and witty man who did not enjoy the highest repute for spotless veracity; and a main purpose of his testimony, as he fought for his life, was to coinvolve Nasser in the military decisions of the prewar

weeks and thus trap him in a position of responsibility for the defeat.
A full transcript of the trial record has never appeared, but *Al Ahram*
published extensive excerpts at the time and other Egyptian sources
made their shorter contributions.

Testifying on February 24, 1968, Badran began his review of prewar events with Amer's proposal in December, 1966, to request the
total withdrawal of UNEF:

"The first time the subject of Sharm el Sheikh came up was in December, 1966, or January, 1967. The Field Marshal [Amer] . . .
and I were then on a visit to Pakistan. At that time the Arab League
Defense Council was in session in accordance with a Summit Conference recommendation. The meeting was in Egypt and the reactionary
Arab nations concentrated their attacks [on Egypt] on the fact that
we had placed UNEF there to defend ourselves. A fierce campaign
was raging in the press at the time. The Field Marshal had an idea to
stop the frenzied campaign. He said that we would send a note to the
President proposing UNEF's withdrawal and that we should occupy
Sharm el Sheikh. There were standby battalions [for the purpose].
No response came from the President because he was not convinced
of the idea then. I told the Field Marshal that if we were to withdraw
UNEF, this would entail the closure of the Gulf [of Aqaba] and
perhaps a war would be touched off. The Field Marshal said he did
not mean to block navigation but just to occupy Sharm el Sheikh so as
not to give anyone any pretext to speak against us. . . . He told me
he would occupy Sharm el Sheikh only, but we would not close up the
Gulf. I said this would be half a solution. . . . Then we returned to
Egypt and then a Syrian report came to the effect that there were
Israeli troop massings."

The President of the Court, Hussein Shafei, a Vice-President of the
Egyptian regime, interrupted at this point and told Badran to skip the
story of prewar events. Badran insisted that these were "the crux of
the whole issue." He resumed his narrative, jumping to May 14, the
day after the Syrians had sent their final false alarm to Cairo:

"After the reports came in from Syria about troop concentrations
around Syria, the Field Marshal held a meeting and sent General
Fawzi to Syria to coordinate the situation. Between us, this was done
on the basis that the Army was ready."

Badran then told the court that on returning from Syria, Fawzi reported there were no Israeli concentrations on the Syrian border.

"The Syrians must be mad," Fawzi had said, and the Russians "must have had hallucinations."

In Cairo on May 16, Mahmoud Riad, the Egyptian Foreign Minister, received the Soviet Ambassador and military attaché. In Gaza that evening, at 22:00 hours local time, the Indian Commander of UNEF, Major General Indar Jit Rikhye, was called to the office of Brigadier Eiz-El-Din Mokhtar, the Egyptian field commander, who handed him a letter in English from the Chief of Staff of the Egyptian armed forces:

"To your information, I gave my instructions to all U.A.R. Armed Forces to be ready for action against Israel the moment it might carry out an aggressive action against any Arab country. Due to these instructions our troops are already concentrated in Sinai on our eastern borders. For the sake of complete security of all U.N. troops which install O.P.'s along our border, I request that you issue your orders to withdraw all these troops immediately. I have given my instructions to our Commander of the eastern zone concerning this subject. Inform back the fulfillment of this request."

Cryptic, peremptory, ungrammatical, Fawzi's letter was also formally unacceptable. Rikhye did not take his orders from the Egyptians. He took orders from no one but U Thant. Why was the message addressed to him? Perhaps, he thought, because he had always maintained such cordial relations with the Egyptian liaison staff; and so the Egyptians may have supposed there was a good chance of immediate compliance. In that case he would have to disappoint them. Fawzi's request did not mention Sharm el Sheikh, the seaside post at the mouth of the Gulf of Aqaba. It referred only to the U.N. observation posts along the Sinai frontier, and it was the troops manning these posts that he evidently wanted Rikhye to withdraw and regroup inside the Gaza Strip. The Egyptians had sent no units into the Strip; the long and narrow region, backed against the sea, was not part of sovereign Egypt and was in any case indefensible. Rikhye at the time had fewer than seven hundred men in the whole of Sinai. At Sharm el Sheikh a garrison of about sixty men watched the Tiran Straits, a reinforced platoon of Yugoslavs with a Greek radio operator and a group of Canadian technicians and logistics personnel to help them. In the Sinai desert facing Israel, the main body of the Yugoslavs lived in six camps, from which they went out to man a series of border posts, some flat against the line, some half a mile or a mile back on a commanding feature. At each post two Yugoslav soldiers kept guard throughout the daylight hours.

Fawzi's letter, it turned out, was only the beginning. Mokhtar made known several urgent requests of his own. He told Rikhye that UNEF must evacuate Sharm el Sheikh and the Yugoslav desert camp at El Sabha, as well as all its posts along the international frontier, by first light the next morning. These troops were to pull back into Gaza. Mokhtar pressed for an immediate answer and immediate compliance, and dwelt on the danger of clashes if the U.N. troops were still on the scene by the time the Egyptians arrived. He made a great point of El Sabha, a bleak prominence more than four thousand feet high, dominating the central east-west road that cuts across Sinai from Israel to the Suez Canal at Ismailia. There was no doubt in Rikhye's mind that Mokhtar was talking about the evacuation of the entire Emergency Force from the entire Sinai Peninsula. The UNEF Commander said he could not comply. He would have to report the matter to U Thant and await his instructions, following consultations in New York and under the mandate of the General Assembly resolution that had created the force.

After the formal discussion in Mokhtar's office, there was the ritual coffee. Conversation relaxed and the Egyptians confided their worry. They had directed their message to Gaza rather than New York because they feared that if they sent it to U Thant, the Israelis at United Nations headquarters would be certain to hear about it and would beat them to the punch. Israeli troops would occupy the two key posts, at Sharm el Sheikh and El Sabha, before Egyptian contingents were able to get there. This conspiratorial thought had apparently come from the highest quarter. A few days later at a meeting in Cairo, Nasser told Rikhye that the decision to address the request to him rather than U Thant had been taken on the cabinet level—by Nasser himself.

Rikhye returned to his headquarters and sent the first message marked "Priorité"—highest emergency—that had ever issued from the UNEF Command in Gaza. U Thant received it at 17:30 hours New York time and spent the next hour and a quarter in consultation with Ralph Bunche, the Political Undersecretary who had been the United Nations' Mr. Middle East ever since his service as mediator during the Arab-Israeli war in 1948. Together they considered Rikhye's report with mystified amazement. Nasser's intentions were

completely uncertain. What was he asking for? A tactical redisposi-
tion of U.N. forces in Sinai? A general withdrawal into Gaza? A temporary redeployment in which UNEF would abandon some posts and
retain others? And why did he send his message through the army
rather than through channels to the Secretariat? U Thant's immediate
concern was that the U.N. troops, by redeploying themselves, should
not become the instrumentality of Egypt. Nasser must not be allowed
to control UNEF by issuing orders to its commander and maneuvering it about for his own purposes. This point must be made clear. But
there were other and greater ambiguities. How was one to decipher
the Egyptian demarche, half written and half oral? Fawzi requested a
partial and limited withdrawal; Mokhtar demanded the abandonment
of Sharm el Sheikh as well and set a deadline. How serious were his
oral additions? Was Nasser, in fact, aiming for a total evacuation? At
18:45 U Thant sent for Mohammed Ahwad El Kony, the Egyptian
representative to the United Nations, showed him Rikhye's report and
asked, "What's this?"

El Kony was flabbergasted. He knew nothing about it.

What should U Thant have done at this point? What could he have
done to salvage UNEF or any part of it? The answer to the question is
cumbered with technicalities and clouded with controversy. U Thant's
critics—Americans, Israelis and Canadians, among others—were bitter in their reproaches. Egypt had an irrefutable right to demand the
withdrawal of UNEF; there was no doubt about that. But, said the
critics, there were many things U Thant might have done or tried to
do when he confronted El Kony with Rikhye's message on the evening
of May 16. Events were moving fast; he should have tried to slow
them down. He could have said: Hold everything; I am communicating directly with Nasser; and have done so immediately. He could
have flown to Cairo. The resources of his office afforded him many
means of trying to gain time—a few days, a few hours. As the General
Assembly's executive agent for UNEF, he could have reported to the
Assembly and sought a debate in which Egypt might be asked to explain her reasons and intentions. The Assembly had created an Advisory Committee, consisting of those nations that contributed troops to
UNEF and certain others. The Committee was U Thant's consultative
instrument; it was empowered to ask for the convening of the Assembly when matters arose that in its judgment were of an "urgency and
importance" requiring the Assembly's attention. U Thant could have

taken the lead in urging that the issue be referred to the body from which both UNEF and he had received their mandate. As Secretary-General, he could have reported to the Security Council on a matter affecting international peace. The point of greatest danger was obviously Sharm el Sheikh. UNEF should be maintained at least there, to head off a reimposition of the blockade against Israel. If U Thant had gained a little time, diplomacy might have gone to work. The interested governments might have tried to find out through a multiplicity of diplomatic channels exactly what was happening. They might have managed to stave off the worst, if the Secretary-General had not acted alone and in haste.

Such was the burden of the exasperated rebukes that were soon to explode around U Thant's head. He was much piqued by them. His critics accused him of abdicating his responsibility. His apologists insisted he had done the only legal and only sensible thing. What he did, in his talk with El Kony, was to lay all his cards on the table at once.

Anxious to prevent Nasser from using UNEF to suit his own designs and pleasure, U Thant restated to El Kony the ground rules of the situation. He explained the legal basis for UNEF's presence in Egypt and hence, as well, the legal basis for an Egyptian demand for its dismissal. He said, first, that the message to Rikhye was improperly addressed and procedurally unacceptable, and, second, that UNEF could not be partially or temporarily withdrawn to one sector. It could not step aside to one part of the front while the armies of Egypt and Israel fought in another. Such a move would open the door to war and was out of the question. The entire functioning of UNEF as a buffer rested on the understanding that there would be no joint occupation of border areas by U.N. and Egyptian forces. If they were stationed side by side, UNEF could not do its job, and this was the reason for the on-the-ground arrangements that had been made with Egyptian local commanders. The Egyptians had agreed not to enter a delimited border zone, two thousand meters deep along the international frontier in Sinai and five hundred meters deep along the boundary of the Gaza Strip. A partial withdrawal would render UNEF ineffective, and if he received a request for such a withdrawal from the Egyptian Government, he would regard it as tantamount to a request for total evacuation. He took the position that he could not give up the integrity of UNEF or consent to split its responsibilities.

U Thant continued: If indeed it was the intention of the Egyptian

Government to seek a complete withdrawal, it should direct its request to him. It would be a legitimate request and he would accede to it. Egypt had the right to withdraw the consent she had given in 1956 to the stationing of UNEF on her territory. If the Egyptian Government addressed such a request to him, he would order the withdrawal of all UNEF troops from Gaza and Sinai, thereafter informing the General Assembly of his decision and his reasons for it.

Such a request, he told El Kony, would be a grave mistake. He therefore proposed to send a personal appeal to Nasser, urging him to reconsider his decision, if indeed he meant to ask for a total withdrawal. El Kony, thus apprised of U Thant's intention, left the Secretariat, hastened to the telephone and called Foreign Minister Riad in Cairo. Within two hours he came back to U Thant with Riad's warning that an appeal to Nasser would bring a "stern rebuff." The appeal was not made.

Thus, while Nasser had concealed his intentions and kept the Secretariat guessing, U Thant had made his fully known. He agreed in principle to the complete withdrawal of UNEF before receiving a request from Egypt, and he advised the Egyptians he would act on his own authority without reference to the General Assembly. On the following day he published his decision to the world. The U.N. spokesman at a noon briefing on May 17 tipped the story of the previous night's exchanges. UNEF, he announced, would have to leave if Egypt withdrew her consent or if "the conditions under which it operates were so qualified as to make it impossible for it to fulfill its functions." U Thant, he said, took an "extremely grave view" of the situation; he had asked for clarification and was still waiting for an answer.

At teletypes in New York and Washington, Israeli diplomats and State Department officials on the Near Eastern Affairs desk read with stupefaction the news story of this announcement. To Avraham Harman, the Israeli Ambassador in Washington, it seemed blindingly obvious what Nasser's answer would be. U Thant had said: All or nothing; and Nasser was certain to accept the challenge. He would feel it left him no choice but to ask for total withdrawal, and how could U Thant think otherwise? Harman telephoned to his State Department friends, who were as appalled as he. The consensus at the Department was that U Thant had led with his chin. He had taken no dilatory intermediate steps, he had consulted no one, and he had moved with expeditious speed to invite the dismantlement of the peace-keeping force of which he was the executive officer and principal custodian. He had followed the line that was the shortest and fastest route to the total destruction of UNEF.

On reading the news Gideon Rafael, the Israeli permanent representative at the United Nations, called Bunche to express his alarm and ask why the calamitous move had been made. If, Rafael said, the Secretariat believed its reply was calculated to force Nasser to back down, it had lamentably misjudged its man; and the United Nations must act urgently to prevent the worst from happening. Later in the afternoon, Rafael saw U Thant. He protested that Israel had not been consulted and reread the Secretary-General's own statement of the previous September in which he had reported to the Assembly that UNEF's buffer role was "still indispensable" and that "relations between the peoples on the opposite sides of the line are such that if the United Nations buffer should be removed, serious fighting would quite likely soon be resumed." He reminded U Thant that UNEF had been created within the frame of an Assembly resolution, insisted on the need for consultations with the Advisory Committee, and proposed that U Thant send an urgent message to Nasser requesting him to reconsider his decision.

Dismay was general in Western ranks at the United Nations. No one had seen the crisis coming and everyone was unprepared for it. Against the background of successive Assembly resolutions and ten and a half years' experience in the field, it was generally assumed that UNEF was an institution that could not be summarily and unilaterally dismissed and disbanded. Nasser had no absolute unfettered right to order it out of his country. But how valid was this assumption? U Thant, in fact, stood on very strong legal ground. Everything he had told El Kony was perfectly correct. Egypt was fully entitled to dismiss UNEF and reoccupy her own territory; this right had never been questioned by the Assembly and no formal limitation had ever been set upon it. Israel had asserted her sovereign right from the very beginning by refusing to allow U.N. troops on her territory. The Israelis did not intend to become the ward of the United Nations or entrust their security to anyone but themselves. They had freely rejected UNEF, and by the same token the Egyptians had freely accepted it. The Egyptian local commanders had agreed not to send their troops into the border zones; but this was a voluntary agreement which they were free to revoke whenever they wanted. There was a further curious legality in the life story of UNEF. U Thant was not bound to consult the General Assembly before deciding what to do. It was true that the Assembly had created UNEF and established its functions. But UNEF had been able to enter Egyptian territory and remain on it only by reason of a separate agreement of consent on the part of Egypt; and this agreement had been concluded with Hammarskjold. The Assembly had had nothing to do with it; and the first U.N. troops, on their way to Egypt in 1956, had had to stand by in Naples until Hammarskjold completed his negotiations in Cairo. Strictly speaking, the question of UNEF's continued presence in Egypt was within the competence of the Secretary-General and not of the Assembly. U Thant could act on his own responsibility if he chose.

The root problem, of course, went much deeper than these technicalities. What were the principles forming the legal basis of a U.N. peace-keeping force? These had been widely pondered and discussed but never satisfactorily defined. Everyone agreed that such a force, established by the Assembly, could operate only with the consent of the country where it was stationed. Presumably it could be withdrawn only after it had fulfilled its functions and "completed the task" for which the Assembly had created it. But who was to decide when the task had been done? The legalists said that such a force could be withdrawn on the sole decision of the host country, whose sovereignty was unchallengeable and could not be limited. The advocates of U.N. peace-keeping activity said that withdrawal should be subject to a process of advice and consultation between the host country and the United Nations. Hammarskjold was firmly of the latter school. Having created UNEF almost overnight, he flew to Cairo and, after a seven-hour argument with Nasser, extracted from the Egyptian Government his famous "good faith" agreement: Egypt agreed to act in good faith whenever she exercised her sovereign powers on any matter concerning the presence and functioning of UNEF. This meant she would not act brutally and unilaterally. The agreement applied only to UNEF's role in supervising the 1956 cease-fire and in securing the withdrawal of Israeli troops from Sinai and Gaza; it was never extended to embrace UNEF's later and greatly enlarged role as a long-term policeman on the Egyptian-Israeli border and at Sharm el Sheikh. However, Hammarskjold continued to wrestle with the problem. He exercised all his ingenuity to devise a formula that would protect UNEF against unilateral destruction. He even wrote a memorandum to himself in which he built a vast legal construction on the ambiguities of United Nations procedure. By accepting the General Assembly's resolution, he argued, Egypt had agreed to limit her sovereign right and to define her sovereignty on the basis of a "good faith" interpretation of UNEF's tasks, and so her freedom of action was tied to a definition of these tasks by the Assembly. But this limitation on Egypt existed only in Hammarskjold's mind. His memorandum was a private paper that never found its way into the records of the Secretariat. It had no legal standing; it was an exercise in intellectual agility by an imaginative statesman who sought to extend the authority of his office to the outmost limits. The root problem thus remained unresolved. Hammarskjold's memo is interesting because it offers a guide to the course he would have taken had he faced the issue that U Thant faced on the night of May 16. Hammarskjold would probably have interpreted his powers very widely and sought to exploit all the resources of his office. U Thant interpreted his powers narrowly and went by the book.

The initiative remained with Nasser, and already on May 17 events were rapidly heading out of control. A series of "Priorité" cables came in from General Rikhye during the day. The Egyptians, fearful of the surprises that Israeli guile might have in store, were moving their troops into the U.N.'s delimited zone along the Sinai border. No request for complete withdrawal had come from Cairo; but at dawn, as Mokhtar had promised, Egyptian troops occupied El Sabha and deployed with their armored cars next to the U.N. observation post there. Two and a half hours later Rikhye reported they had moved in and occupied the post. Already, two of the Yugoslavs' camps were behind the lines of the Egyptian Army. Throughout the day, at other points, Egyptian troops moved up to, around and past the U.N. posts to the border with Israel. At 14:00 hours Gaza time, notwithstanding Rikhye's notice that he took orders only from U Thant, further ultimative messages arrived from Fawzi. The Egyptian Chief of Staff requested that all Yugoslav detachments be withdrawn from Sinai within twenty-four hours, and added that Rikhye might take "forty-eight hours or so" to withdraw the U.N. garrison from Sharm el Sheikh. Rikhye replied that such moves required instructions from the Secretary-General and that in the meantime UNEF could not yield to Egyptian troops. The Yugoslavs continued to man their observation posts as usual, but even without yielding, UNEF was in the process of being overrun. At the United Nations, delegates were communicating urgently with their governments and still talking of preventing the worst—unaware that the worst was taking place and that the peace-keeping force that had stood guard for a decade in Sinai was being engulfed and nullified by the Egyptian Army.

Later in the day U Thant learned that he faced a force in dissolu-tion. India and Yugoslavia counted themselves out: they would call home their contingents at once if Egypt asked for a total withdrawal. This became known at a meeting which U Thant held at 16:00 hours with representatives of the countries that provided troops to UNEF: Brazil, Canada, Denmark, India, Yugoslavia, Norway and Sweden. He informed the group of the Egyptian demands of the previous night and of the position he had taken. George Ignatiev, the Canadian rep-resentative, promptly objected. He made the following points: (1) Egypt could not peremptorily order UNEF's withdrawal. She was bound to act in "good faith" and should make no request without prior consultations. (2) The Egyptian request was ambiguous. There was no reason to assume that Egypt was asking for a complete with-drawal, as U Thant appeared to have done. She might be asking for a partial redeployment of some sort. It would be best to find out before leaping to conclusions. (3) Quite apart from the question of Egypt's legal right, one had to consider the *de facto* situation that would be created if UNEF should leave, thereby enabling the armies of coun-tries "traditionally hostile to each other" to take up battle positions. (4) The *de facto* situation would be particularly dangerous at Sharm el Sheikh, where UNEF's presence guaranteed free navigation through the Gulf of Aqaba. José Sette Camara of Brazil seconded Ignatiev's objections and warned of the "dangerous consequences" of a total withdrawal.

These arguments were being heard twenty-two hours too late. U Thant had taken his decision and had communicated it to Cairo. An *aide-mémoire* embodying the points he had made to El Kony would, he said, be handed to the Egyptian Ambassador as soon as the meet-ing was over. He said he did not intend to consult the Assembly; the decision was his alone. "It is not," he said, "within the competence of the General Assembly to act." However, if Egypt should ask for com-plete withdrawal, the first action he proposed to take would be to appeal to the Egyptian Government to reconsider, without immedi-ately complying with the request or advising the Assembly.

The debate grew warmer and ranged further afield. Ignatiev argued that U Thant should make his appeal to Nasser at once, without waiting for a formal request. Furthermore, in view of the serious consequences of a total withdrawal, he felt it would be unwise to cede to a unilateral request before the Assembly had a chance to discuss the matter. Danilo Lekic of Yugoslavia sharply disagreed. A direct appeal by U Thant, he said, would be an affront, since it would bring into question the sovereign right of Egypt. Indeed, such a unilateral act would mean taking sides; Egypt was within her right and Nasser had used the threat of force as a legitimate political weapon to curb Israel and defend Syria. Gopalaswami Parsatharathi of India was of the same opinion. As for the Assembly, Lekic said, it had no authority to deal with the issue. Parsatharathi concurred. Duly primed by his government, Lekic announced that in the event of a request for UNEF's removal, "we have to abide by that request"; UNEF could not keep its troops on Egyptian soil once Egypt withdrew her consent. When her consent lapsed, the Force lapsed. Parsatharathi concurred. Both he and Lekic made clear that under such circumstances their governments would withdraw their national contingents. Nasser had taken his diplomatic precautions and, as he had foreseen, UNEF was crumbling at the conference table.

As for the General Assembly, U Thant reminded Ignatiev of the procedural difficulties. These were evidently considerable. The Assembly was then sitting in special session on the question of South-West Africa. The Middle East problem was not on its agenda, and the rules required the assent of two-thirds of its members to place it there. How many days of polling this might take! Bunche brought up another difficulty that had always troubled the Secretariat. The Assembly resolution of 1956, he recalled, had asked that U.N. troops be stationed on both sides of the Sinai border, and Israel had not accepted this. The Secretariat felt vulnerable on this account; UNEF seemed a one-sided and prejudicial arrangement. The United Nations, Bunche said, would be in an invidious posture if it questioned Egypt's rights in the matter.

A committee divided against itself could offer no coherent advice to its chairman. The meeting ended with U Thant maintaining his position. Shortly thereafter he gave El Kony the *aide-mémoire* recapitulating his points of the night before and adding that if the Egyptian troop movements to the border continued, he "would have no choice but to order the withdrawal of UNEF from Gaza and Sinai as soon as possible."

On the morning of the next day, May 18, three Egyptian helicopters landed at Sharm el Sheikh. Fawzi, after all, had not waited for forty-eight hours. The helicopters brought a party of eleven officers, including sappers and technicians to look after a desalination plant in the area. The Egyptian major in command announced he had come to take over the post and gave the Yugoslavs fifteen minutes to evacuate. The Yugoslav commanding officer said he had no orders to withdraw. The Egyptian major, alleging that the commander of UNEF had agreed to the withdrawal, was insistent; the Yugoslavs must leave at once, since other Egyptian forces would be coming along soon. They argued it out. It was finally agreed that the U.N. garrison would remain pending the receipt of instructions, and so they all stayed on together. The Yugoslavs radioed to their battalion headquarters at El Arish to ask what to do, and were promptly told they should withdraw "under no repeat no circumstances." In Sinai meanwhile Egyptian troops evicted Yugoslav sentries from two observation posts on the international frontier and forced them out of the area of their post at El Sabha. The Yugoslavs did not resist, having no mandate to do so. The Egyptians were in a great hurry. They turned up at another of UNEF's desert camps, at El Amr, and served a fifteen-minute evacuation notice on the Yugoslav platoon there.

In New York on the same morning, Rafael saw U Thant on the urgent instructions of Foreign Minister Eban. He again asserted Israel's right to a voice in the matter. He reiterated her view that UNEF should not be removed on the unilateral request of Egypt. He stressed the "extreme danger" of an abandonment of Sharm el Sheikh and urged U Thant to save whatever he could of the Force. U Thant suggested it might be a good idea for Israel to accept U.N. forces on her side of the border. And why? Rafael asked. How can troops in Israel protect Sharm el Sheikh? He declared the idea to be entirely unacceptable to his government. U Thant then revealed that he had changed his mind about sending a preliminary appeal to Nasser. The Egyptian Foreign Ministry had requested him not to, since it would cause bad feeling.

The Egyptian request for withdrawal arrived at noon, New York time. El Kony delivered the following letter from Riad:

"The Government of the United Arab Republic has the honor to inform Your Excellency that it has decided to terminate the presence of the United Nations Emergency Force from the territory of the United Arab Republic and the Gaza Strip. Therefore, I request that the necessary steps be taken for the withdrawal of the Force as soon as possible.

"I avail myself of this opportunity to express to Your Excellency my gratitude and warm regards."

To this message El Kony added his oral gloss. He spoke of the deep feelings of resentment in Egypt at what was regarded as attempts to exert pressure and to make UNEF "an occupation force." Word had apparently reached Cairo of the unfriendly stance of the Canadian and Brazilian delegates at the contributors' meeting the previous day. El Kony added a further warning. In the prevailing atmosphere of emotional excitement, Egypt could no longer answer for the safety of U.N. troops.

U Thant said he would comply with Riad's request and would order the complete withdrawal of UNEF as soon as possible; at the same time he wished to warn of the gravely heightened conditions of tension that this would create. He told El Kony of his desire to appeal urgently to Nasser to reconsider his decision.

Advised of this intention, El Kony again hastened to the telephone and called Riad. He returned, later in the afternoon, to tell U Thant of his Foreign Minister's "urgent advice" not to make an appeal and of his warning that if he did, he would be sternly rebuffed. Suitably cautioned a second time, in nearly identical terms, U Thant again changed his mind. The appeal was not made.

At 17:00 hours U Thant summoned the full Advisory Committee —the contributors to UNEF and others—into formal session to announce the receipt of the Egyptian demand and the terms of his oral reply. The general debate was renewed. Ignatiev, protesting, said the position he had taken the day before was now the formal position of the Canadian Government. He did not question the legalities and he fully recognized Egypt's rights, but the understandings of 1956–1957 had called for consultations with the contributors and other interested parties. He urged that UNEF be maintained at least at Sharm el Sheikh. In the confusion of the hour, no one at the meeting was certain whether U.N. troops, in fact, were still there. U Thant, Ignatiev proposed, should send a qualified answer to Cairo, acknowledging receipt of the request, recognizing Egypt's full right to withdraw her consent and indicating that consultations would immediately be set in train pending a definitive reply. Lekic and Parsatharathi sharply objected. Egypt was exercising her sovereign right and must receive an unconditional reply. Lekic said that UNEF "as of this moment" was illegally on Egyptian soil. Was it his contention, Ignatiev asked, that the Egyptians had the right to harass U.N. forces, since their presence was already illegal? Egypt, Lekic retorted, would certainly allow time for UNEF to get out. Bunche again intervened, emphasizing Egypt's "unqualified right": the United Nations had no legal basis for remaining in Egypt and could not insist on remaining illegally.

U Thant told the Committee he intended to comply promptly and he did so at 19:00 hours. His letter to Riad announced he was issuing instructions for arrangements to begin without delay for the orderly withdrawal of the Force, and expressed his "serious misgivings" about a move which he believed "may have grave implications for peace." At 22:30 hours he cabled his instructions to Rikhye. On the same evening he submitted a special report to the General Assembly, and the next day a report to the Security Council. In Gaza, Rikhye received his evacuation order before dawn on May 19; he instructed all UNEF troops to withdraw from their forward border posts as of 17:00 hours on that day. He sought, however, to keep his men at Sharm el Sheikh as long as possible and claimed transport problems to secure a delay. Fawzi granted him a reprieve and the Yugoslav detachment was able to remain at its post for three more days.

But the worst had happened and the decision was irrevocable. Outstripped by events, the foreign ministries of interested capitals were unable to catch up with them. Their messages and their interventions were all too late. On the morning of May 19 Rafael delivered another communication from Eban. It urged U Thant not to condone any changes in the *status quo* pending the fullest and broadest international consultation and entreated him to do his utmost to maintain a UNEF presence at least at Sharm el Sheikh, even if the rest of the line were abandoned. The State Department instructed the Embassy in Cairo to exhort the Egyptians to reconsider their entire mobilization —with the clear injunction not to augment the danger of war by insisting on the ejection of UNEF; and above all to warn them against the extremely grave step of altering the *status quo* at the Straits of Tiran. The Embassy's Counselor found the Egyptians at the Foreign Office in a mood of inaccessible elation. By removing UNEF, he told them,

Egypt was throwing away her insurance policy and taking an incalculable risk. Egypt, he was told in reply, did not need any insurance. The dismissal of UNEF was her sovereign right; the deed was done and it was irreversible; and it was not a subject for discussion. The Egyptians were flushed with pride and confidence; they were anxious to leave no doubt in American minds that they meant business. They were tired, they said, of Israel's acting like a big bully in the town square, intimidating everyone who came along. Now somebody had come who was really big, and it was a very different affair.

At a later date, when the war was over, Egyptian diplomats in New York, Washington and elsewhere put out their own story of these events. It was the authorized Egyptian version of the genesis of the June war, and it soon won general acceptance in Egypt. The story was this:

Early in May the Egyptians were told on the highest level, by Kosygin, that Israel was preparing an invasion of Syria. This warning had to be taken seriously, since it came from the Soviet Summit. It was not just another report of the kind they had been receiving from Soviet military attachés. Besides, Israeli leaders were issuing provocative statements. These made a profound impression in Cairo, with their threat of a showdown on a pan-Arab issue that required a response. Egypt therefore sent her army into Sinai in a political demonstration to help Syria and, in order to clear the decks for a possible Israeli attack, asked UNEF to get out of the way on the Sinai border. Nasser did not want total evacuation; he merely sought the elimination of various border observation posts that impeded the full deployment of Egyptian forces along the line. He intended that UNEF maintain its other positions, including those at Sharm el Sheikh. But then U Thant made his great mistake and forced Nasser's hand with his all-or-nothing demarche. What could Nasser do at this juncture? He could not reverse the mobilization to which he and his army were committed. He was compelled to ask for all. Thus, all of a sudden and before they knew it, the Egyptians found themselves at Sharm el Sheikh. They had never meant to go that far. At Sharm el Sheikh they found a political vacuum which had to be filled; so they filled it by exercising their "belligerent right" and reimposing the blockade. U Thant had catapulted them to the Straits and into a confrontation with Israel.

This story of involuntary and inadvertent escalation skips over several awkward facts and circumstances. It does not square with the testimony of Rikhye, who on May 16 was told by Mokhtar to evacuate all his observation posts in the Sinai Peninsula—including Sharm el Sheikh. It defies the United Nations' record of the following day— the haste of the Egyptian Army in its multiple rush to the border, the further orders to Rikhye from the Egyptian Chief of Staff, and the arrival of an Egyptian advance party at Sharm el Sheikh on the day after that. All these moves occurred before the Egyptian demand for total withdrawal. Nor does it quite square with the methods Nasser used, which were brutal—a combination of political blackmail, military ultimatums and obfuscation to keep the Secretariat on the run, the dark hints of possible violence to U.N. troops, the warnings that any appeal would be an inadmissible affront. Nasser's fierce sensitivity to any slight to Egyptian sovereignty was well known and so was his capacity to mobilize emotion on the issue. He dictated the rules of the game from Cairo, and the Secretariat accepted them. While his generals were busy divesting UNEF of its effective role and meaning in Sinai, his neutralist friends in New York were insisting that any restraining move would intolerably offend a leader who was merely acting within his rights. Nor does the Egyptian story quite square with the experience of American diplomats in Cairo during the UNEF crisis, the flushed and fearless mood of Egyptian government officials, the exultant crescendo, the defiance of Israel. The dissolution of UNEF was not a subject for discussion.

But did Nasser know what his generals in Sinai were up to? Egyptian sources, by way of fuller explanation, later maintained that he did not. The Egyptian military leaders, in this singular version of events, deployed their forces on the border and issued their orders to Rikhye without consulting the political leadership. Nasser was thus unaware of the scope of the deployment they planned to carry out and of their exact designs with regard to UNEF. This explanation invites us to believe that the Chief of Staff of the armed forces, who commanded the operation, was equally unaware of what Nasser intended but went ahead on his own, accepting responsibility for the risks that were entailed in a series of unauthorized actions. The implausible is not necessarily unbelievable, and we are in no position to disprove the story. However, we are in a very strong position to doubt it. We happen to know that Nasser and his generals weighed the hazards of the mobilization in Sinai and recognized the risk of war that was implicit in it.

We also know that they weighed the hazards of dismissing UNEF and, having made their estimate, made their decision. The testimony on this point is again provided by the Egyptians themselves.

The witness on this occasion is Hussein Shafei, the President of the special court that tried Badran and others on charges of plotting against Nasser. Shafei wished to shield Nasser from the insinuation that he had plunged Egypt into war. One witness at the trial had testified that Amer had said he was unprepared for war and that Nasser had overruled him. Shafei's statement of February 19, 1968, was among the published excerpts of the trial record:

"The decision to withdraw UNEF was taken following a meeting attended by the Fieldmarshal [Amer]. During that session the President ruled that it was the right of the nation playing host to UNEF to withdraw the latter at any time, considering that this land was Egyptian [and] Arab, and that the possibility of reactions [from Israel] would increase from fifty to eighty percent. The Fieldmarshal attended that session and his only comment was complete agreement. The operation was not a sudden one. On this basis the decisions were taken. If the Fieldmarshal were to have expressed in that session any objection or observation, no measures with their subsequent hazards would have been taken. I say this in reply to the most serious statements uttered in this case. . . . If this subject is raised, all facts must be clear before public opinion."

Shafei unfortunately neglected to reveal the date of this meeting. Presumably it took place no later than May 16.

While Badran and other defendants sought to place on Nasser a major responsibility for the decisions that led to war, Shafei tried to shift back onto Amer and the generals all the consequences of Nasser's impatience for a political victory. Nasser, the defendants kept implying, was the man who made the gamble. But, Shafei replied, Nasser told Amer the odds and he accepted them. In any case, "the operation was not a sudden one." If we accept Shafei's account, there was no lack of coordination between Nasser and his military leaders on the question of removing UNEF. Far from stumbling toward war with his eyes closed, Nasser measured the odds with a startling lucidity. After the mobilization in Sinai, the chances of conflict were 50–50; with the decision to evict UNEF, they rose from 50 percent to 80. Nasser and his generals moved in concert to secure the total evacuation of UNEF and the Egyptians did not, after all, suddenly and to their great surprise find themselves at Sharm el Sheikh.

If this was Nasser's intention from the outset, what could U Thant have done about it? Probably very little. Egypt had her imprescriptible right, and UNEF could not remain on her territory against the will of her government. Aside from the legalities, the situation on the ground in Sinai was practically irretrievable. The Egyptians were certainly acting as if they were pressing for everything, and already on May 17 UNEF posts in Sinai were being overtaken, passed and rendered useless. Along various sectors of the border the Force had ceased to function as a buffer even before the withdrawal of consent. U Thant had to think of the safety of his troops. Mokhtar had warned of the danger of clashes, and El Kony, on instructions from Cairo, had served notice that the machinery of collective hysteria would be set in motion if the departure of the "occupation force" were delayed. It seemed unlikely that the Egyptians would go so horribly wrong as to open fire on their Yugoslav and Indian friends; but still, the position of U.N. troops was obviously insecure and in the long run untenable. U Thant had to consider that the two nations that had advised him of their intention to defect were those whose contingents actually held the line in Sinai and along a large portion of the boundary in Gaza. The Yugoslavs and Indians were determined to pull out, whatever the Secretary-General or Assembly might do or say. If the Egyptian demand for withdrawal had been resisted, the Force would have disintegrated anyway. The remaining contingents could not have continued to function, and any temporizing action might have exposed them to the dangers of Egyptian harassment and the ignominy of a disordered evacuation. Riad's formal request, in its context of diplomatic threats, was an ultimatum, and El Kony made it quite clear that any attempt to discuss the ultimatum or to appeal for reconsideration would be received as a monstrous offense to Egypt's prerogative. If, as a dilatory expedient, U Thant had sent a qualified reply—saying: Yes, we note your withdrawal of consent, which is perfectly legitimate, but we should now like to consult about it—they would have stormed with rage in Cairo. The Secretary-General by that time had no room left for maneuver.

If U Thant had fully exploited the resources of his office and tried to gain time, could he have changed in some way the course of events? We shall never know, since he never tried. He took his irrevocable step on the night of May 16 at his first meeting with El Kony, when he threw away all his weapons and reserved none. He opened his book of rules and revealed them all, without considering too closely the character of the regime or of the politician he was dealing with. In effect, his answer to Nasser invited the imminent and summary demise of a United Nations peace-keeping force at the very moment that the peace it was supposed to guard was being dangerously threatened. He made no attempt to communicate with Nasser, directly or indirectly; he sought no resource to diplomacy; he held no genuine consultations; and he acted with fulminating speed. The action that he took was calculated to precipitate events. The first thought that leaped to the minds of American and Israeli diplomats was: Sharm el Sheikh. The disaster to be averted was the reinstitution of the Egyptian blockade at the Straits of Tiran, and it was because of this immediate danger that Washington and Jerusalem heard the news of UNEF's final and total liquidation with such boundless dismay. Whatever he had done, U Thant could not possibly have saved UNEF in the shape or the role it had known theretofore. He could probably not have changed the ultimate outcome; he might have managed to delay it for a few days. Conceivably he might have gained a respite—a little time that diplomacy might have used in a race to catch up with events and to forestall the worst, and it was this time that he threw away.

Washington as well as Jerusalem took an outraged view of his conduct, and their censure became even more acrid after the war started on June 5. In retrospect, his all-or-nothing message seemed the decisive precipitating act in the prewar crisis, the disastrous miscalculation and misstep that had unloosed the avalanche. The balance of the evidence does not support this judgment. Rather, the evidence points the other way. U Thant does not seem to have forced Nasser's hand, as so many believed at the time and as the Egyptians later claimed. Nasser was apparently aiming from the start for the complete elimination of UNEF. But the Egyptians may still be right in saying that he got what he wanted much faster than he expected. He was probably gambling his way, as usual, aware of both the risks and the opportunities, testing reactions and ready to exploit them, untied to a final timetable, dissembling his intentions and keeping his options open. The Straits of Tiran and the renewal of the blockade were evidently next on his program of risks and opportunities. He may reasonably have supposed that the issue of free navigation would become a big-power issue at the United Nations and that the scene of the crisis would shift for a while from Sinai to New York. He may have expected a cushion of time before the next gamble. He may not have anticipated an instant victory on the issue of UNEF.

But may-have-beens and might-have-beens have no place in history; they exist only in a world of conjecture. There is a moment in the process of escalation when events take over from men and push forward regardless of their will. In the history of the demise of UNEF, this point was reached at the very beginning, on the evening of May 16, when U Thant announced his decisions to El Kony and lost whatever influence he might have had on the course of events. At that point the events took over and began happening too fast for men to handle.

· 6 ·

Ahalan Wassahalan

L IKE EVERYONE ELSE, when the first reports had come in
from Sinai on the morning of May 15, the Israelis had believed
that "Operation Cairo" was merely a gaudy political extrava-
ganza. They were persuded to believe so precisely because the Egyptian deployment was a parade. Their Western friends hastened to assure them it was only an exercise: the fact that such a fuss was being
made showed there was no reason for worry. Israeli military intelligence reported to the government that the Egyptians' return to Sinai
was a political move carried out in a demonstrative manner in order
to gain the maximum freedom of action and to reap the maximum
propaganda benefit in the Arab countries and the world at large. At
the United Nations, Rafael was instructed to tell U Thant that the
deployment was unjustified and to ask him to assure Cairo that Israel
had massed no troops on the Syrian border and had no intention of
initiating any action. The message was gratefully received, and transmitted.

The Israelis had been looking the other way, north toward Syria
and not south toward Egypt. Their Sinai border on Monday morning,
May 15, was practically naked. Hurriedly mustering troops and tanks,
Rabin filled the gap with units from the standing army. Some armored
contingents were about on maneuvers and there was no need for a
mobilization. The next day estimates at the General Staff were cau-

tiously revised and Eshkol, reporting to the Foreign Affairs and Defense Committee of the Knesset, was careful not to say that the Egyptian massings were merely for show. By the end of the day thirty thousand Egyptian troops and two hundred tanks had crossed the Canal. As Minister of Defense, Eshkol asked Rabin to order a partial call-up of reserves.

On May 17 came the surprise of the Egyptian demand for what seemed a "partial" withdrawal of UNEF. What was happening and why? The request had been made with thoughtful regard for the safety of U.N. troops in the event of war, and those in Sinai were apparently being asked to pull back temporarily to the Gaza Strip. Even this could be interpreted as a theatrical move in the inter-Arab game: Nasser had seized the occasion to demonstrate to the Arab world that he could get along without a protective cordon of foreign troops. In Jerusalem it was still unbelievable that with one foot in Yemen and one foot in Sinai, he would invite a direct confrontation. Without bringing troops home from Yemen, he could not face the hazards of an offensive build-up. The object of the massing in Sinai was evidently not offense but deterrence.

Nevertheless, Jerusalem was uneasy. Eshkol later recalled that at this moment he began to wonder whether the dates emblazoned on Israel's strategic calendar were really reliable. The calendar said Nasser was not ready for a showdown and it cast its spell on people's minds, but wars had a way of getting started before everyone was prepared for them. Israeli intelligence watched the disposition of Egyptian units and the choice of commanders. Cairo announced that General Abdel Mohsin Mortaji had been named commander of the Sinai area, in charge of any land operations against Israel. He was reputedly one of Egypt's leading specialists in tank warfare. By May 19, forty thousand troops, the equivalent of three and a half Egyptian divisions, had deployed in perfect order in eastern Sinai and were ranged in depth along the entire frontier. The number of tanks had grown to five hundred.

By this time the Israelis had made two startling discoveries. Unchallenged by the Israeli Air Force and undetected by Israeli radar until it was too late, Egyptian Migs had crossed Israel from east to west on a number of reconnaissance overflights. The Migs had flown low over Jordan to elude the radar screens, then climbed rapidly to a great height and traversed the country at several points from Tel-Aviv south to the site of Israel's nuclear reactor at Dimona in the Negev Desert. They were not spotted by Israeli radar until they were safely out at sea. The second discovery was made in Sinai: troops from Yemen had arrived in the peninsula. Having left the Yemeni port of Hodeida on May 15 for the three-to-four-day journey the length of the Red Sea, an infantry brigade and two armored battalions had disembarked at Port Suez at the southern end of the Canal. The infantry brigade and one of the armored battalions had immediately crossed the Canal to their staging areas in Sinai. The security of the operation had been well guarded: it was an emergency transfer outside the Egyptians' regular logistic plan for the rotation of their units in Yemen.

So great was the bewilderment in Jerusalem on the morning of Friday, May 19, when the Egyptians achieved the final dissolution of UNEF and at the same moment completed the largest deployment of troops ever recorded in Sinai, that the Israeli Government was at a loss to know what to say. It had misjudged Nasser. Suddenly and unaccountably he had upset the equilibrium of a decade. In the calendar of Israeli expectations his move should not have come for at least another three years. Neither the end of UNEF nor the mobilization in Sinai presented an immediate military danger. The U.N. soldiers at their Sinai posts had been a buffer, never a barrier, and the General Staff knew that Israel could handle Egypt's forty thousand men in war. But UNEF's disappearance sounded an alarm that was both military and psychological: the collapse of the *status quo* unhinged Israeli calculations, brought the armies face to face and fastened Israeli fears on the possible next step, a renewal of the blockade at the Straits of Tiran. At the Foreign Ministry on May 19, Eban wrestled with Chuvakhin for the last time. He warned the Russian that a blockade by Egypt would be a *casus belli* and proposed that Egyptian and Israeli troops carry out an agreed, mutual and gradual withdrawal from the Sinai border. With more than usual acerbity, Chuvakhin replied that Israel had brought the Sinai crisis on herself by her aggressive preparations against Syria; history, he foretold, would judge the leaders of the Israeli Government for their irresponsible actions. For the last time he accused Israel of mobilizing an invasion force on the Syrian border, and for the last time he was invited to inspect the area for himself. Poker-faced and brusque, he declined with his customary formula: "I am here to communicate facts from my government and not to check on them." Late on May 19 Eshkol ordered a large-scale mobilization. It got under way that night and the next morning.

With consternation and perplexity the Israelis suddenly realized that Nasser had mocked and overturned their timetable. Their unpreparedness was not physical but mental. The year 1970 had been set as the earliest possible date for an offensive concentration. Having erred in their national estimate by a margin of three years, they were uncertain of the public stance they should assume in the days immediately following, puzzled as to the exact note they should strike in their public utterances, apprehensive that too weak a stand might encourage Nasser to go on and that too strong a stand might heighten the crisis and incite him. Israeli leaders had made so many bold statements in the days preceding the Egyptian move! Now they fell silent. In instructing their diplomats in New York and Washington to draw attention to the explosive consequences of a blockade, they took care to remind them that these urgent representations should remain private and unpublicized. If, on May 20 or May 21, Israel had clearly warned that a blockade meant war, might there have been no blockade and no war? The Israelis, measuring the character of their adversary, decided not to provoke him. In Washington their Embassy urged that President Johnson make a warning statement. He, too, abstained.

But on May 22 the issue of Israel's response to challenge was put to the test in a violent argument at Eshkol's office. The time had come to draft his first report to the nation, the speech he was to deliver in the Knesset that evening. What should be its tone and purport? Ya'acov Herzog, the Director-General of the Prime Minister's Office, argued that nothing should be said that might be seen as inflaming Nasser, lest in the future the world hold Israel responsible for overreacting and augmenting the tension. Others contended that if Nasser was planning a blockade, he did not need a pretext; only a clear warning would stop him. Herzog's line of argument prevailed. A public warning might be seen as a dare and a challenge, and Eshkol was anxious that Israel should not appear in American eyes to be precipitating a much greater crisis. The extremely mild speech he made in the Knesset that night called for the restoration of the *status quo* on both sides of the Sinai border and spoke softly of the national and international rights of all states. It contained no statement on the dangers of a blockade and no mention of the Straits of Tiran. Had he issued a warning, it would have been too late. The decision had already been taken in Cairo.

In the Arab nations a swell of applause and jubilation had lifted

Nasser to the heights. He was the restored and reconsecrated hero. The triumphs of a single week had swept friends and foes into the anti-Israel campaign and fulfilled yet another of his three conditions for a confrontation: Arab unity. From Kuwait to Algeria the Arab world rallied round him. The sheikhdom of Kuwait, a patch of desert floating on a sea of oil, proclaimed a state of military preparedness and placed its minuscule army at the service of the United Arab Command. From Algiers, President Houari Boumedienne sent a message of unreserved support in the name of the Arab Revolution. Mohammed Achmed Mahgoub, the Prime Minister of Sudan, cabled his solidarity. The Lebanese made known their sisterly concern for Syria, and the Iraquis announced they were ready to send troops to defend the Syrian Republic against Zionist aggression. From Baghdad a military delegation flew to Cairo with a message from President Abdel Rahman Aref, pledging that Iraq would dispatch infantry, armored and air forces to Egypt to participate in the common struggle. The hyperbole of language crowned the excitement of the hour. *Al Ahram* summoned the Arab peoples to a "battle of destiny" against imperialism and its Zionist outpost, and from Sinai General Mortaji announced that his troops, fully prepared for all eventualities, were waiting for the "sacred war" to recover the land of Palestine.

The Egyptian mobilization in Sinai was an intoxicating success; the swift expulsion of UNEF was even more spectacular. Would King Hussein, the despised lackey of imperialism, so recently the object of scurrilous abuse in Nasser's public speeches, be able to stand alone against the tide? During the first week of the crisis the King's radio in Amman had flung its usual gibes in the direction of Cairo. When Egyptian troops crossed the Canal, the Jordanian radio scoffed at this "parading demonstration" and invited Nasser to show his nerve by dismissing UNEF. When UNEF was dismissed Amman jeered again and invited him to prove he was not bluffing and to satisfy Arab national claims by closing the Straits of Tiran to Israeli shipping. "Unless this is done," Amman Radio said, "the Arab cause will be denied the fruits of the UNEF evacuation." Nevertheless, on May 21, the day of this broadcast, Hussein sent his Chief of Staff, General Amer Hammash, to Cairo to inform the Commander-in-Chief of the United Arab Command, General Ali Ali Amer, that Jordan stood ready to do her part and wished to coordinate her operational plans. Nasser was unappeased; he did not intend to let his royal enemy climb on the bandwagon so easily. Hammash was told that "We do not share our plans with traitors" and the next day was sent ignominiously home with the message that Nasser refused to deal with imperialist agents.

The leader was once again in undisputed command. To the goads and traumas of the past—the memory of 1961 when Syria had broken away and the older shocks of 1956—was added the impetus of his triumphant restoration. Encouraged by the exuberant response his acts had evoked in the Arab world and the weak and apparently irresolute response they had drawn from Israel, he took the final step.

When and how was the decision made? Hussein Shafei, as President of the special court in the trial of the postwar conspirators, described the circumstances in his statement of February 19, 1968:

"I spoke in the morning about the withdrawal of UNEF which had led to the decision to close down the Gulf of Aqaba on the basis that this [the Gulf] is part of our territory and that it constituted the last vestige of the 1956 aggression. The President was meeting with all the Vice Presidents at his residence when he raised the question once more. He said this [the reinstitution of the blockade] might induce Israel to perpetrate aggression and would bring the possibility rate of aggression from eighty percent to one hundred percent. To this the Fieldmarshal [Amer] replied, 'I am ready to give my neck, Mr. President.' Now if there had been a desire for a period of grace or for a change [of plan] on the part of the responsible command in view of its estimate of the dimensions of the operation, this situation would have been decisive in taking the decision."

This meeting, then, took place after U Thant had agreed to evacuate UNEF. Nasser knew he was challenging Israel to war; the chances of conflict were now one hundred percent. Amer had his last opportunity to speak up and failed to use it.

The next witness is Badran. On February 24 he recounted a conversation which he, as Minister of War, had with Amer on the eve of the initial move into Sinai:

"I asked the Fieldmarshal whether we were ready to go through with the battle and told him that the withdrawal of UNEF would lead to a confrontation. He told me that he intended to occupy Sharm el Sheikh in place of UNEF and agreed with me not to close down the Gulf [of Aqaba]. . . . Then there were the movements of troops into Sinai to take up their offensive positions in the event of Israel's attack on Syria. . . . When the troop movements took place, the withdrawal of UNEF had to be effected so that we would be ready for attack. UNEF's withdrawal from Sharm el Sheikh was followed by the closure of the Gulf. . . . A meeting took place so that there would be no backing out. We were confident that our Army was ready and that Israel could not attack because intelligence estimates pointed to the fact that we were superior in armored weapons, artillery and air power. It was calculated that Israel would not walk into an open grave. This was the estimate of the situation. The Fieldmarshal went to Sinai and I was with him. He met people there who were angry because they wanted to start operations."

Thus, according to Badran, on the eve of the adventure there were still no plans for closing the Straits. At any rate, Nasser had not communicated them either to his Minister of War or to his responsible military commander. Amer assumed as always that the Egyptian Army would simply occupy Sharm el Sheikh and hoist the flag, without imposing a blockade. When he got the word from Nasser a few days later, he might have demurred but instead he offered his neck. Everyone in the army was keyed up with a sense of prodigiously superior strength; and some front-liners felt frustrated because they wanted to fight immediately. Badran continued:

"When the date for the closure of the Gulf was fixed, the President was supposed to announce it in a speech. The President selected an air base [at which to make his announcement] and met with officers there. They were enthusiastic and wanted to fight. The President spoke to them about the exact political angles. The officers were not satisfied, and the words of the President did not match their enthusiasm. The Fieldmarshal felt this and after the departure of the President, the former said to them, 'Boys, don't worry, you will fight.' . . . The President was speaking political words and he wanted to enlighten them [the Air Force officers]: If there isn't a war, don't be upset because there is the U.S.A., and so on."

What were Nasser's "exact political angles"? His sensible judgment was that Egypt should not strike the first blow, since this would alienate international opinion and could also result in bringing in the Americans on Israel's side. He aimed to preserve his victory without a war, if possible, and with a war, if necessary. He would pass to Israel both the military privilege of the first strike and the political stigma of being the aggressor. Since he expected his army to make a stand in Sinai, his calculations were reasonable and well founded. Badran went on:

"I say this because later on there were rumors that the Fieldmarshal wanted to deal the first blow and the President did not want this to take place. I say that the President was not against our going to war but it was understood from his words that we should not deal the first blow because the U.S.A. would support Israel. As a matter of fact, the Fieldmarshal was convinced of [the wisdom of] not dealing the first blow and said this to Sidki Mahmoud [the Commander of the Egyptian Air Force]."

Amer, however, was of two minds and had to be convinced by Nasser. Badran testified at another point:

"The Fieldmarshal wanted to deal the first blow because he was worried about the boys' morale. Then he saw it would be better if the blow were not dealt."

In the end Amer used Nasser's argument to convince Mahmoud:

"For the record I should like to state that Sidki Mahmoud had objected. The Fieldmarshal said to him, Would you like to deal the first blow and face the U.S.A. or would you like to sustain the first blow and face Israel only? So he said, I agree. The Fieldmarshal asked him about the potential losses [to the Egyptian Air Force in the event of an Israeli first strike] and he said twenty percent. . . . No one believed that the Jews would be so capable of undertaking the operation against us because of our superiority in weapons and air power and our excellent plan which would have obstructed any confrontation. No one calculated that the Jews had secured immense technical facilities from the U.S.A.. . . . The main factor is that the Jews made a detailed reconnaissance by means of the Americans of every nail in our planes. In the first raid on the airports, they picked on the planes equipped with defensive rockets. . . . The Jewish Air Force relied on a U.S. plan."

What was the relationship between Nasser and his highest military commander? On February 24, nearly six months after Amer's suicide, Badran told this story to the court:

"In the name of the people and its right to the Revolution, the people must know. I am not defending a man even though he is dead and has no one to defend him. I am stating facts. A certain date was set to close the Gulf. The date was at very short notice, to the point where it was impossible to effect it. So the Fieldmarshal had to bring in paratroop units and light units to occupy [Sharm el Sheikh]. He had to embark on a quick operation entailing many difficulties. He was upset. I said to him, Why did you agree with him on all this? He said, I gave my word. I told him this was wrong and he should have discussed [the matter] with the President first. . . . The President said to the Fieldmarshal, Can you close down [the Gulf] in such and such a time? and the Fieldmarshal said, I can; but the implementation was difficult for the Fieldmarshal. . . . I am stating facts."

The Court: "But unfortunately there are no witnesses to these facts."

Badran: "The court can accept or reject these statements. The President is there and you can ask him. I accept his verdict."

Like the flashbulbs of a photographer sporadically illuminating an unsuspected scene, the extracts from Badran's testimony offer a bizarre picture of the process of decision-making in authoritarian Egypt. Nasser, riding the crest, was still the calculating gambler, but he misread the odds. He was able to misread them so easily because of the way in which misinformation pervades and characterizes so much of Arab society. He was the supreme and solitary autocrat, separated by his unique prestige and power from the leaders of his military and political establishment, even from Amer, his comrade of the Revolution, his Deputy Supreme Commander and First Vice-President. Even Amer could not say no. Surprised by a sudden question, lacking the troops and the means of overland transport to meet Nasser's deadline for the seizure of Sharm el Sheikh, he could not bring himself to ask for time. So he gave his word. Badran's account, as far as we can judge, is correct. Amer flew troops to the craggy wilderness of southern Sinai and they were parachuted onto the rocks.

Everyone was ready to tell the chief what he wanted to hear. What he wanted was a fast political victory. An immediate decision was taken after summary consultations had confirmed that nobody wanted to back out. How could the generals say that with all their armament they were not prepared? Besides, they had convinced themselves that they were. "The political decision," Badran said, "was taken on the basis of the military situation." Everyone was disposed to join in the self-deception: Amer, hard-pressed but unwilling and unable to draw back, even though he had always excluded a blockade from his reckoning; Badran, quizzically skeptical at times but ready to go along; Mahmoud, glibly offering his estimate of losses no greater than 20 percent; and the air force officers at their base in Sinai, pressing for war, discontent with Nasser's political quibbles, champing and impatient for the battle of destiny to which he had called them. All the leaders had said they were ready to face Israel; they ended by believing it, and acted on their belief.

Nasser, it appears from the trial record, did not blunder into war in a series of unconsidered overreactions. He deliberately sought a confrontation. He knew and accepted the risks, and his strategy was perfectly rational. He expected either an Israeli capitulation and a glorious Arab victory without firing a shot, or a war in which Egypt would hold the line somewhere in Sinai and possibly inflict heavy damage on the enemy.

The brass of Egypt, the ranking officers of his establishment—Amer, Mortaji, Mahmoud and Badran, and three Vice-Presidents, Mohieddin, Sabry and Shafei—foregathered at the Sinai headquarters base of the Egyptian Air Force to hear his announcement. It was May 22, the day of Eshkol's speech to the Knesset. Nasser began:

"What I want to say is that we are in 1967 and not in 1956. . . . Why do I say that now? I am saying it today in facing Israel. Israel today has not got either Britain or France as was the case in 1956. She has America, who supplies her with arms. But the talk that took place in 1956, the conspiracy that took place in 1956, could not be accepted again by the world. From 1956 until today, Israel has been bragging. They talk about excellent training and efficiency. They talk of the Sinai campaign, which was not a battle at all, because we were withdrawing at the time to face Britain and France. Today we have the chance to prove the truth. We actually have the opportunity to show the world the facts as they are. Today we are face to face with Israel—Israel which threatened aggression and was bragging only recently."

If UNEF had tried to remain on Egyptian soil as an agent of imperialism, he said, "we would have considered it hostile and we would have disarmed it."

As always, he flashed his bright sword at the end:

"What is the meaning of the armed forces' occupation of Sharm el Sheikh? It is an affirmation of our rights and sovereignty over the Gulf of Aqaba. The Gulf of Aqaba constitutes our Egyptian territorial waters. Under no circumstances will we allow the Israeli flag to pass through the Gulf of Aqaba. The Jews have threatened war. We tell them: 'You are welcome. *Ahalan wassahalan.* We are ready for war.' Our armed forces and all our peoples are ready for war, but under no

circumstances will we abandon any of our rights. This water is ours."
Ahalan wassahalan. "You are welcome." He had never said that
before.

At midnight in Tel-Aviv the Israeli military monitoring service
picked up Cairo Radio's announcement. The broadcast gave two versions of the decision. Nasser was correctly quoted as saying that the
Gulf of Aqaba was closed to Israeli flagships; the Cairo announcer
went further and said it was closed as well to the passage of all strategic materials, even in non-Israeli vessels. Puzzled at first by so big a
discrepancy in so important a statement, the Israelis shrewdly
guessed it was a ruse intended to head off any sharp, immediate reaction. The military waited until five in the morning before awaking Adi
Yafeh, Eshkol's political secretary. An hour later the Prime Minister
and Yafeh set out by car from Jerusalem for General Headquarters in
Tel-Aviv; and Eshkol decided, on the way, to summon all party leaders, including those of the opposition, to an emergency meeting that
afternoon, with the General Staff attending.

At that moment Yigal Allon, the Minister of Labor, was in the
Soviet Union and Moshe Dayan, who had retired from the army and
held no place in the government, was in the Negev. Dayan had mistrusted the national estimates. By some bold gift of independent insight, he had sensed that war was coming from the first move of the
Egyptians into Sinai. On May 20 he had telephoned to Eshkol to ask
for permission to visit the front: he wanted to see the troops, talk to
the commanders and go over their plans. Eshkol had agreed and
Rabin had provided transport for the tour. Dayan was now at the
front and Yafeh sent a helicopter to fetch him back for the meeting in
Tel-Aviv.

From Ambassador Harman in Washington came a personal message from President Johnson, transmitted by Eugene Rostow, the Undersecretary of State for Political Affairs. The message was urgent:
Israel must hold her hand. Unlike some Presidential notes at critical
times in the past, this one did not overstep the usual limits of diplomacy. It did not suggest that disregard of the American advice would
have damaging consequences for the future of American-Israeli relations. But the tone was imperative. Israel must hold back, in order to
give the United States a chance to enlist the support of the maritime
powers and try to break the blockade by peaceful means. If Israel
took military action, she would be alone; the United States would not

be responsible for the consequences.

The lines of cleavage in Israel's national outlook were drawn in the sharp debate among ministers and generals at the meeting in Tel-Aviv that afternoon. The General Staff was for immediate war—Rabin; his Chief of Operations, Brigadier General Ezer Weizmann; and his Director of Military Intelligence, Brigadier General Aharon Yariv. Believing that war was inescapable and that Israel must respond at once if she were not to renounce the advantage of strategic surprise, the generals warned against the dangers of delay. If Israel failed to react to what she had so often proclaimed to be a *casus belli,* her military deterrent would lose its credit; indeed, the *casus belli* itself would lose its edge and urgency if it went unresisted and unchallenged. Most important of all, the generals said, were the dynamics of the military situation following the blockade. The next step was inevitable. Egypt would move her strategic reserves across the Canal, there would be a further substantial build-up in eastern Sinai, and Israel in a few days would face a massive security threat on her desert border. She could not afford to vacillate; nor could she tie her national security to the problematic hopes and schemes of the United States. She must enter the war under conditions that promised the quickest victory with the fewest casualties. The time to strike was now. The General Staff was in a position to order the strike within forty-eight hours.

At the opposite pole stood the Foreign Ministry. Foremost in Eban's mind was his experience in 1956, when the Americans and Russians had both turned against Israel. In times of crisis, the link with Washington was more vital than ever, and Eban remembered the State Department's injunction, repeated through the years: "If you want us to be with you on the landings, please advise us about the take-offs." He remembered the nightmare of the communications breakdown during the Suez crisis. American counsel had a built-in weight and thrust greater than that of any other power, and if Israel ignored it she might forfeit the political fruits of military victory. For Eban, the first imperative was to keep the lines open to the State Department and the White House.

A prime concern, as the issue was debated, was to establish clearly that a *casus belli* existed. Were the Straits of Tiran really closed? The question was raised and discussed. In the eyes of the world, evidently, Israel should appear to have a legitimate cause for action and not merely a pretext. Should she send a ship through the Straits, with colors flying, to test the reality of the blockade? The proposal was made, but there were obvious objections. The proclamation of a blockade had the same implications as the halting of a ship, and the Egyptians would be certain to see through the stratagem. To make a test ship the precondition for action would be as good as to announce to the Egyptian Chief of Staff by cable the exact moment to open war on Israel. A second concern, more complex and more hazardous, was to assess the exact nature of the threat in Sinai. The danger, at all events, was not immediate. It was still in the future—but how far? While the generals were sensitive to the military implications of the blockade, Eban responded to the pressures of the American relationship. Before going to war, he argued, Israel must demonstrate her readiness to try the diplomatic way.

With the partisans of war ranged against the proponents of diplomacy, Eshkol was caught in the middle. The message from Johnson was the determining factor in his decision. Johnson had once told him that what he said he would do, he did; and though Eshkol doubted that the Americans would indeed be able to open the Straits, he felt he had only one choice. The consensus of his ministers and of the opposition party representatives supported him. Israel should not jump into war and offer explanations later. The American President had said he would do everything possible to ensure free navigation through the Straits of Tiran, and he had asked for time. Very well, he would have it. Israel could afford the time and allow the Americans the opportunity to show what they could do; they would then have no cause for complaints or reproaches in the future. "Therefore," Eshkol reflected at a later time, "I saw fit to put them on the spot." The meeting in Tel-Aviv ended with the decision to give Washington a chance—for two, three or four days.

Thus Israel began her period of waiting. Having agreed to wait on the strength of the American pledge, Eshkol next decided to send an emissary to Washington to put the pledge to the test. There were, however, other Western capitals that were equally committed to Israel on the issue of Tiran. In 1957 a triumvirate of maritime powers—France, Britain and the United States—had solemnly underwritten the settlement that had guaranteed the right of free passage. The French at the United Nations had been particularly forthright, announcing they would take action against any renewal of the blockade and, like the Americans, recognizing Israel's right to act in self-defense against it. Where did the French stand now? The Israelis on May 23 were bewildered and upset by French silence. No spokesman in Paris had ever disassociated France from her engagements of 1957, but on the day after the blockade, no French spokesman bothered to reaffirm them. De Gaulle's position was a mystery, and the Israeli Embassy in Paris was making anxious inquiries at the Palais de l'Elysée in the hope of reaching him.

From London also the premonitory signs were disheartening. What of the celebrated Tripartite Declaration of 1950? In that statement, the same three powers had affirmed their resolve to take action, both within and outside the United Nations, to prevent any violation of frontiers or armistice lines in the Middle East. French government officials now announced that France had no plans to implement the declaration, and in London the Foreign Office said that Britain no longer felt bound by it. The French said, in effect, that the declaration was dead, the British said it was outdated, and both said it was up to the United Nations to preserve peace in the Middle East with its usual procedures.

Was Israel alone or would those who had pledged their help now keep their word? Someone should go and find out. But who should it be? At Eshkol's office on the evening of May 23, a further debate was engaged. The obvious candidacy of Eban was vigorously contested by several Ministers. They mistrusted him precisely because, after his years of service in Washington and New York, he was Israel's leading advocate of the doctrine of American support. The moment he left the country, they said, he would become the government's chief interpreter and main channel of communications with the Western capitals. He might even commit the government to a course of action on which it was not prepared to follow him; he might be understood as saying that Israel would not go to war, and then her friends could later claim that he had sought to mislead them. Others in the cabinet disliked the entire notion of a trip that would tie Israel's hands and prolong her period of waiting. What, they asked, could Eban accomplish? He would travel from capital to capital collecting advice, and it was perfectly clear what the advice would be. Everyone would tell him: Don't go to war. Israel, it was argued, should not place herself in such a position, limiting her freedom of action at a time of danger. The proposed trip was both risky and pointless. It was imprudent for the Foreign Minister of a small power to visit the capitals of the great powers at such a moment. In any case, a state does not ask for the permission of others to go to war, and its most sympathetic friends, whatever they may feel, cannot possibly grant it. If he met De Gaulle, Eban would present Israel's situation and plead her case but he would have no decision to convey. He would listen to De Gaulle's authoritative advice, and the President of France would be enraged when Israel disregarded it.

These arguments were still being pressed when cables arrived from the Israeli Embassies in Washington and Paris announcing that the Presidents of the United States and France would be ready to receive the Foreign Minister of Israel. These messages sealed the decision. At three-thirty on the morning of May 24, Eban boarded a plane and set out on the most controversial mission of his career.

At the Elysée Palace he found De Gaulle—as he later described him—"agitated, very nervous and tense." The Paris newspapers on that morning rang with alarums of war in the Middle East and De Gaulle was apprehensive. It seemed to Eban that what he feared above all was a confrontation between East and West, and may even have conceived that by his advice to Israel he was saving her from the dangers of a Soviet intervention. He repeated his advice many times with evident feeling: *"Ne faites pas la guerre! . . . Ne faites pas la guerre! . . ."*

Magisterial in expression and vague in commitment, De Gaulle saw the Middle Eastern conflict from his own lofty plane of preoccupation. The dispute at the Straits of Tiran was an opportunity for France to lift herself into the Grand Directorate of the Big Four. When Eban alluded to the French obligations in the conflict, De Gaulle swept them away with stroke of a sentence: "That was 1957 and now it is 1967." The engagements of the Fourth Republic did not extend to the Fifth; they were the product of *"la chaleur de cinquante-sept."* To resolve the abstruse legalities of the navigation issue, he proposed that the Big Four convene and seek a reasonable settlement. *"Il faut bien que les Quatre . . ."*

To the best of Eban's knowledge, *les Quatre* were not in the habit of holding consultations. When the Russians were interested in settling matters globally, they went to the Americans, and France was of no more account for them than Paraguay. The Elysée had demoted the issue of the blockade—or elevated it, perhaps—from a *casus belli* to a matter requiring consultations by a Big Four establishment that did not exist. Eban's doubts on this score were confirmed a few days later when the French proposal for a Big Four conference, politely welcomed in Washington, was cold-shouldered in Moscow.

Instead of a commitment, De Gaulle offered a political figment. At a later time he claimed that he had told Eban that if Israel were attacked, France would not permit her liquidation. Eban did not recall the remark, nor did it appear in the Israeli protocol of their conversation; and since Israel could ill afford to wait for De Gaulle to rescue her at the moment of threatened liquidation, the assurance in any case was of only passing rhetorical interest. *"Ne faites pas la guerre! Ne tirez pas la première balle! . . ."* Eban in reply expounded the Israeli point of view. *"Monsieur le Président,* we cannot open war. Egypt has already done so!" De Gaulle asked what he meant. Eban said: "Egypt has opened war by imposing a naval blockade at Tiran." De Gaulle replied that as far as he was concerned, he who fires the first shot is the one who opens war. "There are many ways of liquidating man and state," Eban said, "and strangulation is one of them. A naval siege is a very effective way of liquidating a state!" But De Gaulle refused to withdraw his definition and after Eban had reviewed the major threats to Israel—the Egyptian mobilization, the blockade, the terror from Syria—he insisted that *tout de même* there still was wide room for diplomatic activity and consultations.

At the end De Gaulle wished the state of Israel success and prosperity in her undertakings, explaining that his advice at this hour was inspired by his sentiments of friendship. Israel, he said, was not yet sufficiently stabilized to be able to solve all her problems alone. But Eban had the last word. With a turn of phrase intended for the ear of the leader of the wartime Resistance, he said that "if Israel is faced with the choice of surrender or resistance, Israel will resist."

What did De Gaulle understand from this talk? Did he believe Israel had chosen the path of diplomacy and that all she wanted from him was his help in easing the tension? He himself, of course, aspired to play an Olympian role in the crisis; and having imparted his urgent advice to Israel not to make war, he easily assumed that she would obey and refrain. Soon after Eban left the Elysée, the French Minister of Information defined the government's position. Freedom of navigation in the Gulf of Aqaba, he said, was an extremely complex problem of international law, especially since the Egyptian Government, maintaining its belligerent rights, had never agreed in principle to the passage of Israeli ships. Thus, in another sentence, was the French commitment to Israel publicly disavowed.

From Paris Eban flew the same day to London for a meeting at the airport with Harold Wilson. The British Prime Minister was sympathetic and ready to offer his help, on condition that matters be handled through the United Nations or within the framework of a joint operation by the maritime powers, including the United States. Eban resumed his journey to Washington.

On at least one level of the American Administration, under the shock of crisis on the morning after the blockade, there was already a conviction that war was inevitable—either war or a major Egyptian political victory at the expense not only of Israel but of American positions throughout the Arab Middle East. This was the immediate estimate of political officers on the Near Eastern Desk at the State Department. The prime objective of American policy through the years had been to prevent a Middle Eastern war. Now, as they saw the situation on May 23, the war threatened and the Administration was constitutionally unable to take the unilateral action required to avert it. Since, under the circumstances, the United States would find it impossible to fulfill its commitment to Israel in the only effective way— by a fast and vigorous intervention to force a backdown in Cairo—Israel would either have to fight or capitulate. In these terms at the very start of the Tiran crisis, the men on the Near Eastern Desk foretold and summed up its entire course with synoptic clarity and logic.

But on May 23 the task of the State Department was to find an escape from this logic if it possibly could, a means whereby the United States could honor its commitment and prevent a war. What *was* the American commitment? What exactly did it mean? It was embodied in a long series of documents—in the statements of four American Presidents pledging support of the independence and territorial integrity of Israel, in Dulles' memorandum of February, 1957, on passage through the Straits and in Eisenhower's cabled assurances to Ben-Gurion at the end of the Suez crisis. It had been confirmed in conversations at the White House between Ben-Gurion and Eisenhower and later between Eshkol and Johnson. The American Presidents had clearly encouraged Israel to believe that if she ever found herself in serious trouble, the Sixth Fleet would be there in a matter of hours. But a commitment in the form of general assurances is extremely difficult to define; it is morally binding but its meaning is revealed only when it is put to the test. What are the unforeseen circumstances at the time it is invoked? What is one in a position to do about it? The Americans recognized their obligation but were uncertain as to what it entailed in terms of action. They were committed, alone and independently of their allies, but they could not act alone at the moment of challenge. It came down to the fact that the President could not commit the Sixth Fleet and its fighter squadrons to a Middle Eastern war or authorize American warships to shoot their way through the Straits without the approval of Congress.

For some time the State Department, preoccupied with another war, had been neglecting its long-term planning for Middle East contingencies. It had no plan for the UNEF emergency and none for the renewal of the blockade. In the anxious weekend between those two events, when the danger signals pointed toward Tiran, a contingency plan was conceived. This was the project for the establishment of an international naval force. In the event of a blockade the United States would seek a declaration by the principal maritime powers reaffirming the right of free passage and, more substantially, the creation of a multinational armada to which its major allies would be asked to contribute warships. The Red Sea Regatta, as it came to be called, would serve as an armed escort for Israeli and other Israel-bound ships passing the Egyptian coastal guns at Sharm el Sheikh. The notion was that the regatta would achieve a *de facto* standoff at Tiran and diplomacy would meanwhile seek some compromise formula for settling the dispute. With this project the Americans hoped to honor their commitment.

The Israeli Embassy in Washington got the news of the blockade at 22:00 hours on May 22. An hour later Ephraim Evron, the Israeli Minister, was called to the office of Eugene Rostow, who asked Israel to sit tight so that the United States could pursue diplomacy. Rostow said the issue would have to be taken to the Security Council, since American opinion would not understand or accept a failure to do so; but he assured Evron that the United States stood firmly with Israel and was sending messages of warning and restraint to the three other parties—the Russians, the Egyptians and the Syrians.

The next day the Israeli Embassy waited anxiously for what it wanted most, a clear statement upholding the American commitments of 1957. Various drafts of a Presidential declaration were being composed, compared and rewritten at the State Department. To the Israelis' alarm, one of them omitted any mention of the American position on Tiran; it indicated that no "aggression" had yet taken place and called on all sides to keep calm and use restraint to avoid a conflict. Evron intervened to urge that the declaration contain at least a mention of the blockade and of the American position. This was done in the final draft that was sent to the White House. The President's statement, after expressing dismay at the "hurried withdrawal" of UNEF, said that "the purported closing of the Gulf of Aqaba to Israeli shipping has brought a new and grave dimension to the crisis. The United States considers the Gulf of Aqaba to be an international waterway and feels that a blockade of Israeli shipping is illegal and potentially dangerous to world peace."

But in the twenty-four hours that followed the President's statement, the nature and locale of the crisis dramatically changed, fulfilling the predictions of the Israeli General Staff. The first phase of the crisis ended soon after Eban set out on his journey; the second phase was already under way when he was talking to De Gaulle and Wilson on May 24. When he left Tel-Aviv, there was no immediate sense of danger to Israel's security; when he arrived in the United States, the rapid and renewed build-up of Egyptian forces in Sinai had begun. He heard about it in a cable from Eshkol's office which reached him in Washington on May 25. The message was accented with high alarm and Eban was told to impress on the Americans the new dangers of the situation. Every hour brought fresh intelligence reports of the Egyptian deployment: an armored brigade and a second infantry brigade had returned by sea from Yemen, and in the Gaza Strip the Palestine Liberation Army—"detonator" of the sacred war—had been fully mobilized and placed under Egyptian command. There were disturbing signs of Egyptian overconfidence. Egyptian Migs had made further reconnaissance flights over the Negev, all of them undetected until it was too late, while Egyptian Army units were moving into offensive positions, poised for an attack that might come at any hour. Eshkol sent a message directly to Secretary of State Dean Rusk, emphasizing that the thrust of the crisis had abruptly shifted from the Straits of Tiran to the Sinai border.

The alarm was sounded but Eban was uncertain as to what he was expected to do about it. How was he to interpret the message to Rusk? Was it an appeal for direct military aid? Certain lines and phrases suggested that it was. But Eban had left Israel with one clear assignment and nothing else: to test the American commitments with regard to Tiran and the eventual availability of the Sixth Fleet in the defense of Israel. He was now caught between two briefs, and the message he was conveying to the Americans was equivocal. On the one hand, he was saying: There are burglars in my house; where are the policemen you have promised me? and on the other: Look, this murderer is threatening to cut my throat; will you send your police to help me? If you don't stop him, I may have to deal with him myself. To which the Americans replied: As for your murderous assailant, don't worry about him; we are holding him back; he is making a lot of noise but he won't do a thing. As for the burglar, you must be patient; we are organizing the police force and hope to have it on the way very soon.

In fact, Eshkol was not asking for American military aid. He wanted Eban to stress the growing urgency of military developments and press the Americans for a firm line and early decision on a course of action. At a dinner on May 25 Rostow presented the American project for an international armada. Joseph Sisco and Lucius Battle from the State Department, Eban, Harman and Evron were among those present. Their exchanges were difficult and at times embarrassing. Painful moments were spent in a search for the relevant documents of 1957—the statements of Eisenhower and Dulles—and in a worried discussion as to what they meant. A general confusion of spirit prevailed at table. The Israelis felt the conversation was getting off the track, away from the main issue of the military threat posed by the second wave of the Egyptian build-up. They emphasized the need for early action. The Americans put their stress on the need for Israel to hold off until they could call the armada into being. But to the Israelis' central question, For how long must they hold off? the Americans had no answer. They suggested no date and made no commitment.

In any case, this was a question that would have to be answered by the President. The next morning, at a meeting with Robert McNamara, the Secretary of Defense, and General Earle Wheeler, the Chairman of the Joint Chiefs of Staff, Eban found that the Pentagon, no less than certain quarters at the State Department, had misgivings about the Red Sea Regatta. McNamara asked whether the regatta plan meant that every time an Israeli ship appeared at Tiran, a warship would have to escort it through the Straits and up the Gulf of Aqaba to Eilath. What sense did that make? A good question, but the Americans had proposed the flotilla in the first place. At this point the Americans and the Israelis made their radically divergent estimates of the military situation. Both McNamara and Wheeler felt the Israelis were exaggerating their vulnerability to Egyptian attack. Israel, as the dispatches from Jerusalem made clear, believed she was in day-to-day danger as the Egyptian mobilization gathered strength; the United States believed she was not. The Israelis feared a surprise attack; the Americans were ready to swear that Nasser would never fire the first shot. Wheeler's faith in the Israeli armed forces was invincible. Armed with his astonishingly accurate estimates, he was certain that whoever started a war, Israel would win it singlehanded and her victory would be decisive.

In the midst of Eban's visit a further alarm was heard from Jerusalem. The Israelis relayed an urgent message from their military intelligence that the Egyptian Command was operationally prepared to implement its plans for a coordinated land-and-air offensive. The Americans, disbelieving a message that seemed to contradict their own information, decided to act on it anyway: true or not, it warranted an appropriate signal to Cairo. On Johnson's behalf, Rostow called in the Egyptian Ambassador, told him of the report, expressed the hope that it was not true and warned in the strongest terms of the disastrous consequences of an Egyptian move.

Eban's appointment with Johnson, originally set for noon on May 26, was postponed by the White House in order to give the President more time to inform himself, and no new hour was set. Nerves at the Israeli Embassy were sorely frayed by the uncertainty of waiting. The White House suggested at one point that the Foreign Minister refresh himself with a walk. Evron telephoned to Walt Rostow, the Presidential assistant, to say that the delay was dreadful, since it made it appear there was a crisis between the United States and Israel. Rostow agreed and said a new hour for the appointment would be fixed. Eban resumed his troubled waiting. Evron called Rostow again and asked to come to see him. On arriving at the White House he was told that the President would see Eban at 19:00 hours on condition that he make no statements afterward, that he shun the assembled television cameras and that he come and go by the diplomats' entrance instead of the main door. This was acceptable to Evron provided the Foreign Minister's arrival was not "secret." Just as these arrangements were concluded, the President sent word that he wanted to see Evron immediately. They had met many times and were on the warmest terms.

Johnson had taken his measure of events and he went straight to the point. He told Evron: I am not a king. He was a six-foot-two Texan; he could not give orders. His main point was that he was constitutionally bound and could not act without Congressional consent. He needed a Congressional resolution similar to that of August, 1964, that had empowered him as Commander-in-Chief of the Armed Forces to take all necessary measures to face the situation in Vietnam. He had determined, he said, to seek such a resolution; equally, he proposed to move vigorously ahead on the plan for an international maritime force for the Straits of Tiran. Having thus set out his position, Johnson told Evron that Israel was a sovereign and independent country and he could not tell her what to do.

Soon after Evron left, Eban arrived. McNamara, Walt and Eugene Rostow, McGeorge Bundy and Clark Clifford were there when he went in; Rusk was away on a trip. Johnson had meanwhile received a joint memorandum from Rusk and McNamara that presented two broad policy alternatives. There were obviously only two: either the United States could permit Israel to act alone or it could urge restraint while an effort was made to find a multilateral solution. Johnson held to the second alternative. But implicit in the formulation he had received was the thought that the ultimate decision lay with Israel. If in the end the choice lay between surrender and resistance, who else could make it for her? The United States could exert powerful pressure to prevent a war. In the end it could not tell Israel what to do.

The President gave Eban a memorandum setting forth the American position. It opened with a reminder that the constitutional processes of government were basic for the United States on any question of war or peace. It reaffirmed the American stand on freedom of passage through the Straits as well as the commitment of four American Presidents to defend the integrity and independence of the Middle Eastern states. It affirmed the American intention to support and uphold the principle of free navigation. It warned of the grave consequences of any unilateral Israeli initiative and concluded with an aphoristic formula that had been excogitated by Rusk: "Israel would not be alone if she did not act alone."

In his meeting with Eban, Johnson did not repeat his remark to

Evron about Israel's being a sovereign and independent state. He
spoke of the American commitment. He recognized and accepted the
commitment and proposed to organize international action to implement it. The objective of the action would be to lift the blockade and
secure full freedom of passage for all ships, including of course those
of Israel. He said he needed two weeks in which to pursue the proposal and he asked Eban for that time. Canada had already said she
would contribute two destroyers to the armada, and he would be dis-
cussing the project with Harold Wilson during the latter's forthcoming
visit to Washington. Johnson stressed again his need for a Congressional resolution authorizing him to shoot on behalf of a non-
American ship. What applied to the maritime force evidently applied
all the more forcibly to the use of the Sixth Fleet in the defense of
Israel.

On leaving Washington on May 27, Eban believed his trip had been
a notable success. He had fulfilled his assignment. He had established
an indispensable contact with the Americans, he had involved them in
their responsibilities, and he had vindicated the doctrine of American
support. The line to Washington was open and there would be no
repetition of the communications crisis of 1956. Each side recognized
and appreciated the other's motivation. Moreover, his trip had established that the United States and Israel agreed in their broad assessment of the crisis and its meaning. The sudden polarization in the
Middle East was clearly not the work of Israel but the result of a
Soviet-Egyptian initiative; and the moves of the Moscow-Cairo axis
were aimed at American no less than at Israeli interests. The two
world powers that had acted in concert against Israel in 1956 were
divided in 1967. Another weighty imperative had inspired Eban's trip.
He had wished to ascertain Soviet intentions in the event that Israel
acted alone. Israel reserved her freedom of action but always on the
proviso that the Russians did not intend to intervene with their own
force against her. Evidently they did not so intend. Their warnings to
Israel had been harsh and at times brutal; but they in turn had been
strongly warned by the Americans. Clearly, the two big powers would
neutralize each other in the event of war.

Above all, as he left for home, Eban felt he had an answer to his
main question. The United States was honoring its commitment. But
on returning to Tel-Aviv and going directly to an emergency meeting
of the Israeli cabinet to report on his mission, he found that a substan-

tial number of his colleagues sharply and bitterly disagreed with him. Israel during his absence had entered her trial period of alarm and anguish. In four days the Egyptians had moved a further three and a half divisions—some forty thousand men—into eastern Sinai. They had taken the crucial step: the Fourth Armored Division, the mainstay of their strategic reserve, had crossed the Canal, and between nine hundred and a thousand tanks—more than the British Eighth Army and the Afrika Korps together had amassed at El Alamein— were now deployed in the Sinai Desert. The manner of the deployment argued a sudden decision. Unlike the first wave, that had moved in almost stately order, the second was disorganized, precipitate and pell-mell. Logistics fell apart; units tumbling to their desert stations outran their water supplies and their ammunition. The Egyptian Command was continually changing its mind; orders and counterorders sent the newly arrived units now one way and now another in uncertain shifts up and down the frontier. Of these changes in the order of battle, there was one that appeared particularly menacing. A special armored group commanded by General Saad Shazli, an enthusiast of mobile warfare, suddenly abandoned the northern anchor of the Egyptian lines at El Arish, where Mortaji had anticipated an Israeli drive to isolate the Gaza Strip. Shazli's group, roughly the size of a division and listed as Egypt's crack troops, moved south to positions below the central east-west axis of Sinai; and there it was held in mobile reserve, opposite the southern Negev, an offensive threat that pointed to a possible armored thrust across the Negev toward Jordan with the object of cutting off Eilath. By May 26 the Egyptian build-up fulfilled all the conditions of that massive offensive concentration which, in the doctrine of Allon, entitled Israel to respond with an "anticipatory counterattack."

Allon was in Moscow as head of the Israeli delegation to a conference of the International Social Insurance Federation when he heard the news of the blockade. Forsaking his colleagues, he flew to Paris and arrived there just as Eban was beginning his meeting with De Gaulle. Without waiting to hear the outcome of that conversation or read the diplomatic reports from Jerusalem, he flew on to Tel-Aviv and drove to General Staff Headquarters for a briefing by Bar-Lev, who had been summoned home a few days earlier from his political studies at the Sorbonne to become Rabin's Deputy. The next day Allon went with Eshkol to the Negev to see the front commanders. On returning to Tel-Aviv, he called in Bar-Lev, Yariv and Brigadier General Mordechai Hod, the Commander of the Israeli Air Force, to go over operational plans in the bomb-shelter war room at headquarters. He asked for Hod's plan of action and the time it would take him to carry it out—on the Egyptian front? on the Jordanian front, if Jordan came in? on the Syrian front, if Syria decided to join? and even on the northern frontier, if Lebanon moved as well? What would be the pivoting time from front to front? Hod's answer was in minutes. Allon put the same questions to Bar-Lev with respect to the land forces. Fortified by their answers, on May 26 he went to Eshkol to report his judgment that war was a certainty, that Israel would win it, that she could fight on three fronts—and that she must strike first. The issue, he said, was no longer Israel's rights at Tiran but her security as a nation.

Eshkol was an able and vigilant Minister of Defense; and Rabin, commanding the universal loyalty of his officers and men, a planner down to the last detail, combining thoroughness with extraordinary flexibility, was perhaps the finest Chief of Staff that Israel had ever had. The armed forces were ready. Eshkol knew this; but he was thankful for the judgment of a soldier-politician with whom he had worked for so long and so closely in the councils of government. After his long talk with Allon on May 26, he was convinced that Israel was in mortal danger and that, inescapably, she must go to war. He never looked back.

But the domestic political events which, a few days later, were to cost him half of his job—his position as Minister of Defense—had already been set in train. These events centered on a demand for a government of national union to guide the country through the crisis. They began in a restricted circle of opposition politicians maneuvering for a change of leadership, and they ended with a popular call to Dayan to take command of the nation's security in place of the Prime Minister. Eshkol, seventy-one years old, had done the state some service and he knew it. He had his pride as well as his humility. As Minister of Defense he had brought the armed forces of Israel to an unrivaled peak of proficiency and readiness. He was hurt by the agitation against him. The demand for a new government to face the emergency was a declaration of nonconfidence in his leadership and he resisted it stoutly to the end.

Ironically, at this moment of domestic disarray, the man who had led Israel through her first two wars was firmly convinced that she was unprepared for her third. Six years had passed since Ben-Gurion had stepped down as Prime Minister and during that time he had lost touch with military developments. The information he received during the crisis came mainly from secondhand sources. He believed that a war at this juncture would be unbearably costly, entailing casualties in the army and among civilians that might run into the tens of thousands. Expecting a prolonged conflict, he insisted that Israel should not go to war without a guaranteed line of arms supply from a major power—an expectation that directly contradicted the prognosis and short-war doctrine of the General Staff. He was sharply critical of Eshkol's mobilization of reserves, arguing that a mobilization without a decision to go to war was a dangerous provocation. With these doubts and fears Ben-Gurion urged that Israel dig in, try to hold her position through diplomacy and achieve what she could with regard to Tiran, using the interval to secure foreign military support until she was fully equipped for a war on three fronts.

An implacable antagonism opposed Ben-Gurion to the man who had followed him in the Prime Minister's chair and who had determined to stay there. When the crisis came, he wanted Eshkol to go and saw an opportunity to displace him. No doubt he was persuaded that the Eshkol government was incapable of meeting the test. He may have felt as well that he alone could provide the national leadership that was needed at that hour. When, in 1961, he had withdrawn from office and returned to his kibbutz in the Negev, he had known that Eshkol would become Prime Minister. He had evidently not expected him to *be* Prime Minister. On an earlier occasion, in 1955, Ben-Gurion had yielded up the reins of government and retired to the Negev, but he had remained Prime Minister in effect and before many months he had been called back. Eshkol never called him back. Instead, he took command, and after his many years as trouble shooter in the dominant Mapai Party, he had a strong and solid power base. Homely and sometimes faltering in manner, rambling and proverbial in speech, Eshkol was an easy man to underestimate. His manner belied his strength of resolve and his firmness in decision. In the notorious Lavon affair that had left such a legacy of bitterness, it was Eshkol who had had the last word. In that affair a former Minister of Defense, Pinhas Lavon, was accused by a high-ranking army intelligence officer of responsibility for a misbegotten and discreditable

cloak-and-dagger operation in Egypt. Ben-Gurion upheld the honor of
the army against Lavon, even after new evidence appeared to indicate
that the key document in the case was a forgery. Seven successive
investigations were held and finally, over Ben-Gurion's protests,
Lavon was exonerated by an interministerial committee headed by the
Minister of Justice. Ben-Gurion denounced the verdict and demanded
a full-scale judicial inquiry. But his party, Mapai, and the new Prime
Minister, Eshkol, by then had had enough of the Lavon affair and
refused. Ben-Gurion was unforgiving. He assailed his successor as
dishonest, incompetent and unfit to be Prime Minister.

Now, in their worried agitation for a change of leadership, the opposition parties turned first to Ben-Gurion. Would he be prepared to
return to power as the leader of a national coalition? First to make the
proposal was his inveterate political foe to whom he had not spoken
or nodded for years: Menachem Begin, leader of the militantly nationalist party, Herut, and former chief of the terrorist Irgun. Begin
was ready to forget the rancors of a lifetime for "unity's" sake; and, he
declared, if Ben-Gurion were willing to accept the management of
state affairs, he would propose his candidacy. He directed his appeal
to Shimon Peres, now the secretary of Rafi, a party of Mapai dissi-
dents of the younger political generation who owed allegiance to Ben-
Gurion. Peres transmitted the message and Ben-Gurion replied that
he could not work under the same roof as Eshkol. But Begin insisted.
He proposed that Ben-Gurion return as Prime Minister with Eshkol
as his Deputy. Peres again delivered the message. Urged a second
time, Ben-Gurion agreed to serve—on condition that Eshkol be neither Prime Minister nor Minister of Defense.

On May 24 Begin undertook the delicate mission of carrying the
proposal to Eshkol. The Prime Minister listened politely and firmly refused to demote himself. Begin then advanced an alternative: Eshkol
would remain Prime Minister and Ben-Gurion would join a government of national union as his Minister of Defense. Eshkol again declined. He did not believe Ben-Gurion would be an appropriate Minister of Defense under the circumstances; and besides, how could he
ever collaborate again with his colleague, his mentor and his leader
who had turned against him? "These two horses," he said, "can never
pull the same wagon together." His refusal was final and Ben-
Gurion's candidacy was dead. The obvious alternate choice for Minister of Defense in an expanded government was another Rafi man:
Dayan.

Characteristically, throughout the prewar crisis, Dayan followed his own path and kept his own counsel. His immediate reaction was to go to the front and see for himself. The armed forces were his central and consuming interest and he had always kept in close touch with the men of the General Staff. He went first to the Negev frontier, then to the Jordanian and then to the Syrian; saw the troop dispositions, reviewed the operational plans and made his proposals; and then visited the border settlements to check on their shelters. His conclusion was that the army was in excellent shape. He found the generalship "superb"; the armored corps at a high level of development; the equipment, organization and command all better than he had known in his own day. He was confident of Israel's position.

What he would have done or have urged Israel to do if he had seen the situation in the same fearful light as Ben-Gurion, we do not know. His position in the crisis was the direct opposite and he did not have to face that kind of choice. He foresaw a short war in which the casualties would be serious but not prohibitive. He felt no uncertainty, as others did, about the new and untested generation. He held that the blockade at Tiran was a direct assault on a basic national interest that had to be answered, and he considered that failure to answer it would open the way to further disasters. Nasser would not stop at Tiran. He would strike at the Negev and in time he would strike from Jordan as well; he would aim for the dismemberment of Israel. Since these were the alternatives, Dayan was for war.

His conduct was true to his style, linear and straightforward. He stood completely aloof from the party machinations for a change of government; he disapproved of the maneuvers to return Ben-Gurion to power, believing they would have a disruptive effect on the national leadership; and he took no part in the campaign to promote himself. He knew, of course, that he would probably be called in the end, and if he was, he would accept a position of military responsibility and nothing else. The defense of Israel was his business. Proudly and grandly, his behavior signified: If they want me, let them ask for me and I will serve in a post that is appropriate; if they don't want me, they needn't ask for me.

In an atmosphere of heightened apprehension on the evening of May 26, Eshkol summoned the cabinet to Tel-Aviv for what was in effect the start of a continuous session. The second wave in Sinai had completed the Egyptian mobilization, and during the day the Egyptian Air Force had defied Israel's air defenses with four successive Mig overflights of the southern Negev. The ministers were placed on emergency call. Those of the National Religious Party were advised to remain in the city and not return to their homes, since on the following day, in observance of the Sabbath, they would be unable to travel.

Eshkol returned to his hotel. At his suite he received a delegation of the United Jewish Appeal and went tired to bed, after midnight. At a quarter past two the telephone rang at the bedside of Adi Yafeh. The Soviet Ambassador, through an aide, requested an immediate meeting with the Prime Minister. Yafeh protested: Did the Embassy realize what time it was? what day it was? The Russian insisted. Yafeh suggested that Chuvakhin come to see Levavi, the Director General of the Foreign Ministry, who was also staying at the hotel. There was a confabulation at the other end of the line; the Russian came back, insisted on Eshkol and adjured Yafeh not to take it upon himself to make the decision on so important a matter. Yafeh told him to hold the line, got his dressing gown, walked past the security guard outside Eshkol's suite, knocked and awakened him and asked him to open the door. They consulted Levavi and it was agreed they could not, after all, deny the Soviet request. Yafeh went back to the line and told the Russians to come.

They came immediately—Chuvakhin and a First Secretary. In the untidy room, stale with the debris of the previous evening's reception —the cluttered trays, the drained glasses, the half-emptied bottles of fruit juice—Eshkol and Yafeh received them, demonstratively, in slacks and pajama tops. Levavi, more circumspectly, dressed. Chuvakhin delivered a note from Kosygin. It warned of the responsibility that would lie upon Israel if "circles eager for battle" and "those pushing [her] to the brink of war" gained the upper hand. In one respect, Eshkol noticed, it was more judiciously balanced than previous Soviet demarches. Referring to the mounting tensions on Israeli-Arab borders, "with the two sides increasing their forces," it refrained at least from placing the total blame on Israel. It was signed, "Sincerely . . ."

It was a quarter to three, and for the next two and a half hours Eshkol and Chuvakhin talked in their native tongue. Eshkol opened with his observations on Kosygin's note. He reminded Chuvakhin of the personal invitation to visit the Syrian border which the Ambassador had spurned the previous October. Israel, he said, was surrounded by hostile countries, and her mobilization was in specific response to

Egyptian concentrations in Sinai. What about the Egyptians? Eshkol suggested the Russians would be well advised to direct their pressure on Cairo, where they probably had the best and most intimate relations of any power in the world. He hoped the Soviet Union would see fit to try to persuade the Egyptians to withdraw their troops from the border. The suggestion was not to Chuvakhin's purpose and he dismissed it curtly: "I am the Ambassador to Israel and am not concerned with my country's relations with Egypt."

As the Ambassador to Israel, there was only one question that concerned him. Would Israel "fire the first shot"? He pressed for an answer several times with an inflection of urgency. But Eshkol was not an easy man to pin down. He, too, knew the trick of circumventing a hard question by blandly changing the subject; indeed, Chuvakhin had taught it to him. "I learned from him," Eshkol later remarked, "not to talk about things that were not useful to me. I carried on with philosophical ideas. . . ." But after Chuvakhin had challenged him a fourth time, *Will you fire first?*, the First Secretary interrupted impatiently: "Mr. Ambassador, you have asked the Prime Minister this question four times and he has declined to answer!"

Eshkol sprang from his chair and spoke with passion. "Look at our situation!" he exclaimed. "They have blockaded the Straits of Tiran! Isn't this an act of war? Isn't this a first shot? For the past three days Egyptian planes have been flying over our territory! Isn't this a first shot?" He turned on his interlocutor and poured out his thoughts. The function of an Ambassador, he had always believed, was to promote friendly relations, to the best of his ability, with the country to which he was accredited. It did not seem to him that Chuvakhin had cared or tried to do this. Since this was the case, he would be pleased to welcome a Soviet ambassador who held this conception of his role. True, Israel was a small country; others carried much more weight in the world of culture and politics. But she still had her part to play, and he would be glad himself to meet and talk to Soviet leaders in the hope of promoting Soviet-Israeli friendship.

Chuvakhin listened impassively. Eshkol's fire drew not a flicker of response. But neither did Chuvakhin get an answer to his question. He had probably contributed his share, through the months, to the Soviet misestimate of Israel. Certainly he had been right on one point: he had advised Moscow that a conflict between Israel and Syria was unavoidable. But he had painted a dark picture of Israel's social and political life, which bore so many marks of a sick and contracting capitalist society—the dwindling trickle of immigration, the augmenting flow of emigration, the economic decline, the disaffection of those in the Diaspora who felt it was time that Israel stood on her own feet. There had been so much talk of all this! Chuvakhin probably concluded that such a society, with its parties divided and demoralized, its government wavering, its Prime Minister's prestige at so low an ebb, could not find the strength and the will to react. Yet still, Israel was always an enigma, and when he left Eshkol's hotel in the early morning of May 27, Chuvakhin could not be certain.

War or diplomacy: the issue was to be decided at a meeting of the Israeli cabinet that began on the evening of that day. Eban, home from Washington, sanguine about the prospects for an international armada, arrived in the middle of that session. The debate that followed his report on his trip was stormy and contentious. His critics were appalled that he had placed his hopes in the American project. Quite apart from the feasibility of the maritime force, there was a basic divergence among the eighteen ministers on the substance of the American commitment. In the message he had brought from Johnson, Eban saw and emphasized one part and his challengers another. There was, indeed, an American undertaking. Johnson had accepted the American commitment and affirmed the American objective. But he had not affirmed that the United States would fulfill it *under any circumstances*. On the contrary, he had made explicit reservations. After reading the protocol of the conversation at the White House, some defense advisers asked with dismay, But where is the commitment? There was no commitment to take independent action.The Americans were prepared to organize an armada to resist and break the blockade —not separately but "in concert" with others; and for Allon and other go-it-aloners the vast loophole in the undertaking lay in those two words. Israel, they felt, was caught in the political straitjacket of an American request to wait for two weeks—for the resolution of a dispute that was now of secondary importance. They felt, too, that Eban had failed to bring home to Johnson the full danger of Israel's military position. They may well have been right. Eban had had to carry two briefs. The decisive day had been May 24, when Egypt resumed her build-up and Eban was stopping in Paris and London. Later, in Washington, reading the cables at the Israeli Embassy, he could not possibly have appreciated the atmosphere of grim urgency that had suddenly taken hold at home, where men were reading the intelligence reports and reacting to the hour-by-hour developments accumulating around them.

The debate continued for most of the night. Allon had considered Eban's journey to Washington a mistake and had said so to Eshkol. He decried the armada proposal, mistrusted its applications, feared the delays and demanded freedom of action. Even if the armada were established, what would it mean in practice? It could not in any case represent a solution of the Gulf of Aqaba dispute. One might assume that the Egyptians would not fire on an American warship; Nasser would be wise and patient and say, Please! and let it pass. Every two or three weeks, perhaps, an escorted Israeli ship would traverse the Gulf unmolested; the first oil cargo would probably get through, and then the second and third. But what of the fourth? Nasser could change his mind. But whether he changed it or not, he would of course hold to his position of principle and denounce the United States as the gunboat protector of Israel. Every passage of an Israeli ship would carry the danger of an explosion, and the Americans, under the pressure of shifting circumstances, mindful of their interests in the Arab world, might reverse their views on the future of the flotilla. It was a fragile affair. The issue between Israel and Egypt would remain unresolved and Israeli ships at best would be permitted to pass under American protection and Egyptian sufferance. The armada would be living from ship to ship and Israel would be living in hostage to Nasser. As McNamara had said, what sense did this make? Allon and some others had a deep, instinctive political objection to the whole notion of an American-sponsored armada. Even if it succeeded, they said, it would merely serve to perpetuate Israeli dependence on the United States.

But in any case, these speculations were academic. The scene of danger was no longer Tiran but Sinai. Allon argued eloquently for war. Some who heard him envied his spirit but feared his impetus. To be sure, he said, the element of strategic surprise was already gone. But every day's delay meant a costlier battle and the certainty of heavier casualties, as the Egyptians dug in, consolidated their positions, sorted out their logistics problems and improved their intelligence. Every morning brought the danger of a pre-emptive air strike at Israeli airfields and cities, and every day, as the Egyptians organized, the margin of opportunity for an Israeli initiative diminished.

When all the arguments were heard, the final question remained. Did the circumstances impose on Israel the necessity to act alone? Each of the eighteen Ministers had to find his own answer. Eban saw and emphasized Israel's isolation: she had only one lifeline and that was to Washington, and if she acted alone, she might again find herself alone when the fighting was over. Several others agreed with him that Israel must wait. The armada project should be given a chance: Johnson had asked for two weeks and perhaps he should be granted at least one. The danger was great and the United States was a support, after all.

In essence, the message Eban had brought home was twofold. Johnson had said he could not provide Israel with the air support of the Sixth Fleet without Congressional approval, and with respect to Tiran he had offered the armada. The paradoxical effect of his message was immensely to deepen Israel's sense of loneliness and at the same time to make it more difficult for her to act alone. On the one hand, the Americans said they could not help if war came; on the other, they told Israel to wait while they sought to patch things up.

The night was nearly gone and there was no clear consensus in the cabinet. Eshkol put the issue to a vote. He, Allon and seven others voted for immediate war. Eban and eight others voted for delay. The government was evenly split, nine to nine.

Had Eshkol taken a different view of his prerogatives as Prime Minister and of the processes of government by cabinet, he could have used his authority to enforce a decision. He did not do so. Had he brought immediate pressure on two of his Ministers, he could—as he later avowed—have broken the deadlock and won a majority for war. But he wanted something better than that; he hoped in the end to get a united and if possible a unanimous cabinet. He, too, was certain that Israel must go to war; his practical political sense put him on Allon's side in that argument. But his instinct was to convince and not to impose. He felt the full weight of his responsibility and he no doubt felt, as well, the need to consolidate world opinion in support of Israel. "War is war, after all," he later said, and it was a difficult thing to go to war with a split cabinet.

It was five o'clock in the morning and spirits were numb. He decided to put the issue off for a final decision at a cabinet meeting later in the day.

But when the cabinet reconvened, the situation had changed. At ten-thirty in the morning, the Foreign Ministry brought a message that had been delivered by Ambassador Barbour in the middle of the night: a personal letter from Johnson to Eshkol. The advice from the White House was much stronger than Eban had indicated the previous evening. The insistence on delay was firm and explicit. The United States, Johnson said, was in touch with both Moscow and Cairo, to assure "restraint" on the Egyptian side; and Israel must take no initiative, since the path of diplomacy had still to be explored. Johnson cited a tough phrase of Kosygin's in a note received the previous day at the White House—a warning that the Soviet Union would do everything possible to go to the aid of the attacked. An addendum by Rusk said that military preparations were going ahead —an aircraft carrier was being sent to the Gulf of Aqaba region—and spoke of the dire consequences of any precipitate Israeli action.

The President's letter was decisive when the cabinet met again on the afternoon of May 28. The dominant mood was a sense of loneliness—the fear of going to war without American support. The decision was nearly unanimous. The cabinet voted to delay action in view of the American efforts to find a way out and of the military situation "as it then stood," by which it was meant that according to all the evidence, the Egyptian mobilization in Sinai had reached its height. Even Allon voted to wait. Only one Minister, Moshe Carmel, dissented.

The cabinet agreed that something must be said to the nation, which had not heard from its leader since the day after the blockade. Israel in the interim had begun to feel the moral attrition of uncertainty at the edge of the unknown. The blockade was a denial of her right to exist, as everyone instinctively knew, and the denial had not been answered. The nation had mobilized to reconfirm her existence, and then had stood still. The troops were anxious to hear; the General Staff and the front commanders were impatient to act. In principle, Israel like any other country should be able to order mobilization for a variety of strategic purposes—not only for war, but in order to deter or to warn or to block. But now, in the tension of bewilderment and waiting, the nervous pressures of a nation under siege demanded a definite word. The field commanders, especially those in the Negev, warned of an inevitable deterioration in the morale of their troops if they were held in further suspense, with no decision and no announcement by the national leadership. The strain of indecision was the most wearing and most damaging. Many felt that, having mobilized, Israel must go to war; one thing had to lead to the other, in the logic of a national effort that placed practically the entire able-bodied population in the field. A main purpose of Eshkol's radio speech on the evening of May 28 was to meet these arguments and to explain to the two hundred thousand mobilized civilians and their families why there had to be a further period of waiting and exploration.

Eshkol was exhausted. He had a cold. For a week he had been kept busy with a succession of round-the-clock meetings, with no time for himself and no buffer between him and events. For three days the process of decision-making had consisted of a marathon cabinet session interrupted by snatches of sleep. He asked two of his ministers to help prepare drafts of his speech. The agreed hour for the broadcast was eight-thirty and time was short. Successive drafts were tossed at him and he dictated successive changes. Yafeh and a secretary took down the changes and sped to their typewriters. They were still busy retyping when Kol Israel, the Voice of Israel, telephoned to ask when Eshkol would be ready to pretape the broadcast, and they were still at their typewriters when the sound engineers arrived with their recorders. The minutes flew; the engineers waited; the Prime Minister's desk was strewn with the litter of discarded copies. When the last sheets were ready and all was in order, it was nearly eight-thirty—too late to prerecord. Eshkol drove to the studio, with no time to read over the finished copy.

So an old and tired man, a halting speaker on the best of days, *enrhumé,* after two all-but-sleepless nights, went on the air live. So, too, the greater part of his people were convinced that he was wavering at the very moment that he had made up his mind. He stumbled through the tortuous sentences of his script. At one point he looked up from the microphone and expostulated: "This sentence is no good!" and Yafeh pointed despairingly toward the studio clock to remind him he was on the air. The script was a model of opaque bureaucratic prose. It said that Israel would oppose the blockade "at the proper time" and that the government had "laid down directives for the continuation of political action in the world arena, which are designed to stimulate international forces to take effective measures . . ."

The speech was a catastrophe. It left the country with the sensation that it had no leadership. In the events that led to the creation of a "national" government and to Eshkol's surrender of the Ministry of

Defense, it was probably the turning point.

But Eshkol's chores for the day were not yet done and the most onerous of all lay ahead. He still had to explain to the infuriated General Staff why international considerations were vital and why the cabinet had decided to wait a while longer. The military leaders were unreconciled. They were furious because Eshkol had failed to use his powers as Prime Minister to impose a decision when he had an opportunity to do so; and unreconciled because they held that by agreeing to delay he had risked the life of the nation. It is one of the ifs of history that may long be debated, and nowhere more passionately than in Israel itself.

Eshkol's meeting with the generals—Rabin, Weizmann and others —was tense and difficult. Everyone spoke his mind, especially the exasperated military. The generals said they could not take responsibility for what might happen if Israel held back. They could not, of course, say whether Nasser would or would not strike. But they warned of the unpredictable dangers that hung over the country from hour to hour and emphasized they could give no guarantee against an Egyptian attack. The immeasurable hazards were there—the uncontrollable threat from the air and the prospect of thousands of civilian casualties, and the danger of an overland thrust from Sinai. Every day, as Allon had said, would mean higher casualties in battle, but the greatest fear was of civilian losses in the event of an Egyptian air strike. Whatever happened, whether Israel or Egypt moved first, not one of the military believed that Israel would survive without a heavy toll of civilian deaths.

What was the nature of the threat? No one could say, since no one could answer the question. What kind of war would Israel have to fight? Against how many enemies on how many fronts? Who would begin it? How many civilian casualties would there be? A thousand? Three thousand, ten thousand? Or thirty thousand? What were Nasser's *offensive* plans? The extraordinary demonstrativeness of the Egyptian operation—the troops moving far out to the front, the Migs overflying the Negev, the touted armored reserves of Shazli suddenly heading to the south—all of this suggested that the Israeli deterrent had somehow lost its credibility. Where was the line of danger beyond which Israel could not wait?

To the Joint Chiefs of Staff in Washington, secure in their knowledge of Israel's deterrent strength and their firm prognosis of her performance in war, the alarm in Tel-Aviv seemed exaggerated. What-ever happened, the Joint Chiefs reported to the White House, the war would last between six days and two weeks—depending on the cir-cumstances. Why were the Israelis so excited? In military terms Gen-eral Wheeler was perfectly right and the Israeli General Staff had no quarrel with him. But in human terms, the difference for Israel be-tween a six-day and a two-week war was measured not in days but in lives, and the divergence in the two estimates lay there. The Israelis could not see the dangers mounting about them in the cool light of a military computation. It was all very well for their Western friends to say that they could afford to wait for "the first Egyptian mortar." Contemporary wars, Allon pointed out, began not with a first mortar but with a crushing air strike. The hazards for Israel were incalcu-lable.

But the ultimate computation that Israel had to make was not mili-tary but political and moral. The alternative to war was a political triumph for Nasser that would enable him to initiate a campaign for the progressive curtailment of her national being and national right. Tiran was a metaphor of her national existence. Sooner or later, as Allon, Dayan and Eshkol knew, she would have to go to war because of the dangers of No War; the fatal prospect of political erosion and moral collapse within if a challenge to her right were not resisted. Nasser might never attack: he did not have to. He could simply im-pose on the Israelis a long and costly mobilization which they would be unable to maintain indefinitely. It was beyond their strength to do so; their economy would go under. Neither could they indefinitely postpone action on a *casus belli*. The plausibility of the *casus belli* would wither as the weeks dragged on; and as the weeks dragged, Israel might lose her spine, her nervous force to react, her courage to fight.

Nasser, if Israel failed to meet the test, could create a situation in which compromise would be tantamount to capitulation. And capitu-lation would not be the end of the story; it would be only the begin-ning of an irreversible decline in the destiny of Israel. The end would be gradual dismemberment, physical and moral, and irremediable contraction, as Nasser tightened the ring around her borders and her people lost faith in their future.

Capitulation and slow death, or the terrible destruction of an Egyp-tian first strike, or a plunge into war—these were the alternatives that faced the Israeli Government during the final week of crisis and decision. The government's dilemma was the product of its American involvement. It had agreed to explore the diplomatic way toward a solution of the original *casus belli,* knowing that while it was engaged in this exploration it was losing time and perhaps the vital occasion to act. The *casus belli* was no longer the original one, and there was no political instrument or formula for inducing Egypt to evacuate her sovereign territory in Sinai.

Where was the line of danger? At the meeting with Eshkol on the evening of May 28, at the end of a tough and bitter debate, Rabin acknowledged that the decision to make war lay with the political leadership and agreed to wait a while longer. Within forty-eight hours, the turning point was reached in the alignment of forces on the borders of Israel and what had seemed until then an unavoidable war became an overwhelming certainty.

The Russians were staggered by the announcement of the blockade. So, at least, we may deduce from their behavior. They had dreadfully miscalculated. On the chessboard of their Middle Eastern strategy, they had set the pieces in motion and had not reckoned that, once in movement, the undisciplined pieces would acquire a life and a will of their own. Day after day, during the opening gambits of the crisis, *Pravda* and *Izvestia* had dedicated page after page to resolute support and applause of Nasser's moves. Now there was silence, the silence of chagrin and dismay. The closing of the Straits of Tiran rated a brief and bare news item with no editorial comment. Nasser had violated a cardinal rule of Soviet conduct, the rule that required that nothing be done that might directly involve the United States and lead to a big-power confrontation. This had been the recipe for Soviet adventure ever since the missile crisis in Cuba—to gain footholds wherever possible without challenging the Americans—and the present adventure had been conceived in strict accordance with this recipe. Nasser had now flouted it by introducing an issue on which the Americans had a formal concern, a cause for intervention and a long-standing obligation. Freedom of shipping in the Gulf of Aqaba was recognized by Washington to be a *casus belli.* The Americans were automatically involved. Nasser had not forewarned his Soviet friends of his decision. He had gone ahead and taken the fateful step; and what had been intended as a clever maneuver to squelch Israel and fortify Syria was suddenly a gamble with war—a war in which the United States would have a vital interest.

There were other reasons for the embarrassed silence in Moscow. Nasser based his right to blockade the Straits on the fact that "this water is ours": Egypt was asserting her sovereign right over the Gulf of Aqaba. This raised a question on which the Russians were as hypersensitive as the Israelis. Soviet warships passed freely to the Mediterranean through the Bosporus and Dardanelles; and nobody denied Turkish sovereignty over these waterways. Indeed, the Geneva Convention of 1958 on "The Territorial Sea and the Contiguous Zone" had recognized the right of innocent passage for both commercial and military vessels through "straits which are used for international navigation between one part of the high seas and another part of the high seas or the territorial waters of a foreign State." The Egyptians were not signatories to this covenant; the Russians most certainly were, and it established their right of lawful passage through such straits as the Bosporus and Skaggerak, which gave them access to the warm sea to their south and the open waters of the Atlantic and the world. The Egyptian position was obviously worrisome. The Russians made no attempt to explain it or justify it in their press or their public statements.

Nasser, of course, was not compelled to declare a formal blockade merely because he found himself at Sharm el Sheikh. He had a perfectly feasible alternative. Saying nothing and proclaiming nothing, he could have picked an opportune moment to station an Egyptian destroyer at the mouth of the Straits—and then waited; the insurance rates would have soared and shipping would have dwindled. Or he could have done nothing. But his appetite was whetted by his winnings and he went for the whole pie in an extraordinary hurry. What was the explanation of his sudden notice to Amer that he needed troops at Sharm el Sheikh? Apparently he was prompted by U Thant's decision, immediately after the dismissal of UNEF, to visit Cairo and try to head him off. The Western powers at that moment were mobilizing their diplomatic resources behind U Thant's mission: he was to fly to Cairo, talk to Nasser, persuade him to leave the Straits alone and even, perhaps, to reconsider his decision to send UNEF packing. As usual, Nasser set his conditions: U Thant would be welcome in Cairo provided he came to Cairo only, dropping both Jerusalem and Damascus from his intinerary. U Thant agreed; blandly, Nasser exercised his veto on the Secretary-General's movements. Setting out from New York on the evening of May 22, exhorted by the Western powers to do his utmost to prevent any change in the *status quo* at Tiran, with his briefcase full of urgent representations from the Americans, Canadians and British, all calling his attention in the strongest possible terms to the extremely grave consequences of such a move, U Thant arrived at the Paris airport the next morning to discover that his trip had precipitated the decision it was intended to block. Cairo Radio had announced the closing of the Straits while he was on his way across the Atlantic. He telephoned to Bunche to seek advice. Should he continue his journey or return to New York? After consulting various interested parties, Bunche told him by all means to carry on to Cairo and see what he could do to mend or defuse the situation.

Nasser had been amply forewarned by his delegates in New York of the purpose of U Thant's journey and of the contents of his briefcase. He acted fast and dramatically in order to forestall and disarm this particular application of pressure. He blockaded the Straits so as not to have to argue about it. In Cairo on May 24, at his single meeting with U Thant, he explained that the Egyptian Government had taken its decision on the blockade "a few days" before and that three possible courses had been open to him. He could proclaim the blockade before U Thant's departure from New York, which would have seemed rude and might have impelled the Secretary-General to call off his trip; he could wait until U Thant had come and gone, which would have seemed a gratuitous rebuff; or he could announce the deed while he was en route. And this is what he did. It seemed the least offensive way.

U Thant was puzzled by Nasser's air of blissful confidence. Nasser declared that what he had done was to restore the situation to "pre-1956"; he intended to take no warlike steps. But, U Thant objected, by mobilizing in Sinai and by blockading Tiran he was, in fact, greatly increasing the dangers of war. "We are ready," Nasser replied serenely. The meeting was a jellylike affair. U Thant suggested he might send a special United Nations representative to the Middle East to handle the crisis. This, Nasser said, would be acceptable on condition that the emissary resided in Cairo and abstained from visiting other Middle Eastern capitals. The idea died there. U Thant returned to New York with Nasser's assurance that he would refrain from any action liable to exacerbate the tension.

From the moment of the blockade Soviet diplomacy ran scared. Messages flew and Ambassadors scrambled. Although Moscow relied primarily on the Americans to hold Israel in check, it took the extra protective step of making sure the Israelis received the message directly. "Will you fire the first shot?" Chuvakhin asked anxiously; and in the same early morning hours of May 27, while he was importuning Eshkol, his counterpart in Cairo, Ambassador Dmitri Pojidaev, was closeted with Nasser, striving to freeze the situation after the second big trans-Canal move of the Egyptian Army. The Ambassador's first assignment on this nighttime call was to tell Nasser not to go to war—not to take *any* precipitate action; and his second, to inform him that the Americans were saying the same thing to the Israelis. What else Pojidaev may or may not have said, we do not know. Nasser had pressed on toward his great "pre-1956" objectives and expanded them beyond anything the Russians had advised or wanted. He knew, of course, that he was inviting a confrontation with the United States no less than with Israel. By defying the Eisenhower-Dulles commitment, he was challenging both countries. The Americans accepted the confrontation, and their first postblockade demarche to Cairo, delivered in May by Richard Nolte, the new Ambassador who had arrived at his post only two days before, was straight and strong. Interference with free navigation in the Gulf of Aqaba, Washington told Cairo, was a violation of international law and an act of aggression which the United States would oppose by all possible means. To be sure, there was a cushion: the United States would act first within the framework of the United Nations and later, if need be, outside it and in concert with others. The Americans kept their options open. "All possible means" extended almost but not quite to the use of force.

On every side and on every level, both the Americans and the Russians conveyed their message. The Americans told the Russians they were exerting pressure on Israel; the Russians told the Americans they were urging restraint in Cairo and Damascus; the Americans sought to hold back the Israelis with the assurance that both they and the Russians were holding back the Egyptians; the Russians warned both Americans and Israelis they would go to the aid of the attacked but at the same time assured Nasser that while they were checking him the Americans were checking Israel; and the Americans told the Egyptians they were doing their utmost to restrain both sides.

But above the immediate antagonists, Israel and Egypt, the hovering and committed big powers faced each other. On that level of confrontation, Johnson took personal command. From May 23 until the end of the June War, relations with the Russians were governed by direct messages from the White House. At such moments of crisis, the conduct of relations with Moscow is peculiarly guarded: general positions are made known as clearly and straightforwardly as possible, and the message is repeated to numerous third-party contacts to ensure that it becomes generally known. But no more. Nothing is made explicit with regard to precise intentions.

Thus, in his first message on May 23, Johnson warned Kosygin that the closing of the Straits could mean war and laid down the ground rules of the American position. He said the blockade was an extremely grave matter that challenged a commitment of the United States and would meet with its full opposition; that the Sinai mobilization itself was a grave and dangerous development; and that the two events together constituted a threat to world peace that must be of urgent concern to the international community. He reminded Kosygin that the blockade was a *casus belli* on which Israel had always declared she would fight; warned that it might provoke a conflict, with all the potential dangers of a big-power confrontation; and called on the Soviet Union to use its influence to induce Egypt to reconsider and reverse its decision. Johnson's diplomatic style was carefully balanced: it combined mildness of language with crystalline clarity. Throughout the crisis, he controlled the lines to Moscow with an unerring hand. Quietly but unmistakably he made it clear that a Soviet intervention in the event of war would be intolerable.

But this was all. Both the Americans and Russians sought to prevent war, but neither at any time advised the other what it would or would not do if war came. Both undertook to "restrain" their respective friends, but neither made any commitment to the other. At no time during the crisis was there a promise by either side not to intervene. The presumption was that in the event of hostilities each would do its best to ensure their localization. But this was merely a presumption. The Americans made no commitment as to their course of action. They were never explicit; they did not bind themselves and did not wish to. The basis of trust for a precise commitment did not exist.

· 7 ·

Trial and Decision

THE SETTLEMENT OF 1957 was dead and the Arab nations rejoiced in the prowess of the hero-leader who had destroyed it. The last vestiges of the tripartite aggression of 1956 were wiped away. On only two previous occasions—the nationalization of the Suez Canal and the establishment of the United Arab Republic—had Nasser attained such an apogee of glory in the Arab world. But of the three occasions, this was by far the most giddy and electrifying. From the Arab capitals, in the week following the reimposition of the blockade, he received the tribute of a universal and rapturous ovation. No Arab state could afford to be absent at this hour of triumph, and every Arab state had to be able to say, "We were there, in May, 1967, taking part in the common struggle." Both the willing and the unwilling, those who honored and those who feared, were drawn spellbound into his magic circle. Even King Hassan of Morocco sent his personal emissary to Cairo bearing his message of congratulations, and even King Feisal, the archvillain, announced the mobilization of the Saudi Arabian armed forces since, as he said, no one who held aloof from the battle could call himself an Arab citizen. None could contest Nasser's emotional supremacy. He had not only erased the stigmas of the past but had called the Arab nation to a battle of honor. "War might be a chance for the Jews," he said in his speech announcing the blockade, "to test the strength of their forces and then they will see that all that was written on the 1956 battle and the occupation of Sinai was nonsense and fictitious." Arab imagination exulted and Arab honor acclaimed.

Cairo in those euphoric days was transported into a world of heroic make-believe. "Nasser, the Liberator of Palestine!" "We are ready for the battle!" Periodically, at a signal from the Arab Socialist Union, Egypt's sole political party, a procession of demonstrators churned into the arena of Liberation Square, to shout their slogans, chant their martial songs, wave their banners and listen to appropriately declamatory speeches in front of the headquarters of the Arab League. "The Arabs will fight, with all weapons in their hands!" In the scenario of this make-believe world, the Arab people stood ready to overwhelm the Israeli foe and Nasser was destined to lead their liberating armies through the streets of Tel-Aviv. For the first time since 1948, Arab power was resurrected and Arab confidence reborn. The scent of victory was in the air. Cairo was on holiday. The martial shouts, the swaying banners, the reverberant speeches were the pomp and rhetoric of a victory celebration; they conveyed no sense of overhanging danger or of the stress and tension of approaching war. The time of trial in Israel was a time of jubilee in Egypt; a rally of Arabism, feverishly disassociated from reality; a carnival of myth-making and collective dreaming. In the intense light of Arab fantasy, as Nasser strode from advance to advance and from climax to climax, the state of Israel seemed frighteningly and desperately trapped.

Was the Gulf of Aqaba really closed? The question that had been asked in Tel-Aviv was answered by *Al Ahram* on May 24. The enforcement of the blockade, the newspaper said, had begun at noon on the previous day with the laying of mines in the Straits of Tiran. The scenario of war fever was accelerated by the mobilization of the Arab states. Egypt and Iraq, at the conclusion of military talks in Cairo, proclaimed their resolve to "shoulder their responsibility in this decisive stage of the Arab battle of destiny." In Baghdad on the morrow of the blockade, Major General Shaker Mahmoud Shukry, the Minister of Defense, announced that Iraqi troops would shortly be on their way to take up positions on the Egyptian-Israeli front. The Iraqi military delegation in Cairo, he said, had reported that "the U.A.R. forces have overwhelming superiority in numbers and in morale, as well as a burning desire to crush Zionism." Colonel Taher Zubeir, the Algerian Chief of Staff, brought a letter from Boumedienne offering

Algerian troops. A similar message arrived from the Emir of Kuwait. All such token contributions were gratefully received. On May 24 Shams Badran, the Minister of War, flew to Cairo with a party of senior military officers to determine what the pledge of "resolute resistance by the Soviet Union and all peace-loving states" to any aggression in the Middle East would amount to in practice.

At least in the first days after the blockade, Nasser appeared confident there would not be war, or rather, while recognizing the risks, believed he would be able to get away without one. The international signs were uniformly auspicious. They pointed, as he had expected, to an unqualified diplomatic triumph. Israel was alone; her Western friends had either deserted her or were about to do so; and in the end she would have to adjust herself to the *fait accompli*. The France of 1967 was no longer the France of 1956 but the benevolently neutral France of Charles de Gaulle, clearly bent on shuffling off its commitment to maintain freedom of navigation through the Gulf. Britain, as Nasser said, was the tail and lackey of the United States and did as she was told by her American master; and the United States, as Cairo Radio said, was immersed in troubles and "all washed up." The French had hastened to make known their indifference to the blockade issue with a suitably evasive statement, and a personal message from De Gaulle had assured Nasser of France's disinterested position above the battle. He was further encouraged by the knowledge that De Gaulle, like the Americans and Russians, had told Israel not to act. As for the Americans, he could safely reckon they would not use force to break the blockade, since they had not done so immediately. His underlying assumption that the United States, enmeshed in Vietnam, would shrink from a Middle Eastern involvement and therefore bring heavy pressure on Israel, was proving correct. Many, no doubt, would sympathize with Israel and offer their condolences. None would make a commitment of wartime aid and none would go to her physical rescue at Tiran. The Israelis were caught completely off balance. They were weakly led and badly demoralized. Eban's trip to the Western capitals was proof of their confusion. If they fought, they would fight in isolation. With their limited reserves and resources, under siege on at least two fronts, they would be able to sustain a short war only—a war of days not of weeks. In making this estimate, Nasser was thinking exactly what a number of Israelis, Ben-Gurion and others, were thinking at the time.

He probably believed his tactics with regard to Tiran allowed him ample room for maneuver. He had deliberately raised an international issue of direct concern to Washington. But, as he imagined, he had been careful to leave his options open. At no time did he say that "strategic" goods carried to Israel in non-Israeli ships—Americans ships, for example—would be subject to the blockade. *Al Ahram* and Cairo Radio said so, but not Nasser, and not the Egyptian Foreign Office. *Al Ahram* said one thing and Nasser another. Riad, the Foreign Minister, chose his words cunningly, like a professional: the passage of an Israeli ship through the Straits, he announced, would be an "act of aggression," whereas the attempted passage of a non-Israeli ship with "strategic" materials would be merely "an uncordial act." Was the blockade directed only at Israeli flagships? The question was never really answered. Nor was it ever finally clear just what strategic cargoes Nasser proposed to ban or whether, notably, he would allow the passage of Iranian oil. *Al Ahram* published a long list of prohibited goods, ranging from ammunition and military clothing to meat and fodder. But no such list ever emanated from the Egyptian Government. In Nasser's game, there was still room for maneuver at the brink. He had left a loophole or two for negotiation; and if circumstances imposed a compromise in the end, he could expect the Americans and Russians to huddle at the United Nations, devise a formula and then jointly urge it on the Israelis in order to head off a war. The Israelis would be backed into a corner.

This, presumably, was the rationale of his gamble—a huge gamble compounded of miscalculated risks. The favorable international signs swelled his confidence in his stage management of crisis; the acclamations of the Arab multitude elated him even more. The pent-up energies and ambitions of a long period of barren isolation found release in the crescendo of his moves immediately after the blockade. From that moment the stage was entirely his. He took over the management of affairs from the Russians and conducted the crisis in his own fashion. The Russians had little more to say. They could tell him not to make war—which was not in his plan, in any case; they could try to minimize the war risks of the blockade; but they could not control him. They were impaled on their policy of inflexible support of every Arab cause, and in the present adventure, in which they had played so great an initiating role, they were a committed party. Their prestige and authority in the Arab world were irrevocably entrusted to Nasser.

They evidently did not foresee his flamboyant style of play, the panache and bravura of his action, nor the exultant ferocity with which he was now to press home his triumph and expand his challenge to Israel.

His appetite grew with eating. By blockading the Straits, he had forced the issues to the furthest limit of brinkmanship. He might, at this point, have pulled back, left the next move to the big powers and opened a door to negotiation. Instead, he went on gambling. The blockade at Tiran, in his orchestration of events, was merely the prelude to a greater encounter: Egypt, he proclaimed, was ready for a general war whose object would be the elimination of Israel.

He extended the challenge on May 26, in a speech to a delegation of Arab trade unionists:

"The Arab masses everywhere are keen to fight and to regain the rights of the Palestinian people. . . . If Israel initiates some aggressive act against Syria or against Egypt, the battle against Israel will be a total battle. It will not be limited to a small area opposite Syria or a piece of land opposite Egypt. The battle will be comprehensive, and our principal aim will be the destruction of Israel. . . . I am confident that once we enter the battle, we will be victorious with God's will. . . . The battle is one of destiny and there is no room for argument."

On the same day Mohammed Hassanein Heikal, Nasser's approved spokesman and most sophisticated interpreter, celebrated the achievements of the "ten glorious days" in which Egypt had "altered the balance of power" in the Middle East. Astutely, in drawing the lesson of those days for the readers of his weekly sermon in the columns of *Al Ahram,* Heikal predicted that Israel would be compelled to react to the blockade for reasons that were primarily psychological. War was certain: "The psychological factor makes the acceptance of the challenge to war a necessity [for Israel] not only for reasons of security but for the necessity of survival." He explained: "The closure of the Gulf of Aqaba to Israeli shipping and the embargo on strategic goods going to Israel, even if carried by non-Israeli ships, means first and last that the Arab nation, as represented by the U.A.R., has succeeded for the first time in changing by force something that was imposed on her by force. This is the crux of the problem. . . . The opening of the Gulf of Aqaba to Israeli shipping was a *fait accompli* imposed by imperialist force. And this week's closure of the Gulf was a substitute *fait accompli* imposed and protected by Arab force. The gravest factor for Israel in the situation is the *fait accompli* and [the issue of] who can impose it and has the force to protect it. It is not the Gulf of Aqaba . . . it is the philosophy of Israeli security on which Israel's existence has depended ever since she was born, and on this philosophy her survival hangs. For this reason: Israel must take up arms! And for this reason, too: The armed clash between the U.A.R. and the Israeli foe is inescapable." The ten glorious days were a prologue to the final confrontation: "I am sure . . . that Israel cannot keep silent and accept what has happened. . . . She has no alternative but to deal a blow, and we have to stand ready and buffer the blow and minimize its effect. . . .

"Let Israel start! This will be followed by a second blow from our side which will be the death blow!"

On May 28, Nasser held a press conference in the floodlit, circular council chamber of his Presidential Palace, answering with aplomb and at length the sharpest questions that the wit of correspondents could contrive. The earnest voice was serene and subdued, the tone was one of aggrieved rectitude, and the impression was that of a long, unbroken and insistent monologue in defense of Arab rights. He seemed at times a sleepwalker speaking in an exalted trance of fatalism. Did he expect an Israeli attack? "We expect everything. As regards an Israeli aggression, we expect it every day. . . . As I said to you, we are leaving the initiative to Israel. If they want to react violently or not violently to the exercise of our rights, we are ready. Our sons are ready; our army is ready; the whole Arab nation is ready." Under what circumstances would he consider lifting the ban on Israeli shipping through the Gulf? "Not under any circumstances whatsoever. . . . This is our attitude and I will not move from it by even one inch." Was there any workable settlement for the Middle East? Since the great powers would not allow the destruction of Israel, was there any feasible *modus vivendi?* "Our cause is a just one, hence we do not care one whit for the big states. The big states can only decide on the affairs of their own countries. . . . We are bent on the restoration of the rights of the Palestinian people. . . . We will never accept coexistence with Israel." The dismissal of UNEF and the blockade at Tiran were not subjects for discussion; they were details —"casual incidents" in a much greater affair: "No power, however mighty, can infringe upon Egyptian sovereign rights, and any attempt of this kind will constitute an aggression against the Egyptian people and against the whole Arab nation; and we shall inflict upon the aggressor inconceivable damage." The greater affair was Palestine itself: the "problem of aggression which has taken place and is still taking place against one of the countries of the Arab nation, Palestine, and the constant threat it constitutes to all our countries." Was the moment well chosen for war with Israel? "We are at present fully prepared for the confrontation. In the event of Israel attacking any Arab country, we will not allow it to fight in a limited area but we will launch a full-scale war."

Each time Nasser spoke, fatalism, appetite or brinkmanship expanded the goals of the battle of destiny. The final objective was set on the following day, May 29, in a speech to members of the Egyptian National Assembly. He announced the "resurrection" of the Palestine issue:

"Since we have been able to restore matters to what they were before 1956, then with the help of God we can restore them to what they were before 1948. . . . We are prepared to open the entire Palestine case. The question today is not that of Aqaba, nor the Tiran Straits, nor the Emergency Force. It is the right of the Palestinian people. . . . If the Western countries deny us, ridicule us and despise us, then we the Arabs must teach them to respect us and to take us into consideration. Otherwise all that we say about Palestine and the Palestinian people . . . will be only empty words, cast in the wind."

He was already at the brink, but he stood also at the pinnacle of power. The psychological mobilization he had achieved—by his defiance of Israel, his readiness for a generalized war, his "resurrection" of the cause of Palestine—was politically irresistible. For how long would the King of Jordan be able to resist it? The sense of power thrilled the Arab world and offered the prospect of a further political victory. Fully realizing the nature of his challenge, keeping—as he thought—his options open, believing that his army could achieve a stalemate in Sinai, relying on the Americans to hold Israel back and on both the Americans and Russians to descend, like *dei ex machina,* with a providential formula—he gambled again. The victory that now lay within his reach was the final capitulation of Hussein. In order to achieve it, he had to add yet another *casus belli* to his list: for the military pact which Hussein signed in Cairo on May 30 placed both Egyptian and Iraqi troops on the West Bank of the Jordan River, assigned an Egyptian commander to the King's headquarters in Amman and completed the ring of Arab arms and Arab manpower around the borders of Israel.

For fifteen years, since his accession at the age of seventeen, the gallant tenacity of King Hussein had preserved an unpopular throne and an anachronistic kingdom against the revolutionary tumult of the times and the malice of a horde of enemies. How many treasons he had escaped, how many conspiracies, how many foreign upheavals and domestic dangers he had passed in that time! Fearless and agile, he still held up his crown above the tide. Alone and unbefriended in the Arab world, but romantically animated by a sense of his high mission as the last ruling member of the noblest of Arab dynasties, he still played out his part and craved recognition as a legitimate leader in the Arab cause. He, too, was a nationalist and a patriot. As early as 1963, he had wistfully sought a reconciliation with his most remorseless enemy, the republican autocrat in Cairo. In the spring of that year, amid the ferment of hopes and rumors that surrounded the talks for the creation of an Egyptian-Syrian-Iraqi federation, Cairo Radio invited the Palestinians of Jordan to assassinate their "dwarf king," and the ensuing riots were suppressed with ruthless confidence by Hussein's then 100-percent-loyal Jordan Legion. But after the wild incitements from Cairo and the welter of violence at home, when the wave had subsided, after the Palestinian agitators were safely packed into jail and the Legion stood again in unchallenged control, Hussein blandly said the riots had begun spontaneously enough as a natural manifestation of popular enthusiasm for the projected tripartite federation, which he himself was still ready to join on a basis of "equality and sovereignty." Thus he tried to find an honorable place for himself in the changing and hostile world around him. Like his inveterate enemies, the Syrians, who plotted against him with such unwearying zeal, he looked ultimately to Nasser for his Arab credentials and his title of authenticity.

So he had been the first of the Arab heads of state to answer Nasser's call for a meeting at the Summit, which offered him access to the highest councils, a peer among peers, a sovereign among sovereigns. So, too, he had hoped to come to terms with the Summit's military offspring, the Palestine Liberation Organization, and with the appointed head of that new body, Nasser's creature and stalking-horse, the rampant and venomous impresario of the Palestine War, Achmed Shukheiry. Jordan, tragically, was the host country to the great majority of the Palestinian refugees and, pathetically and forlornly, regarded itself as the successor state to Arab Palestine. The King wished to show that his country was in the very forefront of the anti-Israel struggle; he therefore wanted to settle with Shukheiry and, indeed, to have the Palestine Liberation Army operate in Jordan. He was on extremely treacherous ground and he picked his way cautiously. Eager though he was to win acceptance as an authentic nationalist leader and to integrate the outcast kingdom of Jordan into the fraternity of Arab nations, he knew he could accept Shukheiry's army only under the strongest safeguards—under Jordan's sovereign tutelage and control. He hoped, somehow, both to prove his dedication to the cause and hold in check any organized threat to the Hashimite throne.

Thus began his curious and ill-starred attempt to coexist with a militantly subversive organization sponsored by Cairo. Shukheiry was an insatiable blackmailer; his demands from the outset were extortionate. He wanted freedom to create a state within a state: complete autonomy of political action and the right to recruit, train and arm Jordan's Palestinians, the restlessly disaffected and disloyal majority of the nation. Foreseeing that Israel would not sit on her hands and watch the creation of this new army on her most sensitive border, he demanded that Syrian, Iraqi and Saudi Arabian troops be allowed to enter Jordan and serve as the shield for his Palestinian militia. And even this was not enough. As if to seal the downfall of the Hashimites, he called on Hussein to institute compulsory military service throughout the country and thus convert the faithful Jordan Legion from a regular into a conscript army. Predictably, the officers of the Legion rallied to the King in opposing a transformation of their ranks that would have robbed them of their pay scales and emoluments.

For two years the Hussein-Shukheiry relationship oscillated absurdly between passionate clashes and ambiguous reconciliations, with "pacts" that broke down within weeks, sometimes days, after they were concluded, to be followed by renewed and ever stormier recriminations by Shukheiry and renewed but guarded concessions by the King. Shukheiry bullied, he threatened, he blustered, he fumed; but he never won that coveted position of autonomy that would permit him to arm and agitate against the throne. Hussein handled him shrewdly; his concessions never carried him across the red line of danger. The last of the "pacts," a coexistence agreement signed in February, 1966, was safely nebulous, authorizing the P.L.O. to set up offices in the towns of Jordan, to recruit (within limits), to distribute pamphlets and enjoy the facilities of the Jordanian post and telegraph service free of charge. From these carefully formulated checks and courtesies, it was difficult to say who had got the best of the bargain. But in any case, it did not last long. Two months later in Gaza, the P.L.O.'s annual convention, duly attended by Palestinians from Jordan, loudly chastised Hussein for his perfidies and enjoined him to release immediately the many P.L.O. members whom he was holding as subversives in jail. In a speech on June 16 Hussein declared the comedy was over: P.L.O. activities were banned in Jordan and he would have nothing more to do with Shukheiry. Boldly and for the first time, in that remarkable speech, he said the thing to do with the Palestinian refugees was not to intern them but to resettle them. The refugees, he declared, pronouncing a heresy that no Arab leader in the Middle East had ever dared to utter in public, should not be isolated in their camps behind barbed wire, sitting in squalor and embittered sloth, dependent on international charity. They should support themselves: "We reject the philosophy that says that by keeping the refugees at starvation level, their feelings of hatred will be nurtured and their desire for revenge strengthened. Only a free and thriving people can have the strength to liberate their country."

It was the final breach with Shukheiry. On the "Voice of Palestine" from Cairo, he responded diffusely and furiously, with all his limitless resources of spite and vilification. Hussein, he said, was "a traitor like his grandfather, Abdullah, an arms dealer who took high commission; a man . . . who has no right to live among us, no right to exist in the entire Arab world. He alone, one person and one throne, stands in the way of Arab union. The P.L.O. will cut off both his hands." The King's proposal to resettle the refugees was proof that he was an American agent, since it meant "the liquidation of the Palestine problem and the absorption of the Palestinians into the host countries."

As King and Supreme Commander, Hussein would have only one political organization and one army in his country. His Legion, which had not seen action since 1948, had grown in size in recent years and shrunk in standards. New batches of Western weaponry had come in, Patton M-47 and M-48 tanks from the United States as well as Centurions from Britain—the M-48's on the understanding that they would not be moved across the Jordan River to pose a threat to Israel. The falling-off in quality was the immediate result of reorganization and expansion, the creation of new brigades and the absorption of the National Guard. Nor was the Legion still that perfect buttress of Bedouin fidelity that it once had been. During the years of summitry, when he had tried to keep in Nasser's good books, Hussein had cooperated with the United Arab Command—to a prudent degree; and in June, 1964, when the U.A.C.'s Commander, General Ali Ali Amer, on a visit of inspection in Amman, had had sharp words about the doddering incompetence of certain older officers who were unable to answer any of his questions, Hussein had obliged by retiring more than a hundred of them, causing a momentary flap in Western Embassies. A few weeks later he replaced them with younger, carefully screened and equally loyal officers. But as time went on and the reorganization gained pace, the Legion's officers were selected more and more for their competence and less and less for their loyalty; and unhappily for Hussein, the two attributes were usually in inverse ratio to each other. He still hoped to juggle the props of power somehow. If only, he reckoned, he could improve his political position on the inter-Arab scene, he might be able to dispense with the traditional domestic staff of Bedouin loyalty.

Between him and his neighbors to the west, the formidable Israelis, there existed both an enormous disparity in military strength and a tacit covenant. This unwritten understanding was based on the paramount interest which they shared: both wished at all costs to preserve the Hashimite throne in Amman and neither would willingly countenance any political move that was liable to shake it. For the Israelis that dubious throne was an irreplaceable buffer against the greater enemies, Iraq and Egypt; they could not and would not tolerate any change in the military balance on their Jordanian border; and among their major *casi belli* they had always listed the entry into Jordan of Iraqi or Egyptian forces, a prospect that was equally distasteful to Hussein. He, for his part, saw that peace and quiet along the Israeli frontier was his only possible policy; and sensibly, he did what he could to achieve it. Jordan, unlike Egypt, had no cushion of empty desert; she was Israel's immediate and intimate neighbor, her border areas dotted with towns and villages that were open to Israeli attack and many of her populous centers not far distant. Hussein despised terrorism and knew well enough that it was self-defeating. He tried to check the various Palestinian guerrilla bands, El Fatah and others, that could be used against him no less than against Israel. But he never went all out to suppress them. Jordan was too weak, too close and too exposed to ask for trouble; but the King was too weak to prevent it. Caught between Palestinian passion and the threat of Israeli reprisal, he could only hope that the saboteur bands would be grateful if he did not move rigorously against them and that Israel would be grateful if he moved at all.

By the summer of 1966 his understanding with Israel—the unwritten compact—was already wearing thin. As he watched events on the Syrian-Israeli border, he harbored ever darker suspicions of Israeli designs, and the notion took hold in his mind that if war came, Jordan rather than Syria would be Israel's main target: the conquest of the West Bank would be a far more tempting and tangible prize than the destruction of a few mediocre Syrian brigades. It had always been his premise that Israel wanted all of Palestine to the Jordan River and eventually would strike to get it. Then, on the morning of November 13, the Israelis struck—at Samua. In the aftermath of that calamitous raid, the principal Palestinian towns of Jordan—Hebron, Nablus, Ramallah and Jerusalem—erupted in riot. The great political cleft between the two halves of the country—the West and East Banks—was perilously deepened; and the Hashimite throne on the dusty hill in Amman was more fearfully shaken than it had been for eight years. The Israeli reprisal had demonstrated that the Legion was impotent to protect the border, and there was nothing the King could really say. In the past he had permitted local arsenals in the border villages, presumably under the army's lock and guard; but shortly before Samua he had abolished them in order to prevent border Palestinians from committing him to trouble. El Fatah and the P.L.O. had meanwhile generated a new temper of perfervid militancy among young Palestinians. The reaction now was wild and threatening.

Frightened and angry, the Palestinians in the border villages cried for protection. More angrily still, they clamored for arms to protect themselves. Why were they not given them? Why was Hussein forever quarreling with his Arab neighbors? With the Syrians? The Egyptians? The P.L.O.? Why hadn't his great friends, the Americans and the British, done something to curb the Israelis? Where was the mighty Sixth Fleet? Cairo Radio exhorted the demonstrators to sweep Hussein off his throne, while Amman heaped sardonic reproaches on Nasser for not sending his air force.

Hussein managed to retain full authority over the apparatus of power and to act effectively against the agitators. He sent first his head-bashing police and then his troops into the fray. Well-posted armored cars in the snarled web of Amman's downtown streets forestalled any outbreaks in the capital. The Legion, though no longer the Legion of 1963, met the test and stifled the riots. Nablus, the last of the insurgent towns, was placed under total curfew and finally subdued after its electricity and water were cut off. The P.L.O., officially outlawed five months before but still permitted to lead a kind of twilight existence, was at last conclusively proscribed, its activities suppressed, its offices closed and its agents imprisoned. To be sure, Samua put a severe strain on Hussein's relations with his army commanders. They, too, wanted more arms, and in the extreme alarm of the hour, he turned to the Americans. An emergency airlift delivered the desired equipment at the turn of the year, with the desired heartening effect.

But the chief consequence of these events was political: Samua was a watershed in Hussein's relationship with Israel. The Israelis, badly miscalculating, had presumed to carry out a police job he was unable to do himself and had merely succeeded in exposing his helplessness to an aroused nation. They had humiliated the King whom they claimed they were helping and encouraging to act against the terrorists. Suddenly he found himself under attack from all directions— from the P.L.O., whose West Bank agents were calling for insurrection and demanding arms; from the Egyptians, who were crying for his head; from the Syrians, who were forever proclaiming that the Palestinians needed not a Hussein but a Ho Chi Minh to liberate their homeland; and now—from the Israelis. He was fighting on all fronts at once and thereafter was convinced that Israel's ultimate aim was to ignite a war and seize the West Bank.

Nothing could uproot this fixed idea, so frequently expressed to Western diplomats during this period; and Israeli reassurances were wholly unavailing. Samua had destroyed their credibility. In Hussein's public utterances there was a new and desperately exalted Arab ring. He spoke of personally leading his army against the invading foe, to redeem Arab honor amid "the cannon's roar and the bullet's whine," though he might die in the attempt. He promised his troops he would prove worthy of his blood, as the fortieth in the direct line of descent from Mohammed. Many Jordanians excitedly saw the raid at Samua as a dress rehearsal for the greater incursion to come. Had it not been a combined infantry, tank and air operation? Hussein's conception was equally excited but more subtle. Israel—so he argued and apparently believed—could not invade Jordan as long as he remained on his throne, since the Americans insisted on keeping him there. Hence the Israelis intended to get him first, justifying and clearing the way for a full-scale expedition by means of such turbulent actions as Samua. They had decided he was worthless to them, indeed an embarrassment and an obstacle because of his American connection: they would therefore seek to provoke a leftist coup in Amman and thus polarize the contest between a Soviet-influenced Jordan and a pro-Western Israel. The enemy in the case would then be clearly identified. The unhappy effect of Samua was finally to alienate Hussein, by convincing him of Israel's changed attitude toward himself and unchanged goal with respect to the West Bank. The tacit covenant that had existed for so many years between Amman and Jerusalem was shattered: the line of understanding was cut. It was never repaired.

Nowhere as in the towns and cities of Jordan, the following May, was Nasser's triumphant challenge to the Israeli enemy celebrated with such a fervor of high hope and expectancy. The final battle for the liberation of Palestine seemed gloriously at hand. Such was the atmosphere of mass elation, so flaming were the hopes, so delirious the expectations, that in Jordanian hearts was suddenly rekindled that old, deep-set cultural conviction of impregnable superiority—they, the intrepid warriors, pitted at last against the clever Israelis who had managed to maintain themselves in the usurped homeland only because of their immense foreign backing. Hussein in this atmosphere foresaw a great political victory from which he would be excluded and by which he would fall. His predicament, as he saw it, was simply this: either to be an Arab in an Arab cause or to remain on the sidelines and be identified with Israel forever after. But to join the cause and take part in the political victory meant surrender to Nasser. He knew that in the end a pact with Egypt might prove the kiss of death; but he faced the prospect of almost certain insurrection if he abstained from Nasser's greatest triumph. An ominous report from his intelligence service said that Nasser had chosen him as his next target: sometime in July, according to this grapevine advice, the Egyptians would make a concerted push to topple him. He may well have reckoned that even lacking such help from without, internal pressures would be quite sufficient to overwhelm him. Which way should he turn? At the outset of the crisis he seems, in fact, to have turned in both, such were the shifting and insecure foundations of royal policy. On the eve of the blockade he sent Hammash, his Chief of Staff, to Cairo to feel his way toward an accommodation. But at the same time Jordan apparently wanted war and was doing all she could to provoke it, by her mockery of the dismissal of UNEF and her ceaseless gibes about Tiran. It evidently occurred to Hussein that his one salvation, at this point, lay in war—in the hope that Israel would immediately wage war and knock out the Egyptians. This would have resolved his dilemma. Immediately after the blockade, the Israelis were advised by an intelligence contact that Hussein was waiting impatiently for them to move: the message warned that his position was desperate, his fate lay in their hands, and in the absence of Israeli action, he could not hold out much longer.

Had Israel moved on May 24 or 25, there would never have been a Hussein-Nasser pact or a war on the Jordanian front. But at that moment the role and attitude of the West counted for more in Tel-Aviv than the immediate consequences in the region. The consequences were decisive. Hussein saw the Israelis apparently paralyzed by the mobilization of Egyptian might and worried above all by the repercussions in Washington. They had decided to talk rather than fight. Their hesitant response persuaded him that Nasser knew what he was doing and was on his way to a blazing triumph. The fruit of the Israeli consultations in Washington was Eshkol's radio speech on the evening of May 28, a signal that Israel was still holding off and had not taken a decision for war. So Hussein, isolated in Amman, anxiously waiting to see what would happen, watching Nasser forge ahead while Eshkol tarried, drew his conclusions and made up his mind. The conclusions he drew were mistaken. Had he read Israel's intentions correctly, he might still have held out.

No doubt he made a number of crisscrossing calculations before deciding—quite suddenly, after hurried contacts with the Egyptian Ambassador in Amman and to the surprise of all but a favored few in the royal circle—to take off for Cairo. He saw, for example, that the Egyptian-Syrian defense pact had actually worked: the Egyptians *had* come to Syria's rescue and Israel had, in fact, been deterred. And no doubt, convinced that Israel was the main and permanent threat to his kingdom, he thought it might help matters if he secured a mutual defense pact for himself. But his flight to Cairo was, above all, another *fuite en avant:* his imperative need was to save himself from final isolation in the Arab world and join Nasser's party before it was too late. This was a political and not a military calculation. He could not be absent from a spectacular Arab political victory and survive; and in the ecstatic mood that had then swept Jordan, he probably believed he could not be absent from a general war, if it came. If the war were won, he would be isolated; if it were lost, he would be the traitor responsible for the defeat. Besides, he was a man of honor, an Arab dynast of ancestral pride, and it was better to go down as a loyal Arab in the event of military disaster.

Some diplomats believed that Hussein like other Jordanians was convinced the Arabs would win in a test of arms. Others strongly doubted it. From what he himself later said—wrily, drily and chivalrously, without a word of recrimination or reproach for his Egyptian ally, after he had lost the Holy City of Jerusalem and the whole of the West Bank—he apparently had few illusions about the Arab capacity to meet Israel in war. Given his exalted Arab temperament, we may guess that he, too, was swept along by the romantic surge around him—well aware of the suicidal implications but engaging his royal honor and believing he had to be on Nasser's side in so momentous an encounter.

On the morning of May 30, attired in field khaki as Supreme Commander of the Jordanian armed forces, piloting his own twin-engined jet plane, Hussein flew to Cairo to capitulate to the man who was about to emerge as the maker and breaker of the Arab world. At the military airport at Almaza, on the desert northern edge of the city, he was mellifluously greeted by the Egyptian President and a smiling phalanx of his power elite—Amer and four Vice-Presidents. There followed five hours of talks at Kubbeh Palace. At one point a telephone call was put through to President Aref of Iraq and at another, Shukheiry was ushered in to join the discussion. In his most recent execrations of the King the previous week, Shukheiry had set two "complementary" goals for the Palestinians of Jordan: the destruction of Israel and the destruction of the "Hashimite harlot" who had persecuted Arab commandos, filled Jordanian prisons and by his treachery had turned his country into an American state and a base for NATO. Nasser beamed and Hussein smiled wanly as television cameras were rolled in to record their signing of a five-year mutual defense pact on which, Nasser said, there had been complete agreement from the very beginning. It stipulated that an armed attack on either party would be considered an attack on both, and that in the event of war the forces of both would be placed under the command of the Egyptian Chief of Staff. In a speech after the signing Nasser observed that Arabs knew how to forget their differences when the chips were down. "The Egyptian Army, the Jordanian Army, the Syrian Army and the Lebanese Army now stand on the Israeli border . . . to face the challenge," he said. "Behind them are the Iraqi Army, the Algerian Army, the Kuwaiti Army, the Sudanese Army and the whole Arab nation. The action we have taken today will amaze the world."

For Hussein it was total capitulation. In the defense pact and the various corollary agreements that adorned it, Nasser exacted every imaginable concession. Hussein agreed to open the borders of Jordan to the immediate entry of Iraqi forces; to withdraw his own troops from his border with Syria, which he had closed a week before after a Syrian terrorist's mine had killed sixteen Jordanians at a frontier post (as a result of the incident, he had promptly broken off diplomatic relations with Damascus); to release all political prisoners, those of the P.L.O., El Fatah and others; to accept the P.L.O. on Jordanian territory, on Shukheiry's terms; to admit Egyptian forces; and to place his army under the operational command of an Egyptian general, Abdel Moneim Riad, who would shortly go to Amman to establish an advance headquarters of the United Arab Command.

Six hours after landing in Cairo, Hussein and his party of General Staff officers took off again in the royal jet, carrying an extra passenger on their homeward journey. A circling squadron of Egyptian Migs escorted them until they re-entered Jordanian air space above the sparse fringe of palms along the shore at Aqaba, at the head of the Gulf. Some minutes later, when the plane swept down the runway at Amman airport, turned and taxied to rest, cut its engines and opened its door, Shukheiry followed the King down the ramp. He was free to go anywhere in Jordan that he wished, to raise his Palestinian army, although, of course, the King took the elementary precaution of assigning an accompanying officer, who duly noted his contacts and kept a record for the police. Joy was boundless in Jordan over the King's reconciliation with Nasser. Eager throngs lined the streets as he drove back to his little palace on the hill, and headlines in the Amman newspapers next morning hailed "the Genius Commander, Hussein the Great."

The Israelis had misestimated Nasser's ability to create a solid Arab front overnight. Now for the first time, he commanded a collective Arab strength, achieving a degree of Arab military unity and coordination without precedent in postwar history. Perhaps, had he been a very, very clever man, he would not have gone so far. In reply to Hussein's request to come to Cairo, he might have said: Thank you very much, but right now you must stay home, I have enough and we shall talk about a defense pact sometime later. But, of course, this was out of the question: Nasser was riding high and he had not yet had enough. Indeed, events had taken control and were imposing their own pattern. Washington's intervention had produced Israel's hesitations and these hesitations had spurred Hussein on his journey to Cairo. Nasser's blockade had produced his second wave of mobilization in Sinai, and the evident dangers of the new situation had led him to reconsider his military posture and conclude that Jordan, facing Israel on her most vital strategic border, must be present in any war. So he exacted the military agreement that made the war inevitable. He was confident of his defensive strength, he relied greatly on the deterrent of his air force and particularly of its bomber component, and he now held Israel in the vise of an Arab military coalition of overwhelming numerical weight. But even more than a military expedient, the pact with Jordan was a political act that celebrated his ascendancy on the Arab scene. The confrontation with Israel was the irresistible occasion for extending his sway. In reaching for that further triumph, he set the stage for war.

In Israel a number of developments had heightened the sense of imminent danger in the forty-eight hours following Eshkol's speech of May 28. Egyptian Migs had made further sneak flights across the Negev and, along the boundary with the Gaza Strip, the first shots had, in fact, been fired. Troops of the Palestine Liberation Army, equipped with Chinese machine guns, mortars and bazookas, and occupying the border posts abandoned by UNEF, had mortared the wheat fields of Nahal Oz and neighboring kibbutzim and machine-gunned an army vehicle on patrol. Meanwhile the reports which Eban received from the American diplomatic front were unpromising. The multinational regatta on which he had placed such hopes was fading into the misty future, an increasingly hypothetical and decreasingly

relevant exercise. On the morning of May 30, the third day after his
return from Washington, he summoned a press conference in Jerusalem to announce that Israel could allow only "the shortest possible
time" for international action to "rescind" the blockade at Tiran and
the abnormal build-up in Sinai—"a brief period of suspense" that
would be measured not in months but in weeks or days.

Perhaps, if Nasser had not signed the pact with Hussein later that
day, if he had not given free rein to his exuberant commanders, if he
had not allowed his troops to dig in ever closer to the Sinai frontier
while armored reserves mustered behind them, and had not allowed
the mobilization of arms and passion on Israel's borders to gain such
momentum that it seemed unstoppable—perhaps, if he had not done
these things, war might yet have been avoided. But he did do them,
and the fact that he marched along so confidently on the road of escalation aroused in Israel the phobias of the unknown. Where was he
going? What new and untried weapons did he have? What missiles?
What chemical warheads? What secret political support? What
pledges from the Russians? On the night of May 30 came the awful
realization that he was about to consummate Israel's encirclement.
The key was the command of the Jordan Legion. Israel now faced
Egypt on her eastern frontier, and by a telephone call to Baghdad and
the stroke of a pen the gates of Jordan were opened to the troops of
Iraq as well. For years Israel had lived under the incubus of division at
her waist, in the narrow coastal plain where nine miles of farmland
separated the westward bulge of Jordan from the Mediterranean
shore, and where Tel-Aviv and its populous suburbs, Herzliya and
Netanya, and the Lydda airport lay within easy range of enemy guns.
The threat was now real: the Egyptians commanded Israel's most vulnerable border.

From across that border was heard the voice of Shukheiry, who had
donned a military uniform for his reappearance in Jordan. "Either we
or Israel," Shukheiry said in an interview. "There is no other way and
we shall accept no other solution than the liberation of Palestine. I
cannot imagine that even a single Israeli is going to be left alive once
the battle begins." If any Israelis were left, he said, they would be sent
back to Europe. From Baghdad came the voice of President Aref,
bidding farewell to Iraqi pilots as they left for a forward base. "It was
treason and politics that brought about the creation of Israel," he said.
"Brothers and sons, this is the day of battle to revenge your martyred

brethren who fell in 1948. It is the day to wash away the stigma. God willing, we shall meet in Tel-Aviv and Haifa." From Cairo came the salutation of the commander of an Egyptian air base, as he welcomed Iraqi and Kuwaiti troops: "All you soldiers of Kuwait, Iraq and soldiers of Sudan will be stationed in the front lines and we hope that you return to your countries healthy and by land after the destruction of Israel."

In the dead streets of Tel-Aviv, a city emptied of its youth, the buses had disappeared, the tables at the sidewalk cafés were deserted and the discothèques were silent. The tourists were gone, the big hotels were depopulated. Nearly all of the postmen having left for the front, children delivered the mail; and nearly all of the buses having been commandeered for the mobilization, they walked to school. Downtown hotels were made ready as emergency hospitals, and along the beaches below them, children and mothers came to fill their sandbags and drag them home. Observing carefully the printed instructions they had found in their mailboxes, they took down the pictures from their walls, crisscrossed their windows with tape and made sandbag shields around the air openings of their basement shelters. In Jerusalem the beautiful campus of Hebrew University, on its high hill open to the sky and sun, was hushed and forsaken. Of its Israeli Jewish students, ten thousand were mobilized. Of the nine hundred who remained, the majority were girls. They, too, were away, filling the jobs of drafted men in factory or government office; at schools and hospitals, stacking sandbags; transporting food from warehouses to shops; or giving courses in first aid and stretcher-bearing. And each day, on Israel's borders, the pressures mounted and closed in.

Sabras and immigrants, the young generation and the old, those for whom the Second World War was an immediate and intimate experience and those who were not yet born when it ended; the soldiers at the front, their families at home—all felt the same loneliness and all believed that a battle of survival was imposed upon them. From that loneliness sprang their courage. For Israel there could be only one war and one battle; and no one else would fight it for her. It was war because there was no alternative. In the somber anguish of that time, when all expected bombs on their cities and thousands of civilian deaths, the chasm between the Israeli generations was bridged and the holocaust of Nazi Europe acquired a dreadful and present meaning for those who had been exempt from the experience of their fathers.

With the Arab world united for Israel's destruction, the legacy of the fathers was transmitted to the sons: the holocaust must never happen again, the people of Israel must not die in horror. So they prepared for the ultimate sacrifice in a war in which they believed their only alternatives were victory or extinction.

The political expression of their tension and anguish was the phenomenon of Dayan's return to power. Only a few people in the country, indeed only a relative few in the councils of government—the General Staff, Allon, Eshkol and some but by no means all of his ministers—knew the true balance of military forces and were confident of Israel's strength. The nation at large turned to the man who had become the paramount symbol of leadership in the realm of defense. It was not only that he was a younger man, attuned in outlook to the spirit of the new generation; not only that he was a nearly legendary figure who had been almost continuously associated with national defense since independence—even after his retirement from the army; and not only the luster of his victory in Sinai in 1956. It was the aura of the man himself—his commanding temperament, his natural capacity for independent decision; and this aura of certitude, inborn, individual and unmistakable, gave him a public confidence and moral authority that were somehow his alone. He was the man the country wanted as its Minister of Defense, the man to lead the army if Israel had to fight and equally the man to say "halt" if she had to halt, since all were certain that if Dayan drew back it would be not for lack of resolution or of clarity of vision.

The politicians turned to him, with the mixed motives that politicians have, in their agitation for an expanded cabinet, a "government of national union." Some in Dayan's own opposition party, Rafi, relentlessly inimical to Eshkol, were quite disposed to use the occasion to undermine and discredit the Prime Minister, with alarmed and despondent suggestions that the armed forces were unprepared. Within the government the National Religious Party, without whose votes the Eshkol coalition would lose its majority in the Knesset, was wedded to the proposition that the House of Israel must be united in time of war and that Rafi must be represented by Dayan as Minister of Defense. Politicians scurried and consulted; worried party conclaves were held on every side. Begin, the perennial outsider, the leader of the unreconciled Right, was indefatigable in his crusade for an all-party cabinet with Dayan at the helm of defense.

For several days the campaign proceeded and Eshkol resisted. He clung to his defense portfolio and, indeed, he might have kept it if, in the end, an upsurge of popular feeling had not carried the accolade to Dayan. He was slow to perceive that there was more to the campaign than the impure motives of party politicians. He was upset by the display of nonconfidence in his leadership, certain of his government's ability to meet the test and justifiably proud of his stewardship as Minister of Defense. He saw no reason to surrender half his job.

On the night of May 30, the night that the news came of Hussein's pact in Cairo, Eshkol faced a revolt in his party. At a meeting of Mapai's Knesset deputies, even his closest associates, his most loyal friends abandoned him. Speaker after speaker demanded Dayan; others, less numerous, proposed a military man already in the cabinet —Allon. If he had to part with the Defense Ministry, Eshkol much preferred to make way for Allon, whom he found to be a more congenial and pliant collaborator. But in any case, a large consensus of the deputies called on him to yield the portfolio: the malaise of the country had invaded the ranks of the dominant party. The next afternoon he called Dayan to his office to suggest a number of alternatives.

Dayan's terms were characteristically explicit. Would he, Eshkol asked, join the government as Minister Without Portfolio, to serve together with Allon and others on the cabinet's inner defense committee? The offer was entirely unacceptable. Dayan did not want a government post without authority. Would he agree to be Deputy Prime Minister? This was equally repugnant, for the same reason. He was a man of action, Dayan said, not a man either to give deferential advice or accept a title; and his sphere of action was obviously at the front in the Negev. Would he, then, accept a military command? He would, indeed. Commander of the Southern Front, for example? Dayan chose the front; if he were mobilized, he would assume any duty imposed upon him by the Chief of Staff. But what it amounted to was that if he were given an army command, he wanted the southern front; if a place in the government, then an office that carried both responsibility and authority—the Ministry of Defense. Eshkol, for a few hours at least, saw a way out of his problem. Allon would be Defense Minister and Dayan would go to the Negev. Rabin was consulted and the decision was taken.

But a short while later, on the evening of May 31, Eshkol faced a revolt not only in his party but in his government. The Ministers of the National Religious Party, absolute for Dayan as Defense Minister in an all-party coalition, uttered ultimative threats of resignation. Without Dayan, it appeared, there could be no government of national union.

The next day the wavering struggle hastened to its denouement. With the staunch support of his party's redoubtable Secretary, Golda Meir, and other party elders, Eshkol went before the Mapai Secretariat to seek approval of his plan: Allon as Defense Minister and Dayan as Southern Front Commander. The debate in the Secretariat continued for several hours after Eshkol had said his word and left. His proposal came too late; conceivably, had he made it a few days earlier, the outcome might have been different. Led by its younger members, insisting on its right to authorize changes in the cabinet and defying its all-powerful Secretary, the party council by preponderant vote rejected Eshkol's formula and demanded Dayan as the man of the hour. The last political bastion had fallen and the battle was over.

That afternoon Eshkol summoned Dayan and offered him the defense portfolio. A little later, announcing his decision to a meeting of his Ministers, he seemed cheerfully relieved and relaxed. The loser in the contest was Allon, who a few hours earlier had still expected to receive the mantle he had been offered the previous day and already was in busy consultation with officers of the General Staff. Had Eshkol acted sooner, before he had lost so large a measure of public confidence; had he handed over to Allon a week before when it was still politically possible to do so, or had appointed him his Deputy Defense Minister as some members of his cabinet had suggested, then Allon and not Dayan might have led Israel to war and have worn the laurels of victory. But Allon on the afternoon of June 1 met the occasion with the grace of a practical politician. Withdrawing his candidacy and asking for an end to internal debates that were apt "to distract the public from the war effort and weaken its preparedness at this grave hour," he declared himself ready to serve in any capacity, within or outside the government, that the Prime Minister might designate.

The old Eshkol government convened for the last time at ten o'clock that evening in order to approve the broadening of the coalition. A quarter of an hour later it was joined by Begin, as Minister Without Portfolio, and Dayan, wearing khaki but without his Major General's insignia. After the ritual exchange of greetings and congratulations, the emergency war cabinet sat down to its first meeting.

Away in Washington, while Israel was settling her internal problems, President Johnson was doing his level and loyal best to fulfill his
promise of international action. Only six days had passed since
Eban's visit to the White House, but already Johnson's Red Sea Regatta, bravely showing the flags of the major maritime powers and
upholding the principle of free navigation, was a rapidly receding vision. Israel's period of waiting had served to bring the President face
to face with an intractable dilemma. Factors of predominant importance on the American political scene had intervened to limit his action
—the fallout from the war in Vietnam and the stern insistence of
Congress that whatever the United States did for Israel it must do
multilaterally. The nightmare of Vietnam was on everybody's mind,
and with it the dread of another nightmare in the Middle East. There
could be no more unilateralism; Vietnam was enough. Congressional
leaders, Rusk found, were immovable on this central point: the
United States, in implementing the plan for an armada, must act as a
member of an international club, if possible under the comfortable
umbrella of the United Nations, if necessary outside it, but in either
case in concert with an appropriate array of respectable allies. This
Congressional proviso clearly meant allies of the West, the Europeans
and Canada, and not merely an assortment of Far Eastern confederates such as the Administration had raised, in greater or less force, for
the war in Vietnam. Multilateralism was essential. No doubt the international character of the Maritime Force would be largely symbolic,
but even a symbol must be convincing. Congress was adamant.

Acquainted though they were with American constitutional processes, the Israelis in Washington were taken aback by this development. They had not realized the extent of the Far Eastern fallout or
anticipated the specific condition set by Congress—the supreme importance of being multilateral. Still more they were jolted to discover
the political requirement for a Congressional resolution, which evidently made the prospects of the regatta all the more problematic. As
a model and precedent, Johnson could cite the resolution of August,
1964, that had empowered him to make war in Vietnam; with equal
force Senators William Fulbright, Mike Mansfield and others could
cite that resolution as a reason for not making the same mistake on
the other side of the world. The armada was conceived as a military
escort that would fire if fired upon. The Administration could reasonably assume that so astute a politician as Nasser would not open fire

on an American ship. But what if something went wrong? What if the Egyptians fired? What would the Russians do? The immeasurable risks were there.

The erosion of enthusiasm and support for the Red Sea Regatta among the maritime nations was swift and spectacular. France declined, Canada defected, the Scandinavians got cold feet, and Britain, sympathetic at first, then hesitant, then apprehensive, wobbled and drew back. Already embroiled in the Arab world, caught in the cross fire of rival terrorist organizations in Aden, the British boggled at the prospect of a further scrap at the other end of the Red Sea. Parliament as well as Congress had its qualms, and Wilson, reluctant to proceed with the Americans alone, urged that everybody try, first, to see what could be done at the United Nations. In Paris, the Elysée simply turned its lordly back on a project that flouted both its creed of French "neutrality" and the interests of its new-found Arab friends. The Scandinavians recoiled when a timely statement by Foreign Minister Riad, bristling with references to imperialist domination and nineteenth-century warship diplomacy, warned that any attempt by the maritime countries to impose their mandate on Egyptian territorial waters would be regarded as an act of aggression and would be dealt with accordingly. One by one and two by two, the maritime friends of the United States, reserving their doubts as to the strength of the American resolve, worried by possible Russian reactions, and loath at all events to join a small force, diffidently excused themselves and bowed out of the flotilla. The proposed declaration of principle by the maritime states found few takers and, embarrassingly, those who stepped forward to proffer their signatures—Portugal and South Africa—were the wrong kind of political friends. It was a black day for multilaterialism.

As he had told Eban, Johnson had a verbal commitment of two destroyers from Canada but, alas, these also dropped out of sight. Canada's change of heart epitomized the problem. The Canadians were Israel's good friends and their relations with Nasser were in a sorry state indeed. On May 27, in the aftermath of UNEF's dismissal, the Canadian contingent in U Thant's disbanded army was singled out for special notice, in the shape of an ultimatum from Cairo ordering it out of Gaza and Egypt within forty-eight hours. U Thant acceded in the request, regretting the circumstances that had led to it and asking for a few hours' extension for imperative reasons of logistics. The

Canadians hastily organized an airlift for the evacuation of their eight hundred men and missed their deadline by only one day. This was the penalty that Nasser exacted for the distinctly unfriendly stance of the Canadian Government and the wicked maneuvers of Ignatiev, its United Nations representative, during the hassle over UNEF. Nevertheless, while they had firm views on free passage through the Gulf of Aqaba, the more the Canadians thought about the Red Sea Regatta, the less they liked it. After so many years of United Nations peacekeeping in the Middle East, in which the Dominion of Canada had so loyally participated, the regatta seemed to Prime Minister Lester Pearson a dubious experiment, an untimely throwback to unilateral police action, smacking of imperialist imposition, redolent of gunboats, evoking distasteful and unwelcome memories of the Royal Navy wheeling off Port Said in the distant November of 1956. It seemed a painfully atavistic approach—an independently organized armada, under American patronage, outside the accepted framework of the United Nations. How far should one go in trying to police the world? And besides, there was the lowering shadow of Vietnam. If there were an explosion at the Straits of Tiran, where would the ensuing escalations land the committed parties? Canada withdrew her offer of two destroyers.

Thus, in the span of a few days, the regatta dwindled. Faraway Australia was in the lists, and Britain's name was still down, immediately followed by a large red-penciled question mark. Of the Atlantic allies of the United States, only Holland remained as a sure and resolute starter.

Nevertheless, had a Middle Eastern war not interposed, a regatta of some kind there almost certainly would have been, a minimal multilateral force, to test the issue in the Gulf of Aqaba. Plans would have gone forward and in another two weeks, or three, the fleet would probably have come into being, engaging the ships of four or five nations dedicated to the principle of free passage. Johnson was determined to see it through. There had been, at the various levels of American policy, many widely divergent estimates and contrary advices. Some armada advocates were convinced to the end that whatever the hazards the project was worth a try. There were others who, wildly and mistakenly, ignoring the clamorous lessons of 1956, had at one time fancied the regatta as a way of overturning Nasser, on the upside-down assumption that he could not possibly survive the break-

ing of the blockade. There were others still who from the beginning
had not believed in it at all. Johnson, in any case, intended to go
ahead: not quixotically but for the plain reason that the regatta was
his only option, his only means of honoring the American commitment. He still had a long way to go. Not only was the regatta's membership uncertain; not only was its order of battle undecided—the
nationality of the warship that would actually steam through the
Straits as an escort, the instructions to the Commander in such and
such circumstances; not only these practical problems but the flotilla's
general terms of reference had still to be settled. What exactly was its
mission? Would it escort oil and other strategic cargoes in non-Israeli
ships only? Or would it extend protection to Israeli ships as well? The
eventual partners in the enterprise would have to reach agreement on
these matters. Multilateralism required time and negotiations; and
after Nasser had tightened the noose by his pact with Hussein, there
was no time. Events on the ground had overtaken the multilateral
negotiations, and the drama on Israel's borders had superseded the
crisis at Tiran. A new front was opened in Jordan and Egyptian
troops were heading toward it. In Washington on June 1 Ambassador
Harman decided to fly home to report his judgment to his government: the proposal for a Maritime Force was no longer valid because
the rush of events did not allow the time to bring it to fulfillment. In
Jerusalem Eban was already of the same view. On the evening of June
1 he informed Rabin that he no longer had any political objections to
going to war and that he would vote for war in the cabinet.

Immediate international action organized by the Americans was
one way of resisting the blockade. Conceivably, there was a second
way: a judgment and order by the Security Council. But the Russians,
riveted to their line of unqualified support for their Arab friends on all
occasions, were unwilling to play. Johnson had warned them from
the start that the blockade was a very serious matter, a challenge
which the United States intended to answer, a *casus belli* for Israel,
with the implicit risk of a big-power confrontation. The Russians at
the United Nations professed the opposite view. Where, they asked,
was the crisis? Why the excitement? Why, asked Fedorenko, the Soviet delegate, this "artificially dramatic climate" so disingenuously
fostered by the Western powers? With a brotherly arm around Arab
shoulders, Fedorenko scolded the Americans for raising such a bogus
commotion. At the request of the Danes and Canadians, the Council

was summoned on May 24 to consider an anodyne resolution supporting U Thant's mission to Cairo and requesting all parties "to refrain
from any steps which might worsen the situation." The Arabs saw this
call for restraint as being aimed one-sidedly at Nasser and were wildly
against any resolution at all. What was Nasser doing but exercising his
legitimate rights and discharging, as El Kony said, his "national obligation and inescapable duty" in response to Israeli provocations? The
resolution failed to get off the ground.

   Nasser's lawyers had been studying the legalities of the Tiran issue
for many years. They based their case primarily on Egypt's state of
belligerence with Israel, but they also prepared a defense in depth
with a series of fallback positions. Egypt was within her rights, they
argued, because the Straits were Arab territorial waters, with the three-
mile limits of Egypt and Saudi Arabia overlapping in midstream and
with the navigable channel on the Egyptian side. Further, the Gulf of
Aqaba was in its entirety Arab—if one accepted the overlapping of
twelve-mile limits, which the United States did not; and, of course,
said the Arabs unanimously, Israel had no right to be in Eilath anyway. In the argument on these points, the Indians were active as Nasser's international lawyers, affirming—as all acknowledged—that the
waters of Tiran were Arab; and the Americans busily needled the
Russians by reminding them of their adherence to the Geneva covenant on free passage through international straits. The Russians,
mindful that the waters of the Bosporus and Dardanelles were Turkish,
were careful not to get locked in on an argument that could be so
easily turned against them.

   A resolution by the Security Council with the Russians voting
"Aye," calling on Egypt to renounce her "belligerent rights," might
have given Nasser pause. On returning from Cairo, U Thant searched
for a point at which to defuse the crisis and came up with the perfect
diplomatic formula in his report to the Security Council: he requested
all parties in the dispute to "forgo belligerence" so that the Council
might deal with the underlying causes of the crisis. In the language of
the United Nations, the euphemism had a very precise meaning. It
meant the lifting of the blockade. If Nasser forwent the exercise of his
"belligerent rights" at Tiran, the blockade would remain in suspense.
There would be a breathing spell, technically without prejudice to the
issue of who controlled the Straits or who had the right to pass through
them; and international diplomacy might then go to work. The Ameri-

cans, striving to gain time to mobilize their Red Sea Regatta, picked up U Thant's formula and made it the central and operative part of a draft resolution. Again, the Russians interposed their roadblock.

The Russians were now coasting comfortably, as they believed, on Nasser's succession of victories. They had good reason to seek to "de-dramatize" the crisis; they wished to sit tight on their gains and not debate them in public, especially as the theme of Tiran was so embarrassing. As the crisis broadened after the blockade, they sniffed a still greater Middle Eastern triumph, thanks to Nasser, who had raised the stakes: a triumph of unexpected dimensions in which American authority would be humbled and American prestige broken in the Arab world, while their own position and influence, as the patrons of the game, would be commensurately enhanced and expanded. True, Johnson had warned them they were playing a dangerous game. But what probably impressed them most at this stage were the misgivings of the American Congress; the eloquence with which American Senators were insisting that every possible use be made of the United Nations—the standard way of evading national commitments; and the flagging interest of the maritime states in the President's regatta.

Nasser was winning his gamble on the international scene. The statesman's calculations had been cannily correct. Shielded by his Soviet friends from any effective international pressure, he saw no impelling reasons to give anything away in negotiation. UNEF had vanished, at a word from him; Tiran had been blockaded, and not a shot from Israel or a warship from the United States; and if the Israelis could be contained, he had every prospect of getting home free. When, on May 29, the State Department's special emissary, Charles Yost, arrived in Cairo to explore Nasser's loopholes, he found the Egyptian Foreign Office supremely uninterested. Yost's mission was to search for palliatives—a suspension of the blockade, if possible, or at least some sort of mitigation. The Egyptians would hear of neither. Nasser was holding his face-saving concessions in reserve and felt under no pressure to open any of his loopholes. He was so unconcerned at this moment to talk to the Americans that he had not even troubled to catch up on his White House correspondence. On his desk lay an unanswered letter he had received from Johnson the previous week. "I have received a nice letter from President Johnson," he informed the French Ambassador in Cairo, "and I don't intend to answer it for the time being." The impasse in high-level communications between Cairo and Washington was complete. Johnson's letter had been very nice indeed, restrained in tone, friendly in spirit, urging Nasser to take no precipitate action, amiably acknowledging that American-Egyptian relations had not been of the happiest, and suggesting that he would be ready to send Vice-President Hubert Humphrey to Cairo in the hope of improving matters. Nasser kept the letter for future reference.

During Yost's conversations in Cairo, there were waffling hints on the Egyptian side that Nasser might agree to arrangements similar to those of the United States Battle Act, permitting trade in certain goods between belligerent countries, possibly including oil—but always in non-Israeli flagships. In time something might well have been worked out along these lines but it would, of course, have been entirely unacceptable to Israel. For the Israelis, discrimination was the vital issue—the denial of their existence—although, oddly and foolishly, they had neglected through the years to establish regular Israeli shipping through the Gulf of Aqaba. In the decade since 1957, fewer than ten Israeli commercial ships had journeyed through the Straits; the last flagship engaged in international trade had passed three years before the reinstitution of the blockade; and in the year immediately past, there had been only two Israeli fishing boats. But such statistics, for Israel, were beside the point. The point was her sovereign right and national existence. Moreover, under the Battle Act arrangements, her oil shipments from Iran would have been perpetually at Nasser's mercy. The Israelis took a poor view of Yost's mission to Cairo. The State Department had not advised them of this particular gambit and they were persuaded that its intent and bias was to turn up a formula that would save Nasser's face at their expense. It was a portent, they surmised, that Israel in the end would be asked to pay the price of the crisis.

The sense of power attracts sympathy to its side as well as interest, and the success of Nasser's showmanship was yet another phenomenon that deepened Israel's feeling of loneliness. It was a virtuoso performance. Rising from a dismally low ebb in his political fortunes, he had not only mesmerized the Arab world but for a brief, dizzy time had convinced many Western capitals of his strength and dominance. The Russians were not alone in believing in the defensive capacity of the Egyptian Army, and the Arabs were not alone in succumbing to the spell of his triumphs. Military attachés at Western European Em-

306 *Encounter with the Middle East*

bassies in Cairo began retouching and recasting their estimates, impressed by the logistical feat that had produced such a rapid concentration of modern armament in the Sinai Desert. Some were ready to concede they had been operating on a cliché in accepting the idea of Israel's preponderant deterrent power. In Paris, Foreign Minister Couve de Murville was heard to ask how many Israeli ships had been passing through the Straits of Tiran recently, and to suggest that while Nasser would evidently balk at Israeli flagships he might still allow the passage of strategic cargoes. Even the Danes, so friendly to Israel, were unconvinced that Tiran was a *casus belli;* and Avriel, now Ambassador in Rome, found that even the Italians, so warm and sympathetic, could offer only their commiseration. It was widely accepted by Israel's Western European friends that she must acquiesce in the inevitable. "The music that was being played to us," an official at the Israeli Foreign Ministry later said, recalling the mood in Western chancelleries during the last week before the war, "was the same that was being played to Czechoslovakia in 1938. The same tone, the same key."

Beyond the Atlantic, in New York and Washington, diplomats from the Soviet-bloc states were jubilant. They freely imparted their advice, telling the Israelis they must really dedramatize their predicament, which was not so bad, and reminding them that international circumstances had altered since 1956—the British and French gone from the Middle East, the Russians no longer distracted by a Hungarian revolution. They urged them, too, to consider that all that was being asked of them was a return to pre-1956—with a compromise on Tiran, of course, so that non-Israeli ships would be free to pass with "innocent cargoes." No doubt, these Eastern diplomats speculated, appropriate arrangements would be made so that Venezuelan oil could be delivered to Haifa, with the United States paying the difference in price. "Let's not overdramatize. . . ." The *mot d'ordre* was everywhere.

Meanwhile, in the theater of Middle East operations, the big powers swung into position. Through the Bosporus and Dardanelles, during the final days, Soviet destroyers with their suggestive batteries of surface-to-surface missiles headed for the eastern Mediterranean to join the new Soviet fleet already stationed there and carry it to its highest peak in history. Intended though it was to impress the Israelis, this offshore demonstration served mainly to excite the imagination of the Arabs and to fire their expectations of Soviet support in the event of war. Nasser himself knew better—or should have. The Russians were his secret weapon in the war of nerves, but, in cold fact, Badran on May 28 had returned from his mission in Moscow with the advice that if war came and anything went wrong, Egypt and her Arab allies would be on their own: on no account would the Soviet Union intervene with its own force. A similar firm warning had been delivered to the Syrians.

As a countersignal to the Kremlin, the ranging Sixth Fleet, for which the Soviet Mediterranean naval units were no match, converged and consolidated in the eastern Mediterranean; and as an earnest of American determination to press on with the regatta project for Tiran, Johnson ordered the aircraft carrier *Intrepid* to proceed through the Suez Canal to the Red Sea. Its southward journey from the Port Said roadstead began before dawn on June 1 and was completed late that afternoon. The carrier glided evenly and noiselessly—piloted by Egyptians, all hands below deck—like a grand and ponderous apparition or a prodigious token of intent, while astonished Egyptians clustered on the Canal bank to watch its passage with a kind of angry awe.

On June 2, in his Friday lecture in *Al Ahram*, Heikal analyzed the nature of the challenge to Israel with a perceptiveness that was wanting in many a Western chancellery. Israel, he wrote, had only two choices, war or internal disintegration. She must strike fast to shatter the Arab blockade and re-establish her psychological security or she would crumble from within. In Heikal's mind there was no doubt that the *casus belli* for the Israelis was their national survival. When would the Israelis strike? On the same day—the morning after the first meeting of the national union government in Jerusalem—Amer alerted his troops and field commanders to prepare for an impending attack. Nasser and Amer appear to have suddenly realized at this time that by deploying the entire might of Egypt in the flat expanse of Sinai they had offered the Israelis both a pretext and an opportunity: it was a setup for a Middle East Pearl Harbor. At any rate, Amer explicitly told his commanders to expect it; his "War Command No. 2" of June 2 was evidently intended as an emergency alert. Iraqi forces at this time were on the move toward Jordan to take up positions on the West Bank. Amer's reading of the situation was lucid enough:

"Israel will not be able to support the burden of mobilization for a long period. The mobilization has already caused a general paralysis of its economy.

"The following are two important events which took place recently: 1. Jordan's joining the mutual defense pact. 2. The participation of Iraqi forces in great strength in the battle from Jordan's borders.

"My analysis of the situation, particularly since the formation of the emergency government in Israel, which includes extremists who are calling for war, is that Israel is likely to think that the Iraqi forces will not be effective on the Jordan front for another fortnight. Israel is planning to confront Egypt before this concentration of troops is completed.

"Therefore, I have prepared my plan and have given my instructions to organize operations. I call on each and every one of you to fight with the maximum of violence, to carry out devotedly orders and instructions within the framework of the established general plan, until the Command has completed its mission.

"Our aim will be to rout the main armed forces of Israel. Our armed forces with their numerous and powerful means are able to do this.

"I bless you all. . . . The battle is the battle of destiny of the United Arab Republic and the entire Arab people. . . . I have complete confidence in our victory."

On the same day Nasser decided the time had come to step back from the brink and open the way to negotiation. The initiative had come from the Americans. In their search for a passageway to peace they had been operating on three levels: telling the Israelis to hold tight, trying to organize their multilateral flotilla and meanwhile making their overtures in Cairo. Ambassador Nolte on June 2 was called to the Egyptian Foreign Office to receive Nasser's reply to the letter from Johnson that had been delivered ten days before. Everything in those ten days had encouraged Nasser to stand firm, including the many hints of possible concessions; and in picking up Johnson's letter and reopening the line to Washington, he looked for a big-power compromise. He was not wrong. The immediate fruit of his correspondence with Johnson was an agreement that Vice-President Mohieddin would fly to Washington on June 7, with the understanding that at a propitious time his visit would be reciprocated by Vice-President Humphrey. In initiating the Mohieddin trip, the Americans hoped, indeed, to reach a compromise that evidently would have excluded Israeli flagships and perhaps oil cargoes as well—a formula that for Israel was the equivalent of capitulation. As Nasser knew, the key historical document in the matter of Tiran was the memorandum that Dulles had given Eban in February, 1957. In that document the United States undertook to exercise the right of free passage for American flagships—and for no others—subject only to an eventual contrary ruling by the International Court of Justice; and in it Nasser probably saw his terms of reference for a compromise settlement. He could presumably hope to meet the American position by saying: Yes, we will permit United States flagships to pass pending a judgment by the World Court, but not the ships of Israel. This would have left the Israelis high and dry, but the Americans might well have been induced, on balance, to accept it. Before world opinion, it would then have been difficult for Israel to go to war on the issue.

The news of Mohieddin's forthcoming trip was thus, for the Israelis, yet another incentive to go to war quickly, if they needed one. Undoubtedly they acted on the conviction that they could no longer stand by while the momentum of the Arab build-up around them mounted. That momentum alone might eventually have carried the Arab states into war. But at the same time, the meaning of Mohieddin's visit to Washington was unmistakable: for Israel it represented the dangers of No War, the certainty of a compromise that would hand Nasser his political victory and the equal certainty of an irreparable decline and contraction of Israel's national right. Was it this news that triggered the final decision? Why did the Israelis choose the morning of June 5? Did they strike protectively, fearing that Mohieddin might succeed and hastening to achieve their war objectives? We do not have a conclusive answer, because we do not know the day or the hour at which they took their decision, or the course of the deliberations that led to it. The Israelis have kept the secret.

On the official record the decision for war was taken at a cabinet meeting on the late afternoon of June 4; and this no doubt was the time of no recall, after which it became impossible to reverse the plans that had been set for the following morning. But we may guess that the Ministers had already taken their contingency decision at an earlier time, in the knowledge that there would be a strong majority for war at the cabinet session of June 4, at which the decision would be made formal and final. Certainly in the stress of those final days, when the country was encompassed by immeasurable risks, both present and future, Israeli leaders were responding to many different pressures under the multiple barrage of events; and the most impelling ones were evidently those that were closest to home. Israeli officials who lived through these events and who knew their pressure said later that neither the news of Mohieddin's trip nor the waning prospects of the Maritime Force prompted the government's decision or its timing: the immediate and overriding factor was the danger that weighed on Israel's borders. True, the Israelis were perturbed by the eleventh-hour news of Mohieddin's mission and its implications. True, they were persuaded that the Red Sea Regatta had no useful future and that the notion that the Americans would find a way out of the crisis was dead. But both the projected mission and the projected naval force—these Israelis said—were already beside the point. "Tiran was a dead duck," as a Foreign Ministry official later put it. The threat was in Sinai, where eighty thousand Egyptians were powerfully dug in. Even if the regatta had been real, fully mobilized and ready to steam up the Red Sea, what guarantee was it for the future? How could Israel indefinitely rely on its protection? And even this familiar argument was beside the point. Of what use would the Red Sea Regatta be in the Sinai Desert? The idea of a test ship, now proposed again by some of Israel's friends, presented greater risks than ever. On June 3, Mortaji in an order of the day told his troops on the Sinai front: "You are now entering a most holy battle against Israeli and imperialist aggression against your homeland. The world is waiting for the day of your sacred struggle for the return of the stolen right. You will restore this right by force of justice, by force of arms and by force of faith." How was Israel to interpret such proclamations? No hot line, no instrument of contact, no possible communication existed across the gulf from Jerusalem to Cairo: the two capitals were as inaccessibly and incomprehensibly distant from each other as Washington and Peking.

Throughout the final week, and especially after the formation of the national coalition government, a major Israeli concern was to see that all the military facts gathered by Israeli intelligence reached the desk of President Johnson. The Israeli and American intelligence pictures tallied. Iraq was a full and active partner in the Nasser-Hussein pact long before she sent a delegation to Cairo—on the last day, June 4—to add her signature to the protocol of the agreement. Several days earlier the Iraqi Eighth Brigade was on the road and on June 2 it crossed the frontier into Jordan. Two Egyptian commando battalions were dispatched to Jordan the same day. In the plan of General Riad, now in command at army headquarters at Amman, these reinforcements were destined for the West Bank, the Egyptians to bolster the Jordan Legion and the Iraqis to carry the offensive against Israel while the Jordanians provided the shield on their home ground. Both the Egyptian and Iraqi Air Forces were alerted for immediate offensive action.

In the end Israel saw that she alone would have to make the decision. It was her life and her danger; and no one else, no big power, could make the decision for her. And in the end, the fear of destruction was greater than the fear of loneliness. "Our house was on fire," Ya'acov Herzog later said. "We were no longer thinking of the great powers." Away in Paris, the great power that had provided Israel with 70 percent of the arms with which she would presently go to war announced that it was not committed in any way nor on any question to any of the states in the dispute. A government statement on June 2, issued after a cabinet meeting under De Gaulle, said that whoever first employed arms in the Middle East, wherever it might be, would have neither the approbation of France nor, for all the stronger reason, her support. "France considers that the worst thing would be the opening of hostilities." Having repudiated her commitments, France now renounced her neutrality. Firmly basing his policy on his doctrine of France's role in world affairs and on his ignorance of Israel, De Gaulle pursued his dream of a four-power conference at which the Great Oracles would reveal the terms of a permanent settlement in the Middle East: an Olympus to which he could aspire only if the conflict did not degenerate into war. The next day the Quai d'Orsay advised the Israeli Embassy of De Gaulle's decision to impose an embargo on all arms shipments to the Middle East. It was a startling reversal of alliances, since Israel was the only significant recipient of French arms. As an act of policy designed to influence the immediate course of events, it was an empty and irrelevant gesture. The embargo was presumably intended to deter the Israelis from war. It merely deepened their sense of utter isolation.

As for the Russians, there was no need to give particular thought to them. The Israelis had already made their reckoning, and the question of possible Soviet intervention did not even arise when the time of decision came. There was, of course, the underlying assumption that the Russians' primary concern would be to avoid a collision with the United States; and to give teeth to the assumption, there was the material presence of the athletic Sixth Fleet. There was the knowledge that Johnson had sent his unequivocal warnings to Moscow; and on the immediate scene, the fact that the Russians lacked the military means to intervene in the only way they effectively could—in a manner that would tip the scales swiftly and finally. They had no aircraft carriers, no possibility of air support, no overflight rights across Turkey or Iran and no marine commando units in the area. The maneuvers of their Mediterranean fleet were a political and psychological demonstration. If there were a protracted Middle Eastern war, they might be able to assemble a credible force in the Mediterranean, and the danger of Soviet intervention under Arab prodding would then, of course, become more real. Ultimately, just as the Russians relied on Washington to keep Israel quiet, so Israel relied on American power to keep the Russians out. The Israelis were right in their assessment and the Russians were mistaken. The deterrent capacity of the United States, its persuasive force in the crisis, was more effective against the Russians than against either the Israelis or the Arabs.

A large majority in the Israeli cabinet were already prepared to vote for war when Dayan took over the Ministry of Defense. The war would have been waged and it would have been won without him, but he was intimately involved in every aspect of its management, as a rather extraordinary Defense Minister who was not only endowed with keen political sense but was as versed in military matters as his Chief of Staff and personally familiar with all the commanders down to the battalion level and often, indeed, even further down than that. Rabin was immensely grateful to have him. The immediate requirement was to determine the priorities—to set the precise military and political shape that a war with Egypt would take; and in this area of decision Dayan played a cardinal role. Earlier in the week, at a meeting with Rabin, Gavish and others in Beersheba, he had already proposed that the whole of the Sinai Peninsula be set as the war objective. He had then merely made the "suggestion" in his capacity as a qualified private person; on becoming Minister, he authorized the operational change. In its earlier contingency planning, the General Staff had envisaged El Arish and Sharm el Sheikh as the major objectives of a campaign that would aim to expel the Egyptians from eastern Sinai.

On the evening of June 2, Dayan and the General Staff reviewed the plans. The result of their discussion was a broadly expanded program that called for a general Israeli offensive along the three main axes of Sinai, the liquidation of Egyptian arms in the desert and the conquest of the entire Peninsula to the Suez Canal. The Canal was the limit set by military expediency and political prudence; the Peninsula was the territorial prize that Israel needed in order to bargain for peace.

The next day, June 3, Dayan held a press conference. As a man who rarely made a public utterance without a definite intent, he offered to the envoys of the world press his nutshell assessment of the prospects for war or peace. It was too late, he said, for a spontaneous military reaction to the blockade, and still too early to draw any conclusions as to the possible outcome of diplomatic action. This seemed a most plausible synthesis of the situation as it then stood. Dayan said he doubted that diplomacy alone could lift the blockade or compel the Egyptian Army to leave Sinai; but, he reasonably added, "If anyone tries again to achieve freedom of passage through the Straits of Tiran by diplomatic means, I think he should be given a chance." So clear were his ideas, so crisp and easy his sentences and so persuasive his manner, that many a special correspondent, American and British, at once booked a seat on an outgoing plane and departed from Israel the next morning, shrewdly convinced that war was still a distant possibility. Dayan seemed to turn every question to advantage. "I would not like American or British men to be killed here, and I do not think we need them." His words hit the mark. To Israelis, for whom his return to office had been a tonic at a time of harrowing tension—"Having Dayan is worth more than an extra division"—his remark was an assurance that Israel could indeed rely wholly on herself and needed no one to fight for her. The effect on American Congressmen was similarly bracing. They realized they were not, after all, being asked for a resolution committing American soldiers to the defense of Israel.

Four days earlier, on May 30, Eshkol had written to Johnson, advising him of Israel's decision to delay any unilateral action, in view of Eban's report on his Washington talks. These further days of suspense had notably strengthened Israel's position in the forum of world opinion, in France, Britain and especially the United States, arousing her friends to alarm and exciting many to ask, Why doesn't she act? For how long will she stand and wait? Washington as well as Jerusa-

lem saw the dilemma in a harsher light: on the one hand, the rising
threat to Israel's security and on the other, the dwindling credibility of
the American search for a solution. The Americans took a realistic
view of the situation; they, too, knew that it was Israel's life and danger and that in the end it would be her responsibility to act. "With
their nineteen hundred years of exile," Ambassador Barbour later observed, "and with their memories of the concentration camps, these
are not men who can be ordered what to do." This final human recognition was, as always, implicit in the American attitude.

But at the critical juncture Johnson was placed in an even deeper
dilemma: either to press ahead with the international armada, a
doubtful venture with evident military risks, involving a possible clash
with Egypt and an unforeseeable Soviet response; or to fail in an
American commitment of honor, with disastrous consequences for the
American position in the Middle East and for the value of American
commitments everywhere. There was no third choice: it was either the
risk of a Middle Eastern military involvement or a political-moral collapse from Teheran to Addis Ababa to Rabat. The bedrock problem
of obtaining a Congressional resolution had barely been scratched.
The Administration had had to make a soft sell to Congress, with
assurances that any armada would be multinational and that, indeed,
no commitment had yet been made to anybody; and in the final days it
seemed that a resolution would be forthcoming only if Israel were
actually being overrun. Through the week the intelligence reports were
piling in from Israel and the Arab states; the Arab coalition was functioning, the Arab ring was closing and every day Israel's position became more vulnerable. At this point, some in the Administration must
obviously have thought of the obvious thing: the feasibility of unleash-
ing Israel. The easiest way out of the dilemma was to let the Israelis
handle it themselves. The United States could not find a way out; Israel
could. The possibility of an Israeli initiative could not, in any case, be
excluded and in contemplating that prospect, the Administration was
fortified by the stout advice of the Joint Chiefs, who said that Israel
would win in short order, whatever happened, and would win on her
own. Johnson knew that if war came, it would present neither the
need nor the risk of American intervention.

But, of course, Washington could not unleash Jerusalem. The
Americans could not give a green light any more than Israel could ask
for it. Their position at the end was precisely what it had been at the

beginning: war must be averted. They continued to press for restraint in Jerusalem (though perhaps in tones that were less peremptory); they accepted gratefully Israel's assurance that she would not, for the time being, operate; they continued to assure the Russians they were doing their best to contain Israel and even advised them (on the basis of what Israel had said) that they did not expect an Israeli attack. And, indeed, they did not. When the attack came, its timing was a surprise in Washington. The Americans on June 4 believed they still had more time—to mobilize their regatta and to talk to Mohieddin.

The last official communication in the exchange between Washington and Jerusalem was a model for the diplomatic archives. At the State Department at four o'clock on Saturday afternoon, June 3, Rusk handed it to Evron: the President's reply to Eshkol's letter of May 30. It was both a thank-you note and a progress report on the making of the armada. Johnson expressed appreciation of Eshkol's decision to delay and of Israel's steady resolution at a time of grave tension. He then cited in full the text of the *aide-mémoire* he had given Eban at their White House meeting, the memorandum that opened by stressing the basic importance of American constitutional processes on matters of war and peace, and ended with the key formula according to which Israel would not be alone if she did not act alone. Johnson then reviewed the situation. The United States was "vigorously pursuing" the "British" suggestion for an international naval force. Johnson by then must have known of Britain's second and third thoughts on this project, but he evidently did not wish to appear, on the record, to be taking any initiative without Congressional approval. He went on to say that certain nations were reluctant to join such a force until all remedies at the United Nations had been exhausted, and declared it was the unanimous feeling of American leaders that the United States must not act in isolation.

Studying the letter, carefully noting what it did and did not say, Evron took it as a document for the historical record, confirming that the United States was still handling the crisis along the agreed lines and establishing that there had been no collusion. It was significant, he reflected, for what it omitted. To be sure, the *aide-mémoire* spoke of the grave consequences of any unilateral Israeli action; but in the body of the letter, signed by the President that afternoon, the imperative call for restraint was not repeated. The red light, perhaps, was shading to amber. In any case, he concluded, in the light of Johnson's straightforward account of the difficulties, Israel could no longer rely on her American ally. She was alone and time was running out. She had, after all, demonstrated to the world that she had tried the diplomatic way. Evron transmitted the letter to his government, together with his judgment that events had reached the point where Israel must act on her own, and that the time had come.

But until the very end, until the very morning of the war, Israelis and Americans both strove to limit it to a single major front. On the highest level in Jerusalem, at the office of the Prime Minister, even after the Nasser-Hussein pact, it was still hoped and believed that Jordan could be induced to stay out when and if the time came. This belief was encouraged by a memorable precedent: in 1956, too, a defense agreement had proclaimed the unity of Jordanian and Syrian forces under Egyptian command—and Jordan had managed to sit out the Sinai war. Would Hussein act in time to serve his own interests? Perhaps he would, even though the Arabs seemed to have a genius for not doing so. Thus, in the last week, a series of messages passed from Jerusalem to Amman, carried by third parties, assuring Hussein that in the event of war nothing would happen to Jordan if she just sat tight. The Americans took the initiative in this final endeavor, proposing to neutralize the Jordanian front by a double Israeli-Jordanian engagement of nonbelligerence. They secured such an undertaking from the Israelis and conveyed it to Amman. The Jordanians refused to buy the arrangement.

On the evening of June 3 Eshkol appointed an inner cabinet committee to act as a consultative defense council. In the event, it was the body that was largely responsible for the conduct of the war: Dayan, Allon, Eban and Yigael Yadin—archaeologist, writer and former Chief of Staff—with Ya'acov Herzog as their coordinator.

At the cabinet meeting the next afternoon, a consensus of the Ministers entrusted responsibility for the operation of the Defense Forces to Eshkol, Dayan and the General Staff. Such was the final formula. Two Ministers, members of the left-wing socialist Mapam party, asked for permission to consult their party colleagues before giving their vote. All the other Ministers voted for the proposal and Eshkol, at the last, secured the near-unanimity he had hoped for.

The trial of waiting was ended. The decision, it was later said, was taken not in a mood of eager confidence but in a spirit of No Alternative.

· 8 ·

Victory

F OR SEVERAL MINUTES, from our high rooms in our multi-storied hotel, we could hear the deep and labored pounding in the distance, off to the north and northwest of the city where the airports were, and occasionally what seemed to be a sonic boom, before, below our windows, there burst the familiar panting noise, half wheeze and half bellow, of the air-raid alert. The day was calm and clear; the early morning mist from the river had already burned away. There had been several mock raids and trial blackouts in recent days and nights, and now, at nine-twenty in the morning, this might well have been another exercise. But unlike the others, this alert had not been announced. Traffic stopped in the looping arteries of Liberation Square; the lights continued to flick green and red; and as silence fell on the streets, the smothered pounding of the ack-ack batteries grew more distinct. Hotel boys knocked violently at our doors and, with their floor keys, irrupted excitedly and ordered us to take shelter in the basement.

But for correspondents and others who had errands to do or deadlines to meet, it was better to take a walk. Beyond the square, in the business center of the city, the radiating avenues were flowing with life. The hurry and clatter of traffic were gone; trams and buses were halted; and in their place was the hectic vivacity of the Cairo crowd. Unmolested by traffic, people roamed the streets. In knots around the radios of parked cars, in bands around the transistors of newspaper-and-cigarette kiosks, they listened to martial songs and poetry and waited for the first war bulletins, exhilarated and expectant. "Israeli forces have begun attacking Egypt and our forces are striking back." Cairo itself was under air attack, the radio said, and so, too, were several other Egyptian cities. The announcer's voice was exultant and hoarse: "Our armies have only one cry: On to Tel-Aviv. One Arab army, one Arab nation. Forward, forward on the road to liberation and unity under the hero, Gamal Abdel Nasser." From upper balconies and rooftops, men and women watched the sky: now and then, off to the north and west, they saw the puff of an ack-ack shell bursting black or the glint of a fighter's wings, very high. Soon came a bulletin from the air force, a "first indication of victory": twenty-three Israeli planes had been shot down. Men cheered, danced on the sidewalk and climbed on each other's shoulders. War songs followed on the radio, demonstrators gathered, banners unfurled. The voice of the announcer returned with a call for "the destruction of Israel and a giant Arab onslaught on Tel-Aviv." Men and boys broke from the crowd and swung in a pack down Kasr-el-Nil, marching under the festive streamers and repeating their shout: "Tel-Aviv is finished. Tel-Aviv is finished." Policemen gave up trying to wave people off the streets or usher them through the wire-meshed gates to the underground shelters. In the general ignorance of war, the reality of fear was unknown.

Through the day the score in the air war mounted—the figure of twenty-three leaping to forty-two and forty-four, then to seventy-three and finally to eighty-six Israeli planes destroyed—and the victory celebrations on the sidewalks multiplied. The High Command announced that Egyptian armor, after storming the Israeli border positions opposite El Kuntilla at the southern end of the Sinai line, had carried the battle deep into enemy territory. All believed that Nasser had reversed the positions of force in the Middle East; all expected he would now administer to the Americans the lesson he had taught the British and French in 1956. Only the evening before, in his speech celebrating Iraq's accession to the Egyptian-Jordanian Pact, he had said that "we are burning with impatience for this battle to begin in order to avenge the perfidy" of the tripartite aggression at Suez. It seemed, indeed, in the shrill air of Cairo, that Israel had been driven into war by the wild promptings of desperation.

At midnight, having sent our last dispatches or met our last radio circuits, we walked back through the blackout to the Hilton cafeteria, still knowing only what the Egyptian communiqués had told us. Over soup and sandwiches we tried to focus our thoughts. Egypt could not stop the Israelis, we all agreed; but neither, most of us believed, could Israel possibly win. She would be forced back to the old lines by international pressure. Nasser would lose his war but he would win his crisis; and he would keep his blockade at Tiran. Why, then, had Israel struck? Because, we felt, she had to fight to save her moral future, and hence her physical future as well. Had she remained passive, accepting a posture of defense, she would have sunk into despair and in time have been squeezed out of existence. Nevertheless, the balance of big-power interests being what it was, she could not win. So we believed on that night.

Nasser himself learned what had really happened at four o'clock on the afternoon of June 5. Not until then, he later claimed, did his generals dare tell him the truth—nearly the entire Egyptian Air Force wiped out on the ground in the first two hours and fifty minutes of war that morning. On the previous weekend the Russians had flapped and told both him and Washington that they had information of a coming Israeli attack; and he himself (so he claimed) had alerted his air force commanders. Unexplainably, the urgency of the message had failed to get through. A witness at Badran's trial was later to testify: "Military intelligence informed the Armed Forces on June 3 that an attack could be expected within forty-eight hours. But nobody did anything." Migs and Sukhoys, Ilyushins and Tupolevs—not dispersed or in revetments and apparently flying no cover—were obliterated at their bases from El Arish to Cairo to Luxor.

Informed of the disaster, Nasser appealed to the Algerians for air reinforcements: Algeria, too, had been liberally supplied with Soviet aircraft. Toward four A.M. on June 6, he telephoned to Hussein and General Riad at Army Headquarters in Amman. Their radio-telephone conversation was intercepted and taped by Israeli military monitors, and portions of it were promptly published. The Jordanians on the first day of the war had misread the signals on their highly sophisticated radar equipment. They saw masses of planes taking off on their screens, wave after wave ascending from Israel, and concluded that American or British fighters had flown in from nearby aircraft carriers to reinforce the Israelis. How else explain Israel's inexhaustible supply of planes? The Jordanians could not imagine that Israeli pilots were flying up to eight missions a day. Hussein was full of this story and Nasser seized on it during their early morning collo-quy. The two rulers discussed whether they should accuse only the Americans or should extend the charge to include the British. Hussein agreed that Britain should be included in a joint denunciation. Nasser then nailed it down: "By God, I will make an announcement and you will make an announcement and we will see to it that the Syrians make an announcement that American and British airplanes are tak-ing part against us from aircraft carriers. We will issue an announce-ment, we will stress the matter and we will drive the point home." Hussein: "Good. All right." The conversation included other flour-ishes. Before hanging up, Nasser assured Hussein that Egyptian planes were attacking Israeli airfields that very morning while his army was engaged in a counteroffensive into the Negev, and he urged the King to do his part.

For Nasser the story of Anglo-American intervention was a gold mine that offered many possibilities in the hour of grave setback. It would light the fires of Arab anger and would provide a 1956 way out of military defeat, converting the destruction of the Egyptian Air Force into a heroic stand against another tripartite collusion. Nor could so sharp-witted a politician have been insensible to the further implications of the story. Clearly, if the Americans had come in on Israel's side, the ball was now in the Russian court. At his press con-ference a week before, Nasser had said he did not want a big-power confrontation in the Middle East: he would leave it up to his "friends" to decide what to do when the time came. The desperate time had now come. The asserted American intervention was a challenge to the Russians to show what they could do for the Arabs, a way of testing their intentions and of prodding them to act.

The announcement of the Egyptian High Command on the morning of June 6 said it had been conclusively proved that large-scale assist-ance was being rendered to Israel by American and British aircraft carriers. Evidence showed beyond a shadow of doubt that American planes had been providing an air umbrella over Israel, thus releasing Israeli planes for combat; and Hussein had personally confirmed to Nasser that American planes, in direct support of the Israeli Air Force, were taking part in air combats on the Jordanian front. How else explain the four hundred Israeli sorties which, Hussein said, the

Israelis had made over Jordan alone on the first day?

The Russians were enraged by the announcement and for many good reasons. In the eyes of the entire Arab world, they were reneging on their promises of "resolute resistance" to aggression, while the Americans were loyally rushing to the aid of their Israeli friends. Worse than that, Moscow was being provoked to take a hand. The Soviet reaction, sharp and immediate, was the opposite of what Nasser had apparently bargained for. Kosygin on June 6 summoned Murad Ghaleb, the Egyptian Ambassador, to the Kremlin, to inform him that the accusation was untrue, that the Russians had their own means of knowing it to be untrue and that Egypt was seeking to involve them in war. The Soviet Union, he advised the Egyptian sternly, would have none of it.

The American Embassy in Amman had already got wind of the radar-screen story the previous day and had frantically entreated the State Department to knock it down. American officials in Washington began putting out the truth fast. In Cairo, Nolte hurried to see Foreign Minister Riad to tell him the charge was false, warn him that it would prove immensely harmful to Egypt, and beg him to reconsider and to reserve at least a margin of doubt, so as not to take an irretrievable step. It was a characteristically inconclusive diplomatic exchange in the frank-and-sober vein. Nolte asked that the campaign of anti-American invective in the Egyptian press be called off and that Mohieddin's visit to Washington be permitted. Riad, the most impeccable of diplomats, was his gentle and humorous self. But even Riad, Nolte surmised, was convinced of the truth of the accusation. He gave no hint of the break that was about to come.

Four hours later, in the early evening, Nolte was called back to the Foreign Office, where he was notified by a sheepish and apologetic Undersecretary, El Fekki, of the rupture of relations with the United States. The break was oral: no written statement was presented. The Ambassador told El Fekki that the action was based on an erroneous assumption and that in the long run Egypt would be the loser. The Egyptian version was that the Americans were not only providing protective cover for Israel but were replenishing the Israeli Air Force to offset its losses in combat. But no precise charges were ever made. "Your planes and ships are killing Egyptians," an American Embassy official was angrily told at the Foreign Office. Formally it was a rupture without a cause.

When we read the High Command's announcement at the Press Center at the U.A.R. Radio and Television Building, we realized how wrong we had been in our own assumptions the night before and we knew that Israel had won. The Israeli victory was already a fact, since this army handout was the alibi. The Egyptians, too, as they gathered at their radios, knew it was the signal of a still unavowed defeat. They were being robbed of victory by the Anglo-American imperialists. The old impassioned cry of imperialist treachery had too many associations in Arab memory, too deep an anchor in Arab imagination not to be understood in all its ominous significance. For three weeks Cairo had been held to a strident pitch of unreality, and now, after one day of wartime delirium, the city collapsed into a nervous gloom, probably about to degenerate into anti-American outbreaks. That night, when we walked back again through the darkened streets and across the silent square to the hotel, a security officer was waiting for us at the reception desk. He had a list of names, twenty-one American newsmen to be expelled from Egypt or, if physical eviction was impossible, to be placed in internment until some means of travel became available. The next morning we packed our bags, paid our bills and made our way under escort to our place of confinement on the little street bending back from the river, a rather less restful hotel, with its bewildered inmates, its bare lobby, its tin ashtrays and its faded color photograph of a youthful Nasser, clear-eyed and confident, on the wall of its gray and meager lounge.

Forty-eight hours earlier, at nine o'clock on the morning of June 5 in Jerusalem, General Odd Bull, the Norwegian head of the United Nations Truce Supervision Organization, had received an urgent call from the Israeli Foreign Office. The Israelis asked him to convey a message, a short note from Eshkol to Hussein. It was Israel's last attempt to keep Jordan out of the war. "We shall not initiate any action whatsoever against Jordan," it read. "However, should Jordan open hostilities, we shall react with all our might, and she will have to bear the full responsibility for the consequences." A similar message was entrusted to Ambassador Barbour for transmission to Amman, and in a radio broadcast at noon Eshkol repeated his assurance that Israel did not want war with Jordan. It was then too late.

Hussein was no longer the sole master in his own house. He was already the half-captive of the Egyptians, who had firmly planted themselves at his side. He was probably even more the captive of his own temperament, far too impulsively romantic, and fatalistic as well, not to be swayed by the war enthusiasm mounting around him. For the first few hours he still had a choice. He was Supreme Commander still, never leaving for a moment his army headquarters throughout the first day and night of the war and working closely with General Riad, who officially and formally was in charge of operations and was giving orders to Hammash, Jordan's Chief of Staff. It was evidently a wavering and ambiguous line of command.

Hussein's mistake on that first morning was to believe the reports the Egyptians were feeding him: that the Egyptian Air Force was bombing Tel-Aviv and attacking Israeli airfields everywhere, and that a land offensive from Sinai was heading for Beersheba. At eleven o'clock, when he received Eshkol's message, the Egyptian Air Force was already destroyed but he did not know it. The Israeli radio was not telling him; the Israelis had a host of political and military reasons for not revealing the extent of their gains. The Egyptians assured him there would be an early cease-fire and urged him to gain all the territory he could in order to strengthen the Arab bargaining position. So he went ahead—misled by Nasser, with Riad at his side, evidently expecting a big Arab push, believing, in any case, that an overland drive into the Negev had begun and that the Israeli Air Force was in the process of being bombed to pieces. Perhaps, had he known the truth, he might have reversed his decision and pulled out on that first morning while there was still time. Perhaps, in the emotional stampede of the hour, it would have been difficult, even impossible, to hold back the Jordanian troops. Had the order to fire never been given, they might have opened fire anyway.

Hussein's action was a surprise to the Israelis, just as his pact with Nasser had been the week before. They had expected he would probably fire a few shots to celebrate Arab solidarity and adorn the Arab record, and let it go at that. They had not expected him to go all out. On the morning of June 5 they were ready to meet an attack on the Jordanian front, at Jerusalem and elsewhere, but they were not prepared to take the offensive. Jordanian guns heavily shelled and mortared Israeli Jerusalem from positions around and above the old Arab city; Jordanian planes rocketed Netanya on the coast; and the command in Amman capped its folly by directing Jordan's one and only land offensive across demilitarized territory on the fringe of Jerusalem to occupy the headquarters of General Bull, Government House, a

building whose name acknowledged its origin as the residence of the
British High Commissioner in the days of the Palestine mandate. This
attack on an international sanctum drew a stern reproof from U Thant;
if it meant anything, it seemed to mean that Jordan had repudiated
the Armistice Agreement of 1949. And since the stately building,
sheltered in a grove of evergreens, commanded a broad view of the
entire southern section of Israeli Jerusalem, its seizure on the first
morning of the war was even more intolerable to the Israelis than it
was to the Secretary-General. They moved in with a battalion largely
composed of Hebrew University students and expelled the Jordanians
from their perch.

Israeli tanks and busloads of parachutists were already streaming
up and across the Judean hills to Jerusalem that afternoon and
Eshkol, caught in the movement on the roads as he returned from Tel-
Aviv, was late for the early evening meeting, in the basement of the
Knesset building, at which the cabinet was to take its decision. Dayan
had other things to do: he did not wait for the meeting to start and
drove back to his headquarters in Tel-Aviv. A difficult choice confronted the cabinet. Israel's objective in the war with Jordan would be
the capture of the entire West Bank. But what of Jerusalem? The old
Arab city, the Holy City of three faiths, was a fortress; and within its
narrow gates, behind its sixteenth-century Turkish walls, lay a dense
labyrinth of roofed and vaulted alleys, an ancient jumble of stairways,
courtyards, battlements and sudden culs-de-sac. The Old City could
not be taken in a day, perhaps not even in a week; Israel's air superiority, even her preponderance in armor, would count for little in that
maze of moldering stone. Dayan had made his position clear. Fearing
a long and murderous fight among the Holy Places that would excite
the concern of the international community and prompt the intervention of the powers—inducing them, perhaps, to impose an international administration or even some form of condominium that would
inevitably raise the question of the status of Israeli Jerusalem itself
—he proposed that the Old City be bypassed. The political risks of a
frontal attack were too great. The Israeli brigades, he argued, after
completing the encirclement of Arab Jerusalem, should stand by for
its surrender—leaving the road to Jericho and the Jordan River open,
both as a way and as an invitation to the Jordanian troops to retreat.

Good reasons must, perforce, give way to better: Dayan's view was
strongly contested by Allon and others at the cabinet meeting. Allon

advocated a direct assault. He, too, thought of the international repercussions but drew the opposite conclusion. Arab Jerusalem, he believed, would not in any case surrender. The Jordanians would organize for a siege and during the uncertainty of waiting, pressure would
mount on Israel from the Vatican, from France, from Washington,
not to touch the Holy City. From this it followed that Israel should
strike at once. Allon's position was generally upheld by the Ministers.
They settled on a broadly permissive formula, authorizing the armed
forces to proceed to the conquest of the entire West Bank, including
Jerusalem, and leaving it to Rabin to decide on the tactics.

At two-twenty the next morning the parachutists opened their attack on Jordanian positions outside the walls in the northern quarter
of the city. They suffered heavy losses, advancing head on under violent artillery fire, across rough-breaking ground where the enemy was
solidly entrenched and down tangled streets where every rooftop had
its gun post. Fighter-bombers with flickering lights flew ahead over
Arab Jerusalem, tempting the Jordanians to open fire and expose their
positions, then dropping flares and flying low to bomb them. After a
seven-hour battle, the parachutists by midmorning were looking down
on the Old City of Jerusalem, invested with sun and splendor, from
the broad height of Mount Scopus. The next morning they captured
the Mount of Olives and the encirclement of the walled city was strategically complete. Having been informed at dawn by General Uzi
Narkiss, commander of the eastern front, that time was of the utmost
importance to the state of Israel, Colonel Mordechai Gur, the
commander of the parachutists' brigade, led the frontal assault on the
walled town by smashing his half-track into the half-closed gate of
Saint Stephen's. In the Via Dolorosa that opened before him, not a
Jordanian soldier was in sight. Above and around him, the stone ramparts were deserted. The Jordanian Governor of the city soon presented himself to announce that the Jordan Legion had left. It was the
morning of June 7, a moment of return and recognition in which the
sufferings of the past met the radiance of the present—nearly nineteen
hundred years since the destruction of the Temple, more than two
thousand years since the Jews had last been the masters of Jerusalem.
When Dayan visited the city that afternoon, and stood by the Wailing
Wall, his words had, for Israelis, the blaze of a redeeming sword:
"We have returned to the holiest of our holy places, never to part
from it again."

Why was Jerusalem abandoned? Many a retired officer of the Jordan Legion later asked that question, knowing that if the city had prepared for a siege, the bitter and costly fight—gate by gate, roof by roof, wall by wall—would have lasted many days. Organized resistance from behind the parapets of Arab Jerusalem might have saved the third most holy shrine of Islam for Jordan and the King. The Jordanian troops who fought outside the walls fought stubbornly and well. Apparently, though, they and their commanders had underestimated the Israelis' capacity for nighttime battle. They had expected a night of rest; by the second day they were demoralized and, disposed for the attack, were unable to change plans and posture or reorganize for the defense. So, at any rate, one might suppose. Perhaps, anticipating a general Arab offensive and an early cease-fire, Jordan had no contingency plan for a siege or, if she had one, was too overwhelmed by the violent reversal of events to act in time. This, too, is supposition.

On June 6, it was finally known in Amman that Egypt, the only power capable of confronting Israel, had caved in; that the enemy everywhere ruled the skies; and that the Syrians' reported bombing of the oil refineries at Haifa, like their claim to be marching across the hills of Galilee to Nazareth, was a fatuous fiction. On that day the order went out from headquarters in Amman for a general retreat, to salvage whatever could be salvaged of men and equipment all along the line, and Jerusalem was included in the order. No one thought beyond that. As the Israeli brigades struck into and across the bulge of the West Bank from north and south—one of them transferred for the purpose from the Syrian front—the chain of communications between Amman and the field broke down and with it the chain of command. Some field units, deserted by their officers, pegged out. In the confusion Amman announced thousands of casualties; in fact, fewer than five hundred soldiers of the Legion lost their lives.

Yet none of this quite explains the giant puzzle of the failure to defend Jerusalem, a failure of the will and reflexes as unfathomable as that of the Egyptian generals face to face with the reality of war. The responsibility lay not with the men and officers on the scene but with the high command. Dayan saw at once the immense political potential, to Israel's harm and Jordan's advantage, of a protracted fight for the Holy City; Hussein, Riad and the Jordanian generals evidently did not. Had they had Dayan's or Allon's political imagination and alertness, they would have seized their opportunity. Dayan's objections to a direct attack proved, in the event, to be unfounded and he stood at the Wall of the Temple less than forty-eight hours after he had made them. But his hesitations honored his foresight and his prudence. The flamboyant taker of risks whom we all had known so well in the popular legend was, in the flesh, a statesman of practical vision.

Nasser may well have believed the reports with which he filled Hussein on the first morning of the war. They evidently corresponded to the well-laid plans of the Egyptian General Staff for that day, and so he recited them. He had not yet been undeceived. But he could not possibly have believed what he told Hussein over the radio-telephone on the morning of June 6. By then he knew the truth of the colossal defeat and had already sent an S.O.S. to Algiers. Hussein's troops were the best and bravest the Israelis met and, gallantly, he never chided Nasser for having sought to lure him into a still greater disaster. "We are flying our planes over Israel today," Nasser had said in that talk, "our planes have been striking at Israel's airfields since morning." In fact, during the four days of war on the Sinai front, not a single Egyptian bomb fell on an Israeli air base, nor on Tel-Aviv, Haifa or Jerusalem, nor anywhere else in Israel. Years of staff planning had gone into air force commander Hod's single throw, on which he staked all in order to meet Israel's first imperative in war, the annihilation of Egyptian air power. From that strike on June 5, he held back only twelve interceptors for the defense of the homeland. In view of the flexibility of his force and the extremely short distances, he did not believe he was taking a desperate gamble.

As Amer had foreseen clearly enough in his Order of the Day, Israel did not wait for the announced Arab build-up on her eastern border to proceed very far. She struck not only because of Jordan's opening shots but because of the arrival of the first Iraqi forces. Elements of Iraq's Eighth Brigade were already on the West Bank on June 6 but had not yet reached their assigned positions. Reconnaissance units of the two Egyptian commando battalions crossed the river late on June 5; the others were due to join them the following night. Iraqis and Egyptians alike were overrun in the battle that broke the back of the Legion on June 6 and their surviving remnants fled. By the evening of June 7 the Israeli line was on the Jordan River.

For the Americans on the outbreak of war, the first requirement was to inform the Russians that the United States had no foreknowl-

edge of the Israeli attack. This was urgently done. The Russians, no
doubt, suspected collusion and we have no way of knowing whether
they believed the American assurances. They had always raised their
eyebrows and laughed incredulously when State Department people
had tried to impress on them that the United States could seek to
influence and persuade the Israelis but ultimately could not control
them. Perhaps, in the end, their own experience with the Arabs helped
to disabuse them of their notion of the all-powerfulness of big powers.
The Americans, at all events, enjoyed an inestimable advantage on the
opening day of the war. Their intelligence system, outdistancing the
Soviet services by many hours, supplied them with nearly instantane-
ous reports on the course of a battle that was proceeding in perfect
accord with the estimates of the Joint Chiefs. Before dawn on June 5,
it was already known at the State Department that five Egyptian airfields had been rendered inoperative. The world at large had to rely on
the Israeli communiqués for its news, and the Israelis were being sys-
tematically unhelpful. The Russians' Mediterranean fleet included an
intelligence ship, but they were apparently relying also on their military mission in Cairo, where the Egyptian commanders were holding
back the news even from Nasser. The Israelis, knowing their Arabs,
were meanwhile counting on Egyptian claims of victories in Sinai or
the Negev to confuse the picture still further. In such fashion many
hours of battlefield time would be gained before the Russians at the
United Nations got their bearings. These calculations were not disappointed. When the Security Council convened on the morning of June
5, Arthur Goldberg, the American delegate, was ready to support a
pure and simple cease-fire resolution. The Russians stalled. "There's
not yet a clear picture," they said in effect, "let's see first what is
happening."

By that night in New York, the results of the air war were known
but the progress of the land war was not. The Arabs were stunned and
the Russians bewildered. Federenko and his delegation were apparently clueless, uncertain what to do and lacking precise instructions.
For the Israelis, the American decision to support an unconditional
cease-fire—with no provision for a withdrawal—was the hoped-for
assurance that the United States was with them in seeking to preserve
the political fruits of their victory. The Russians, harassed by the
Arabs, unenlightened by the Israelis and trailing in their intelligence
reports, refused to commit themselves to a simple cease-fire. More

than ever they were the prisoners of their wayward and intransigent
friends and—how could they know?—conceivably the Egyptian claim
was true and some Egyptian armored columns might have penetrated
into the Negev somewhere. So they hewed to their Arab line and insisted on a cease-fire resolution demanding immediate withdrawal of
the Israeli aggressors to the positions of June 4.

Rafah in the Gaza Strip, El Arish at the northern end of the Sinai
line, Abu Agheila at the center, El Kuntilla in the south—in tumbling
succession the Egyptian strongpoints fell to Israeli arms while Americans and Russians hassled in New York. The crux of their argument,
which continued late into the night of June 5, was the precise political
significance of "June 4." For the Russians it meant not only a return
to the old lines but the maintenance of the Tiran blockade and of the
Egyptian mobilization in Sinai. They indicated they had no choice but
to go along with the Arabs, and at one helpless point suggested that
the Americans try to talk to El Kony themselves. The two powers
were back again in the old prewar argument; the blockade was the
first issue to be unknotted and they never got beyond it. There was
long bickering over the terms of a larger package resolution that
would require both an Israeli withdrawal and a renunciation of force.
Evidently, to be acceptable to the Americans, such a resolution would
have had to include a guarantee of "nonbelligerence" by Egypt—the
renunciation of her famous "belligerent rights" at Tiran. The Americans insisted on a common interpretation whereby "June 4" would
not mean a restoration of the blockade, and the Russians replied they
would reserve their own interpretation as to that. At this dead point
the argument ended.

But matters changed radically in the next few hours. On the morning of June 6 the Russians were not merely harried and perplexed but
totally adrift, floundering and alarmed as no one at the United Nations had seen them since the Cuba missile crisis of 1962. By then
they knew the extent of an Israeli victory that had cut across all their
calculations at the very moment they had seemed so close to a victory
of their own. All their options were disastrously unpinned. Reversing
their stand, they expressed interest in a simple cease-fire. However,
still waiting for explicit instructions, they asked the Americans for
time to consult Moscow. Goldberg assured them they would have all
the time they needed.

The Russians had ample reason to be alarmed. As they now discovered, the entire Arab "revolutionary" world was in collapse and the Israelis were overrunning that immense outlay of Soviet equipment in Sinai, capturing masses of it intact—including the desert sites of ground-to-air missiles—and thereby blasting the prestige of Soviet arms, Soviet friendship and Soviet commitments. These losses and liabilities were appalling enough. Much more critical, at this particular moment, was the immediate risk that opened before them. The Russians quite evidently feared that if they were unable to stop Israel somewhere, they might soon find themselves in a position where they would be compelled to honor their pledges of support to Cairo. It was at this point on the morning of June 6 that Moscow opened the hot line to the White House.

Johnson later called it the most awesome moment of his Presidency. The message from Kosygin demanded that Israel accept a cease-fire and withdraw her forces to the positions of June 4 or, as he implied, face the prospect of Soviet action on behalf of the attacked. Johnson looked down his barrel and measured the threat. In language both moderate and unfaltering, he assured Kosygin that the United States wanted a cease-fire and would use its best efforts to secure one. He made no mention of an Israeli withdrawal; the cease-fire that he sought was unqualified; and the force of his message lay exactly in what it did not say. However, the reply to Kosygin was twofold. Simultaneously, Johnson sent a meaningful signal: he ordered the Sixth Fleet, already stationed in the eastern Mediterranean, to move farther eastward, closer to the coast of Israel; and to buttress the warning, he dispatched another aircraft carrier to the Mediterranean. The double message was received and understood. The Russians were being told that they must choose between confrontation and cooperation, between continued identification with the Arabs and accommodation with the United States. Kosygin chose cooperation and accepted Johnson's terms. The reply from the Kremlin said the Soviet Union, too, would seek a cease-fire—plain and simple.

This was the full extent of the American-Soviet entente during the week of war. But the exchange on the hot line was the turning point in the crisis between the powers, for implicit in the joint agreement to seek a cease-fire was the undertaking by each of them not to intervene in the conflict. In the late afternoon of June 6 the Soviet delegation at the United Nations received its new instructions and at midnight an unqualified cease-fire resolution was unanimously adopted by the Security Council. The Arab states rejected the call and insisted on an Israeli withdrawal: once again they were clearly resolved to act too late to serve their interests. Had they accepted the Americans' original proposal the previous day, the war on the Jordanian front might have been shortened and the war on the Syrian front might not have taken place at all.

For the first time, in voting for a straight cease-fire, the Russians dissociated themselves from the Arab line. They tried to make up for it by vociferously denouncing the Israelis. Moscow rumbled with solemn threats to sever diplomatic relations with Israel if she did not immediately obey the Council's call. At the United Nations, Federenko demanded a further resolution condemning the aggressors and ordering them to withdraw to the 1949 Armistice lines. But these were verbal thunderbolts for the Arab gallery, and the Arab states knew it. The truth was that their Soviet patron was accepting the Israeli military victory, and they had been foolish indeed ever to imagine that Moscow would invite the risks of a nuclear confrontation for their sakes.

The Russians' next concern was to halt the rout in Sinai and secure a cease-fire before the Israelis pivoted northward and carried the war to Syria. On June 7 Ambassador Pojidaev delivered a message from Kosygin to Nasser, and in New York that evening, in a desperate attempt to save Syria from Egypt's and Jordan's fate, the Russians introduced a second unqualified resolution, more urgent than the first, setting a deadline and calling for a complete cease-fire on all fronts at 22:00 hours that night, Israel time. This resolution, like its predecessor, was unanimously adopted. Jordan, knocked out of the war, accepted it. Israel agreed to comply on condition that her enemies did the same. Egypt, Syria and Iraq steadfastly refused. There was, as Eban observed, "unilateral and so far unreciprocated acceptance" of the Security Council's call. The war with Egypt and Syria continued.

On the Egyptian front, Israel had a fixed objective that was both military and political—the Suez Canal. On June 7 Dayan visited some of his field commanders in Sinai and briefed them with his customary clarity. The main question they put to him was: Shall we go on to Cairo? He said: No, certainly not. The sound practical sense of his reasoning was obvious the moment he stated it: Israel did not need Cairo. She did not want to hold down a hostile population, and it was not territory she was after—she would hold enough in Sinai once she reached the Canal, all that she wanted in order to bargain for peace. But Dayan was in no haste to announce this limited objective to the world. Quite the contrary. At a press conference in Tel-Aviv later the same day, he said his forces would stop somewhere in Sinai short of Suez. Israel could get to the Canal easily enough if she wanted to but "it was not our aim to get there. Our problem was Sharm el Sheikh," he plausibly observed, "so why should we go straight on to Suez? It was our business to settle the problem of free passage to Eilath and the concentration of Egyptian forces in Sinai . . . we were not fighting now to use Suez." These remarks, intended in part to throw the Egyptians off the scent, seem to have been inspired mainly by the prudent thought of forestalling any international—or Soviet—intervention. Israeli forces, after all, had been to the Canal once before and the powers had not permitted them to remain there.

He was wary, too, when it came to extending the war to Syria. On June 7 Eshkol was visited by delegations from the northeastern border settlements that for two days had been under heavy shelling from the Syrians on the Golan Heights. Dayan's birthplace, Degania, was one of them. The kibbutzniks pleaded for war and protection but, in spite of that, at a midday cabinet meeting on June 8, Dayan said No. He was not yet ready. A number of anxious considerations detained him. He wanted, first of all, to secure a "working" cease-fire on the two other fronts, particularly in Sinai along the line of the Canal, before turning against the Syrians. He wanted more troops; he did not feel safe with the two and a half brigades that were then in position opposite the Golan Heights. With more troops there would be fewer casualties, and he needed time to gain this extra insurance. He did not forget the Russians' jealous concern for Damascus and he was worried by what they might do—shades of November, 1956, of Bulganin's brutal sally at that time and the vagrant threats of Soviet planes and "volunteers." Nevertheless, the cabinet overrode his qualms and voted to open the Syrian front, authorizing him as Minister of Defense to set the time of the action. Dayan returned to his headquarters command post outside Tel-Aviv, reviewed the situation with the General Staff and, not bothering to inform the government (and thereby rasping the sensibilities of some of the Ministers), ordered General David Elazar, the commander of the northern front, to open the attack on the Syrian heights at dawn the next day.

Several developments had helped and spurred him to change his mind. Rabin pivoted his troops faster than Dayan had anticipated. Infantry reinforcements were hurried from the Jordanian front and the Tenth Armored Brigade sped north to Galilee, covering some sixty miles in thirteen hours, the tanks moving on their own power since no transports were available. In Sinai, an Egyptian counterattack with tanks and parachutists had been broken on the afternoon of June 8, and by nightfall the Israelis were in El Kantara, on the Canal. During the night Egyptian armor fought and lost its last rearguard battles: by three o'clock on the morning of June 9 nearly the entire east bank of the Canal from the Mediterranean to the Red Sea belonged to the Israelis, and at five-fifteen, a telegram from Gavish, the Southern Front Commander, announced to Rabin that the whole Sinai Peninsula was theirs. With four divisions destroyed and three others ravaged, Egypt was out of the war and the working cease-fire that Dayan wanted was assured.

By now it was a formal cease-fire as well. The counterattacks of June 8 on the approaches to the Canal had been Egypt's last fling, and during the night Nasser threw in his hand. Word of his decision to accept the United Nations resolutions, telephoned to El Kony while the Security Council was in early evening session, was passed by the Egyptian delegate in a handwritten note to U Thant, who at once read it to the relieved and astonished members. They had expected to hear a speech by El Kony setting forth Egypt's reasons for continuing the war. The Syrians, the last of the Arab coalition, now deserted by their allies, fell into step later the same night. They, the agents and begetters of the drama, for whom war with Israel was the fulfillment of their wildest dreams, had shunned the battle when it came. They had shelled the Israeli border settlements and had made two armored sorties down from the hills that had been repelled at the first line of border kibbutzim; but their main forces, sitting tight in the fortifications of the Golan Heights, anxiously watching the course of the battle in Sinai, had never risked a major assault. Now with fearful haste they sued for a cease-fire. They were unable to get the appropriate orders to their field commanders in time, and the Israelis were undisposed to allow them to escape. On the morning of June 9 it was Syria's turn.

Thus the conflict completed its circuit and returned to the ground of its inception. The Israelis battered their way into, around and past the thick net of trenches and cement bunkers that Syria had spent so many years building and perfecting under the supervision of Soviet engineers and technicians. The dismayed voices of Russian officers, apparently trying to redirect the Syrian artillery fire, were heard by the Israelis on their field radios, loud and clear in the midst of battle. The Syrians fought fiercely in their entrenched positions. Their defense crumbled once these were overrun and the fortified line was breached. The Israeli battalions mounted the crest, and wide before them stretched the plateau of southen Syria and the road to Damascus.

The Russians in these final hours of the war, not knowing how far the Israelis intended to go against the most pampered of their protégés, had their second seizure of high alarm. They sent thunderous notes, laden with menace, to Jerusalem and Washington, and on June 10 announced the rupture of relations with Israel amid threats of economic sanctions. Chuvakhin drove for the last time to Jerusalem to carry the news to Eban. The Syrians reiterated their acceptance of the cease-fire and the Israelis replied that they, too, would accept it—whenever the Syrians stopped firing. The battle was engaged and only Israel was in a position to halt it. The Russians, fearing for Damascus, not only pressed, as did the Americans, for a Syrian cease-fire resolution in each of its successively more peremptory versions, but also gave in on what for them was a matter of constant principle. They had always sought to limit as much as possible the authority of the Secretary-General, and now they sought to subject to the Security Council such questions as the nationality, composition and weaponry of the United Nations observers on the Syrian front. After a six-hour argument they yielded the point, agreeing to full freedom of movement for the observers under the authority of U Thant and their commander, Odd Bull. But in the end it was neither the Americans nor the Russians who dictated a halt to the fighting. The Israelis themselves halted it, at a time and a place of their choosing.

On the morning of June 10 Dayan helicoptered to the Syrian front. The Israelis then were about four miles west of Kuneitra, the headquarters of the Syrian Southwest Command and the last town on the road to Damascus. Elazar wanted to move on and take it, and put up a strong argument. Dayan said no; he was not interested in Kuneitra. He wanted Elazar to join up his forces, straighten his line north to south and secure a belt of territory, about twelve miles deep, that would give the Israeli border settlements permanent protection from Syrian artillery. But as Dayan spoke, new reports came in and the opportunities of battle shifted: Syrian civilians were fleeing from

Kuneitra and armored units were forming up north and south of the town, apparently for a counterattack. Dayan changed his mind and Kuneitra was taken. Then came the inevitable next question: What about Damascus? It was late in the morning and Elazar reckoned he could reach the city by nightfall. But Dayan did not want Damascus. "We don't need more territory; we don't need an Arab city to hold down. We have achieved our objective." Odd Bull, as U Thant's deputy for the occasion, was meanwhile pressing for a cease-fire. The Israelis answered: Good, you name the hour and we will accept it; just be sure to get the Syrians to stop firing at the same time. Bull demurred. It took the Syrians longer to get the word to all their units. The Israelis were sorry. "As long as they keep firing, we will fire back at them."

An observed cease-fire finally came at 18:30 hours and the war was over. The Syrian battle cost the Israelis a hundred and twenty men killed and more than three hundred wounded. But, as it turned out, Dayan had overestimated his need and had called for reinforcements far beyond his requirement. The battle was fought and won almost entirely by Elazar's two and a half brigades, and the men of the Tenth Armored, who had rushed up from the south and were present in support of the action, were never needed in combat.

Four days of battle in Sinai, two days on the Jordanian front, twenty-nine hours on the Syrian—Israel had attained all her objectives in the limited political time that the balance of world forces afforded her. She herself, in effect, drew and set the cease-fire line on each of the three fronts, accomplishing irreversible facts by the swiftness and finality of her victory. Had her troops pressed on and seized more territory, the big powers at the moment could have done very little to stop them. Israel stopped herself. Eshkol, Dayan, Eban and the others responsible for the political conduct of the war went as far as they deemed it judicious and profitable to go and stopped in just the right places. Their realism established the cease-fire lines as the new *status quo* in the military geography of the Middle East.

The Israelis accomplished several other things. By defending their vital interests and saving themselves and their future, they defended the position of the United States and saved their great Western friend from a clamorous defeat in the Arab world. They solved Johnson's insoluble problem. He had earnestly sought to discharge a solemn American obligation and had found himself unable to do so. The Is-

raelis saved both the honor and credibility of the American commitment by fulfilling it themselves. To their great satisfaction, they demonstrated to Nasser (and themselves) that they could handle the Arab
armies singlehanded under nobody's patronage but their own. In the
impasse of the big-power relationship, only they were able to take the
initiative that turned the scales and stripped Nasser of his expected
triumph. In defeating him they humbled his great patron and wrote
finis to a series of Soviet intelligence errors and policy miscalculations
so fundamental and far-reaching that a major Middle Eastern adventure had crashed, at a blow, in derisory fiasco.

The great patrons, the June war showed, were not ready or willing
at the showdown to identify themselves with the cause of their clients.
And by the same token, the clients—Israelis and Arabs—could not
rely on their patrons. Nor, at the test, were the great powers able to
have their own way and order the small powers around. In that respect the nexus between Jerusalem and Washington was not unlike
that between Cairo and Moscow. Even in an age of intercontinental
ballistics missiles, small powers were not powerless, and there were
still situations in which the big powers, as they faced each other, definitely were. A great power might still have the capacity to annihilate
another, but precisely for that reason it no longer had the option of
gunboat diplomacy. Its armory abounded in weapons that were meant
not to be used. An IBM rising in the air out of the Soviet Union was
first and foremost a signal of confrontation with the United States,
even though it might be aimed at Israel. With the armories of the two
great powers neutralizing and canceling out each other, a small power
determined to fight for its existence could still Go It Alone.

The Russians, surveying the humiliating mess after the crash, could
reflect on the folly of entrusting their interests in so great an enterprise
to unreliable friends they could not possibly control. The irrational
escalation of the crisis, Nasser's special and personal contribution
once he had taken over its management, they had obviously not reckoned on. Now, with bewildered chagrin, they had to face the complaints of their disenchanted Arab friends. In Arab eyes they had iniq-
uitously reneged. The Russians, the Arabs reflected bitterly and belatedly, were just another big power after all, interested in the Arab
world only for their own unaltruistic purposes, for the opportunities
and weapons that it offered in the contest with the West. Indeed,
many an Arab concluded, the disaster proved that American credibil-

ity was better than Russian credibility, American friendship more valuable than Russian friendship, since the Americans had not really restrained their Israeli friends and indubitably would have sped to their aid in an hour of mortal need, which was more than the Russians were prepared to do for Egypt. The friends of the Soviet Union had been left to their fate; the friends of the United States had prospered and triumphed. The Americans evidently knew what they were doing. Nasser himself was soon to complain that the Americans had deliberately held him back while the Israelis hit him. After all, there had to be a plot somewhere to explain the incredible débâcle.

Others, too, both great and small, had played their leading roles in the snowballing process of miscalculation. For reasons wholly unrelated to the Straits of Tiran or the Egyptian mobilization in Sinai, De Gaulle had annulled an alliance of more than ten years' standing in the romantic belief that France had the strength and authority to remake the power balance in the Middle East. Had the crisis followed his prescription and his view of history, it would have brought dramatic support to the Gaullist doctrine of how the contemporary course of European events and of East-West relations should be shaped. For years he had been telling the Europeans they could not rely on the United States, which was far away, and must settle their own accounts with the Soviet Union, which was the world power present in Europe. The concept of Atlantic obedience, outworn and archaic, must yield to an eastward shift in the global balance involving a rapprochement with the Russians; and this salutary trend was about to be confirmed by the denouement in the Middle East, where the Americans were destined to stand aside and do nothing while the Russians widely improved their positions and the French, somehow, managed to insert themselves into the altered setup. Israel by her victory defied De Gaulle's view of history and refuted his doctrine in action. She was guilty of historic insubordination, and this, it seemed, was the profound reason for his anger. Unlike Johnson, he had believed he could issue orders to a sovereign state; and had meanwhile given dangerous encouragement to Nasser. On the eve of the war, he had imagined he might restrain the Israelis by imposing an embargo on the delivery of French jet-fighter aircraft. As a result of the war and of Israel's disobedience, he maintained the embargo as a permanent penalty. Yet when the dust had settled, it was as clear as ever that only two powers really mattered in the Middle East. There was no third.

French support of the Arab-Soviet line meant little in practice to the Arabs and was at best a diplomatic convenience for the Russians.

Romanticism of a less cerebral and more visceral kind hastened the undoing of Hussein, whose road to disaster was similarly paved with miscalculations. Had he been a brighter statesman and a less ardent man of honor, Jordan might have been spared. Of all the defeated Arab leaders he, at least, had no recriminations afterward and guarded no grudges. Alone among them, he took the whole responsibility upon himself. On the third day of the war, Syria, Iraq, Algeria, Sudan, Yemen and Lebanon leaped, at Nasser's cue, to sever relations with the United States in an access of outraged solidarity against the imperialist power that had sent its war planes into the fray. But Hussein preferred to forget that unsavory story, cooked up in Amman and served to the world in Cairo, an early-morning fantasy unwisely dropped on Nasser's eager plate. Honorably Hussein retracted the accusation and prudently he maintained relations with the power that was eminently able, and—sooner or later—would probably be ready, to help him to his feet. His country was still indispensable in the weird equilibrium of the Middle East, even though in brutal fact the Israeli victory had destroyed the state of Jordan and re-created, precisely, the desert kingdom of Transjordan over which his grandfather, Abdullah, had first ruled. If in the passionate confusion of the prewar crisis Hussein had read Israel's intentions correctly, if he had not been tricked into thinking she was too distraught to act for her survival and had not been stampeded by Nasser's showmanship, he would not have flown to Cairo. And if, in the days that followed, he had determined to stick it out, taking up the Israelis and Americans on their proffered guarantee of Jordanian neutrality, the entire West Bank might yet have been his, Iraqi troops would never have gained a foothold in his country, and four hundred thousand Palestinian refugees would not, in time, have carried their fears, their dreams, their hopes of revenge across the Jordan River eastward, to camp in destitution on his wind-swept hills. Jordan would not have known this agony. And the Hashimite descendant of the Prophet would still have been the Guardian of the Holy Places, the King of Jerusalem.

And what, in the end, of Sharm el Sheikh, the lonely post among the rocks on the farthest uninhabited rim of Sinai? The crisis had turned on the three syllables of that fanciful and alluring name. "What is the meaning of our occupation of Sharm el Sheikh?" Nasser had asked rhetorically in his speech to the Egyptian airmen. In the Foreign Offices of world capitals, the meaning was that he had changed his line of action and had decided to go all the way by defying both Israel and the United States. The Israelis on the third day of war organized a parachute drop to seize the head of rock above the Straits but, as it happened, a navy torpedo boat out of Eilath, accompanied by a few troop transports, got there first; and what was to have been a drop was a routine landing on the old UNEF airstrip. For the parachutists, a sorry anticlimax. The bulk of the Egyptian forces had already departed and only two companies remained. The Egyptians scampered and scattered at the first sight of the Israeli Navy, some trying to put out in little boats. The place fell without a shot.

Then, as the Israelis settled down and inspected their surroundings, they made the strangest discovery. The Egyptians had never mined the Straits of Tiran. The waters in the navigable channel on the Sinai side were open and clear. No Egyptian destroyer was standing by. To be sure, officially and authoritatively, *Al Ahram* had mined the Straits, just as it had dispatched an Egyptian destroyer, several submarines and several torpedo boats to the scene. The horizon offered no sign of the Egyptian Navy; and—*Al Ahram* to the contrary—there was no sign, either, of Egyptian coastal artillery on the rough stone escarpment overlooking the entrance to the Gulf of Aqaba. Later, in another part of Sinai, other Israeli troops found two big coastal guns, abandoned at the edge of the desert road, nearly a hundred miles short of their destination. Indicating, perhaps, a sudden decision? Who was to tell? The blockade had never been enforced; it had merely been proclaimed and imposed by *Al Ahram*. And that had been enough.

Our forces in Sharm el Sheikh have joined our main forces stationed in Sinai. In the cramped and cheerless lounge of our hotel, the one place where we could keep each other company during the long idle afternoons of our internment, we heard the Egyptian Command's laconic announcement on the English-language channel of Cairo Radio. Heads bent over a transistor, we waited for more. The one bare sentence, saying so little and so much, and repeated like a knell at intervals, was apparently the only news from Sinai, the only war communiqué we would have on that afternoon of June 7. It was still more than enough—the single bulletin repeated without comment in a dead voice, tolling the crack-up of Egyptian arms and the end of the

tragedy of Arab make-believe. The reversal was too swift and the ca-
lamity too complete not to be felt as a physical shock. In my mind
were the shrill impressions of recent days. I thought of the victory
shouts and victory streamers, the organized hysteria, the maelstrom of
collective emotion that had filled the air; and looking up, my eye
catching the photograph of Nasser on the wall, the faded image of the
faded hero, I was suddenly appalled. It was not the physical devastation of the war, though this was obviously too great even to be measured—the divisions routed and destroyed, their survivors racing
frantically westward, seeking escape across the Canal; the Israelis out-
stripping them, blocking the way ahead and shutting the trap; the
Canal itself, the prize of Egypt, now closed indefinitely and its revenues lost; the Egyptian oil fields in the Gulf of Suez, now overrun and
added to the victor's spoils. It was not the physical wreckage that
appalled but the huge fantasy Nasser had created in rearing his house
of cards and in leading his country and his people to this disaster.
The Arabs must say and believe in order to survive; it was their charm
and their tragedy. Belief had overpowered reality and the magic of the
word had usurped the place of action. The clever statesman had dra-
gooned some and duped others, while the hero had expressed and exploited the frustrations and failings of his people and built his power
on them—their thirst for glory, their burning need for self-assertion,
their passionate credulity, their immense capacity for self-deception.
Who would pay for the débâcle? War was the army's and air force's
department but, I thought, it would hardly be good enough to try to
pin all the blame on the generals. From his place on the wall, Nasser
still fixed a clear, commanding gaze on the distant future. He was, I
ventured to think, finished.

In my head there echoed at that moment something he had once
said, I could not recall when or where, in one of his speeches on some
anniversary or other—a statement somewhere in the past that gave
the measure of the present. I remembered the general sense of that
utterance but not the exact words or the occasion, and the thought
that I might still have it sent me back to my room to search among the
old texts and clippings I had saved. It was a short passage from a
speech dated June 26, 1962:

"Whoever wants to go to war ought to prepare for it. Whoever
wishes to achieve his goal ought not to gamble with the future of his
country or with that of others. . . . We ought to get ready, instead

of making speeches. . . . We must prepare not only insofar as power and strength are concerned but also morally. Lack of moral considerations was responsible for our 1948 disaster."

The cease-fire having been accepted at last, the war in Sinai ended at twelve noon on June 9. Nasser, the radio said, would address the country at half-past seven in the evening. Intermittently and inexplicably that afternoon, the air-raid alert panted its warning to a city that was already numb and pulseless with the shock and stupefaction of defeat. On the southern outskirts, visiting friends told us, troops were digging in around the military hospital and to the north, around the air force base at Almaza. But except for the fitful groan of the alert, not a murmur, not a vibration reached us from the estranged city outside our hotel, only a tremor of repressed tension in the vacant streets as the hour approached for Nasser to speak. Cairo lay becalmed in the soft air of early evening and the broad corniche, handsome and desolate, stretched away along the bank of the slow-bending river, northward, to join the old Delta road leading east across green plantations to Abu Suweir, Ismailia and the narrow waterway where the guns of Israel pointed at the heartland of Egypt.

· 9 ·

The Sequel

THE THIRD ARAB-ISRAELI WAR, as the world soon came to know, was only a spectacular episode in a tragically prolonged encounter. It led to an impasse more rigorous and more violent than any the Middle East had yet known. The war the Israelis waged was devastating, conclusive and short; it fulfilled brilliantly the immediate requirements of their security and the precepts of their military doctrine. It brought under Israel's control a territory nearly four times the area of her own, it actually shortened her military boundaries, and it lifted the threat of direct Arab assault against most of her border settlements. The Israelis breathed safely, with a new-found sense of national confidence, behind strategic frontiers that were nearly all their military leaders could ask for. Yet, in the long term of the unfinished encounter, the war gained for Israel only a temporary advantage. The victory she achieved was not a war victory in the ordinarily understood sense, for beyond the cease-fire lines lay the great unoccupyable and irreconcilable Arab world. The victors asked for peace, and their adversaries, defeated but rejecting the consequences of defeat, denied it to them with renewed and immitigable passion.

"Our central purpose is that this war should be the last." So Eban said at the war's end and other government leaders repeated after him; and all in Israel concurred. Peace for the Israelis, after so great an ordeal, meant acceptance of their existence and recognition of their national right. Recognition meant a formal settlement to be concluded directly in negotiations between themselves and their neighbors. Such is the normal way in which wars between nations are terminated. In the fullness of victory in June, 1967, it seemed to the Israelis that this way was now open. They drew from their experience the harsh lesson that they could not rely on international guarantees or on the commitments of their closest friends: the guarantee of their survival lay in their own strength and in their capacity to win a peace settlement themselves. "Arrangements reached outside contractual agreements between the parties involved," Eban said further, "can be blown away overnight, and so they were blown away." The insistence on a formal peace, on something more than a tenuous skein of international assurances, was not merely procedural; it was the heart of the matter for a government and a people that asked for confirmation of their existence. In the first days of jubilation even the time-hardened realists, even Ben-Gurion, believed that the objective conditions for peace had been won. Peace at that moment seemed inescapable: so great a military victory must lead to a final political settlement. But it was not so. Israel had won a battle but her existence was still unacknowledged and unconfirmed.

The war destroyed the greatest of the Arab armies but it remobilized Arab emotion and refired Arab pride. The defeat was a provocation that humiliated and inflamed. For the Arabs, the existence of Israel was still and always a historic crime, an aggression, an unredeemed injustice to which the perpetuated misery of the refugees bore witness: all the greater a provocation now that Israel had seized the whole of Palestine and had imposed the rule of an occupation army on a captive population of more than a million Arabs. Each of the Palestinian Arabs on the West Bank of the Jordan River was a defeated person, isolated from the Arab hinterland and cut off from the mainstream of Arab life. For how long, none could tell. "They have robbed us of our homes, our lands and our country," one of them said in occupied Ramallah, a surgeon, trained for his high profession at a great university in the United States, "and they now think that because they have won a single little battle, they can have *peace*. Never!" The Arabs might lose still other battles and the Israelis might overrun still other territories, but there would be no peace. Arab righteousness took shelter in the evasions of language from the facts of war and politics and the pangs of self-examination and self-reproach. The war, in official and in common speech, became known as "the aggression" and the defeat was disguised as "the setback." Haunted by their humiliation, sustained by their fatalism, the Arabs could live with their injuries but they would not accept the insult. They refused to accept the fact of Israel.

The Russians, after the war, recuperated swiftly. Which of the great powers had come out first in the engagement? Israel had determined the immediate issue, and her triumph had seemed at the time a success for the West. And so indeed, at the time, it was. But with the passage of months, the balance sheet in the Middle East began to look very different. The immensity of the military defeat left the Arab states more than ever susceptible to Soviet penetration and offered the Russians an unprecedented opening. The great void left by the destruction of Egyptian arms, the bankruptcy of the Egyptian state and the ejection of the Americans from half a dozen Arab capitals, the Soviet Union hastened to fill. The Arabs had only the Russians to turn to and the Russians, after the débâcle, sped to their aid. A first emergency airlift of arms to reaffirm Nasser's authority, preserve the Egyptian regime and refreshen their own battered status in the Arab world began within hours after the last shots in the war had been fired. Arms were the standard and traditional way in which the powers established, maintained or recovered political influence in the Middle East. Soon the Russians were more firmly entrenched than ever in Cairo and Damascus, while Egypt and Syria more than ever were the dependents of Moscow. The expelled Americans, having set their policy squarely against any return to the *status quo ante,* had few advantages they were in a position to exploit. In any case, they were clearly not eager to return to Egypt with their usual bounty except on hard-and-fast political conditions. Israel, having lost France, was increasingly dependent on Washington. In the space of a few months, the Arab-Israeli war led to a radical alteration in the Middle Eastern stance of the two powers and, as it turned out, the Russians achieved, after all, one of their main objectives in the region—the political polarization that it had been the Americans' constant purpose to avert. Provisionally, at least, the Russians appeared to have reversed the balance of gain and loss. So startling was the change and so lively was Arab political fancy that many Lebanese and others, regretting the general rupture of ties with the West, easily convinced themselves that the war had been a Soviet-Syrian plot to demolish the Egyptian armed forces and place Nasser in Moscow's power.

In the course of months, the Russians rebuilt Nasser's war machine under the guidance of a greatly expanded mission of Soviet instructors and technicians. Egyptian arms on land and in the air were restored to approximately their prewar level. The Soviet Mediterranean naval squadrons were progressively strengthened, with the advertised role of defending the Arab states against Israeli aggression. Ideology stiffened. The fiasco of June, 1967, provoked a wide-ranging and restless debate among the Communist Parties of Eastern Europe, some of which were profoundly unpersuaded that Egypt, Syria and Algeria were "socialist" states, genuinely deserving of so large a Soviet commitment. It was evidently in order to meet such doubts that the Russians again rechristened the anti-Western Arab regimes, scrapping the pretentious name of "revolutionary democracies" and designating them, more cautiously, as "noncapitalist progressive states." But the Soviet role in the war as well as Soviet postwar policy required an ideological warrant. The leading journals of Communist theory in Moscow insisted on the new official reading of the Arab-Israeli dispute: it was henceforth pictured not as a dispute between nations but as a transborder class conflict between the imperialist-directed state of Israel and its neocolonialist Arab victims.

In Egypt after the catastrophe, the generals paid and Nasser remained. He was the faulted hero, no longer blindly admired but loved and clung to still. After the shame and the insult, he was all that Egypt had left. For the mass of Egyptians—and this was perhaps the most striking change—he had lost his hero's invulnerability. Before the war, people had blamed his advisers and lieutenants when things had gone badly wrong; now they blamed him. Still, in a way, he gained a new sentimental glory in defeat. His halo gone, he became human; and where there had once been adoration and awe, there was now sympathy and attachment. The Israelis had not really won the war as long as he was there and Egyptians could say, "They failed in their great objective; they wanted to overthrow him and the Arab people stopped them."

But the move to depose him had actually come from the Egyptian generals, even before the war had ended, and he, the master conspirator, manuevering with speed and guile, had neatly eluded them. On June 8 the agonized search for culprits had begun, at a meeting called by Badran, at which Nasser and Amer were present. The military commanders, alarmed and at bay, blamed the political leadership for pushing them into a war they had not wanted and of which they had been given so little advance notice. Seconded by the generals, Badran demanded that Nasser vindicate their honor and Egypt's by stepping down. It was either he or they. At the end of that uncomfortable discussion, if we may believe Badran, Nasser and Amer agreed they would both take responsibility for the defeat and would abdicate together. Then followed the machinations that culminated in the *coup de théâtre* the next night—Nasser broadcasting his speech of renunciation and Ali Sabry, his trusted bravo, alerting the youth groups of the Arab Socialist Union to get out their banners and posters and stand by for the demonstrations. Nasser bowed to the will of the people, reneging on his bargain of the previous day; and Amer, dismissed and disgraced, was the first to pay for the defeat. The service chiefs who rallied to him were promptly fired; and as disaffection spread, several hundred officers were purged. Never remarkably bright or exceptionally able, Amer tried to plot his way back to his former eminence as Deputy Supreme Commander, but Nasser's police kept several steps ahead of him. This was presumably not too difficult, since nothing could have been more amateur or inept than Amer's conspiracy to organize an army march on Cairo. Disgruntled commanders of the old swaggering elite congregated at his mansion in the capital, the headquarters of the stillborn coup; meeting followed meeting in the house, leaflets multiplied, arms caches proliferated—and this in the Middle East! Nasser's intimate friend of nearly thirty years was placed under house arrest to face trial for conspiracy. Already during the war, it was rumored, he had meditated suicide. Late in August, 1967, a few days before his interrogation was to start, he died of poison and the world was informed that he had killed himself.

How great a debt, unacknowledged and unavowed, King Feisal owed to the defense forces of Israel! The Arab-Israeli war brought to an end Nasser's participation in the war in Yemen. The Egyptian defeat revived the art of summitry. At a meeting of the Arab heads of state, held in August at Khartoum in order to hoist Egypt and Jordan from the pit of insolvency, the Saudi monarch and the Egyptian President finally settled their accounts in the Arabian Peninsula. Feisal contributed his handsome share to a rescue fund established by the three most affluent of the Arab oil states, Saudi Arabia, Kuwait and Libya. It was conscience money, freely donated by the oil monarchs to affirm their devotion to the common Palestinian cause; and since the payments were popular in the Arab world, they were also political insurance. To Nasser went ninety million pounds sterling—at that time, 252 million dollars—and to Hussein, forty million. It was a small price to pay to rid the Peninsula of Egyptian troops, and Feisal made the timing of their withdrawal a firm condition of the compact. Bankruptcy would doubtless have constrained Nasser, in any case, to recall the rest of his expeditionary force from Yemen; but the Saudi contributions to the fund, paid out in installments in the course of a year, were Feisal's guarantee that Nasser would keep his part of the agreement. Punctually as promised, on November 30, 1967, the last Egyptian units sailed for home from Yemen while on the same day, by one of those fortuitous strokes of history, British troops, taking off by plane and helicopter, saw their last of the black and sharp volcanic rock of Aden and the dusty expanse of the Aden Protectorate. The two foreign antagonists in southern Arabia, the revolutionary and the imperial, departed together. In the Aden Protectorate, amid a tumult of rejoicing on the day the British left, the victorious National Liberation Front, a passionately conspiratorial, militantly nationalist, pan-Arab terrorist movement, proclaimed a new independent and sovereign state, the People's Republic of Southern Yemen. The leaders of the new republic owed nothing to Nasser. In their grenade-throwing, machine-gunning rise to power, they had eliminated their Cairo-financed and Cairo-directed terrorist rivals and had established themselves alone.

The powerful weapons against the West which the Arabs had always counted in their armory—the oil boycott, the withdrawal of Arab holdings from British banks, the closure of the Suez Canal—were of no avail when the reckoning came after the June war. So the Arab states were compelled to recognize at their Khartoum conference. For years the notion of an oil boycott to bring the imperialists to their knees had been fostered in Cairo as a tenet of Arab nationalist faith. At Khartoum the Arab states, both the haves and the have-nots, betrayed their faith in order to save Nasser and Hussein and to maintain the haves, at least, in the style of living, unpinched in the pocket, to which they were accustomed. A boycott would be merely a self-boycott: the oil revenues were more important to the Arabs than the oil shipments were to the West. The heads of state sensibly decided to resume oil production and pumping operations immediately. Only the unappeasable Syrians dissented. In addition to a total ban on oil exports, the Syrians demanded a total withdrawal of sterling balances from London and a total diplomatic breach with the West. The conference rejected their proposals and ignored their protests.

The channel of East-West commerce, the waterway that linked the worlds, the Suez Canal, remained closed after the war and, through disuse, diminished in importance. Nasser kept it closed because of the bargaining power that he believed it gave him. He overestimated the Canal's effectiveness as a lever to impel the Western powers to induce Israel to withdraw from Sinai. Every day that it languished, as the Egyptians were well aware, it sank further into obsolescence and became less essential to a maritime world that soon learned to adjust itself to the inconvenience of getting along without it. From the Canal's eastern bank the Israeli Army interdicted its use except on Israel's terms. Insisting on freedom of passage for her ships as for those of everyone else, Israel shrewdly announced her readiness to make a separate deal so that the Canal might be reopened. But the Egyptians ignored this offer: the passage of Israeli ships within sight of Port Said and Ismailia would have meant visible recognition of the state of Israel. The Egyptians thereby appeared the more stubborn and the Israelis the more reasonable. Nasser's subsidy from the oil states was more than enough to replace his lost revenues at Suez. But even so, in the end, his country would be the loser. The waterway that in its heyday had been a historic necessity, a world feature for the sake of which armies had marched, fleets had mobilized and Western powers had carved out protectorates and conjured up mandates, became a neglected moat slowly accumulating the sand-silt of the desert—a place of convenience for a cease-fire line in a protracted stalemate. It seemed unlikely ever to regain its pre-eminent place in commerce and history.

After the rout of the Arab armies there followed the renewal of Arab terrorism and the militant resurgence of El Fatah. The Israelis at the end of the war expected that so decisive a defeat would have the effect of reconciling the Arabs to the idea of coexistence. The defeat, instead, rearmed their intransigence. The saboteur group that had been the cosseted creature of Syrian Army Intelligence emerged as an autonomous organization that professed to be the core of the movement to liberate not only the West Bank region but the whole of Palestine. By the spring of 1968, there were thirteen Palestinian commando groups operating from Jordan, and El Fatah was the most prominent and popular. Along with the others, it helped to satisfy a fierce psychological need. Arab youth had seen Egyptian tanks flee back across Sinai and had watched Jerusalem go without a fight. The smart of defeat and the shock of losing the whole of Palestine engendered a militant Palestinian nationalism of which El Fatah became the symbol and the standard-bearer. The generals and the politicians had failed; the *fedayeen* were the one group that were keeping up the struggle, moving independently, without waiting for discredited governments or shattered armies. They were the only people that were fighting to get back Arab honor and self-respect. Recruitment was widespread among young Palestinians, reaching outside the refugee camps to new strata of Arab society: for the first time educated young Arabs, university students, enlisted in the liberation cause. Women in Jordan donated their jewels and bracelets; contributions flowed in from Palestinians and others in Kuwait, Saudi Arabia and Libya, and from businessmen in Beirut who wanted to give though not to fight. El Fatah was able to make generous settlements on the widows and children of its martyred saboteurs. Arms came from Egypt and Iraq by way of Damascus—some came even from China—while training for new recruits was provided in Syrian and Egyptian camps and, for the more advanced, in Algeria. El Fatah sought to instill a new military discipline in its expanding ranks, and of all the commando groups it was politically the "purest," telling its members to forget their party affiliations, Baathist or Communist, and sink their identities in the patriotic fight.

Soon the *fedayeen* organizations, though their operational accomplishments were meager, became a legend in Jordan. The aura of heroism in the Palestinian cause passed from Nasser to the activists. Like other such movements before them, the *fedayeen* exploited Arab miseries and traded on Arab delusions. They brought with them their familiar baggage of gimcrack ideology, their apocalyptic cult of unending guerrilla warfare, their pretensions as leaders and saviors in a struggle which they conceived as the uprising of a conquered people against foreign invaders and oppressors. Israel, in the mythology of the movement, was an inherently weak and unworkable nation, manufactured and synthetic, lacking the stamina for a prolonged conflict and destined to disintegrate under the blows of the commandos. On the strength of this doctrine El Fatah summoned Palestinian youth to

an illusory battle to bring down the state of Israel by means of guerrilla actions that were supposed to make the Israeli people lose their
nerve and despair of their existence. The *fedayeen* were of small account as a military challenge. Their strategic goals were beyond them;
they achieved nothing that could properly be called guerrilla war
against the Israeli occupation forces. They were unable to establish
bases in Israeli-held territory west of the Jordan River or to inspire a
civil-resistance movement among the Palestinian Arabs of the West
Bank. Their raiding parties and saboteur squads were regularly
tracked down and wiped out by the Israeli Army within days or within
hours after they had crossed the river from their Jordanian camps.
The extent of their achievement was a campaign of sporadic terrorism
aimed chiefly at civilians—the shelling of Israeli border settlements
from posts beyond the river, the exploding bomb in a marketplace in
Jerusalem or at a bus station in Tel-Aviv, the packed Israeli airliner
machine-gunned and grenaded at an international airport in Europe.
What was a source of deep concern in Israel was not the presumed
military threat of El Fatah—even resolute and sustained guerrilla
warfare could offer no serious challenge to her survival or her functioning as a state—but the fact that Israelis for an indefinitely extended period would have to accept terrorism as a part of their lives.
They would have to accustom themselves to a new reality in which—
so Harkabi concluded in a study of Arab postwar strategy—El Fatah
would have to be lived with and the deaths of its victims would, perhaps, come to be looked upon as something senseless but familiar and
statistically ineluctable "like the toll in traffic accidents which modern
societies have to pay."

El Fatah had indeed come to stay, for as long as anyone could
confidently foresee. Ineffectual as a military force, it was a political
success. In the aftermath of the defeat the immediate role of the
fedayeen was to assuage Arab pride with imagined victories; their
greater and more deadly achievement was to revive the wish-dream of
Israel's destruction. It was quite unnecessary for their purposes to
mount a credible guerrilla operation; given the emotional and moral
reactions of the Arab temperament, it was sufficient to stoke the
dream with terrorism. The *fedayeen* groups in Jordan became not
only a legend but a power and, with the magnification of their deeds,
were able to impose on the conflict their temper of implacable violence. Hussein was as aware as anyone that El Fatah might be turned

against him as well as against Israel. He was, as always, under the double pressure of internal passion and external blackmail, and at first, as in years past, he oscillated between defiance and accommodation. He was dismayed by El Fatah's tactic of exposing Arab women and children to Israeli reprisal shelling by establishing its terrorist posts inside the Jordanian refugee camps. He sought, in the beginning, to control the *fedayeen*. At one point early in 1968 he boldly announced he would proscribe them, but he at once reversed himself and acquiesced in their activity. Finally he came to terms with them. Such was their popular ascendancy in Jordan that he did not care, or dare, to move decisively against them, and in the end El Fatah, with his consent, operated under the protection of both his army and his police and often with their active support and connivance. He became the political hostage of the activists.

The Israeli retaliations, fierce and systematic, inflicted heavy punishment and at times gained a respite but they did not effectively deter. On the contrary, they incited. Every large-scale Israeli reprisal against the *fedayeen* heightened their prestige in Arab eyes; every bombing or shelling of their camps in Jordan swung mass feeling behind them and made it more difficult for a timorous government to try to curb them; and when Israeli tanks crossed the Jordan River on a punitive raid against terrorist bases, Hussein sent his own troops and his own tanks to meet them. Through the months and then the years, the lengthening cycle of violence—of raid, retaliation and counterraid —served to widen the abyss of passionate estrangement which the Palestinian militants, above all, sought to place between the Arab peoples and Israel. With the *fedayeen* setting the pace, Hussein sought to demonstrate he was no less militant than they. First the Jordan Legion and later the Iraqi army units that had remained in Jordan after the June war turned their guns against Israeli border settlements on the West Bank. When, in the end, Hussein publicly espoused the *fedayeen,* he echoed the language and the arguments the Syrians had made familiar in their bellicose days before the war. Protecting the terrorists and aiding them on his territory, he nevertheless disclaimed responsibility for the consequences of their actions. It was not his job, he said—as the Syrians had said before him—to safeguard Israel's security or to protect her against *fedayeen* violations of the United Nations cease-fire that he had accepted. It was not his task to lighten the burden of the Israeli occupation army by controlling El Fatah. He was not Israel's keeper.

In June, 1967, the Israelis had expected that victory would bring, at least, safety for their civilians in the settlements along their previously exposed frontiers. Had not the Syrians been driven from the Golan Heights? The kibbutzim in the plain of northern Galilee, below the dismantled Syrian fortifications in the hills, were indeed safe at last from Arab artillery; but the settlements facing Jordan south of Lake Tiberias, in the Jordan and Beisan river valleys, were now in the line of fire, dangerously exposed to Jordanian or Iraqi or terrorist shelling. More than ever, exasperation pushed the Israelis back to their bedrock military policy, their conviction that their only defense lay in offense. Their retaliatory shelling depopulated the east bank of the Jordan River. Many Jordanians abandoned their farms and evacuated their villages, moving eastward as refugees into the desert hinterland. But on the Israeli side of the valley the civilians held on, men, women and children, and continued to live in their frontier settlements: for them to forsake their kibbutzim would have been to relinquish a part of their national life and to diminish the moral presence of Israel.

So, too, on yet another frontier that ultimately, in any decisive encounter, would be the primary frontier in the balance of Arab-Israeli military strength, the Israeli victory brought not a respite but an intensification of the struggle, fixing the confrontation with Egypt on the banks of the Suez Canal. The ultimate meeting in war, like the ultimate meeting in peace, must be with Egypt; and Egypt's intense involvement in the conflict, consuming her emotional and political energies after the ignominy of defeat, absorbing armaments, resources, money and manpower to rebuild the military power of a humiliated nation, was of far greater importance for Israel and her future than the re-emergence of the *fedayeen*. The third Arab-Israeli war tightened the coils of tension around all of Israel's tormented frontiers; it brought to the conflict a new severity of passion. The confrontation was harsh and rigid. In the short term Israel's position was secure behind the lines of the new military *status quo;* and for a period of years she would doubtless continue to be decisively superior because of her knowledge, her proficiency and her moral cohesion. But she was still a garrison without reserves, still embattled and alone, an enclave without a hinterland, enclosed by enemies who sought her destruction. The Israeli fortress was still under siege, after a swift and brilliant counterattack.

Once again it fell to the lot of the United Nations Secretariat, through the offices of a Swedish diplomat, to seek to mediate the conflict. In his months of shuttling to and fro between the Foreign Offices of Jerusalem, Amman and Cairo, Gunnar Jarring, as U Thant's special representative, was unable to discover an exit from the impasse. The Arab states refused to pay the price of recognizing Israel or of negotiating with her in order to recover their lost territories, while the Israelis refused to renounce their conquests without a formal peace treaty to ensure that war would not happen again. For the Arabs there could be no concessions without a prior Israeli withdrawal; for the Israelis no withdrawal without prior negotiations and a contractual peace. On the one hand the Arabs insisted on no recognition and no peace treaty; on the other they presented a novel diplomatic formula, "the elimination of the consequences of aggression," to press their demand for an unconditional withdrawal of Israeli troops. The implications of the formula were plain enough: Israel had committed aggression and the occupation of Arab territory was its consequence. Thus the aggression should be undone and its consequences reversed. The Arab states proclaimed they would not be bludgeoned to the conference table by Israeli arms and would not allow Israel to dictate terms from a position of force. They would enter into no discussions until the dishonor of the Israeli occupation was removed. Which was more important to the Arabs, to recover their lost lands or to persist in denying Israel's existence? The Arab states, imagining that events could be erased and their results unmade, wanted to do both. At their conference in Khartoum, where they staked out these policies, they proposed to regain Sinai and the West Bank without political surrender, evidently in the belief that American-Soviet mediation would win back their territories for them and secure a settlement that would rescue Arab honor but would involve no final commitment to peace. Nasser, too, seems to have believed it would be possible to extract a settlement in this way, thanks to the great powers and above all to the Americans, who he oddly assumed would be willing and able to persuade the Israeli conquerors to give up their conquests. But history could not be undone so easily.

From their third war with the Arabs, the Israelis learned precisely what they had always believed. The war confirmed their national attitudes and fortified their basic convictions: Israel was a nation ultimately dependent on her own strength and on her readiness to go it alone, and she could place no trust in the United Nations. The Israelis talked to Jarring as a friendly interlocutor but not as an official mediator between them and the Arabs. They accepted his mediation only as a means of bringing about direct negotiations that would destroy the Arab myth of their nonexistence. They rejected the United Nations as the guarantor of their future; they refused to give up the occupied territories with nothing better than an international guarantee of the kind that had failed them in 1967. They would not return to the *status quo ante* of a United Nations-sponsored armistice, as they had done under American and United Nations pressure after the Suez War. They had been burned once; they would not repeat the mistake of entrusting their future to arrangements patched up by the powers and sanctified by the General Assembly. From their third war the Israelis sought to win what they had failed to win from their first and their second: secure and recognized borders, a permanent settlement, a genuine peace.

If only, the Israelis often contended, if only the great powers would leave the Middle Eastern countries to themselves, the way to a final settlement would in good time be found. But this was a purely speculative line of argument. No doubt the Arab-Israeli conflict, if it were not enmeshed in a great power conflict, would have seemed less desperately insoluble than it did. If the Russians immediately after the war had not set out in hot pursuit of their long-term interests in the region; if they had not hurried to restore their position and Nasser's; if they had not gone on to renew the arms race and re-create his military establishment—if they had not done all this, no doubt the prospect of the Arabs and Israelis coming to terms would have been brighter. But the Russians, acting like a great power, did do these things, and in the new Middle Eastern alignment after the war Israel was caught more closely than ever in the toils of the big-power relationship. Self-reliance was one lesson she had learned; but the war had brought home, also, the countervailing lesson of her ultimate strategic dependence on the United States. Washington had always been the capital that counted above all others; as a consequence of the war the American connection, politically and militarily, was more vital than ever. It was the only connection that mattered. The Americans became Israel's principal supplier of arms—her only important one; they also became the moral protector of her victory. To be a small power, trusting in its own strength to achieve its national objectives, but finally dependent on the good will and support of a great power on the opposite side of the world—this was an abnormal and precarious condition. The dilemma was heightened for Israel by the war and its aftermath. In the new pattern of conflict, she had to think both of the possible emergence of an isolationist America and of the perils of being surrounded by hostile Arab states, some of which were coming increasingly under Soviet influence and tutelage.

In the long term it was by no means certain that a small power determined to fight for its survival could always go it alone. In June, 1967, yes; but the circumstances that surrounded the war were peculiar and they would not necessarily happen again. The Israelis, in saying their survival depended on their own strength, spoke with the moral courage without which they would not have survived. But they were, perhaps, generalizing from the particular circumstances of 1967. What the war showed was that a small power could go it alone when the hostility of one big power was balanced and held in check by the benevolence of another. The Israelis were able to fight and win the war, without risk of Soviet intervention against them, thanks both to their own strength and to the firepower of the Sixth Fleet. In going to war, they relied on themselves and on the American presence. In time, the strengthening of the Soviet Mediterranan fleet and the development of more sophisticated weapons might increase rather than decrease the importance of the American protective cover. How permanent or how provisional was the balance of military forces in the eastern Mediterranean? For how long would the Sixth Fleet be a credible guarantee? Israel's future depended on such remote and problematic contingencies as these.

It depended also on the interests and intentions of the two great powers in the area. For how long would the Americans stand by while Israel consolidated her hold on the occupied territories and Arabs and Israelis, month after month, shelled and rocketed each other across the cease-fire lines of 1967? The two powers, divided by the antagonism of their long-term aims in the region as well as by their basic commitments, nevertheless shared one paramount concern. The primary interest of both was to avert the catastrophe of a fourth Arab-Israeli war in which they would face the risk of involvement against each other. The war of 1967 had presumably been a sobering lesson for the Russians and they would thereafter tread with greater caution in the Middle East. Presumably they would not again place their interests in Nasser's keeping. Yet this was more easily said than done, since they were increasingly entangled with his. It was a treacherous and tricky game, as they themselves must have recognized: by their rearmament of Egypt and their political support of the Arab position, they had not only given fresh incitement to Arab belligerence but had expanded their commitment to a leader whose adventurism was unpredictable, whose actions were beyond their control and whose aims were by no means identical with their own. Soviet and Arab objectives were parallel up to a point: patrons and clients were allies in the struggle to evict the United States from its Middle East positions. But with regard to Israel their objectives were quite different. The Arabs generally still wanted and sought Israel's extinction and still saw it as possible in a term of years. Nasser was fatalistically committed to the anti-Israeli cause by his involvement in the war and the defeat. The Russians did not want Israel's destruction: they knew the United States would not permit it and they wished, in any case, to preserve a state named Israel as their instrument for implanting themselves in the Arab world.

The Russians could not be happy with the new situation they had managed to create in the Middle East. The price they would be willing to pay for an Arab-Israeli settlement would depend, finally, on how badly they needed and wanted a global entente with the United States. There was in their position a built-in ambiguity that seemed to preclude any genuine concerted effort by the two powers to bring about a final peace. The fear that events might get derailed and that the cycle of violence along the Suez Canal and the Jordan River might, in time, erupt again in war, prompted the Russians and Americans, seconded by the French and British, to get together at the United Nations and explore the possibilities of a Middle East arrangement. But if the Russians' principal concern was to prevent a fourth Arab-Israeli war, with the awful hazards of big-power involvement, it was not their concern to achieve a permanent political settlement. Their interest was to damp down the fires of conflict in the Middle East; to bolster Nasser's regime by getting the Israeli Army off its neck in Sinai; to spare Nasser the political mortification of going to the conference table and recognizing Israel; and to maintain Israel herself as a pariah state, as a threat and an irritant enabling them to continue to build and enlarge their Middle East establishment. But it was not in the Soviet interest to bring about a definitive settlement that would liquidate the conflict. The Arab states continued to hope that the big powers, in their parleys at the United Nations, would devise a face-saving scheme and impose it on Israel; while the Israelis, with their rooted distrust of big-power shifts and expedients, viewed the dialogue in New York with alarm and misgiving. The Israelis were not in the market for a new set of international guarantees, since they were convinced that any compromise would be made at their expense. The recognition they wanted was not the recognition of the Big Four but that of their neighbors. What they apprehended above all was a move by the powers to negotiate over their heads and enforce a setlement which, in their view, would be makeshift, insecure, and inimical to their interests; and they looked to the United States to resist such a move and to protect them against it. In this expectation they seemed to overestimate American willingness to accept the risks of unresolved and unremitting conflict in a region of the world where Americans and Russians confront each other.

As the price of victory, the soldiers of Israel became an army of occupation. How could the Arabs realistically expect the Israelis to give up their gains without a direct settlement? But how, on the other hand, could the Israelis realistically expect the Arabs to recognize them? To the second question the Israelis soberly replied that recognition and peace were unattainable in the foreseeable future, and they as readily accepted the consequences. They entertained no illusions; they were prepared, indeed determined, to pay the price. Although the Israeli Government declined to formulate its peace terms unless the Arabs themselves sat down to discuss them, the general shape of the settlement that Israel envisaged was clear. The essential points on which there appeared to be wide agreement were these: Israel would make substantial territorial concessions for peace, but there would be no withdrawal from the conquered lands without a treaty; the Golan Heights must remain under Israeli control; the Egyptians must not be permitted to return to the Gaza Strip; the Suez Canal must be opened to Israeli shipping and Israel must have direct control over the Straits of Tiran; and, finally, the reunited city of Jerusalem must remain under Israeli soverignty. The future of Jerusalem and control of the Golan Heights were the two issues which Israel formally declared to be beyond negotiation.

Their victory placed on the Israelis something more than the heavy psychological burden of a long military occupation. The occupation itself carried the further challenge of requiring Israel to determine the kind of nation and society she wished to be: her relationship with her captive Arabs imposed complex and difficult moral choices, a new and critical search for national identity. Israel before the war still had to resolve the problem of the 250,000 Arab citizens who lived as social and spiritual strangers within her borders; after the war she ruled over a million other Arabs who were asked to accept a new reality for her sake. So it would be for the duration of the uncertain impasse. What kind of Israel would emerge from the experience?

The Israelis after the war spoke with many voices, even within the ranks of their government. The annexationists of the Zionist right, imbued with nationalism and religiosity, invoked "the historic rights of the Jewish people" and dreamed of a Greater Israel, fulfilling the promise of the mythical rejuvenating land which they identified with historic Palestine. The annexationists, to be sure, were a minority. The Jewish character of Israel would be foredoomed by the incorporation of a million Arabs who, within two or three generations, might come to outnumber the Jews by natural increase; and the majority of Israelis abjured the notion of a binational state in which the Jews would be compelled to rule as military overlords and the Arabs condemned to live as their subjects. Evidently, too, if the Zionists talked of history, they should be expected to take it seriously—that is, to recognize and respect the experience of the Arabs in the populous region of the West Bank and their long identification with it. In this context it was irrelevant whether the political power under whose jurisdiction they came was an Arab monarch named Hussein or another.

History had woven for both peoples in the land of Palestine a tissue of human claims and rights, of rights irrefutable and incompatible, which no political settlement could reconcile or requite. Juridically, there was no solution that could be just to everyone. Where, then, should Israel's borders be drawn? Security demanded a revision of grotesquely inadequate frontiers that offered no means of immediate defense—on the Golan Heights and on the approaches to Tel-Aviv and Jerusalem. The Gaza Strip was a peculiar case, an area without a separate self, which the Egyptians had never sought or wished to integrate. But the greater portion of the West Bank area, with its Arab people and Arab history, Israel would have to relinquish in any final settlement, if only in order to save her own humanity and her own character as a democratic Jewish society.

Yet, in the world of political realities, history is made of the present no less than the past, and for the Israelis the war of 1967 made at least one of their Palestinian conquests irreversible. What was true through the centuries of the Jewish attachment to the land of Palestine was most intensely true of Jerusalem. Within weeks after the war's end, exercising their conquerors' rights, the Israelis annexed Jerusalem by formally reuniting it under their rule. For nineteen years they had survived well enough in their half of the city, and had been able to live with it, in tension but not in fear, accustomed to the sight of cement roadblocks and dividing walls, the waste and rubble of no man's land under the lookouts of the Jordan Legion. But once the fortunes of war placed the entire city in their hands, it became impossible for them to part with it. The conquest of Jerusalem was a signal and profound experience both for those who captured it and for all of Israeli youth—indeed, especially for the youth, who with this experience rediscovered the historic roots and associations of their people. It mattered little whether they believed or not: the indissoluble connection, the overpowering bond was there. Israel, if peace came, would be ready to accept international arrangements for the custody and administration of the city's Christian and Moslem Holy Places. But never would an Israeli government willingly give it up.

The third Arab-Israeli war determined a new and rigorous pattern of conflict in the Middle East in which, in the perspective of the years, Israel's position was more precarious than ever. The war discredited belligerence as a means of gaining peace. If the postwar period was a time of excited nationalist hopes for some in Israel, and for others a time of anguished disappointment, it was for others still, particularly those of the new generation, a time for probing the future and for taking thought. The lesson that was impressed on Israeli youth was that there could be no short cut to a solution, not even in the most brilliant victory in the field; that the conflict would be severe and long; that it would yield to no quickly arranged or dramatically enforced settlement; and that reconciliation with the people among whom they must live forever and with whom they must win their peace would require a great investment of energy and patience. The war and its sequel brought not hatred of the Arabs but, among many, a deepening recognition that the conflict was a conflict of rights. For the Arabs the issue was the restoration of lost lands and lost homes; for the Israelis it was their existence. There was no solution in belligerence, not in the long term of the quest for peace and not even in the short term, in confronting the week-to-week dangers of terrorist subversion. The cruel realization for the young of Israel lay there: the war had discredited belligerence as a concept and had perpetuated it as a fact. Israel would have to live indefinitely under the stress of hostility and violence, her existence denied by her neighbors; and the full burden of assuring her survival would lie on her new generation. Belligerence was still her way of life after victory in her third war and would continue to be so for a period of years that had no foreseeable term, perhaps for the years of their lives.

Index

Third Arab-Israeli war (*continued*)
  United Nations and, *see* United
    Nations
  U.N. troop evacuation and, *see*
    United Nations Emergency
    Forces
  United States and, *see* United States
Thoughts (Mao Tse-tung), 139
Tiberias, Israel, 157
Tiran Straits, 98, 116, 205
  closing of
    American initiatives and, 246,
      250–52, 274, 329
    as *casus belli*, 245–46, 270
    diplomatic negotiations, 329
    Egyptian legal case, 303
    international accords, 246–47,
      278
    mine-laying claim, 277, 339
    Nasser's blockade policy, 272–73,
      279
    Red Sea Regatta plan, 251,
      253–56, 265–66, 299–302
    Russian fears, 270–71, 274–75
  Egyptian blockade of, 232
  importance of, 122
  Israel and
    capture of Straits, 339
    Israeli claims, 357
    Israeli rights, 56
  Suez invasion and, 101, 104
  U.N. troops at, 215
Togoland, 111
Tolstoy, Lev, 77
Tours, France, 32
Transjordan, *see* Jordan
Truman, Harry S, 113
Tunisia, 28, 33, 34
Turkestan, 34
Turkey, 86, 87, 131–33, 151

U Thant
  Arab terrorism deplored by, 209
  denies massing of Israeli troops, 210
  Third Arab-Israeli war and, 272–73,
    303, 324
  U.N. troop evacuation and, 216–19
    Canadian troops and, 300–301
    conferences on issue, 223–27
    criticisms, 232
    decision to withdraw troops, 219
    El Kony's interview, 217, 218
    lack of maneuverability, 231
    Rafael's interview, 220, 225
    withdrawal order issued, 227

Union of South Africa, 59
United Arab Command, 145, 149
United Arab Republic
  aftermath of war in
    Arab financial aid, 345–46, 348
    closing of Suez Canal, 348
    conflict between Nasser and gen-
      erals, 345
    dependence on Russia, 344
    Russian arms, 344–45
    settlement policies, 353
  aid to Congolese rebels, 188
  arms aid for, 23, 52, 344–45
  British-French-Israeli invasion of,
    8, 54, 97–108, 180
  Cold War and, 130–31
  Czech aid to, 23
  diplomatic boycott of Germany, 111
  economy of
    American aid, 181–82
    internal difficulties, 147–48, 153
    nationalization of property, 143
  Ethiopia and, 29
  fedayeen arms from, 349
  formation of, 54–55
  France and, 40–41, 50, 95
    De Gaulle's courtship, 109–10
    Suez invasion, 8, 54, 57, 97, 101
    internal difficulties of, 147–48
  Iraq and
    conflicts, 29
    Jordanian-Egyptian alliance and,
      292, 294
    Nasserists suppressed, 55
    pro-Nasser forces, 97
    talks with Egypt, 277
  Israel and
    anti-Israel rallying point, 143–46
    appraisals of strength, 195–96,
      205
    Arab Summit meetings, 145–46
    competition in Africa, 112
    denial of Israel's existence, 58–59,
      146
    early cordiality, 93–94
    Egyptian concessions, 56
    inevitability of war, 172–73
    Jordan River issue, 144–45
    military conflicts, *see* Egyptian
      Air Force; Egyptian Army;
      First Arab-Israeli war; Nasser,
      Gamal Abdel; Second Arab-
      Israeli war; Third Arab-Israeli
      war
    military forces, 204
    Nasser's miscalculations, 197, 207

Winston Burdett

A native New Yorker, Winston Burdett graduated from Harvard and later studied at Columbia. He began his impressive journalistic career reviewing films and books for the old Brooklyn *Eagle*. In 1940 he went to Europe as a free-lance reporter and made his first news broadcast from Stockholm in May of that year, during the Nazi invasion of Norway. As the war progressed he reported for CBS News from Bucharest, Belgrade, Ankara, Cairo, Algiers, Rome and Paris, and followed the Allied armies from the Western Desert in Egypt to the Apennines and the Rhine.

Since 1943 he has been a staff correspondent for CBS News, with worldwide radio and TV assignments ranging from the United Nations in New York to the Congo, and from Vatican City to India. For the past fourteen years he has served as Mediterranean correspondent, with headquarters in Rome. Though often traveling far beyond the bounds of that region, he still regards the Middle East as his chief and most absorbing responsibility. Mr. Burdett currently lives in Rome with his wife and two children.